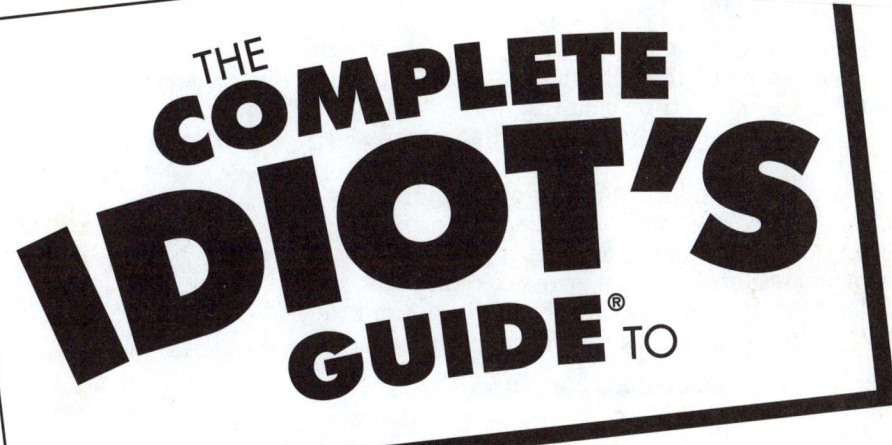

GoldMine 5

ASAP GoldMine Consultancy

A Division of Macmillan USA
201 W. 103rd Street, Indianapolis, IN 46290

The Complete Idiot's Guide to GoldMine 5

Copyright © 2000 by Que

All rights reserved. No part of this book shall be reproduced, stored in a retrieval system, or transmitted by any means, electronic, mechanical, photocopying, recording, or otherwise, without written permission from the publisher. No patent liability is assumed with respect to the use of the information contained herein. Although every precaution has been taken in the preparation of this book, the publisher and authors assume no responsibility for errors or omissions. Nor is any liability assumed for damages resulting from the use of the information contained herein.

International Standard Book Number: 0-7897-2350-6

Library of Congress Catalog Card Number: 00-101710

Printed in the United States of America

First Printing: August 2000

02   01   00   4   3   2   1

Trademarks

All terms mentioned in this book that are known to be trademarks or service marks have been appropriately capitalized. Que cannot attest to the accuracy of this information. Use of a term in this book should not be regarded as affecting the validity of any trademark or service mark.

Warning and Disclaimer

Every effort has been made to make this book as complete and as accurate as possible, but no warranty or fitness is implied. The information provided is on an "as is" basis. The authors and the publisher shall have neither liability nor responsibility to any person or entity with respect to any loss or damages arising from the information contained in this.

Associate Publisher
Greg Wiegand

Acquisitions Editor
Stephanie McComb

Development Editor
Gregory Harris

Managing Editor
Thomas F. Hayes

Project Editor
Tricia Sterling

Copy Editor
Sossity Smith

Indexer
Mary SeRine

Proofreaders
Jeanne Clark
Lauren Dixon

Technical Editor
Deb Newell

Illustrator
Judd Winick

Team Coordinator
Sharry Gregory

Interior Designer
Nathan Clement

Cover Designer
Michael Freeland

Production
Darin Crone
Stacey Richwine DeRome
Ayanna Lacey
Heather Hiatt Miller

Contents at a Glance

Part 1: GoldMining for Beginners — 3

1 Staking Your Claim: Opening Up the GoldMine — 5
Don't forget to unearth the stored wisdom when you are unpacking GoldMine software.

2 Scratching the Surface: Setting GoldMine to Work — 21
How to get the system to do what you want it to.

3 Your Treasure Trove: Storing Contact Information — 33
Contact management depends on getting, keeping, and finding again, the information that could make or break a sale.

4 The Right Look: Making Things Happen — 45
Take charge of what you see and what you do.

5 24-Karat Printouts: Generating Paper by Printing and Faxing — 63
Find easy ways to write to your contacts, to other users, and to your manager.

Part 2: Communicating Through the Internet — 81

6 It Beats a Tin Can on a String: Managing Email — 83
Get GoldMine to talk nicely with the e-world outside.

7 Are There Spiders in the Mine? Using the Web — 95
Gather ye contacts where ye may.

8 Remote Control: Updating GoldMine from the Web — 109
You can upgrade your copy and arrange licenses for your various users.

9 Pretty Up the Place: Customizing Startup and Settings — 117
Fine-tune everyone's working environment.

Part 3: Managing Contacts Efficiently — 133

10 Look, Then Leap: Scheduling Your Activities — 135
Make time for you and your work.

11 Panning for Gold: Filtering Contacts from the Database — 151
Pick people for particular processes by pulling out certain records to work on.

12 At the Corral: Building Contact Groups — 165
Put like with like—know how and why your contacts are grouped.

Part 4: GoldMine in Business — 177

13 At the Mill: Generating the Reports You Like — 179
There's good news and bad news—it's best to get reports that are quick and to the point.

14 Round Up a Posse: Building a Sales Team — 191
Who gets the keys to the GoldMine?

15 Looking for the Real Seams: Using the Opportunity Manager — 207
If you think you know where the gold is, why not put your best people to work there and give them all the support they need?

16 At the Assayer's Lab: Analyzing Leads — 223
It might seem unfair to kill off the messenger who brings bad news—but it might make sense to kill off marketing efforts that are fruitless and to put more effort in those that bring in the business.

Part 5: Administering a GoldMine Installation — 231

17 Be the Boss of the Territory: Maintaining Databases — 233
GoldMine housekeeping includes frequent sorting of data and the throwing out of rubbish.

18 Share the Wealth: Distributing Nuggets of Information — 253
Keep valuable information where you can find it.

19 High Noon: Synchronizing Records — 271
Keep everyone up to date with the entire contact database—especially when many different users could unearth something valuable or somebody interesting.

20 A GoldMine Assembly Line: Automating Processes — 287
Fine-tune your working environment. Capture patterns for setting up GoldMine to work harder for you.

21 Line Please: Creating Telemarketing Scripts — 303
Talk to a purpose—have GoldMine tell you what to say and help you capture the essence of each answer.

22 Boom Town: Extending GoldMine by Adding on Software — 309
If somebody has already invented a clever device, why not have it in your outfit?

23 Getting Tricky: Installing to a Network
and Troubleshooting 317
*Your team will need to network anyway—why not get
them on an electronic net and make communication into
a normal way of life? There are very few problems that
have not been solved already and probably documented.*

Glossary **325**

Index **331**

Contents

Part 1: GoldMining for Beginners   3

1 Staking Your Claim: Opening Up the GoldMine   5

What Is GoldMine, and What Does It Do? 5
   Being Polite and Businesslike 6
   Remembering Every Single Contact 6
Preparing to Install GoldMine..6
   Installing to a Single-User System 7
   Checking System Requirements 8
   Initiating the Install 8
   Licensing Your Installation 10
   Starting GoldMine 12
   Exploring the GoldMine Main Menu...........................12
   Accommodating Remote or Travelling Users 14
   Separating License Types 14
   Inspecting the State of Your System...........................16
Using Free Support 16
   Consulting the Online KnowledgeBase 17
   Downloading from the GoldMine Web Site 18
   Using GoldMine Premium Support Services 18

2 Scratching the Surface: Setting GoldMine to Work   21

What GoldMine Can Do for You 21
   Exploiting Your Computer...23
Noting Useful To-do Activities 24
   Completing a To-do Activity 27
   Setting and Recording the Time 27
   Setting a Date 28

3 Your Treasure Trove: Storing Contact Information   33

Controlling Contact Data 33
   Commanding Files 34
   Commanding Edits 35
Finding a Contact Record 36
   Cloning an Existing Record..37
   Toggling GoldMine Options 38

    Adding Notes to a Contact Record *39*
    Entering Standardized Data *40*
  Improving a Browse List *41*
    Putting More Than One Entry in a Field *41*
    Attaching Descriptions and Explanations *41*
    Using Zip Codes *42*
    Getting Around Your Tabs *42*
    Editing Contact Record Properties *42*

4 The Right Look: Making Things Happen   45

  Preparing Your Workspace *45*
    Controlling What You See *46*
    Commanding Your Windows *46*
    Resizing Your Record Display *47*
    Configuring Your Toolbars *48*
    Editing Your User Preferences *49*
    Commanding Views *51*
    Commanding Lookups *53*
  Controlling What You Do *54*
    Commanding for Your Contact *54*
    Customizing Templates *54*
    Commanding Your Schedule *56*
    Completing Activities *57*
    Commanding Tools and Wizards *58*
    Helping Yourself *59*
  Making Macros *60*
    Giving Your Macro Its Own Icon *61*
    Editing Macro Properties *61*

5 24-Karat Printouts: Generating Paper by Printing and Faxing   63

  Linking to Word 97 or 2000 ....*64*
    Installing the Link *64*
    Setting Link Preferences *65*
    Working GoldMine from Word *66*
    Emailing, Messaging, and Even Writing *66*
  Making a GoldMine Template Form *68*
    Identifying a New GoldMine Template *68*
    Developing a Template *70*

      Placing a Microsoft Word Field *70*
      Placing a GoldMine Field *71*
      Saving a Correspondence Template *72*
      Writing with a Template *72*
      Linking a Document to a Contact *73*
   Initiating a Merge 74
      Starting a Paper Merge *75*
      Starting an Email Merge *75*
      Recording a Document After Dispatch *77*
      Managing Form Printing *78*
      Setting Up Signature Bitmaps *79*

Part 2: Communicating Through the Internet   81

6 It Beats a Tin Can on a String: Managing Email   83

   Mastering Messages 84
      Emailing Another GoldMine User *84*
      Emailing Contacts *85*
      Setting Options for Email *86*
      Specifying Queue, Calendar, and History Options *88*
      Targeting a Mail Merge *88*
   Setting Up Internet Email Accounts 89
   Operating from the E-mail Center 90
   Sending an Outlook Message to a Contact 92
   Sending a Pager Message 92

7 Are There Spiders in the Mine? Using the Web   95

   Contacting the World Wide Web 95
   Finding What 96
      Exploring the GoldMine Search Engine *98*
      Managing Web Site Addresses *99*
      Making Contacts Through Your Web Site *100*
      Collecting Data from the Web *100*
      Controlling Web Import *101*
   Prospecting with Web Site Messaging..102
      Creating the Web Form *102*
      Interpreting an HTML Form *104*
      Understanding the Web Import File *104*
      Formatting the Web Import File *104*

Interpreting the Instructions Section *105*
Interpreting the Data Sections *105*
Matching a Password for Web Imports *106*

8 Remote Control: Updating GoldMine from the Web — 109

Exploring the Licensing System 109
   Configuring Your GoldMine License *110*
   Registering GoldMine Licenses *111*
Understanding Net-Update Now 113
   Installing the File Download on a Network *113*
   Installing a Network Update Locally *114*
Checking Your Details 114

9 Prettying Up the Place: Customizing Startup and Settings — 117

Tightening Your Records 117
   Reviewing How Your Fields Are Used *118*
Administering a GoldMine System 119
   Customizing Processes *120*
Managing the Users' Master File 120
   Selecting the GoldMine Home Directory *121*
   Configuring a User's Time Clock *122*
   Configuring User Groups *123*
   Configuring Resources *123*
   Rebuilding Your Screens *124*
   Creating a New Field *127*
   Creating a New Screen *129*

Part 3: Managing Contacts Efficiently — 133

10 Look, Then Leap: Scheduling Your Activities — 135

Planning Things to Be Done 135
   Contemplating Your Activities *137*
   Reviewing Your Past *140*
   Completing an Activity *141*
   Replying to Another User *141*
   Linking to the Active Contact *141*

Dating an Activity 142
　　　　Recording Activity Details..143
　　　　Allocating Time to an Activity 145
　　　　Using Your Calendar 146
　　　　Rescheduling an Activity 147
　　　　Deleting an Activity 147
　　　　Muddling Your Schedule 147
　　　　Locating Another User 148
　　　　Alarming Activities 148
　　　　Making a Private Call 149
　　　　Restricting a Private Entry 149

11 Panning for Gold: Filtering Contacts from the Database 151

　　Finding Particular Contact Records...............................151
　　　　Searching on Basic Information 152
　　　　Searching on Indexed Fields 153
　　　　Narrowing a Search for Contacts 154
　　　　Calling for Another Record Window 154
　　　　Spinning for a Record 155
　　　　Finding Records Using Their Details 155
　　Exploring Filters...156
　　　　Tagging Contacts for Immediate Use......................156
　　　　Building a Filter 158
　　　　Building a Filter Expression 158
　　　　Editing a Filter 159
　　　　Using a Filter 161
　　　　Optimizing Record Selection 161
　　　　Reviewing the Scope of a Filter 162
　　　　Previewing Filtered Records 162

12 At the Corral: Building Contact Groups 165

　　Working with Contact Groups 165
　　　　Tagging Your Gang..166
　　　　Building a Group with a Filter 167
　　　　Activating a Group...167
　　　　Using the Membership Local Menu 170
　　　　Adding Group Members 172
　　Controlling the Group Building Wizard..........................172
　　　　Using the Optional Settings 173
　　　　Building from a Set of Contacts 174

Part 4: GoldMine in Business — 177

13 At the Mill: Generating the Reports You Like — 179

Introducing the Report Generator 179
   Choosing a Report Category *180*
   Scrutinizing a Report Template *181*
   Looking at a Report's Layout *182*
Using the Report Generator 183
   Using the Reports Local Menu *184*
   Choosing What to Report About *185*
   Reporting History Data *186*
   Reporting Calendar Data *187*
   Saving Report Options *188*
Sorting Report Data 188
   Printing a Report *189*
   Inspecting a Report Onscreen *189*

14 Round Up a Posse: Building a Sales Team — 191

Pressing a Posse 191
   Assigning Users *192*
   Assigning Group Membership to a User *193*
Controlling User Access 194
   Owning a Record *194*
   Checking on Memberships *195*
   Letting Users Operate Particular Functions *196*
   Granting User Access to Records *196*
   Permitting Special Functions *197*
   Seeing What Others Are Doing *198*
   Controlling Users' Menus *199*
   Saving a Menu Template *199*
Inspecting a User's Timekeeping 199
Controlling Access to a Contact Database 201
Hiding User Screens 202

15 Looking for the Real Seams: Using the Opportunity Manager — 207

Forecasting the Odds 207
   Scheduling a Forecasted Sale *209*
   Inspecting Forecasted Sales *210*

Dealing with an Entire Opportunity 211
   Tasking an Opportunity *212*
   Viewing the Opportunity Calendar *213*
   Providing Opportunity or Project Details *214*
   Differentiating Projects and Opportunities....................*214*
Identifying Influencers 215
   Assembling a Team *216*
   Documenting the Competitors *217*
   Documenting Issues *218*
Analyzing the Sales Pipeline 219
Assigning and Analyzing Quotas 220

16 At the Assayer's Lab: Analyzing Leads   223

Preparing to Analyze Leads 223
   Interpreting Lead Analysis *224*
   Costing the Source of a Lead...*225*
Using Leads Analysis in Cunning Ways 227
   Maintaining Leads Analysis Files *229*
   Deleting a Leads Analysis *229*

Part 5: Administering a GoldMine Installation   231

17 Be the Boss of the Territory: Maintaining Databases   233

Maintaining GoldMine 233
   Backing Up *234*
   Identifying GoldMine Files *235*
   Preventing Corrupt Indexes *235*
   Copying and Moving Records *235*
Directing the Maintenance Wizard...................................236
   Rebuilding...Packing...Sorting *236*
   Arranging Automatic Maintenance *237*
Administering Records 239
   Consolidating Duplicate Records..................................*239*
   Driving the Merge/Purge Wizard..................................*239*
   Setting Up Merge Criteria *240*
   Selecting Field Comparison Methods *241*
   Whisking Away the Dross *242*

Making Global Changes to Contact Records 243
   Extending Global Replacements 245
   Logging Updates in History 245
   Viewing the Contact Files Logs 245
   Viewing the GoldMine Files Logs 246
   Substituting a Value from Another Field 246
   Updating a Field with Advanced Options 247
   Replacing with a dBASE Expression 248
Deleting Records 249
   Deleting All (Filtered) Contact Records 249
   Removing Old History 249
   Using the Record Wizards 250

18 Share the Wealth: Distributing Nuggets of Information   253

Linking to Another Data File 253
   Linking from the Links Tab 254
   Editing a Linked Document 255
Nurturing Organizational Trees 255
   Adding Branches 257
   Depicting the Competition 259
   Rearranging the Furniture 259
Using the InfoCenter 259
   Authoring a Book 260
   Searching the InfoCenter 261
   Extracting Information 263
   Printing and Faxing a Topic 263
Fulfilling Literature 264
   Creating a Contribution to Literature 266
   Reviewing Literature Requests 266
   Reviewing Queued Documents 267
   Reviewing Recently Printed Documents 267
Working with the Information Facilities 267

19 High Noon: Synchronizing Records   271

Synchronizing with GoldMine 271
   Setting Up a Session 272
   Rousing the Synchronization Wizard 274
   Synchronizing When Disconnected 274
   Synchronizing by Sneaker Net 275

Filtering for the Transfer Set 276
  Browsing a Transfer Set 276
  Defining a Transfer Cutoff Moment 277
  Defining Send Options 277
  Defining Retrieval Options 278
 Synchronizing with Microsoft Outlook 278
  Defining Options for Outlook Synchronization 278
  Setting Advanced Options for Outlook...................279
 Synchronizing with Palm Pilot 281
  Installing the GoldMine Pilot Conduit 283
  Selecting Data Categories to Purge 283
  Selecting Contact Records for Pilot 284
  Confirming HotSync Settings 284
 Synchronizing with a Windows CE Device 284

20 A GoldMine Assembly Line: Automating Processes 287

 Making GoldMine Work for You 287
  Identifying Useful Processes 289
  Performing Administrative Tasks 289
 Working with Processes..290
  Interpreting a Process Listing 291
  Defining Track Properties 292
  Defining a Track 293
  Triggering Actions 294
  Sequencing Events 294
  Attaching a Track to a Contact Record 295
 Executing Processes by a Scan.....................................296
 Building an Automated Process 297
  Selecting What to Trigger On 298
  Choosing an Action for an Event 301

21 Line Please: Creating Telemarketing Scripts 303

 Selecting a Script 303
  Editing a Script 304
  Saving the Questions and Answers 305
 Changing the Questions and Answers 306
  Creating a New Script...306
  Directing Data Entry 307

22 Boom Town: Extending GoldMine by Adding on Software — 309

Using GoldMine Industry Templates 309
   Choosing an Industry Template *310*
   Installing an Industry Template *311*
   Copying and Moving Records *312*
Exploring the Add-On Categories 313
Sampling the GoldMine Tools Catalog 314

23 Getting Tricky: Installing to a Network and Troubleshooting — 317

Installing to a Network 317
   Sharing the Directory *319*
   Configuring the Workstations *319*
First-Level GoldMine Troubleshooting 320
   Interpreting an Insufficient Memory Error *321*
   Interpreting a BDE Error *321*
   Troubleshooting the Link to Word *322*
   Exploring GoldMine Support Services *322*
   Consulting GoldMine Newsgroups *323*

Glossary — 325

Index — 331

About the Authors

Jonathan Blain is the Founder and Chief Executive of ASAP International Group Plc and ASAP GoldMine Consultancy. He is a leading authority on technology-driven change and Customer Relationship Management (CRM). He is a regular speaker and author on CRM issues. He has co-authored six other books published by Macmillan USA, including the international bestseller, *Special Edition Using SAP R/3*.

Jonathan is a keen yachtsman and has been instrumental in the development of the "Hy Tech Sprint" yacht, a revolutionary 43-foot light displacement, water-ballasted ocean cruiser.

Bernard Dodd graduated and mastered in Psychology at Aberdeen University, Scotland. He founded the Programmed Instruction Centre for Industry at the University of Sheffield, England, to develop methods of retraining adults who were changing jobs as the result of technological developments in the manufacturing and processing industries. He was appointed Principal Psychologist to the Royal Navy to develop training and selection procedures. He has been an independent technical author for 15 years, writing computer-related training materials for many companies.

Publications include *Special Edition Using SAP R/3* (Que, 1998); *Administering SAP R/3: The Production and Planning Module* (Que, 1999); *Administering SAP R/3: HR—Human Resources Module* (Que, 1999); *Administering SAP R/3: The SD—Sales and Distribution Module* (Que, 1998); *Administering SAP R/3: MM—Materials Management Module* (Que, 1997); and *Teaching Machines and Programmed Instruction* (Penguin Books, 1965).

Bernard lives with his wife Hazel near the home of the Royal Navy, Portsmouth, where they keep a steady family sailing cruiser that introduces the grandchildren to the coastal waters of England and France.

Dedication

We dedicate this book to all those telesales people and marketing managers who phoned without a result because they either did not have a contact manager system or else did not know how to purge it of useless contacts.

Tell Us What You Think!

As the reader of this book, *you* are our most important critic and commentator. We value your opinion and want to know what we're doing right, what we could do better, what areas you'd like to see us publish in, and any other words of wisdom you're willing to pass our way.

As an Associate Publisher for Que, I welcome your comments. You can fax, email, or write me directly to let me know what you did or didn't like about this book—as well as what we can do to make our books stronger.

Please note that I cannot help you with technical problems related to the topic of this book, and that due to the high volume of mail I receive, I might not be able to reply to every message.

When you write, please be sure to include this book's title and author as well as your name and phone or fax number. I will carefully review your comments and share them with the author and editors who worked on the book.

Fax: 317-581-4666

Email: consumer@mcp.com

Mail: Associate Publisher
Que
201 West 103rd Street
Indianapolis, IN 46290 USA

A Note from the Authors

GoldMine 5 is a magnificent product that stands head and shoulders above its competitors. It is as the manufacturers describe: an extremely powerful system that is easy to use.

GoldMine started life as a relatively basic contact management system. It has now developed into a very smart product that creates a whole host of solutions for different areas of business, including contact management, sales force automation, customer relationship management, filters and groups for targeting, sales and marketing management, and so on. GoldMine currently has more users than any other CRM vendor (approximately 700,000 user licenses). It is used by companies of all sizes, from small family businesses to giant global corporations. Its success has been due to the fact that the product delivers and users like it.

I am convinced that CRM (Customer Relationship Management) will be the deciding competitive differentiator for all businesses in the new millennium. Customer relations should now be placed at the center of all business strategies and objectives. This means a 180-degree turnaround in contemporary business practice.

The benefits are clear and all sections of the business community can participate in a win-win situation. If the customer base is successfully retained, profitability is sustained and shareholders as well as staff can share in the rewards. More importantly, it is the staff and the customers who together will drive the business and determine the future.

The GoldMine Suite, including GoldMine 5, opens the way for theory to become practice. GoldMine has developed an excellent relationship management tool that can change your business thinking and practice.

We at ASAP have always been aligned to the interests of the end user. We deliver CRM solutions that impact business infrastructures in sales, marketing, and service operations. We help you to listen to your staff and customers more closely.

In our commitment to service excellence, we train our consultants for a month at our international training center on GoldMine and CRM. Our ASAP GoldStrike methodology provides best practice procedures in CRM and GoldMine implementations. Further details can be found at the end of this book.

I hope you find this publication useful and that you will help to make a difference with us in the world of CRM.

Jonathan Blain

CEO, ASAP GoldMine Consultancy

Introduction

If you are thinking of buying GoldMine, or have a copy already, you will know that it is a system designed to help you keep track of your contacts—even if they move from company to company. Meeting new contacts and keeping track of them means exchanging communications by phone, letter, email, encounters at trade shows, introductions, referrals, and by following up inquiries from advertisements.

The beauty of GoldMine is that it will help you manage any and all of these different kinds of activity and keep records of what has happened and your plans for the future. The neat trick of programming is that every event is associated with a particular contact person whose details are kept in the central item of GoldMine—the contact record.

This book is a straightforward guide to show you what you have to do to get the very best from GoldMine.

How to Use This Book

The style of this book is to suggest how you can use the programmed functions of GoldMine and also to tell you exactly what has to be done to get the best results.

There are three kinds of notes:

Mine Safety

Do not try this, unless you like aggravation.

Learn the Lingo

These boxes define computer or contact management terms that might come in handy.

Strike It Rich

A prudent idea or something that might be fun to try.

Make sure you know where the front cover is because it holds the complete idiot's spare brain cell. If the second page is apparently cut out or torn, an enemy hath done this. Get an unmutilated copy with a tearcard that you can consult. (I am told that *tear* rhymes with *bear* not *beer*.)

For extra effect, career promotion even, acquire mastery of the local menus unlocked by right-clicking the mouse.

Here comes your first note, something that might be fun to try:

Flick Out a Local Menu

Experiment with a right-click when you are pointing at something. Your keyboard may have a Microsoft Windows Local Menu key that does the same. It looks like a Dagwood multidecker sandwich with an arrow.

Not that you will need it, after reading this book, but the inside of the back cover demonstrates how to unlock the wisdom secreted in the GoldMine Help files.

We assume that you will be considering whether to have a GoldMine system installed and what it will be like to use when it is up and working. Perhaps you are not yet going to be responsible for installing and setting to work such a complex installation. However, it is not a bad idea to have an overview of what is entailed in making sophisticated systems yield their full potential. Therefore, some space is devoted to the essential mechanics of working with existing data sources upon which much useful customer information may well already reside.

The book is divided into five sections:

- Part 1, "GoldMining for Beginners"
- Part 2, "Communicating Through the Internet"
- Part 3, "Managing Contacts Efficiently"
- Part 4, "GoldMine in Business"
- Part 5, "Administering a GoldMine Installation"

The 23 chapters each begin with some suggestions of what you will learn in that chapter and end with a few facts that sum up the contents. The Contents at a Glance pages give you the theme of each chapter.

Let's begin!

Part 1
GoldMining for Beginners

You have a new GoldMine? Or you have a new GoldMine job and you think you could put more into it? Maybe you have an old method of managing contacts that could do with the GoldMine treatment? Perhaps you would like to get a GoldMine job?

Don't answer any of these questions—the reasons don't matter. The important thing is you're ready to manage your contacts and sales force more efficiently. Get your safety kit on and plunge into the GoldMine. Get the lights on and see where the tools are kept. Find the pit ponies or whatever they use to haul out the stuff.

See to it that all your helpers are up to scratch, preferably with the best scratchers in the business.

Chapter 1

Staking Your Claim: Opening Up the GoldMine

In This Chapter
- What GoldMine is, and what it does
- Installing GoldMine in your machinery
- Licensing yourself and your team
- Getting help—if you need it

You can install and run GoldMine from the delivery disc without personalizing or customizing. If you want, you can also customize the installation as you go along. This chapter introduces GoldMine and covers its installation process.

What Is GoldMine, and What Does It Do?

GoldMine is about managing information about those who could lead you to a successful sale—again and again throughout your company's trajectory and perhaps throughout theirs. It's a trust-building system.

When you, as a potential customer, make contact with a firm, you expect to give a little information about yourself—certainly your name, probably your phone number, perhaps the delivery address for a brochure. If you later make a second contact with this firm, you would like to believe that the person who dealt with your first inquiry is still there and remembers you or at least your name, your topics of interest, and your address. If that person is not still with the company, you expect that your contact information was preserved in some way and passed along to someone else.

If this firm does indeed remember you, you might get the impression that you are dealing with an outfit that knows what it is about. You have found an organization that is trying hard to meet your requirements, and that is using the very best means available.

If you have ever worked with a card index box containing a motley collection of customer contact information, of uncertain authenticity, then you know why the GoldMine designers have made so many improvements. Your cards were almost certainly not annotated with profitability information. They were difficult to search rapidly, particularly when trying to hold the telephone. They were almost never shared with others in the sales or marketing departments.

Being Polite and Businesslike

Try putting yourself in the position of a prospective customer. You've undoubtedly been subjected to the famous "We are dealing with your request" technique. This means they have lost, at least for the moment, all trace of you and your previous inquiry. Even the copious business you have conducted with them over the years has left no trace on their corporate or departmental memory. Why should you have to spell out in detail the specification of your requirement since you have bought it from them in the past and have already submitted a precise definition of what you need this time?

Being helpful to customers and prospective customers is what companies have to aim for. It is often more profitable to sell again to a previous customer than always seek fresh prospects. GoldMine is a compendium of excellent computer procedures that can be linked together in many different ways and which can be precisely adjusted to suit exactly the way your company does business, and perhaps even to the way your company ought to be doing business.

Remembering Every Single Contact

It's such a little matter, getting your system to remember the name and address of a contact, and what they were previously interested in. Of course, a big firm (or department of government) cannot have individual employees who remember everyone who makes contact—there could be thousands. But whistling through thousands of data records is just what computers are supposed to be good at, and GoldMine is exactly the tool you need do to it.

Preparing to Install GoldMine

GoldMine 5.0 is a *contact manager*. This term means that the software lets you keep records for each contact person, even if he changes his company or his position in it. You're about to install this system to manage more effectively information about your prospects, customers, and perhaps suppliers.

You also can manage documents and other forms of stored information which you might want to consult when dealing with a contact or might need to send to that person. For example, you could use GoldMine to view a parts list when consulting a vendor or attach an electronic catalog to an email for one of your clients.

A complex letter, fax, or email message can often be used for several contacts. In such cases, it is convenient to store a master or model as a template. The precise details can be filled in by GoldMine during a merge operation that takes data from the appropriate contact records. You will probably want to review any such templates and forms already available before using them in your new system.

In particular, you should consider whether your contacts can be grouped so that each group might be managed in the most appropriate way. For example, you would not use the same correspondence templates to a prospect as to an existing customer.

If you think through a sequence of events, beginning with the first encounter with a contact, you will see where a computer could be helpful—keeping records, supporting forward planning and the scheduling of appointments, and sending confirmations and reminders. GoldMine is able to help in all of these tasks.

The more imagination you have devoted to devising a picture of yourself working comfortably and efficiently, the easier the task of installing GoldMine Sales and Marketing will be.

Now that you know how you want to use this contact manager, you are prepared to install. Let's begin!

Learn the Lingo

Don't Expect Installation Here!

GoldMine works very well with a team of users, but installing is then a job for the administrator—not a process covered in this book.

Installing to a Single-User System

As the user and installer, there are some basic technical matters to think about before inserting and running the GoldMine installation disc.

Find your specific GoldMine license card and copy the number—you will need it to complete the installation.

Also in your delivery parcel might be a CD-ROM and other sales material directing you to add-on products compatible with GoldMine 5.0.

Part 1 ➤ *GoldMining for Beginners*

Upgrading to GoldMine 5.0

If your system already has a version of GoldMine, make a complete backup of it before you attempt to install GoldMine 5.0. You can then import your existing data into GoldMine 5.0. Upgrading requires at least 50MB of spare space for the installation, and hard disk space of at least 2.5 times the size of your largest existing database file.

Checking System Requirements

Besides the software, you'll need to have certain components on your computer for optimum efficiency. Your business system will need at least a printer and a backup device. GoldMine without email would miss many of the benefits—so you will need an account with an Internet service provider (ISP) and a modem to connect your computer to the phone. If you already have a fax or a pager, GoldMine will be able to integrate with them. With a modem installed, you can dial directly from your workstation. If your work includes paging other people, GoldMine will help you page and document your action.

Each workstation should have a Pentium or higher processor with 32MB of RAM and a video card and monitor that can display 800×600 resolution in 256 colors. Most Pentium computers have this kind of graphic display, but you might want to check your memory. Your computer should display how much memory it has as soon as you turn on the power, so if you're in doubt, reboot and watch the screen.

The operating system needs to be Windows 95/98/2000, NT4, or Terminal Server. And we mean it—some Macintosh and Linux computers feature *emulators* that let you run Windows software, but GoldMine won't work on such a system.

Initiating the Install

GoldMine 5.0 is delivered on a single CD-ROM that will display an installation image, shown in Figure 1.1, containing active component titles that you can click.

Chapter 1 ➤ *Staking Your Claim: Opening Up the GoldMine*

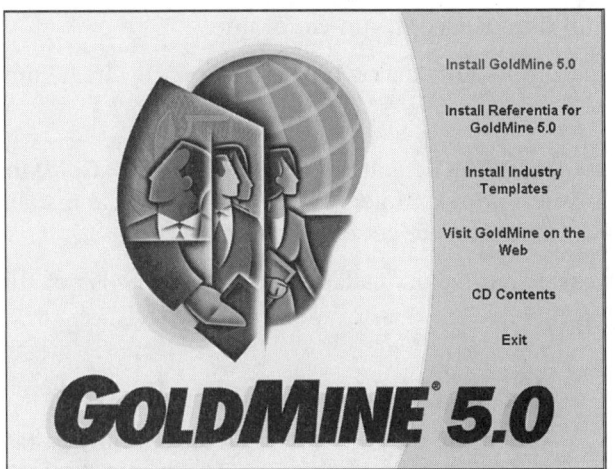

Figure 1.1
Welcome to GoldMine 5.0.

No Action from the Disc?

If your installation disc doesn't start by itself, click **Start** (or press the "Windows logo" key) and select **Run**. You'll want to open the file GM5SETUP on your CD-ROM drive, so type *d*:\GM5SETUP, replacing *d* with the letter used for the CD-ROM drive in your system. Mine happens to be F because I have three hard drives—C, D, and E.

You might be curious to see what is on the CD, or to visit the GoldMine Web site, but the Install GoldMine 5.0 option is the one you should choose right now. You can visit the other options at any time simply by inserting the CD-ROM into your drive.

Referentia Tutorial is an excellent self-teaching package that allows you to operate GoldMine while viewing the lessons. This package can be installed from the GoldMine 5.0 disc now or later. It will then be accessible from the Help menu.

The welcome procedure invites you to read and accept the Software License Agreement before selecting the type of installation you require:

> **Typical**—Complete functionality, with a set of screens and facilities useful for most types of business.

9

Part 1 ➤ *GoldMining for Beginners*

Compact—The minimum files needed to run GoldMine.

Custom—Offers a Select Components dialog box to determine which components are to be installed.

The destination folder to house GoldMine defaults to C:\Program Files\GoldMine. You can change this default location; for example, I have sent my typical installation to D:\GoldMine because my C: drive tends to get overcrowded.

The installation program will create a directory called GoldMine if one is not there already.

Licensing Your Installation

When the files have all been successfully installed, you are required to supply information that will be used to register your license, and also to personalize letters, faxes, and email templates. The following data will be requested:

Organization name

Your name or contact ID

Your email address

Your phone and fax numbers

Your organization's address, city, state, ZIP, and country

Read Your License Number

Beware of the difference between zero and the capital letter O.

Select **Next** to get another dialog box that asks where and when you purchased GoldMine, how you learned about it, your current contact manager, and your software dealer. (You can click **Next** to bypass this screen, if you want.) The next screen requires you to enter the GoldMine serial number and key code, which you should copy from your license card.

Tab Between Fields

If you press **Enter** when completing a GoldMine form of any kind, the system will process the form without letting you finish. Select fields with the **Tab** and **Shift+Tab** keys or by pointing and clicking.

You are advised to move the stickers carrying the essential number and code from the license to the inside of your "At a Glance" manual because GoldMine technical support will ask for them if you call.

If you have purchased GoldSync, a similar number and key code have to be entered. If you check **Automatically Register**, GoldMine will try to dial the GoldMine registration Web site and store your license details there.

When GoldMine is satisfied with your numbers and keys, it will invite you to identify yourself by a username of up to eight characters, to which you can add a password of up to eight characters. If you click **Finish** without giving yourself a username and password, the username will be MASTER, and this will require the password "access". The user who installs GoldMine gets master rights.

You might find it convenient to use the same name to log in to Windows and to GoldMine. You don't have to have a password to log in to GoldMine, but if your username has been associated with a password, you will be obliged to use it. If you are the user with Master rights, you can create another username and then simply press **Enter** after typing it in during login.

You Can Bypass the GoldMine Login

Users who have no passwords can press **Esc** to log in. Their preferences can be edited to bypass the login banner to make GoldMine start up immediately, adopting the username previously logged in.

However, the Master user can arrange for any parts of the system—menus or entries in specific fields—to be withheld from individual users, including those without passwords. In particular, the Master user can determine whether any specific user is allowed to edit their login preferences—which is where you set up permission to log in without a password.

If you are a single user, it might be sensible to have two accounts: one as MASTER, and one under your everyday username. A Master user is automatically created at installation using the issued password. The Master should then change this password and refuse to assign any subsequent users the Master rights, which are to create new usernames and determine where they are allowed to enter data. I am a lazy user—so I sign on with a single letter username and a very simple password. GoldMine defaults to my Windows login name and then bypasses the login banner. I am allowed to access all the screens and fields. I can edit lookup lists. What I cannot do under my everyday username is redesign the layouts and functions of GoldMine.

Starting GoldMine

Your installation program puts a shortcut icon on your desktop. Click and drag this icon to drop it into another toolbar—perhaps an Internet Explorer Quickstart toolbar or a Microsoft Office toolbar. If you drag an icon on to the Start button, the Start menu will pop up and allow you to continue dragging the icon to where you want it to be.

Double-click the shortcut icon to start GoldMine, or select **Start**, click **Programs**, find the **GoldMine** program group, and then navigate to the program and select it.

Shuffle Your Windows Icons

Right-click a space in any Windows toolbar and select **Customize**. While the Customize dialog box is open, you can drag any icon, including GoldMine, and drop it elsewhere in the same or in a different toolbar. To drop a copy, press and hold **Ctrl** until you have released the mouse button.

If you try right-clicking while you are pointing to a GoldMine toolbar, you will not get the Windows options. See Chapter 9, "Pretty Up the Place: Customizing Startup and Settings," for advice on changing the GoldMine toolbars.

Exploring the GoldMine Main Menu

Two of the tools you'll become quite familiar with are the main menu and the Basic toolbar, which appear at the top of your GoldMine screen by default. (You can move them around, but doing so will only confuse things, so don't bother.) Figure 1.2 shows these two components as they look after you install GoldMine.

Chapter 1 ➤ *Staking Your Claim: Opening Up the GoldMine*

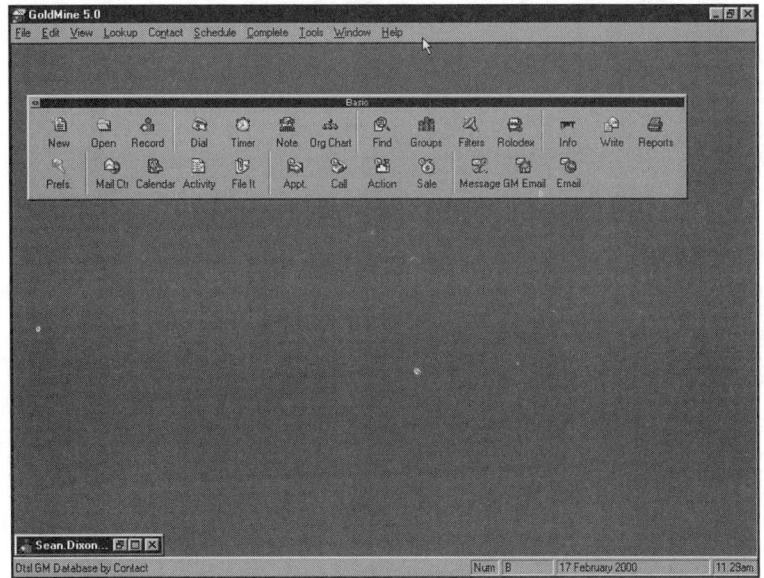

Figure 1.2
You can get most things to work from the main menu and the Basic toolbar.

Each of the main menu options has a drop-down sub-menu. Some items are shown with a function key or shortcut key combination that can be used when the menu is not dropped down. The ellipsis (…) on a submenu item indicates that a dialog box will follow. The drop-down sign (a little triangle) shows that there is a further set of choices to be considered.

Here are the main menu's options and what they contain:

➤ **File**—New Record, Open Database, New Database, Maintain Databases, Print Reports, Setup Printer, Synchronize, Configure, Log Away, Log in Another User, Exit

➤ **Edit**—Undo Ctrl+Z, Cut Ctrl+X, Copy Ctrl+C, Paste Ctrl+V, Copy Contact Details, Edit Contact Ctrl+E, Delete Contact, Record Properties, Record Details, Timer, Toolbars, Custom Templates, Preferences

➤ **View**—New Contact Window, Contact Groups, Calendar F7, Activity List F6, E-mail Center F5, E-mail Waiting Online, InfoCenter, Projects, Personal Rolodex F11, Literature Fulfillment, Sales Tools, Analysis, GoldMine Logs

➤ **Lookup**—Company, Contact, Last, Phone1, Indexed Fields, Detail Records, Filters, SQL Queries, Text Search, Go To, Internet Search

➤ **Contact**—Dial Phone, Insert a Note Ctrl+I, Write, Create E-mail, Take a Phone Message, Assign a Process, Browse Web Site

➤ **Schedule**—Call, Next Action, Appointment, Literature Request, Forecasted Sale, Other Action, Event, To-do, GoldMine E-mail

13

- **Complete**—Scheduled Call, Unscheduled Call, Message, Next Action, Appointment, Sale, Other Action, Event, To-do, Correspondence, Pending Activities
- **Tools**—Automated Processes, Server Agents, Import/Export Wizard, Global Replace Wizard, Territory Realignment, Merge/Purge Records, Delete Records Wizard, Strategic Solutions, BDE Administrator, Year 2000 Compliance, System Performance
- **Window**—Tile, Tile Wide, Cascade, Arrange Icons, Close All, Tool Bar, Status Bar, [1,2,…the windows open in the workspace]
- **Help**—Help Topics, How Do I, Referentia Tutorial, Release Notes, Newsgroups, GoldMine Web Site, Update GoldMine, About

Accommodating Remote or Travelling Users

A GoldMine database is intended to be shared by all users who work with the same set of contact records that it contains. Some or all of these users might go on the road from time to time and collect fresh information about the contacts by entering it into their little electronic friends—luggables, portables, laptops, palmtops, and even curious attachments on their mobile phones. In this section, we'll show you how to set up GoldMine for a portable device.

The key to understanding what kind of installations you can perform is the serial number on your registration card. (Did you save a copy of the serial number? We told you it was important!) A GoldMine Master License bears a three-part code:

D	-0005	-12345678
License type	Number of users	Serial number

Separating License Types

There are two types of Master Licenses that are installed only on an organization's primary network:

D GoldMine dBase License (D-*xxxx* users)

G GoldSync License (G-*xxxx* sites)

Each Master License can be distributed in various ways. For instance, you can add more GoldMine users or GoldSync sites to your existing license. You also can create a sublicense for any users that run GoldMine on an offsite PC.

There are three types of sublicenses for remote sites and remote users:

GoldMine Undocked (U-0001 user)

GoldMine Sublicense (S-*xxxx* users)

GoldSync Sublicense (Y-*xxxx* sites)

Chapter 1 ➤ *Staking Your Claim: Opening Up the GoldMine*

Any sublicense inherits the ID code of the Master from which it was created.

You can inspect your Master License from the main menu by selecting **File**, **Configure GoldMine**, **License Manager**. Figure 1.3 shows my license—well, almost.

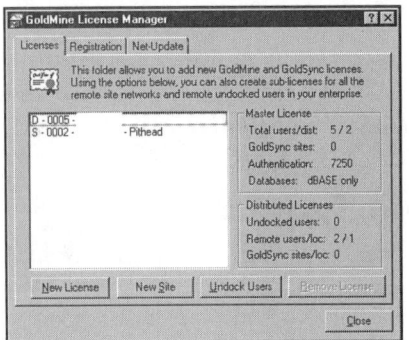

Figure 1.3

My license allows up to five users.

From the GoldMine License Manager screen, there are buttons to create or remove sublicenses:

New License

New Site

Undock Users

Remove License

Each of these options offers a dialog box to identify the user or site. The GoldMine software generates a license number and key code that has to be used when you are installing GoldMine on the remote PC for which it is intended.

GoldMine uses this system of license numbers and key codes to synchronize the data between the various sites and users associated in the Master License. It does so by using a built-in function called Remote Synchronization. For installations where there are many users who need to be frequently updated, there is a separate program called GoldSync. This can harmonize all the contact databases without attention from a user.

GoldSync is an add-on program that can automate the remote synchronization of many GoldMine systems using standard telephone, network, or Internet connections. Normal synchronizing occurs when the various workstations are able to be connected directly with each other. Remote synchronization is the process of preparing files of data to be sent by a communication medium that is not dedicated as part of a GoldMine network. For example, sets of data can be transferred to remote sites and users, and related transfer sets are returned to the master workstation so that all sites are updated as the process is repeated.

15

You can purchase GoldSync from GoldMine software suppliers. Its list price is $215 for a one-site license.

In all of these arrangements, the Master License serial number is copied to all the satellite sites. When remote synchronization is initiated, GoldMine checks this serial number to make sure that no updating can occur from or to installations that are not part of the distributed license.

A user who has a portable computer would need an undocked sublicense created from the license used in the main office. This would allow the user to work in either place without changing licenses. Synchronizing contact records would be simplified.

Inspecting the State of Your System

It helps to know some information about your computer to use GoldMine efficiently. Fortunately, GoldMine is happy to provide this information. You can use a simple technique to check your computer's available memory and disk space, and also to verify your license status.

To view your current license, select **Help**, **About**. This will show you the login banner screen showing your license. There are three buttons. If you click the **GoldMine** button, you will see more details about the GoldMine head office and support services. The **System** button shows how your system is configured and offers you a **Copy All** button. Clicking this button will load your Clipboard with the details. Open a Word or Notepad document and paste the Clipboard contents there.

My system is clearly running short of free disk space on drive C. I think I might have filled it with stuff from the Internet! Check out Figure 1.4 to see more.

Figure 1.4
Information about my system is revealed.

Using Free Support

GoldMine is a complex program, and it's understandable that you'd need help from time to time. That's probably why you bought this book! Fortunately, GoldMine also provides several ways to get information if you're stuck, and they're all free!

Chapter 1 ➤ Staking Your Claim: Opening Up the GoldMine

The first line of free support is the Help button on your GoldMine screen. Try pressing **F1** when your pointer is in the part of GoldMine that you need advice about. From the help screens, there are usually several active buttons to guide you to pertinent advice.

Consulting the Online KnowledgeBase

There are two portals to online knowledge: the GoldMine Web site (http://www.goldmine.com/), and the KnowledgeBase that was delivered to the InfoCenter on your computer when you first installed GoldMine. You can select **InfoCenter** from the **View** drop-down menu, or you might have an **InfoCenter** icon on your toolbar. Figure 1.5 shows the kind of information available from this handy resource.

> **Learn the Lingo**
>
> **Go Deep to Get the Best Help from F1**
>
> Go to a menu option or a relevant dialog box to get the most focused response from F1.

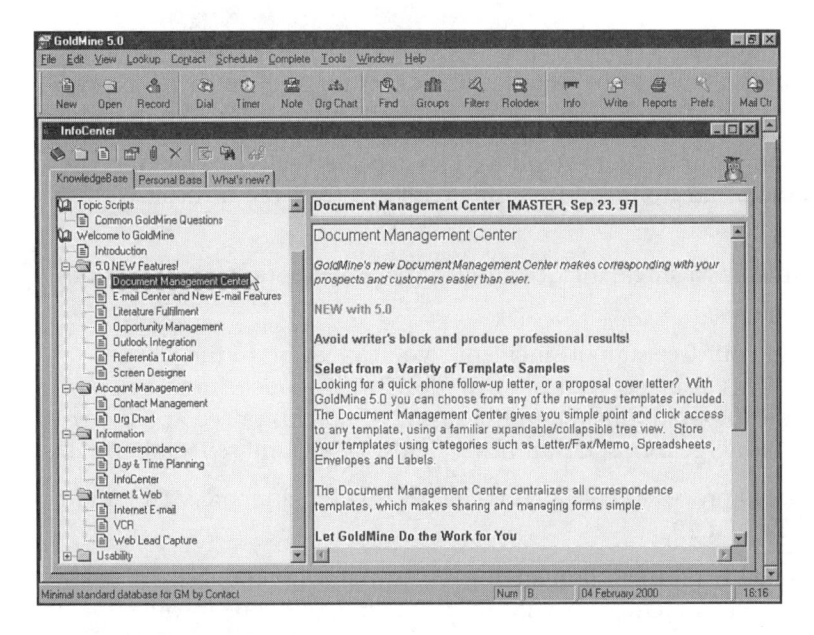

Figure 1.5

Almost everything you need to know can be found in the InfoCenter.

Although GoldMine is delivered with operating know-how in the KnowledgeBase, you can replace or supplement it with information particular to your line of work. The Personal Base tab in the InfoCenter opens doors to information that is visible only to the user who put it there. Chapter 18, "Share the Wealth: Distributing Nuggets of Information," discusses how to be an online librarian in the InfoCenter.

17

Part 1 ➤ *GoldMining for Beginners*

Downloading from the GoldMine Web Site

Wisdom from the Web comes via the **GoldMine Web Site** option, which appears in the **Help** drop-down menu. Free downloadable documents come in three varieties: strategic white papers, manuals, and tips.

My suggestion is to dig every last nugget of information from the GoldMine on your desk before crawling over the Web. You might get caught in the publicity materials, which include some very attractive demonstration packages.

The FactsBack Document Service is available as downloads from the Web or as Fax on Demand. Call 310-459-1222 from a fax machine with a handset and select **3** for this voice-guided service. FactsBack #998 is an index of the documents available.

Using GoldMine Premium Support Services

A premium service is defined as support that you have to pay for, although you might be allowed the first few calls for free. The premium phone support service is available 7:00 a.m. to 5:00 p.m. (Pacific time) Monday through Thursday, and until 4:00 p.m. on Friday.

A single-user GoldMine system is allowed three incidents; a 10-user system, seven. GoldSync for three sites is allowed two technical incidents for free, and a 10-site system is allowed five.

Each issue is assigned an Issue ID that is used to track repeated calls on the same incident. Minor matters might be grouped into a single issue if they can be dealt with in about 10 minutes.

Support by fax is counted as a single incident unless it entails more than 10 minutes of the technician's time.

If you get to the end of your free support incidents, you can go on to the pay-per-incident arrangement. This also gets your problem dealt with sooner than free incidents. Premium support for GoldMine 5.0 in the spring of 2000 is priced at $35 per incident in the realm of merge forms, customizing fields, views, and scheduling.

Problems with automated processes cost $55. Incidents involving reports and remote synchronization are charged $95.

GoldMine 5.0 is delivered with an accompanying CD containing products and services that are designed to complement GoldMine. Chapter 22, "Boom Town: Extending GoldMine by Adding on Software," looks at some of these add-ons.

Chapter 1 ➤ *Staking Your Claim: Opening Up the GoldMine*

The Least You Need to Know

➤ GoldMine 5.0 installs itself from a CD-ROM—but you need to have your license card ready.

➤ You can install a single-license GoldMine to one base computer and one portable.

➤ The License Manager dialog box will encourage you to register your installation online to the GoldMine Web site.

➤ Copious help is available from the Installation guide and from the Help menu after you have installed GoldMine.

Chapter 2

Scratching the Surface: Setting GoldMine to Work

> **In This Chapter**
> ➤ What should I get GoldMine to do?
> ➤ How to tell myself what to do
> ➤ How to press the right buttons

In the previous chapter, you installed GoldMine. So now you have a glistening GoldMine running on your desk (or at least an icon sitting on your desktop, begging to be clicked). Brand new? New to you? Why not start by putting it in its place? Show it who's boss.

What GoldMine Can Do for You

GoldMine is an extensive system of files and automatic procedures—a super card index. One way to remember and look after your contacts is to keep a set of paper index cards each with the details of one contact. If you are tidier than I am, you will probably write the surname of the contact on the top line of the index card so that you can keep all the cards in alphabetical order.

GoldMine offers the better way to keep track of your contacts. As you'll see, it's faster and more flexible than maintaining boxes of index cards—and less of a fire hazard, too.

Part 1 ➤ *GoldMining for Beginners*

If you want to see what the GoldMine equivalent of an index card is, select **File**, **New Record** from the main menu, or click the **New** icon button in the toolbar. Figure 2.1 shows the kind of starting information you will need for a contact record to be useful. Figure 2.2 shows how this information appears in a new contact record when you select **OK** to create it. As you can see, GoldMine lets you add much more information than the basic contact details.

Figure 2.1

Starting off a new contact record with the fundamental information you will need to manage this potential business connection.

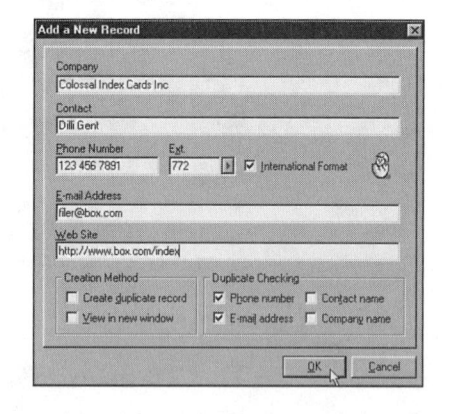

Figure 2.2

All the primary information is in place, ready for you to enlarge it by recording the department of your contact.

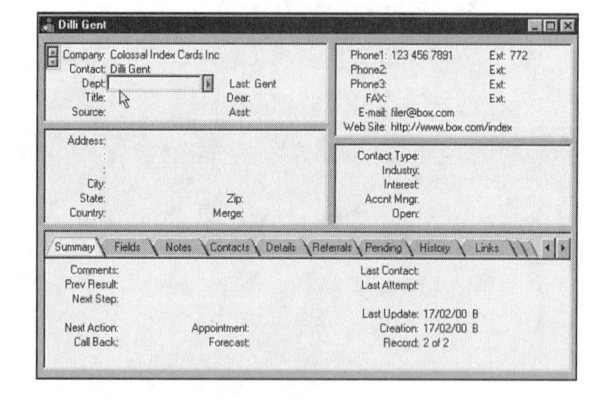

GoldMine must always have a contact database open. It will use the contact file set used on the previous occasion, which might be the default Common Contact Set with which it is delivered.

Having seen how extensive a GoldMine contact record can be, you might yearn for something simpler. Having a lot of information is wonderful, but it can be distracting if you're just looking for a phone number. Fortunately, GoldMine offers a display that is not only simpler but also more private.

Personal Rolodex is a GoldMine function that allows you to have a private set of names and telephone numbers that can be dialed from your screen, but which cannot be accessed by any other user. Figure 2.3 shows what you get if you select **View**, **Personal Rolodex** from the main menu. As you can see, simply type a keyword and

GoldMine displays the matching contacts, just like looking up names in a phone directory. Also in Figure 2.3, I have right-clicked for the local menu and selected the **Output to** submenu. Doing so lets me print a concise contact list.

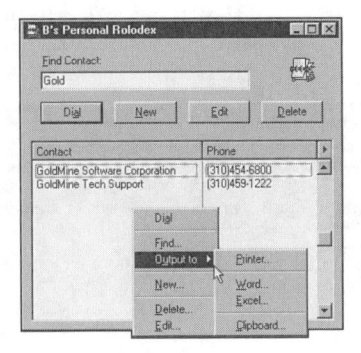

Figure 2.3

You can search the Personal Rolodex for handy private telephone numbers, and use the local menu to make a copy of the full list.

The point about a networked system such as GoldMine is to be able to share information between everyone who needs it for business. Any shared information ideally should be linked to a contact record or placed in a public information store where any user can get to it. Because the Rolodex stores records no one else can access, it should be reserved for telephone numbers that are not part of business.

All your Rolodex entries have to be made by you. GoldMine will not collect numbers for you.

Exploiting Your Computer

You don't need to know exactly how the GoldMine software works. What you do need to be absolutely clear about is how your organization should be managing its customer contacts and the information that is available from them. After that's straight, GoldMine can help you implement this strategy by making the information available to the ones who need it.

Computerized card index systems have been around for years, but GoldMine has developed the concept in many interesting directions. For instance, you can define a sequence of tasks that are to be performed at certain times and under specified conditions. You can then set this sequence to be triggered automatically by a defined occasion or calendar event. You also can arrange the system to assign the various work elements to the persons most able to perform them at the moment when they are needed. And, as in all GoldMine activities, an exact log of the events and outcomes can be recorded and analyzed.

A modern customer contact management system has to expect incoming messages on all channels—and must be able to transmit over the same range. Thus, voice, fax, and Internet communications are regarded as the normal components of a fluctuating mixture of messages. GoldMine routinely associates all messages connected with a customer, regardless of his or her medium of communication, by automatically making an entry for each message on the relevant contact record.

Noting Useful To-do Activities

If you are working hard and long, you had better keep a list of things you need to do to avoid being ejected from your work, family, or society at large. GoldMine allows you to schedule a To-do activity, which is a task that has a priority but no date. Figure 2.4 shows the dialog box for creating a To-do task.

Figure 2.4

I am planning to do an important task that is not specifically time-tabled, nor is it associated with a particular contact.

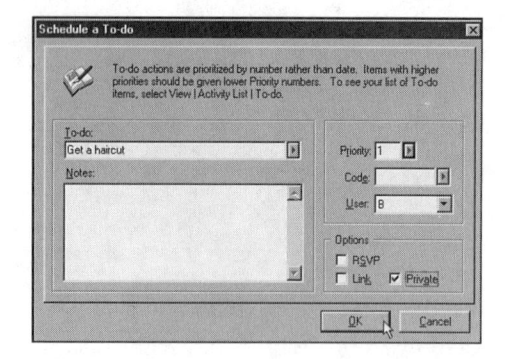

The following sequence will enable you to start making your own To-do list:

➤ You have to meet Auntie Alice at the airport. From the main menu, select **Schedule**, **To-do**.

➤ In the **To-do** field, enter the name or description of the task you want to do, or select one from the drop-down browse list. Auntie Alice is top priority—but not business. No contact record.

➤ Press **Tab** to move to the next field, **Notes**, and record any helpful text. Auntie's flight number and arrival time must be noted.

➤ Press **Tab** and adjust the priority of this task. Nine is lowest, 1 is highest. Would you dare leave her stranded?

➤ Press **Tab** and enter or select an activity code. This field might be left empty. Can you claim business mileage for this trip?

➤ Press **Tab** and select another user if you are assigning the task to someone else. Impossible, under the circumstances.

➤ Press **Tab** and toggle the **RSVP** check box, by pressing the **spacebar**, to have GoldMine automatically set up a request to the user to acknowledge that a task has been scheduled for him to do.

➤ Press **Tab** and toggle the **Link** check box to signify you want the task to be linked to the contact record that is currently open in your workspace. Not for Auntie Alice.

➤ Press **Tab** and toggle the check box to mark this activity as **Private** if you don't want other users to inspect the details of this task. Perhaps.

➤ Press **Tab** and press **OK** to have this To-do task recorded in your activity list. If you don't record this activity, your to-do list will not show it as a reminder.

Chapter 2 ➤ *Scratching the Surface: Setting GoldMine to Work*

In GoldMine, the To-do list is not just for you, the user that is logged on. You can use it to give yourself reminders of private tasks or activities that are not connected with any particular contact or group of contacts. However, you also can assign a To-do task to another user. You can link any To-do task to a contact if you want to plan work in connection with this contact that has a priority but no scheduled timetable. Come to think of it, perhaps Auntie Alice should have been a scheduled appointment.

Figure 2.5 illustrates the To-do list for user B. B's To-do list shows all the unfinished tasks. As you can see, B also can view notes by right-clicking and then selecting **Options**, **View**, **Detailed View** from the resulting menu.

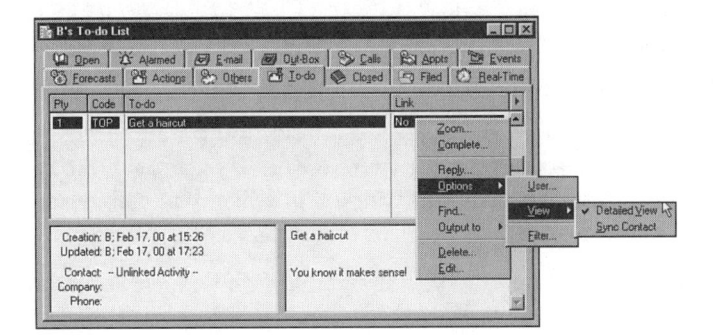

Figure 2.5

I am making plans for important things I must do, sooner or later.

To see your outstanding activities—I mean uncompleted, not award-winning—select **View** from the main menu, and click **Activity List**. Here you can see Auntie Alice in the To-do tab and all your pending activities in the Open tab.

Strike It Rich

Ace Is High

GoldMine likes to work with priorities from 1 (top priority—must do it now) down to 9 (get around to it some day). You must assign the priority number. Your planned activities will get sorted in this order unless they have been scheduled with a date. Some users try to schedule a date to draw attention to the need to get started on an activity.

> ### Strike It Rich
>
> ### Pop-Up Menus Offer Many Useful Options
>
> Like most Windows programs, GoldMine lets you access a host of useful options by right-clicking. GoldMine is special, however, in that it also offers quick keyboard access to these choices. GoldMine takes note of where your cursor is pointing and displays the most appropriate local menu—the most useful set of choices—if you right-click or press **F2**.
>
> For example, if you are pointing at the space next to a field title on a contact record, the local menu will be the browse list, if there is one. If no browse list has been compiled, you will be offered the Lookup window in which you can generate or edit new items for the browse list.
>
> Your keyboard might have a special menu key that gives you one-touch access to the Windows Start menu. This key also works like F2.

The personal To-do list appears as a tab in the activity window. You access the activity window by selecting **View**, **Activity List** from the main menu or by pressing **F6**. GoldMine defines an activity by an activity record comprising at least an activity reference text. If you first created this activity record, your username will be recorded on it with the date and time you finished entering the details. By default, an activity is scheduled for immediate action, but you can specify a different time and date. The essential feature of an activity is that it remains open until you execute a **Complete** command to show whether you have done what was intended.

To see your activity lists, press **F6**. You'll see 12 activity list tabs. The tab on top will be the one you used previously, or **Open** (the default tab) if you haven't used another tab yet. You can bring any tab to the top by clicking it.

You can view the details of any activity on any tab by highlighting the line entry and selecting **Zoom** in the local menu. Zooming in on an activity offers you the same details that appear in the Detailed View, but with more space to read any notes you made when you first scheduled this activity and assigned a priority to it. Chapter 4, "The Right Look: Making Things Happen," discusses activities in more detail.

So there you have it. All you need is a Rolodex and a smart To-do list. You could just keep building your list on the basis of what happened during the day. But what if you could not remember everything that had happened? Suppose you worked with a team who shared some of the same contacts? Is this muddle familiar? You need some way of noting which items on the To-do list have been completed. Fortunately, GoldMine rides to the rescue with the technique we'll discuss next.

Completing a To-do Activity

GoldMine always has a contact record active, even if you have minimized the contact window. Unless you select another contact, the details of this active contact will be used if necessary in any activity you schedule.

When you have done all that you can do in relation to a planned activity, you should select **Complete** from the main menu or from a local menu (remember, you access those by right-clicking or pressing **F2**). Identify which type of activity you are finishing off. Figure 2.6 shows me recording the fact that I carried out this planned To-do task and declared it to be a success. Select **Complete**, **To-do** when you are finished with something on your To-do list.

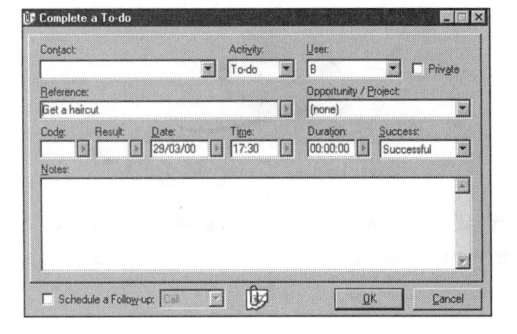

Figure 2.6

Even an unscheduled private To-do activity can be recorded as completed.

If you have not linked a To-do activity to a specific contact, GoldMine will remove a To-do activity after you complete it. All that will remain will be a record in your Closed Activity tab as a permanent notation that you finished the task. If you did link the To-do with the contact active at the time, the details of the complete activity will be recorded in the History tab of that contact.

Setting and Recording the Time

You will need to type in the time, both for scheduling a planned activity and when reporting on an activity that has been completed. You will see a dialog box in each case that includes a time field.

If you are pointing at a time field, you can right-click or press **F2** to reveal a clock on which you can adjust the time in steps of 15 minutes. Select an option button to show a.m. or p.m. Click **OK** to have the time entered in the time field.

From the keyboard, press the up arrow or the down arrow when you have selected a time field. GoldMine changes the time entry by five-minute increments.

Setting a Date

GoldMine always assumes you are living and working in the present moment. The default date is today—even if you are scheduling a major task that will take months.

When you have clicked a date field, the F2 or right-click browse routine will bring up your calendar. You have to move the highlight to set up the date you want entered.

You might have the date copied into your Clipboard, in which case you can highlight the contents of a date field and select **Paste** from the **Edit** menu (or from the right-click local menu) or press **Ctrl+V**. Typing a date will replace the highlighted entry.

Where's Your Month?

Check the date format used by your installation. Europeans and Americans use different formats for noting dates and both are easily confused. For example, April Fool's Day could be 1/4/00 or 4/1/00.

The date format is decided for all users when GoldMine is first installed. Changing it would entail a major rebuilding of the files.

The **Today** button will restore the date that was there by default—that is, the current date. Be sure to confirm that you have moved to the right month and year before you enter your decision by pressing **Select**.

Up and down arrows change the value in a date field by one day per press.

> ### Strike It Rich
> ### There's More Than Meets the Eye After ...
> The row of dots (...) after a menu or sub-menu item lets you know that choosing that command will invoke a dialog box presenting a further series of options—and probably a chance to change your mind.

Any menu can be altered, both in its layout and in the items displayed. GoldMine 4.0 has a slightly different main menu system from GoldMine 5.0. After your system is installed, you can change the layout and contents as you please.

GoldMine 5.0 is delivered with the GoldMine standard main menu and the basic toolbar docked close beneath it. Unfortunately, at the Windows default 800×600 resolution, there's not room to display all the menu if you have the icon labels in place. Figure 2.7 shows the Basic toolbar undocked from its default place below the main menu. As you can see, in its undocked form, there are several more icons you didn't see before.

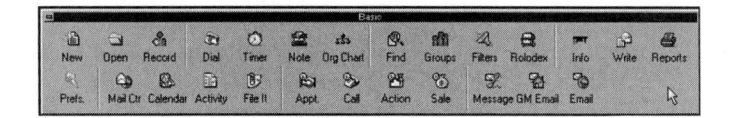

Figure 2.7

You can get most things to work from the main menu and the Basic toolbar, but you won't see all the toolbar icons when the Basic toolbar is docked.

Giving Yourself a Little Help Text

Fortunately, there's a way you can have GoldMine display everything in the docked Basic toolbar. But doing so means you'll have to sacrifice the helpful help text associated with each icon that you saw in Figure 2.7. If you omit these texts, the toolbars are shorter and take up less workspace.

Don't worry about not being able to tell what the icons mean. The same text appears in the status bar at the bottom of the screen, if you have chosen to have this status bar displayed. And as you edit your Preferences to eliminate the toolbar text, you can tell the cursor to display the text when you point to an icon.

Part 1 ➤ *GoldMining for Beginners*

> ### Strike It Rich
>
> ### Toolbars Can Be Undocked and Moved
>
> To undock any toolbar, click its handle bar, usually at the left end, and drag the toolbar into the GoldMine workspace. You can then reshape the toolbar by clicking a border and dragging until you have the shape you require.
>
> If you drag a toolbar away from its default location beneath the main menu, it will display its name and show a button at the top left to close the toolbar. The handle bar will disappear. If you click the title bar and drag an undocked toolbar back beneath the main menu, it will lose its title bar but regain its handle.

In addition to letting you choose how to display help text, GoldMine offers you several layouts of toolbars that range from Getting Started to Advanced. Because the Master user controls what other users can see and what they are allowed to do, you need to be logged in as the Master user in order to edit toolbars. To change how GoldMine displays your toolbars, select **Edit, Preferences**. Click the **Toolbar** tab. Deselect the **Show button text** check box, and make sure both **Show bubble help** and **Show status bar help** are selected. Figure 2.8 shows how I've made those changes.

Figure 2.8

You can adjust Toolbar preferences to display help text on the button, the status bar, or when you point to a button with your mouse.

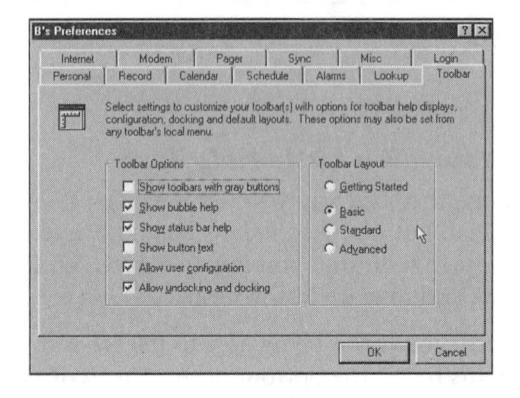

After you have chosen a toolbar layout in the Preferences dialog box, it will be displayed whenever you log on. You can adjust it to suit the kind of work you are doing. This is referred to as *customizing*, and you will be warned that your temporary alterations will be lost when you log off. Customizing is discussed further in Chapter 9, "Prettying Up the Place: Customizing Startup and Settings."

> **The Least You Need to Know**
>
> ➤ GoldMine can be made to record anything about you and your contacts.
>
> ➤ To-do activities are given priorities but not dates.
>
> ➤ Menus and toolbars can be customized to display more icons and helpful text.

Chapter 3

Your Treasure Trove: Storing Contact Information

In This Chapter

➤ Getting your hands on existing contact records

➤ Adding information

➤ Making new contact records

➤ Making better contact records

GoldMine has many mechanisms that help you manage large amounts of information. But all these mechanisms depend on you being able to create contact records that you can find again when you need them. This chapter starts by exploring the File and Edit functions (these spring into action if you work from the main menu). This is usually along the top line of your GoldMine window—but it is possible for it to wander elsewhere.

Entering contact data is pretty straightforward, even if you're new to GoldMine. However, like most computer programs, GoldMine has its funny little ways—some of them well worth getting acquainted with.

Controlling Contact Data

In a contact manager system, virtually all data is connected in some way with at least one contact record. There are various types of records in GoldMine, but they are all marshaled as a set of files that is usually referred to as a *database*.

Commanding Files

The File menu offers commands to work with databases organized around a set of contact records (see Table 3.1).

Table 3.1 The File Menu

Option	Function
New Record	Creates a fresh blank contact record in whatever database you have open at the time.
Open Database	Shows you the list of contact databases that live in your default location. You can move around until you find the one you are looking for, and then have it opened. Your previous database will be closed with the data saved as entered.
New Database	Perhaps you should check with your supervisor before making a new database. The GoldMine philosophy is to have all the contact records together in the same database—just pull out the ones you need for a particular purpose. This option calls up the Databases Wizard.
Maintain Databases	What a good idea! Makes sure that GoldMine fetches contact records as quickly as possible. See Chapter 17, "Be the Boss of the Territory: Maintaining Databases."
Print Reports	There are millions of reports waiting for you. You get to see their outputs on the screen before cluttering up any printer. See Chapter 13, "At the Mill: Generating the Reports You Like."
Setup Printer	Allows you to confirm or change your default printer or its habits. See Chapter 5, "24-Karat Printouts: Generating Paper by Printing and Faxing."
Synchronize	Reveals a submenu described in detail in Chapter 19, "High Noon: Synchronizing Records." The last item allows you to Copy or Move contact records to another database in your collection.
Configure	Opens a door to commands reserved for a supervisory personage with Master rights who can change how all GoldMine users do their work. See Chapter 9, "Prettying Up the Place: Customizing Startup and Settings."
Log Away	The associated icon shows you the exit door. You are expected to say how long you will be gone.
Log in Another User	This shows the GoldMine opening screen with your username in place—but another user can take over, or you can enter again as somebody else.
Exit	Off goes GoldMine, leaving you looking at whatever rubbish has accumulated on your desktop.

Commanding Edits

The first four items in the Edit menu are essentially for messing about with the Clipboard. They work the same as in Windows; Table 3.2 provides a quick summary.

Table 3.2 The Edit Menu

Option	Function
Undo (Ctrl+Z)	Can be used for going back a step although it isn't always obvious what it's going to undo!
Cut (Ctrl+X)	Cut out the highlight text and copy it to your Clipboard for later.
Copy (Ctrl+C)	Copy the highlighted text to your Clipboard.
Paste (Ctrl+V)	Empty the contents of your Clipboard into the field or note space beginning where your insertion point is blinking—which might not be where your cursor is pointing unless you recently clicked there.

> **Strike It Rich**
>
> **See What Your Clipboard Has to Offer**
>
> Windows comes with a handy Clipboard Viewer that can let you see what the Clipboard contains before you paste it. It isn't always installed by default, though. To see if you have it, click the **Start** menu, and then click **Programs**, **Accessories**. If you see the Clipboard Viewer's icon, you can click it to view the contents.
>
> If you are running Microsoft Word 2000, you can click **View**, **Toolbars**, **Clipboard** to get the Clipboard toolbar. You can choose from 12 of the most recent clips to paste. Just point to each item to see the first 50 characters of text, or a temporary label if the item is a picture.

Table 3.3 shows the three editing commands that are special to GoldMine contact records.

Table 3.3 GoldMine-Specific Editing Commands

Option	Function
Copy Contact Details (Alt+E,S)	Offers you a dialog box in which you can check which aspects of the contact record are to be copied to the Clipboard.
Edit Contact (Ctrl+E)	Jumps you back into wherever you were last working in the contact record on top of your workspace.
Delete Contact (Alt+E,L)	Offers you a dialog box to confirm exactly what you want to get rid of.

Finding a Contact Record

You can search for something useful to do in many ways, but a good way in a sales office is to work from your contacts. From the main menu, select **Query**, **Contact**. This will give you a contact listing you can scroll through. You can also type the first letter of your contact to jump to that part of your listing.

> **Mine Safety**
>
> **Soundex Word Matching Is Not Infallible**
>
> For example, Hazel will not be found if you type in azel. You should try to get the first letter correct.

You might not be able to remember the exact name of your contact. As you start to put letters in the **Find Contact** field, the list display will immediately move to the best match it can find according to the first letters, or according to the Soundex match. If it cannot find a match using the letters you type in, automatically the Soundex lookup software will try to find a name that more or less sounds like the spoken sound of these letters, even if the target name is much longer.

When you find your target contact, click on it and your worktop will bring the contact record to the top. If there are any outstanding things for you to do, they can be inspected by clicking on the **Pending** tab.

Of course, if you are very methodical, your target contact record will already be actively sitting on top of your GoldMine workspace.

The contact record that is on the top of your GoldMine workspace is assumed to be the one you are working on—the record most likely to be altered as a result of your actions. This is called the *active record* or the *record with input focus*.

GoldMine is always trying to be helpful, so it will open with the collection of records you were last using and with the final record you were looking at as the active record.

Figure 3.1 shows how I have called Lookup to search my records according to the entry in the Contact field.

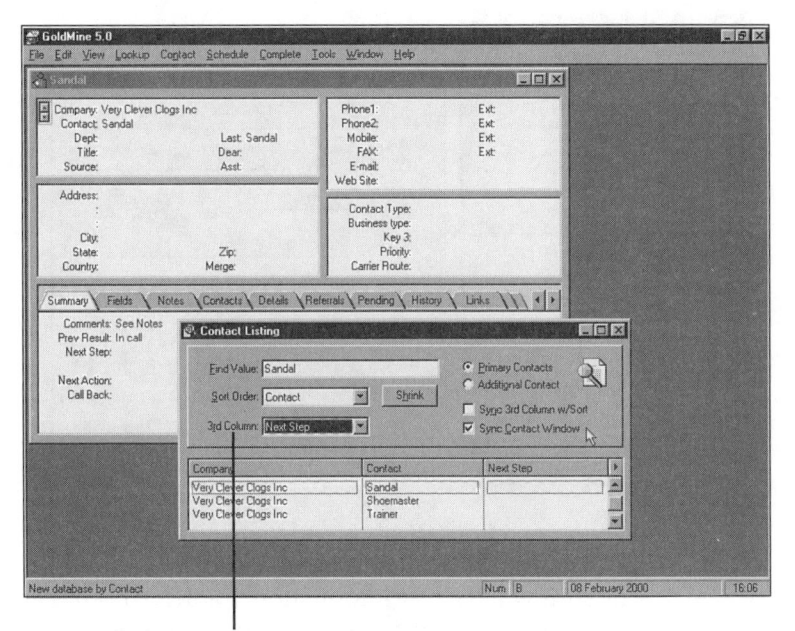

Chapter 3 ➤ *Your Treasure Trove: Storing Contact Information*

Figure 3.1
I spy someone beginning with S in the Contact Listing.

Column 3 will tell me my next step.

Sync Contact Window has been checked to ensure that whichever line I highlight will open the contact record. To select another record, move the highlight bar with an up or down arrow. If you see whom you want, try a click.

Cloning an Existing Record

From the main menu, select **File**, **New Record**. Doing so opens the Add a New Record dialog box, as shown in Figure 3.2. If you click the **Create Duplicate Record** check box—twice if it is already ticked—you will find that your new record will have the basic information copied from your active record.

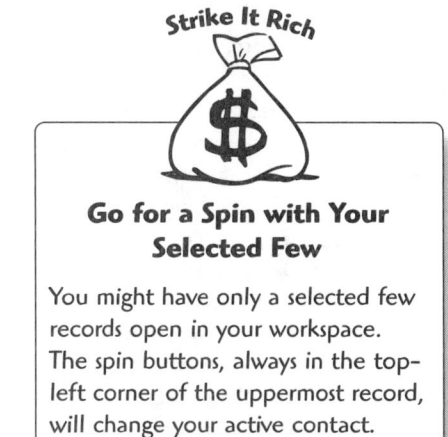

> **Strike It Rich**
>
> **Go for a Spin with Your Selected Few**
>
> You might have only a selected few records open in your workspace. The spin buttons, always in the top-left corner of the uppermost record, will change your active contact.

There is a check box that displays the new record in a separate window. There are also four check boxes that control how you want the check for duplicates to be conducted.

Figure 3.2

Create a new contact in the same company by partially duplicating the active record.

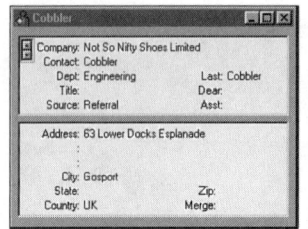

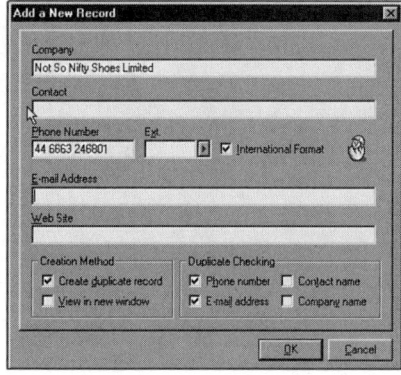

Beware the Enter Key!

In a contact record, you can press **Enter** after typing in field data, but do not press Enter until you are finished with a dialog box because GoldMine will assume that you do not want to edit anything else in the display. For example, use **Tab** and **Shift+Tab** to move about, or click the field you need. Up and down arrows are also very useful because they move your data entry window through the sequence of fields—without leaving any out.

When you click **OK** in the Add a New Record dialog box, the system will create a new contact record containing whatever information you have been able to supply. GoldMine automatically copies the last word of the Contact field into the Last (name) field.

When you select **OK**, or press **Enter**, GoldMine creates a contact record with a unique account number. The Summary tab will show your ID as the user who created the record and today's date. You can generate a record with little data or even a blank record. Obviously, you will need to come back to fill in some fields.

Toggling GoldMine Options

To activate any toggle option in GoldMine using the keyboard, press **Tab** to advance to the option, and then press the **spacebar**. To deactivate a toggle option, press the **spacebar**. The check mark disappears from the box.

Another method is to press **Alt** plus the underlined letter of the option. Doing so locates your pointer. You can then toggle the option on and off by using the spacebar or by clicking.

If you select a menu with keystrokes, GoldMine will highlight the first command. For example, **Alt** will highlight the first item in the main menu, **F** will open the options of the File menu, and **N** will open a new record.

The same thing happens if you click the **New** icon in a toolbar.

Adding Notes to a Contact Record

You can add a note to a contact record by selecting **Contact**, **Insert a Note** from the main menu. On the Basic toolbar there is a jolly picture of a manual typewriter that will do the same. Or you can press **Ctrl+I**. Whichever method you choose, Figure 3.3 shows what happens.

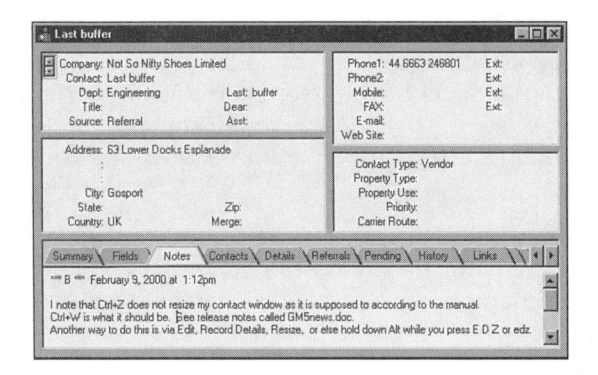

> **Mine Safety**
>
> **Are Your Options Dimmed?**
>
> A menu option will be dimmed if it is not going to do anything—perhaps because you have not previously selected any text, or because there is nothing in your Clipboard. Dimmed options cannot be executed.

Figure 3.3

Add a timed and dated note to the Notes tab prefixed with your user ID.

Your notes will be saved automatically.

Your status bar will briefly display the number of character bytes saved as notes. There is space for 64,000 characters. You would need to use the scroll buttons to read this much text.

Another way to save a note entry or alteration is by clicking outside the Notes tab. Curiously, you don't have to make a deliberate save if you are using the local menu—you could right-click in the **Notes** tab or press the keyboard's local menu key. You can select **Paste** and your notes will be updated permanently by the addition of whatever you had stored on your Clipboard.

Part 1 ➤ *GoldMining for Beginners*

Always Visit Your Local Menu

Right-click to invoke a local menu that depends on where your pointer is at the time. The local menu will probably contain just the very command you need next. Some keyboards have a Local Menu key that is also called the Application key. It carries an icon of a menu with a pointing arrow and also invokes the local menu that is relevant to the place where you last clicked.

Entering Standardized Data

There are some parts of a GoldMine record that you have to type in exactly or import from a file where someone has typed them—names and addresses, for example. But other fields are much more useful if everyone enters the data by selecting an entry from a lookup table. In that way it is easy to call up a report and let GoldMine tell you how many of your contacts have a particular entry in a specific field. Standardized data is information that is made up from one or more options on a lookup table. If you allow your users to freely enter text or numbers in a data entry window, then you don't have standardized data in that field.

If you are pointing at a record field, right-clicking will open a small window to receive your entry. To select a standardized value for this field, right-click on the space where the data will be displayed, or click the right arrow button.

You will see a lookup table or browse list. This list might contain only the entry Lookup window. In these circumstances you can either type in the entry you require, or you can click **Entry window** to get to the Field Lookup dialog box. Here you will be able to create a lookup entry that can be used over and over again, by you and by other users.

If your installation has been in use for some time, or if the administrator has installed a template for your particular industry, the lookup list might already contain a suitable entry, which you can highlight and click. Figure 3.4 shows the existing choices for the Department field. If the list is very long, you can jump closer to certain entries by typing in the first letter of the value you seek.

Figure 3.4

Find a standardized entry for this Department field from the lookup table.

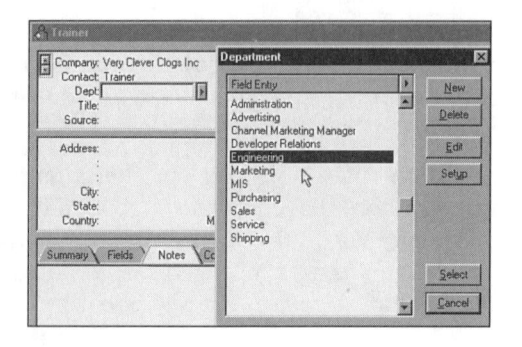

Chapter 3 ➤ *Your Treasure Trove: Storing Contact Information*

It's sensible to always create a lookup item if you think you might need it again in this field.

Improving a Browse List

Click a field and display the lookup table by pressing **F2**. The Entry dialog box appears, headed by the name of that field. Select **New** or **Edit** when you have highlighted an item to be changed.

Type or edit the characters for the entry, and click **OK** when you're done.

Putting More Than One Entry in a Field

You can place more than one value in a single field of a record, if you have created suitable entries in the lookup table.

A standard entry that ends with a semicolon (;) will be added to whatever is already in the field, and separated by a comma. The semicolon is not shown in the browse list.

A standard entry that ends with a percentage sign (%) will be placed in front of whatever is already in the field. Leave a space in front of the % if you want the entries to be separated.

Not all users are allowed to amend the F2 lookup setup. For instance, it might not be a good idea to let users enter text of their own composition and spelling! Chapter 14, "Round Up a Posse: Building a Sales Team," shows how the supervisor with Master rights can control which users are allowed to create new lookup entries.

> **Strike It Rich**
>
> **Set Up Your Pop-ups**
>
> You can arrange for a particular field to pop up the Browse List window when you click in the space where the field window will appear. Click **Setup** in the Browse List window to adjust your lookup possibilities, field by field.

> **Mine Safety**
>
> **Unpunctuated Lookups Overwrite**
>
> Selecting a lookup entry that does not have a semicolon or percentage sign will overwrite any existing field entry.

Attaching Descriptions and Explanations

When you first come to a menu, it might not be immediately obvious what each item means. You can attach a description or explanation to each entry by editing the entry to include two forward slash marks (//). These will not appear in the record, nor will any text that follows them.

Using Zip Codes

The zip code of the contact's address can be configured in various ways. For instance, you can configure GoldMine to expedite an address entry by filling in city and state information from a zip code entry in the browse list.

If you type a zip code that has not been previously recorded in GoldMine, the Zip Code Profile dialog box appears. Here you can record information about the zip code so that it can be used in the browse list procedure.

Getting Around Your Tabs

GoldMine is delivered with a standard set of tabs that holds various data fields that belong to the contact record. Each tab has a title that is visible and you can click on this title to bring the fields to the top of the tab display. Some partial tabs might be visible. They give access to further tabs.

Your GoldMine implementation might have some extra tabs that have been installed as an industry template, or were created by a user with Master rights.

You can also view the standard tabs by pressing Ctrl+ the initial letter of the tab name. After you have selected one tab you can move to another by using the left and right arrow keys.

Some of the tabs contain fields that are controlled directly by GoldMine. You can't enter data into these fields; they'll appear grayed out. The rest of the fields are available for contact data.

> **Learn the Lingo**
>
> **Look After Your Properties**
>
> *Properties* refer to the various details associated with a GoldMine object. Just as in many software systems, a GoldMine property is an attribute of a field, record, or file that has been assigned one or more values, which might be numeric or alphabetic.

Editing Contact Record Properties

The Edit menu also includes commands to access contact record properties and details.

The Record Properties option displays a dialog box with three tabs:

Phone Formatting allows you to choose between USA and non-USA phone number formats for the currently active record.

Ownership lets you assign ownership of this record to specific users and arrange for some of the fields to be "curtained" so that some users cannot see their values.

Alerts offers a dialog box to create or activate alerts, which are Record Alert messages that will appear on any user's workspace if this contact record becomes active there. The user is obliged to acknowledge a Record Alert—the user will have studied the reason why the alert has been activated. The alert name will appear in the Previous Result field of the Summary tab.

You can freely create alerts and then choose which ones to attach to your currently active record. Details of new alerts are automatically stored in the What's New? tab at the InfoCenter. You can transfer any alert to the KnowledgeBase if it is to be a permanent part of your working method.

A particular alert can be attached to a contact record, but no Record Alert message will appear unless the Enable Alerts check box has been ticked. The list will be grayed if the alerts are not enabled.

The Record Details menu offers a drop-down list of all the tabs in the current database. The standard tabs are shown in Figure 3.5. A tab is a collection of fields that have been grouped for a particular purpose. For instance, if you click the **Notes** tab, you will see a display of any notes that users have attached to the current contact record. If you cannot see the tab you require, try clicking one of the tab fragments at the right of the labeled tabs—this might reveal what you seek.

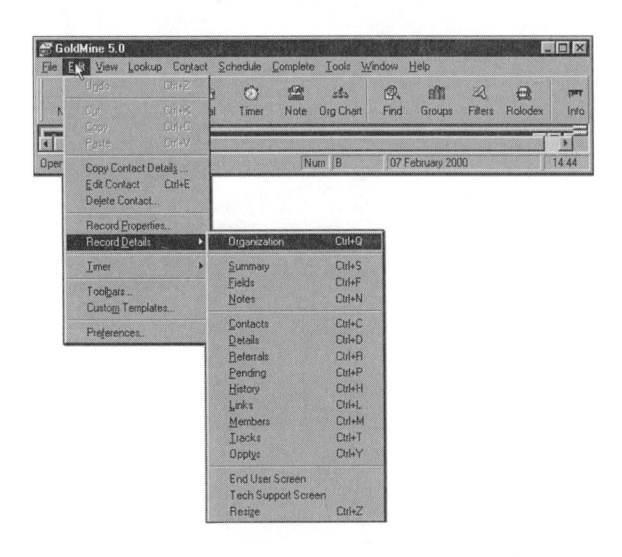

Figure 3.5

Go immediately to any tab in the current contact record.

Some fields in some of the tabs are updated automatically by GoldMine and might not be edited by users. Subsequent chapters discuss how working with the various functions will leave entries on the different tabs.

> **The Least You Need to Know**
>
> ➤ The File submenu item is mainly about databases.
>
> ➤ The Edit submenu is mainly about contact records.
>
> ➤ Contact records can usually be given sensible data by using the F2 lookup routine.
>
> ➤ GoldMine usually looks after itself and your contact records—no matter what you try to do.

Chapter 4

The Right Look: Making Things Happen

In This Chapter

➤ Having your GoldMine window show you exactly what you need

➤ Taking charge of what you plan to do and when

➤ Making some handy devices that will save you work

I sometimes wonder who it is that designs computer command screens. Why don't they ever contain what I want in the places I expect to find them? You have no excuses with GoldMine. Just about everything can be given a make-over.

As you would expect with a Windows system, there are menus with command names that appear when you point to them. There are drop-down and pop-up menus that can be highlighted. There are toolbars with a selection of jolly pictures that you can click. And all this comes as standard GoldMine.

This chapter will remind you of the kinds of adjustments that are possible and the various ways in which GoldMine can help you do your work—from setting up your workbench to enrolling little gremlins to press keys and buttons at your bidding.

Preparing Your Workspace

You might find it amazingly comforting to shuffle all the bits and pieces of GoldMine. Put every button and command thing where it is most comfortable to use. Make your own toolbars, or drag icon buttons about within the standard toolbars. There is no penalty for moving your furniture on a daily basis, and the GoldMine workspace offers you the same flexibility. More experienced operators might have a different setup for each type of work process. Other knowledgeable operators seem to leave everything where it was when the stuff was delivered. At least you get to drive your cursor off in the right direction when looking for a clever command.

They say that icons are good for productivity—yet many professionals hardly use their mice at all. My habit is to know the main menu pretty thoroughly and keep on trying to remember those whizzy hotkey combinations. For example, Alt+F4 shuts down GoldMine. F10 is even more useful because it highlights the first item at the left of the main menu—from there you can move the highlight using the arrow keys.

You've heard about the centipede syndrome—don't try to think too much what every leg is supposed to do or you may never walk again. It is possible to spend so much time using a system like GoldMine that you never actually have time to make any sales.

Controlling What You See

Putting your personal touches to your workspace is more than just cosmetic. Having a timer running when making a call may focus your attention. Arranging to have no more information displayed than you actually need may speed up work and reduce certain types of errors.

The timer increments by the second and has a display in your status bar at the bottom of your GoldMine window. To display the status bar, select **Window**, **Status Bar** from the main menu.

The Edit menu includes a pointer to the Timer submenu. You can set the timer going from zero with the **Start Timer** button. But, to stop it you must select **Stop Timer** from the **Timer** submenu, or else use one of the following keyboard shortcuts:

Shift+F8 to stop the timer.

Alt+F8 to stop and reset the time.

Ctrl+F8 to begin timing again after a stop with Shift+F8.

These shortcuts work only when GoldMine is the active window in your workspace. You can set the timer going for any purpose. Quite separately, your activities while logged on are recorded automatically in the Real-Time tab of your activities list.

Commanding Your Windows

GoldMine adapts the standard Window command to rearrange your open records and other windows such as Calendar and Activities. Try such patterns as Tile, Tile Wide, Cascade, Arrange Icons, Close All, Toolbar, or Status Bar. The lower part of this Window submenu will list the contact name of the active record in each of the record windows you have open—you must have at least one—and the titles of any other

GoldMine windows open in your workspace. For example, you may have two record windows, your calendar and your activity lists, all sharing your GoldMine window.

The Window menu item allows you to tick to view the toolbar or combination of toolbars that you were previously using. In this same way you can also view or obscure the status bar, which is at the lowest line of your GoldMine display. My preference is to always view the status bar because it often (but not always) gives me useful help messages about the open database or a command my cursor is highlighting.

Resizing Your Record Display

A neat way to resize the active record window in your workspace is **Ctrl+W**. You can also do this via **Edit**, **Record Details**, **Resize**, or else hold down **Alt** while you press **E**, **D**, **Z**. Hold down **Alt** and repeat these three letters until what you see is what you want.

The record resize command cycles the active contact between three layouts:

➤ Basic contact information alone

➤ Basic information plus phone numbers

➤ All standard fields plus the tab display with the last used tab open on top

Because it is a Windows window, you can click and drag any border of a contact record until it looks like you want it to.

Any other contact records you may have open will not be affected by a resize command. If you click on the **View Another Record** icon, your next record will be displayed full size, in a new record window. But if you use the spin buttons on the active contact window, you will make the next active contact appear in this same window—whatever its size.

Learn the Lingo

Close All Leaves One Open

There is always one record open in your workspace. It may be minimized, but not removed. It will usually be the last one you used in the current database.

However, you can open additional record windows, each with its own spin buttons and active record. Select **View, New Contact Window** in the main menu, or click the **Record** icon.

Strike It Rich

Please Excuse This Boring Advice: What a Drag!

Drag your window borders and move them to get the data you are working with as close as possible to where you need it.

> **Learn the Lingo**
>
> **Commands Can Change—Read GoldMine News**
>
> Your Record Details submenu might say that Resize is Ctrl+Z. This will not work on my installation, which is 5.00.041. Ctrl+W is the correct hotkey combination. Look through the GoldMine release notes on your installation disk and possibly online at gm5news.doc in your GoldMine root directory. This document will point out differences between GoldMine 4.0 and 5.0 and direct you to all known problems.

Configuring Your Toolbars

Select **Toolbars** from the **Edit** menu and you will get a list of the available toolbars. If you want to change your toolbar layout, select whichever one you prefer. Come back and deselect any unwanted toolbars.

If you want to make several changes to your toolbars, there is a better method. Select **Edit** from the main menu. Click **Toolbars** to get a dialog box that shows the available toolbars with a check mark against any you have open. Scroll through this list and click any toolbar name to check or uncheck it. This Toolbars dialog box has a **Reset** button—click it to restore the toolbars to the default GoldMine layout. Click **New** if you want to create a new toolbar.

The **New** button in this toolbar dialog box allows you to create the name of a new toolbar. GoldMine will show this in your workspace as an empty toolbar with the name you created. Now you must put some icons in your empty toolbar. From the **Edit** menu, choose **Toolbars**, **Insert Item**. This action opens the Insert Toolbar Item dialog box with a scrollable display of the icons in the Standard menu. Click the down arrow of the window containing the word Standard and click a different toolbar layout if the icon you want is not available in the Standard toolbar. See the inside front cover of this book for some suggestions of where the icons can be found. As an alternative to looking in an existing toolbar for an item, select **All Items** from the list of toolbars and scroll down until you find what you want.

When you see the icon you want, click and drag it to your new toolbar—or to any other toolbar you have open. The Insert Toolbar Item dialog box will remain open so that you can select another icon and drag it to a toolbar. Click **Close** when you have finished working on your toolbars.

Figure 4.1 shows how I have created a new toolbar and inserted two items from the Standard toolbar, and how I am now going to add one from the E-mail toolbar.

Only one window can be selected at a time, so only one of the contact windows will contain the active contact record. Click the window you want to activate.

Still in the **Edit** submenu, you can choose to work with **Custom Templates**. This command takes you straight to the Document Management Center (DMC), which is a list of the ready-made templates for just about any kind of communication.

Chapter 5, "24-Karat Printouts: Generating Paper by Printing and Faxing," provides an introduction to document templates and the Document Management Center.

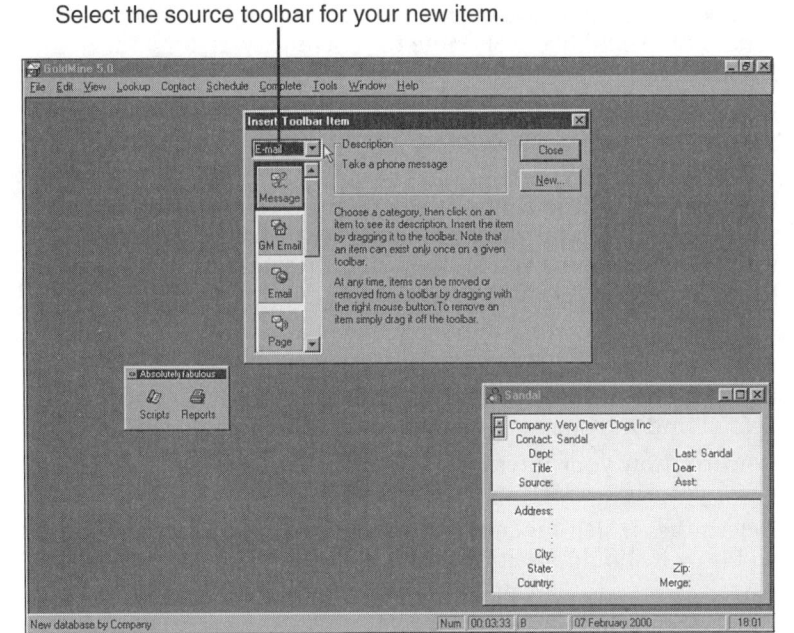

Select the source toolbar for your new item.

Figure 4.1
I have made an absolutely fabulous toolbar, and I am going to add to it some commands from the E-mail standard toolbar.

Editing Your User Preferences

You might sometimes want to modify some of the basic ways GoldMine operates. You access this capability by choosing **Edit**, **Preferences**. The icon for the Preferences command is a triple-flavored ice cream cone. The Preferences tabs described in Table 4.1 offer many choices that will be applied as defaults throughout GoldMine when you are signed on as the user.

Table 4.1   Preference Options

Tab	Choices
Personal	How you want to be titled and named in automatic document creations, including phone and fax numbers; you can also change your login password here.
Record	How GoldMine will display contact records and handle zip codes. Allows you to get rid of any tabs you never use. If you have tired eyes, you can show records with gray backgrounds rather than bright. Would you prefer a larger font? Colored field labels? You can change those settings here, too.

continues

Table 4.1 CONTINUED

Tab	Choices
Calendar	Can be told which days of the week and between which times you would like GoldMine to schedule work for you. Holidays can be arranged.
Schedule	Controls whether timing conflicts are to be reported and whether the timer is to clock in automatically while you are completing activities.
Alarms	GoldAlarm is a little control-freak treasure you can sit on your desktop. Alarms can be audible—with your choice of sounds! They can be verbal popups or messages in your status bar. Snooze delays can be structured.
Lookup	Controls how records will be sequenced and displayed while you are working with a contact listing view.
Toolbar	Lets you choose which standard toolbar layout to have by default and how those little help texts will be deployed.
Internet	Controls how your Internet service provider will be contacted while you are working down the GoldMine.
Modem	Determines which modem will stand by—ready for action—and how it should function when dialing.
Pager	Publishes your pager's PIN number and arranges to send emails for paging, if necessary.
Sync	Specifies what is to be done when documents must be linked to GoldMine records. Not the same as Remote Synchronization, which is between databases that may contain the same contacts. See Chapter 19, "High Noon: Synchronizing Records," for more details.
Misc	Oddments such as choice of 24-hour time format.
Login	Determines where the GoldMine root directory is to be found and where the global or master default database is. Sets which username shall be offered as the default login. Allows you to bypass the GoldMine login advertising banner if you are the sole user.

Many preferences are applied as soon as you click OK on any of the tabs. However, changes in login preferences will require that you login again. You will be quickly returned to your work in progress.

Commanding Views

A GoldMine view is like a portal to a set of functions. The Contact Record view opens a window into the data held on a contact person. The Activity List view is a separate window that shows you what work is waiting for you alone—the signed-on user, although you may have been assigned permission to view the activities planned for somebody else.

If you want more than one copy of a view, just give the command again. Figure 4.2 shows that I have set up two sets of contacts by having selected **View**, **New Contact Window**, even though GoldMine had already given me a contact window by default. When I first open a second contact window, it will refer to the same set of contacts that were available to the first window. But I can spin one set, or otherwise locate a contact, without disturbing the contact window that is not active.

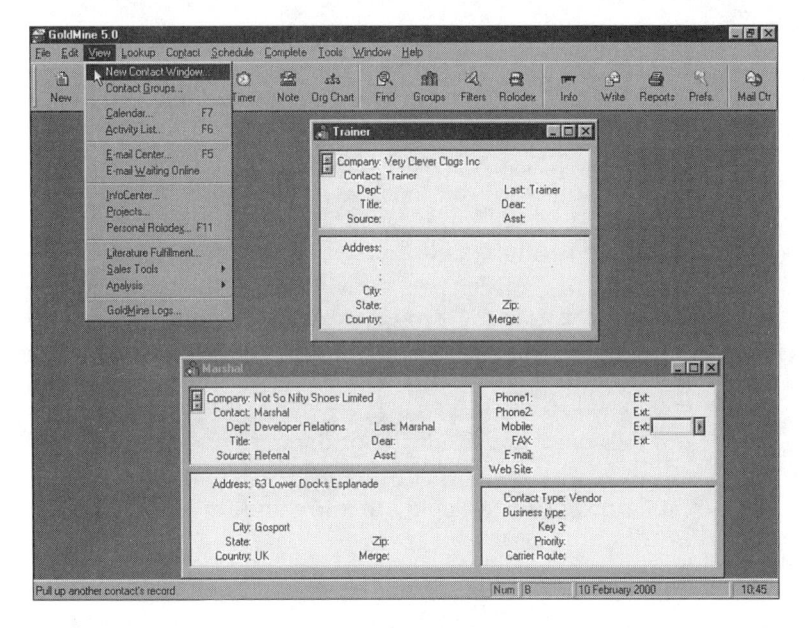

Figure 4.2

My new contact window allows me to play with two sets of contact records at once.

You can have many different contact windows open, but all the records in them must come from the same database. If you create a new record in one window, the same record can be accessed from all the other contact windows.

These are different views that can be accessed, appropriately enough, from the View submenu (see Table 4.2).

51

Table 4.2 Options Found Under the View Submenu

Option	Function
New Contact Window	Takes another contact record and opens it in a fresh window.
Contact Groups	Selects a previously defined group of contacts or builds a group using the Filters and Groups dialog box. See Chapter 11, "Panning for Gold: Filtering Contacts from the Database," for more details.
Calendar (F7)	Shows your calendar in the layout you were using previously.
Activity List (F6)	Shows your 14 activity lists with the last-used tab open on top.
E-mail Center (F5)	Shows your E-mail control center. See Chapter 6, "It Beats a Tin Can on a String: Managing Email."
E-mail Waiting Online	Shows your E-mail control center and automatically connects to your mail server. See Chapter 6 for more.
InfoCenter	Shows the KnowledgeBase and other folders of stored information, with the tools available to use and improve the InfoCenter. See Chapter 18, "Share the Wealth: Distributing Nuggets of Information."
Projects	Opens your Project Manager window so that you can see and control your projects and sales opportunities. See Chapter 15, "Looking for the Real Seams: Using the Opportunity Manager."
Personal Rolodex (F11)	Shows your private rolodex of names and telephone numbers and allows editing or dialing.
Literature Fulfillment	Opens your Literature Fulfillment Center where you can control the available literature and the planned distributions of it.
Sales Tools	Opportunities (or press F9) opens your Opportunity Manager. See Chapter 15 for more.
	Scripts opens your Telemarketing Scripts dialog box where the data for the currently active contact will be automatically available. From here you can select and maintain scripts and consult the InfoCenter. See Chapter 18 and Chapter 21, "Line Please: Creating Telemarketing Scripts."
Analysis	Accesses a range of procedures for analyzing contact data. See Chapter 16, "At the Assayer's Lab: Analyzing Leads."

You can pick and mix these view windows as you please, opening duplicate views if necessary.

Commanding Lookups

If you opt for Lookup from the main menu, GoldMine invites you to choose among the many ways of picking out contact records according to the value or character sequence in particular data fields. Company, Contact, and Phone1 are examples of primary fields that can be used for selecting records. They are available for all records. Chapter 11 discusses the many ways of locating a contact record or set of contact records.

Some fields are automatically indexed so that GoldMine can rapidly scan for the contacts you are looking for. Other fields contain details that can also be used to locate contact records, although the search will be slower because there is no automatic indexing.

Table 4.3   Options in the Lookup Menu

Option	Purpose
Company	Offers the Contact Listing display with the Company field as the sort basis. The default in the Find Value window will be the company name taken from the active contact record.
Contact	Offers the Contact Listing with the active contact as the default value for a search by contact.
Last	Offers the Contact Listing with the entry in Last as the default value for a search by the contact's last name.
Phone1	Offers the Contact Listing with the value in Phone1 as the default for a search by Phone1.
Indexed Fields	Offers the Contact Listing when you have chosen a field for the basis of the search. Allows you to specify a value for any of the fields that are automatically indexed. The chosen field will default to the value in the active record.
Detail Records	Allows you to select the name of a detail field. GoldMine will default to the value for the active record.
	Lookup displays a list of all the records that have any value in the chosen detail field. View makes the chosen contact active.
	Previous and Next will change the active contact to adjacent items on the list.
Filters	Allows you to choose a filter or group in order to identify a set of contacts.
SQL Queries	Allows you to define a search specification to scan the database using logical combinations of retrieval commands.

continues

Part 1 ➤ *GoldMining for Beginners*

Table 4.3 CONTINUED

Option	Purpose
Text Search	Allows you to confine your search to:
	Primary Fields
	Fields Below Tabs
	Notes
	All Fields
Goto	Offers a variety of ways to move about the contact set already open on your worktop.
Internet Search	Offers a predefined array of search engines and search specifications for searching the Web using data from the active contact record.

There are clearly many different ways of getting around the fields and records in GoldMine.

Controlling What You Do

After you and your E-mail Center have built up a set of contacts, you will be looking to move them on towards a sale. There are at least two aspects to bear in mind: You may have to do a lot of routine work, and you are likely to be short of time.

GoldMine helps you by setting up semi-automatic processes connected with your contact records. You can help yourself by scheduling your work and by sensibly completing each activity. Commands have been efficiently programmed for virtually anything you might want to do with your contacts and their records.

Commanding for Your Contact

The **Contact** button opens a nest of functions that use the data in your current contact record, or add to it. Figure 4.3 shows the Contact menu and the Create E-mail submenu.

When one of these activities entails composing a message that will or could be printed as a document, GoldMine offers a range of document templates.

Customizing Templates

You can add to the collection of templates by copying and editing an existing model, or by composing one from scratch. Select **Customize Templates** from the submenu that is relevant to the type of communication you are preparing. You will be taken to the Document Management Center, from where you can select your preferred template for use or editing, as shown in Figure 4.4.

Chapter 4 ➤ *The Right Look: Making Things Happen*

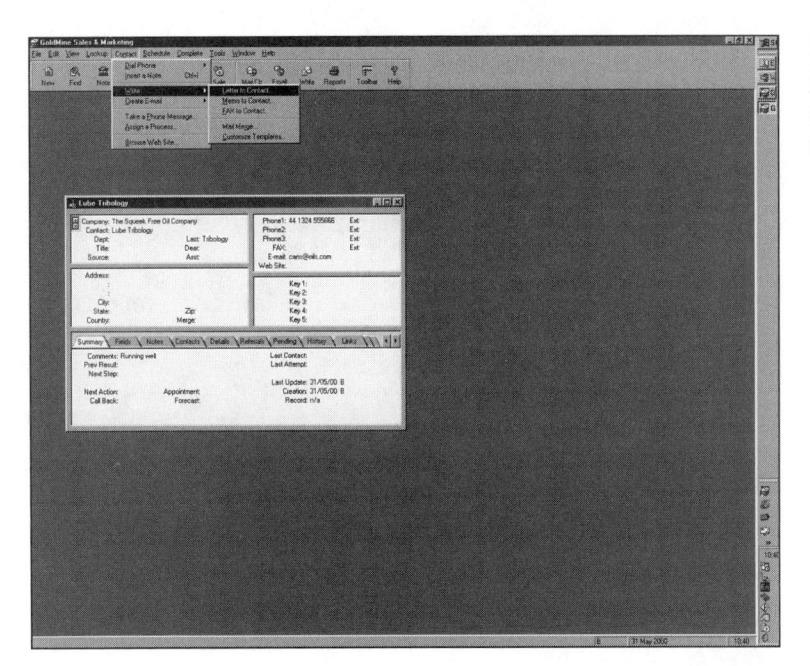

Figure 4.3
Preparing to do something useful in relation to this contact.

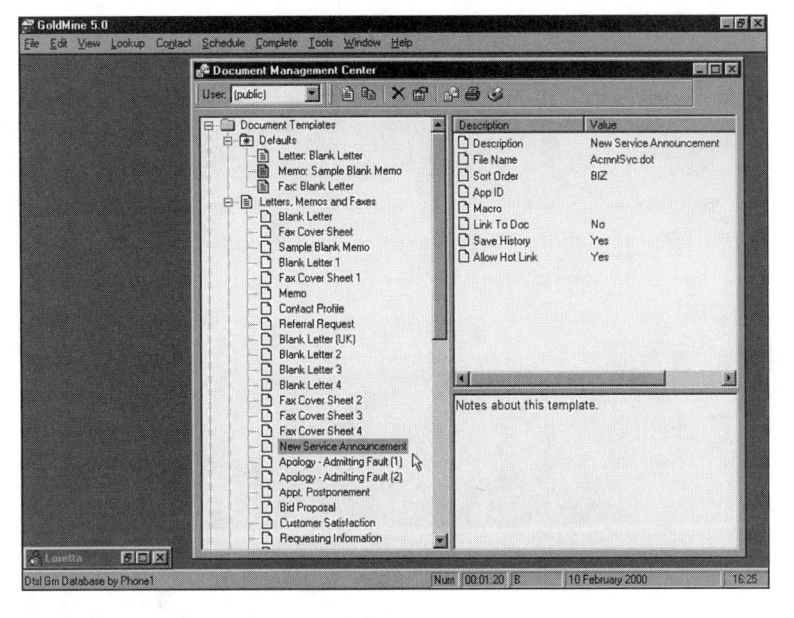

Figure 4.4
The Document Management Center holds a template for just about anything legal.

55

Part 1 ➤ *GoldMining for Beginners*

> **Mine Safety**
>
> **Document Templates Might Include Macros**
>
> A *macro* is a programmed routine that can be executed when the macro is run. A template often includes one or more macros.
>
> GMLink.dot is a document template that includes macros to set up links between GoldMine and your installation of Microsoft Word.
>
> Your system may be set up to warn you about opening a document that could contain a macro, in case this macro includes a virus that could harm your system. If you open such a document, the macros in it will run.
>
> Copy a template only from a source that you are sure is trustworthy because you will need to open this template to make use of it.

A clever template will contain commands that will automatically transfer the value of a particular field from the active contact record—name and address, for instance. Then you can have the template applied to a collection of contact records and so generate a flux of similar but particular messages, faxes, or documents.

Document templates are edited and saved much like ordinary documents. Begin by adjusting one that is already working. See Chapter 5 for more information.

Commanding Your Schedule

Your activity schedule is a device for looking into the future—not the real future, but the future as you have planned it. Figure 4.5 shows the Schedule an Appointment dialog box being used to plan a future meeting.

The difficult part of scheduling is to decide on a suitable time—bearing in mind the wishes of the other people who will be at the meeting.

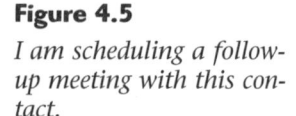

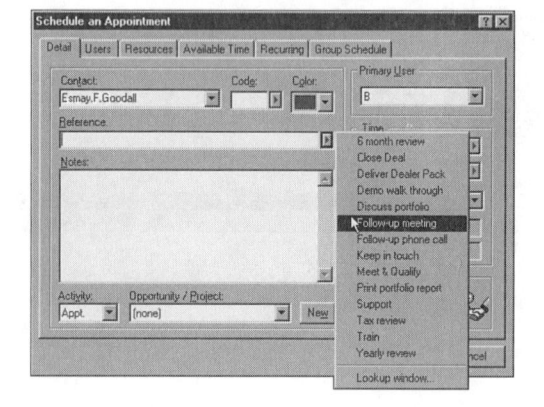

All the scheduling dialog boxes offer similar tabs that can refine the planning of the activity (see Table 4.4).

Figure 4.5

I am scheduling a follow-up meeting with this contact.

Table 4.4 Tabs in the Scheduling Dialog Box

Tab Name	Purpose
Detail (default)	Offers data entry windows for you to enter or a reference text and notes. You can select the date and time of the scheduled activity and set up an alarm.
Users	Opens a list of the users in your GoldMine system whom can be assigned for this activity.
Resources	Lists places and equipment that need to be reserved, such as meeting rooms.
Available Time	Allows you to enter the duration and preferred times, days of the week, and date span for the intended activity. You can initiate a scan, which will consider the schedules of the users and the resources and then display any time periods that would be suitable for the intended activity. When you have settled on the best slot, all the booking, recording, and notifying will be carried out automatically when you click the **Schedule** button.
Recurring	Allows you to specify the pattern and date span over which you want the same activity to be scheduled.
Group Schedule	Sets up the activity or recurring activity for a set of contacts defined by an active filter or active contact group. GoldMine shares out the appointments between the users you have nominated.

As soon as you click the **Schedule** button on any of these tabs, GoldMine will put the necessary appointments and activities in the **Pending** tab of each of the contacts targeted. Each user will also find entries in the activity list under the appropriate tab. User calendars will be blocked off according to the schedule. Chapter 10, "Look, Then Leap: Scheduling Your Activities," discusses these processes in more detail.

Completing Activities

The best thing to do with a pending activity is to complete it. You will expect GoldMine to assume you are most interested in the active contact, so when you select Complete on the main menu, you will have to choose which type of activity you want to bring to a conclusion.

From a listing of the outstanding scheduled activities of your selected variety you have to choose one. If the activity was not scheduled, you have a chance to check an option button to identify what type it is. When you click OK to accept your choice, you will get a form to fill in to record how successful the activity was, when you completed it, how long it took, and what you intend to do next in relation to it.

One of the nice things about completing a scheduled activity is that it is automatically taken from your Calendar and from the Pending tab of you and your contact. The respective History tabs have the honor of keeping a record of what you have done and what has happened to your contact.

Commanding Tools and Wizards

The Tools menu contains various commands that set up how your system is to manage standard and user-defined automated processes. See Part 5, "Administering a GoldMine Installation," for more details on these commands.

Table 4.5   Options in the Tools Submenus

Option Group	Option
Automated Processes	Execute Processes initiates all active processes for a chosen selection of contacts.
	Set Up Automated Processes allows creation and editing of processes and their trigger conditions.
Server Agents	Start Server Agents initiates processes according to the schedules specified in the Agents Administrator.
	Agents Administrator allows you to specify a week's timetable for each process agent:
	Print/Fax
	Automated Processes
	Sending/Retrieving E-mails
	Synchronizing with Microsoft Outlook
Import/Export Wizard	Import Contact Records copies records from another database.
	Export Contact Records copies records into a format suitable for another database.
	Import Zip Codes copies zip codes from another database.
	Clean Up DOS Notes removes spurious characters from texts written by GoldMine for interpretation by DOS programs.
Global Replace Wizard	Allows you to specify a change of value in a specific field in a designated set of contact records. Accepts many such changes per process.
Territory Realignment	Allows you to reassign the activities for a designated set of contacts to another user and record owner or account manager.

Option Group	Option
Merge/Purge Records	Merge/Purge Wizard combines duplicates and deletes unwanted records.
	Merge Visible Records combines the data from all the visible records into the record that is currently in the foreground. The others are deleted.
	Merge Tagged Records combines the data from a collection of records you have tagged by Ctrl+clicking the Contact Listing. The first record tagged receives all the information. The others are deleted.
Delete Records Wizard	Removes unwanted contact records, scheduled activity records, or old history records from your database.
Strategic Solutions	Connects to the GoldMine Software Corporation Web site.
BDE Administrator	Activates the Inprise Corporation's Borland Database Engine Administrator, which controls access to dBASE, Excel, FoxPro, MS Access, Paradox, and Text data sources.
Year 2000 Compliance	Tests your installation for year 2000 compliance, with the exception of the Real Time Clock and the BIOS.
System Performance	Runs data processing tests using current GoldMine data to provide a benchmark in the form of a number of records processed per second. Used to compare different workstations.

Helping Yourself

The Help command on the main menu offers two sets of Windows style help files under the headings of Help Topics and How Do I.

The Referentia Tutorial is a separate application—delivered as part of GoldMine 5.0—that presents basic teaching materials concentrating on the operation of the system:

Tutorials comprising audio commentary on a demonstration of each topic. The presentation can be stopped and selectively replayed.

Fast Answers, calling on audio-visual presentations as appropriate.

Concepts, calling on audio-visual presentations as appropriate.

Help on using the Referentia system.

These excellent lessons can be taken with an active GoldMine running in an adjacent window.

Making Macros

A macro is a set of orders to mastermind some software functions or typing actions. You can build a macro with clever programming commands—or you can tell Windows or GoldMine to pay attention to what you are doing and make a recording until you tell it to stop. We will look at the GoldMine routine.

Mine Safety

Watch What You Record

When you begin recording a macro, you record every action from that point until you stop. So, be sure to take only actions you want recorded. You might want to practice the procedure you plan to record so you don't inadvertently add something unwanted to your macro.

Point to a blank space or separator between toolbars, or to the handle bar at the beginning of a toolbar. Right-click and select the option **Record Macro**. The macro commands are also reachable by selecting **Edit**, **Toolbars**.

After you have started recording, you can move your cursor, click on icon buttons or menu items, and type merrily away as you please. GoldMine will be recording all this—every single click—until you click the **Stop** button on the macro control window. If you want to do something "off the record," select the **Pause** button—then deselect it when you want the recording to begin again.

For example, you can right-click the space or handle in any toolbar and select **Record Macro**. You will see the Start, Pause, and Stop icons. Start will have been selected automatically. Point to a blank field on the currently active contact record and type in an entry. For instance, point to **Dept** and type in `maintenance`. Point to **Title** and type in `Maint Mgr`. Point to **Source** and type in `Maintenance 2000`, because this is where you acquired this contact. Point to **Phone1** and type in the number. Then click the **Stop** icon to end the recording of your new macro.

Now you will see the Define Macro Button dialog box where you must click an icon for your macro and enter a pop-up, quick help text, a status bar description, and optionally, a hotkey to launch the macro from the keyboard. Before you click **OK** to close this dialog box, be sure to click your chosen icon and drag it into one of your open toolbars.

To test your new macro, click **New Record** from the **File** menu and type in at least a company or contact name. If you have made the Maint Mgr macro and assigned it an icon, which you have dragged to a toolbar, now is the moment to test it. You will get all the typing done at full speed across the various fields you used when you recorded the macro. If you have made several type-in macros, you can select them one after the other to fill out your contact record and avoid repetitive typing—along with the errors that sometimes creep into them.

Giving Your Macro Its Own Icon

When you select **Stop** you will be invited to scroll through the available icons (including numbers 1 to 20) and select one for dragging to your chosen toolbar position. Before you are allowed to exit the Macro dialog box, you must enter something for the button text and for the entry to appear in the status line. You can also assign a hotkey combination to trigger this macro from the keyboard. Playback speed can be Full Speed or Recorded Speed.

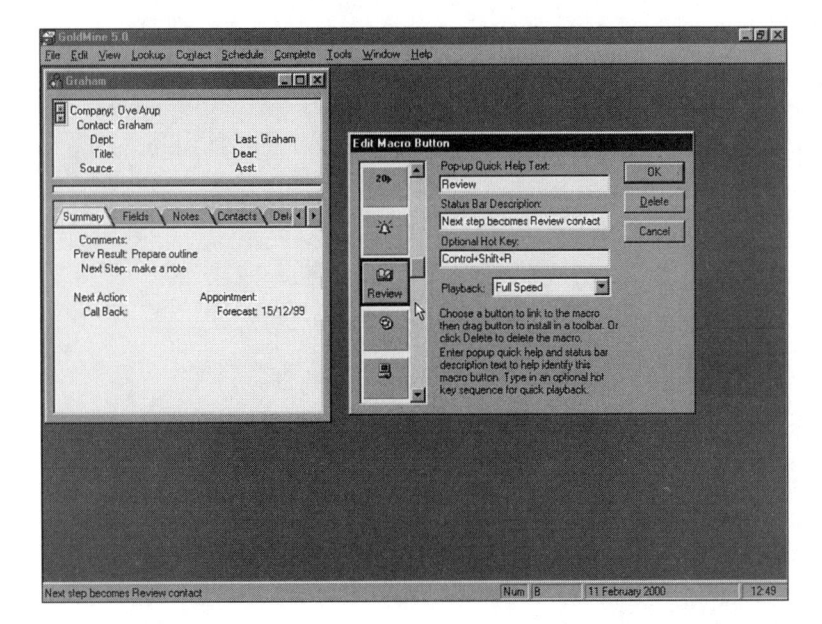

Figure 4.6

I am defining a little task as a macro with its own icon and hotkey.

You are allowed to make up to 10 assignments of recorded sequences to the same macro button. They will all be executed when you select this button or its hotkey.

Editing Macro Properties

The **Edit Macro** command allows you to go back to the Edit Macro Button dialog box and change any of the macro properties, or drag its icon to an open toolbar. However, there is no convenient way to alter the individual steps in a macro, like there is in a Windows macro. You will have to rebuild a GoldMine macro if it does not serve.

If you delete a macro, the icon will remain in place on the toolbar where you put it, but the Pop-up Quick Help Text will vanish, as will the status bar description.

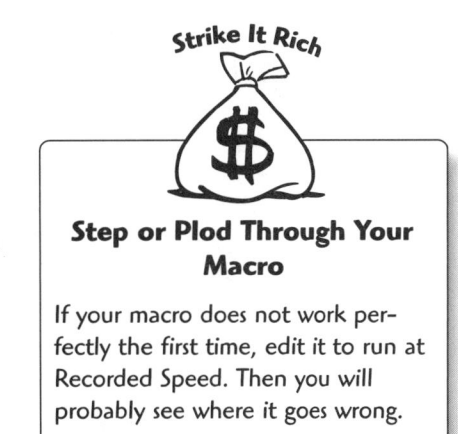

> **Strike It Rich**
>
> **Step or Plod Through Your Macro**
>
> If your macro does not work perfectly the first time, edit it to run at Recorded Speed. Then you will probably see where it goes wrong.

The Least You Need to Know

➤ Adjust your GoldMine workspace to make your job easier and more efficient.

➤ The Help menu has an easy section called How Do I, a beginners audiovisual Referentia Tutorial and a very thorough section called Help Topics. To go deeper still, consult the GoldMine Web site, also accessible from the Help menu.

➤ Semi-automate and accelerate your work with macro sequences that make no errors.

➤ There is no limit to the extent of private automation you can set up by using macros.

➤ Put your best macros on a new toolbar.

Chapter 5

24-Karat Printouts: Generating Paper by Printing and Faxing

> **In This Chapter**
> ➤ Connecting GoldMine to Word for Windows
> ➤ Creating master form templates
> ➤ Merging your contact data with your prepared documents

It seems that there are not enough words to go around. Take the word "document," for instance. A Microsoft document is an electronic file representing a paper document of some kind. Yet the contents of a document file might never actually appear on paper, but instead only be read onscreen. The point is that a Word file can be printed. But so can a spreadsheet. So there has developed the usage that something printable is called a document. Your file folders might therefore contain printable files with names such as Myletter.doc and Myspreadsheet.xls.

Now a fax can be printed, and it can contain pictures. Audio files are objects that can appear in a document. Such a document could not be fully understood by reading it because you would not know what was in the sound file. You can send a document by email to another GoldMine user—but they will need to have an active sound card to hear any audio messages or comments you have stored in the document.

Please expect the word "document" to include anything printable plus any audio elements that have been included in it. A printed document may not reveal the entire message.

Linking to Word 97 or 2000

Your word processor is obviously important when it comes to composing documents and messages. GoldMine can be set up to call upon almost any outside application to process some data and return a result. However, it is convenient to take advantage of this ability to provide a much closer link between your favorite word processor and GoldMine.

If your favorite is Word 97 or Word 2000, the creation of this link is a matter of getting hold of a template. Fortunately, GoldMine provides one for you. For any other word processor to be linked directly to GoldMine, you have to purchase an add-on package. The document template you're looking for is GMLink.dot. If you have recently installed GoldMine, this rather special template will be found exposed at the end of your GoldMine folder listing—not in the GoldMine Template folder, as you might expect.

If you change your fax machine, or add one to your system after installing the GoldMine link to Word, you must run the GMLink.dot template again, because the template goes through a step where you have to identify your fax application and name the macro that GoldMine will run to dial the fax machine. The following fax applications are compatible with GoldMine:

- RightFax, a network faxing system
- Delrina WinFax PRO 8.0, or WinFax 7.01 or later
- FaxRush, an integrated fax support system

Standard GoldMine offers these applications as options when running the GMLink to Word. To connect with any other fax application you have to follow the installation instructions provided by the manufacturer. Updates to GMLink can be downloaded from the www.goldminsw.com Web site.

Installing the Link

After GoldMine has been installed you will be able to navigate to the folder named GoldMine. When you have highlighted GMLink.dot, select **Open** or double-click the filename. In the resulting dialog boxes, select **Install** and agree to Enable Macros. The link will be put in place. If you attempt this when it is not needed, you will simply be shown the readable text of the template. This is also what you get if you select **View Documentation** just before the end of the procedure, or the **About GoldMine Link** option in the GoldMine main menu item that appears after the link is installed.

There is another way of installing the link to Word. Select **Contact** from the main menu. Highlight **Write** and click **Letter to Contact**. If GMLink has already been installed, you will be offered the default letter template already addressed to the active contact and finished by the your full username. If GMLink has not been installed, you will be asked if you want to have it installed. Click **OK** and GoldMine will set up the link.

Setting Link Preferences

During the installation of the link, you will be invited to make some decisions that will be saved as your GoldMine to Word link preferences:

> Select the language in which the process will be controlled and errors reported when the link is running.
>
> If you want to save any merged database file after it has printed a mass mailing, uncheck the box titled **Delete Merge DBF when Done**.
>
> You might want to keep the list of linked GoldMine fields in synch with those in your GoldMine application. Place a tick by the **Always Auto Refresh Field List**.

There is a prompt to confirm the destination when mailing to a group of contacts. If you don't want to have to confirm every item, don't check **Prompt for Group Merge Destination (Print Only)**.

At this stage you have to confirm or re-select the name of the application that looks after your fax. You also have to confirm or re-select the name of the **Fax Number Macro to Use** for dialing the actual fax number of each targeted contact.

There is a sending status report screen that you can have on your workspace if you check **Show Send Screen**.

The resolution of your fax will be at Draft quality unless you check **Use Fine Resolution**.

Mine Safety

Look Before You Link

You must not attempt to install the link if you are running more than one copy of Word. I have just lost half a day because I had not saved this chapter before playing with GMLink.dot. Now I can advise you to shut down your word processor and let it put away the Normal.dot template with your most recent changes. Then open Word without any unsaved document. GoldMine has to be running. If there are GoldMine commands on your Word main menu, the link is already in place. If you have upgraded from GoldMine 4.0, you will have to reinstall the link. Check that your fax system has already been installed, if you have one, before you begin.

You must select **Save Preferences** before leaving the GoldMine Link Preferences dialog box, if you have altered any preferences.

Working GoldMine from Word

When the link has been installed, you will find that your word processor has some extra menu items and several additions to various submenus. These new items all identify themselves as GoldMine additions by their names.

You can change the behavior of a GoldMine link from the GoldMine Link Preferences dialog box. From Word, select **GoldMine**, **Setup GoldMine Link**.

The GoldMine link preferences dialog box offers you the chance to specify or change the fax equipment installed in your system. Choose **Save Preferences** when you are satisfied.

Choosing **GoldMine**, **Uninstall GoldMine Link** will remove the link and all its components, including the GoldMine menu items in Word.

About GoldMine Link displays information about the GoldMine Link and gives you access to the **View Documentation** command.

Emailing, Messaging, and Even Writing

To communicate by paper mail to your currently active contact, select **Contact**, **Write**, **Letter to Contact**. Your word processor will open automatically, if it's not already open. The top window will be a new document window that consists of your default letter template, into which has been poured all the relevant data from the contact record currently open in GoldMine.

> **Learn the Lingo**
>
> **Forms Are Document Templates**
>
> GoldMine makes no distinction between forms and document templates. They are both scanned to see if the user or GoldMine has to insert any information.

There is still time to edit this particular letter before sending it. If you want to edit the template, select **Contact**, **Write**, **Customize Templates**. Up will come the Document Management Center (DMC), where you can change or edit the default letter template, as shown in Figure 5.1.

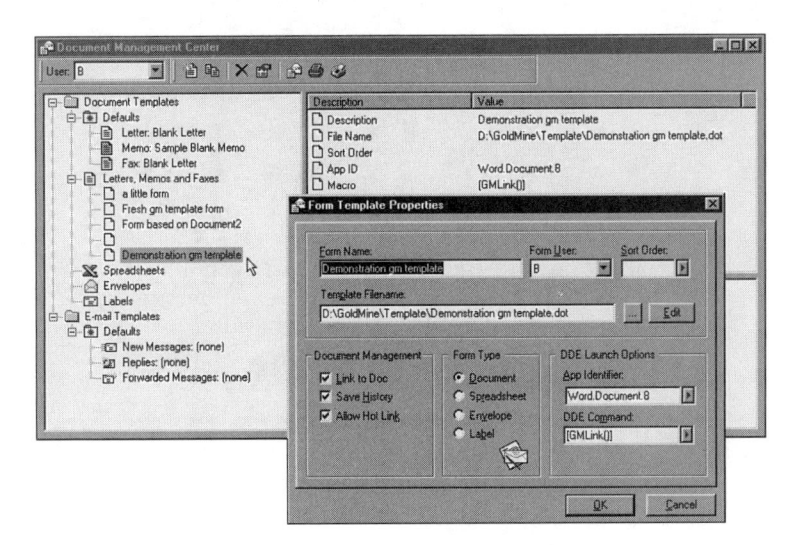

Chapter 5 ➤ *24-Karat Printouts: Generating Paper by Printing and Faxing*

Figure 5.1

The Document Management Center can hold templates to help create just about any document, fax, spreadsheet, diagram, picture—you name it!

The DMC is a GoldMine window offering a structured tree-list of the available form templates, together with some tools for finding, creating, and editing templates. You can also fax and print directly, or have the contact data merged into the template. When the merge takes place, the result is presented in your Word window so that you can edit just this one communication.

Templates are available for writing a memo to your currently active contact or dashing off a fax. In each case, if you highlight the template you need, your word processor will get the default template, replete with the data from the contact record. The result will be waiting in your word processor for you to add the finishing touches, if they are needed.

If email is your style, select **Contact**, **Create E-mail**. Now you have a choice (see Table 5.1).

Table 5.1 Options for Creating an Email

Option	Effect
Message to Contact	This presents you with a standard Mailto message form already addressed, if the data is in the contact record. All the email functions are available as if you were in the GoldMine email center.
Outlook Message to Contact	Offers a Mailto message form, this time in your Microsoft Outlook window as if you were using your Web browser.

continues

67

Table 5.1 CONTINUED

Option	Effect
Pager Message to Contact	Offers the Send a Pager Message dialog box ready to page your active contact. You can elect to page a GoldMine user rather than your contact.
E-mail Merge	Takes you into the Document Management Center, where you can set up an email merge using the set of contacts you specify.
Customize Templates	Takes you to the Document Management Center so that you can alter an email template.

See Chapter 6, "It Beats a Tin Can on a String: Managing Email," for a discussion on how to control incoming and outgoing emails.

> **Learn the Lingo**
>
> **What Happens to Field Names?**
>
> A field name is like a placeholder for some data that will be put there just before printing begins. Merging is getting some data, such as names and addresses, and sprinkling this information over a document master template. Each pass over the template generates a new specific document.
>
> Some field names can come from Word, such as the date and time when the merging or editing is taking place. Other field names can come from GoldMine, such as the particular contact information and the products in which that contact is interested.

Making a GoldMine Template Form

If you want to start with an existing Word template, you have to open it and then put some GoldMine field names in among your text and graphics before you save it as a GoldMine template form. This is so that the merge process can transfer the details from GoldMine when preparing a mailing. Your template design can begin with a blank document, provided you save it as a GoldMine form. Alternatively, you can select a GoldMine blank template or a predesigned GoldMine template from the Document Management Center. You are advised to clone a standard template and save your edited copy under a different name, rather than risk upsetting the standard.

Identifying a New GoldMine Template

Although GoldMine is delivered with many pre-designed templates, most users want to use templates that carry their own imprint—not only the company letterhead and logo, but also the style and appearance of the finished communication to a valued customer or business associate. The following sequence will register a new template:

1. From GoldMine's main menu, select **Contact**, **Write**, **Customize Templates**.
2. Highlight a category, such as **Letter**, **Memos and Faxes**, to display the list of available templates.
3. Select the template you want to clone or edit. If your chosen template is written in Rich Text Format (RTF), WordPad will open it automatically. The template will reside in a file with the RTF suffix and the Document Management Center (in the lower-right pane) will allow you to scroll through the text before you open it to begin work.
4. Right-click and select **New** from the local menu to get the Form Template Properties dialog box in which you must specify the details. Refer to Figure 5.1 for an example.
5. Uncheck the **Link to Doc** check box so that no automatic link to a contact record will be made every time you merge data into the template. This link would cause the contents of the linked document to be printed with your message. You can also uncheck **Save History** unless you want to keep records of all merges with this template. **Allow Hot Link** refers to the link command that would associate this template with your currently active contact.
6. The **DDE Launch Options** section of the template properties contains two fields:

    ➤ **App Identifier**—The Application Identifier determines which program will be launched to process the template. This will usually be where the template was first created.

    ➤ **DDE Command**—Nominates a macro to perform some special Dynamic Data Exchange operation when GoldMine starts up the application in which the template is designed to function. Figure 5.1 shows that the [GMLink( )] macro is needed to control Word when GoldMine fields have to be provided with contact data.

    These launch options are only needed if GoldMine cannot determine which application will process the template. An RTF template will open WordPad automatically.

7. Having established the properties of a template, if you do not want to edit the template itself at this time, select **OK** to close the Properties dialog box. Alternatively, you can click on the **Edit** button to launch the parent application.
8. When you have finished editing the template in the parent application, save the template. If you are in Word and the GoldMine link has been set up, you will be able to select **GoldMine**, **Save as GoldMine Form**.

When you close the Template Properties dialog box after entering new information, you have added a template entry to the Document Management Center (DMC). You might like to assign a code word to each of your new templates so that they will be sorted in convenient categories. My experimental templates are all given the Sort Order entry Trial, which I have placed in the lookup table for this field.

Developing a Template

You have the choice of either creating a new template or cloning (copying) an existing template. Choose the icon from the toolbar of the Document Management Center. Assign a cloned and edited template a new name while the Properties dialog box is still open.

Edit the text and graphics of the template and place the fields that will attract the particular data that you want to embed.

Save a brand new template by selecting **GoldMine**, **Save as GoldMine Form**.

Save an existing GoldMine template you have edited by selecting **GoldMine**, **Update GoldMine Form**.

Placing a Microsoft Word Field

A field in Microsoft Word is a placeholder for a value or result that can be computed in the word processor or imported into it from an associated application, such as an Excel spreadsheet or Access database.

Fields Can Automate Your Writing

Some fields are updated as soon as they are inserted into a document—for example, the author of a document is inserted as {AUTHOR*MERGEFORMAT}. Highlight a field code, or the result inserted by a field code, and right-click. Choose **Toggle Field Codes** to move between code and result. Choose **Update Codes** to command the field to recompute its result. You can update a field code for inserting a table of contents this way if you want to see what is in the document you are writing.

Other fields that are typically used in templates are updated automatically when the document containing them is merged with one or more contact records in the GoldMine Document Management Center.

You might want to insert text such as the date on your template in a Microsoft Word field. With your template open in Word, click where you want the entry to begin. Select **Insert**, **Field**, **Date and Time**, **Date**, and then choose **OK**. What you will get will be either today's date from your system clock or the corresponding field code, for example 12/02/00 or {DATE*MERGEFORMAT}.

If you work on an existing Word template, it will probably have several codes in place already.

Many fields will allow the possibility of choosing among options. Click **Options** and select the preferred item, such as a particular data format. Further choices can be taken if the field is programmed for switches—you can tell this when you are selecting a field in the dialog box because there is a display of the code for the highlighted option. Switches appear in brackets like [\@"Date-Time picture"]. This switch for a date field, for instance, will assign whatever date format was last used by the **Insert Date** command.

> **Strike It Rich**
>
> **Toggle All Your Field Codes**
>
> Toggle between field codes and their latest values for your whole template by pressing **Alt+F9**. Go into **Tools**, **Options**, **View** to make one of these the default display option.

Placing a GoldMine Field

With your template open in Word, point and click to where you want to put a field of GoldMine data. Click the GoldMine option, which was inserted by running the GMLink template. The drop-down menu offers the choice to **Insert GoldMine Field**. Choose this and you will open the Insert GoldMine Field dialog box. There you can either type in the field name, such as **&Contact**, or select from the drop-down browse list of all GoldMine fields that could possibly appear in a GoldMine template.

When you press **Enter**, the field will be inserted in your template at the insertion point. What you will see depends on how you left the toggle field codes when you used Alt+F9. Your template will show the field codes or their values according to the contact record currently active in GoldMine.

> **Learn the Lingo**
>
> **Dynamic Data Exchange**
>
> An inserted GoldMine field code will usually include the letters DDE to show that the field is to be processed using this data exchange procedure that can communicate between many Microsoft and compatible applications, such as Word, Excel, Access, PowerPoint, and GoldMine.

The Insert GoldMine Field dialog box is listed as a toolbar so that you can view or hide it as you please, or just drag it somewhere out of the way.

Saving a Correspondence Template

When you have finished creating a new GoldMine template, you must save it from the main menu by choosing **GoldMine**, **Save as GoldMine Form**. The filename will default to something like Document5 unless you have already assigned something different. Figure 5.2 shows a tiny form being registered for the GoldMine Document Management Center.

Figure 5.2

A new prose masterpiece is about to become a registered GoldMine form.

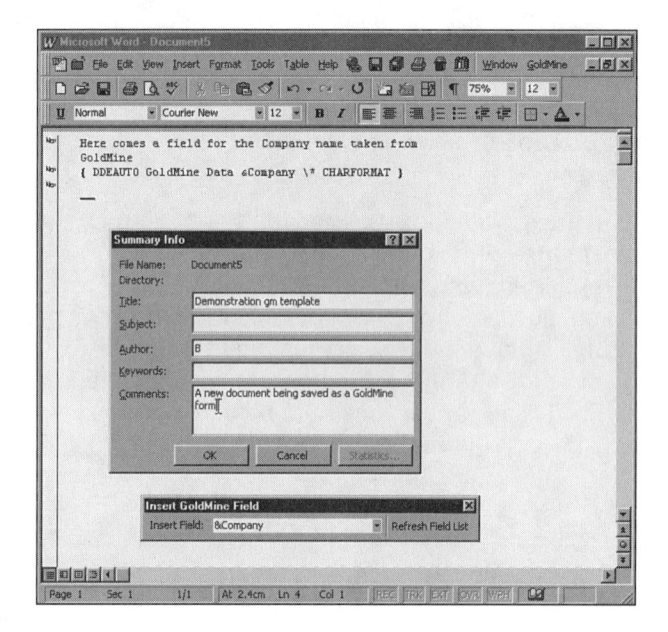

Writing with a Template

When you write something for a contact, whether for mail or fax, you will be directed to the Document Management Center (DMC). The **Write** toolbar icon is actually named **Print Merge Form** in the pop-up help text.

The Document Management Center, shown in Figure 5.2, reveals that my Demonstration GM template has been registered in the DMC under Letters, Memos and Faxes with my user ID—thankfully not a public publication! To check or edit the details, highlight the form title and selected **Properties** from the local menu.

When you inherit a GoldMine system, there will probably be some templates there already. You might start by cloning one or more of these.

Linking a Document to a Contact

One way to have large amounts of information associated with a particular contact is to link one or more documents to the contact record.

From the GoldMine window, click on the **Links** tab of a contact record to see the existing links, if any. Right-click and select **New** from the resulting menu to access the Linked Document dialog box, where you can assign a name for the linked document and identify it by path or by browsing. Chapter 18, "Share the Wealth: Distributing Nuggets of Information," discusses this linked document procedure in the context of various ways of accessing information that might be needed by many users and in relation to many contacts.

> **Strike It Rich**
>
> **Updating GoldMine 4.0 Templates**
>
> The **Update GoldMine Form** command on the **GoldMine** menu scans the open document for DDE fields and saves a field list that is used for group merges. Any document previously used for a GoldMine merge with Word 95 should be opened and saved by this Update command.

You can link a document to the active contact record while you are still in Word—perhaps because you have just created or edited the document. Select **GoldMine**, **Save as GoldMine Linked Document**. This will generate a new line entry in the Links tab of the currently active contact that will access the document you have opened in Word.

The Links tab line entry will include the title you assigned in the Linked Document dialog box before saving the link. There will be date and time information, and your user ID.

The local menu from a Links tab item enables you to launch the application, edit, email, and output, in various formats, the data in the linked document.

Figure 5.3 shows that the Edit command, used when a line entry in the Links tab is highlighted, will show you the Linked Document dialog box. Here you can see details of the file and the link—where the document file lives, how large it is, who made the link and the file, and when they did so. The Edit button in this dialog box will open the document itself so that you can check it and perhaps edit it before any other user consults it again or sends it to a contact. If you do edit a linked document, GoldMine will update the contact record and the document. The Linked Document dialog box will show updates in the Link Creation and File Information properties.

Figure 5.3

This link will be prepared to open a particular spreadsheet when this contact is active.

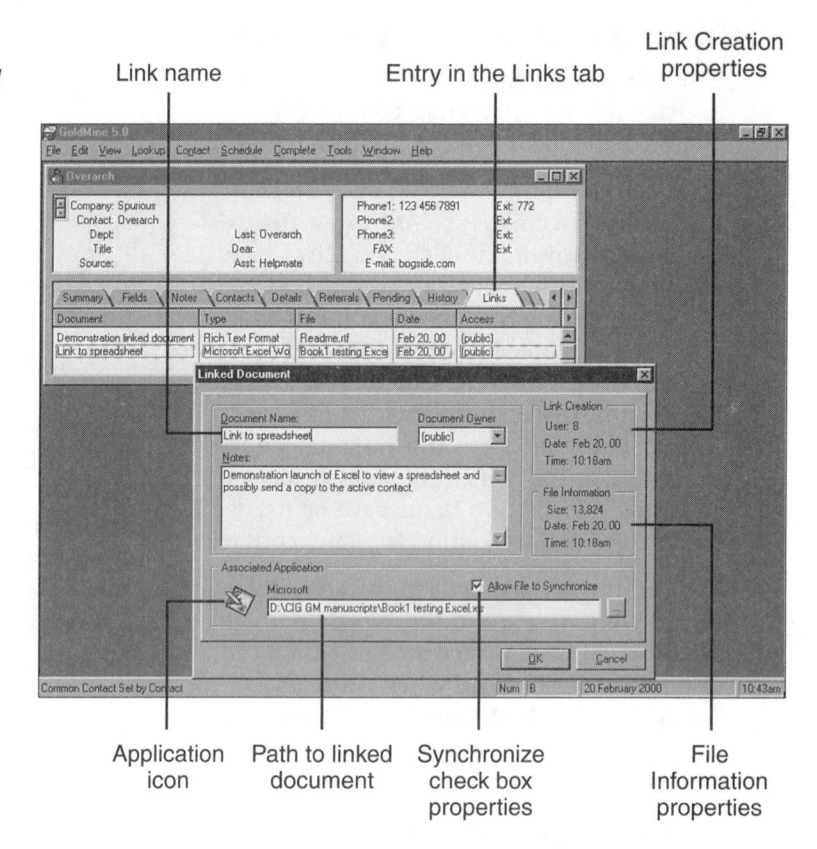

Initiating a Merge

A merge in Word is controlled by a useful toolbar called the Mail Merge Helper. You can access this toolbar in Word by clicking **Tools**, **Mail Merge**. The Helper invites you to edit or create a master document; then you have to say where the target names and addresses are coming from, and then you launch the merge process. This process does not need GoldMine unless the template contains field names belonging to GoldMine.

GoldMine templates or forms are managed from GoldMine, even though they might have been created elsewhere. In GoldMine you select the master template according to what type of communication you want. From the Document Management Center, you can click an icon or right-click for the local menu, which contains the **Merge** command.

There are some differences in procedure between letters, emails, and faxes.

Starting a Paper Merge

A message that is to be printed before being sent or printed via a fax can be prepared by merging into it the name and address of the intended recipient. The same communication can be sent to many addressees. This process can be called a paper merge to distinguish it from an email merge.

Figure 5.4 shows how to begin a merge of letters or faxes. Select **Contact**, **Write**, **Mail Merge**.

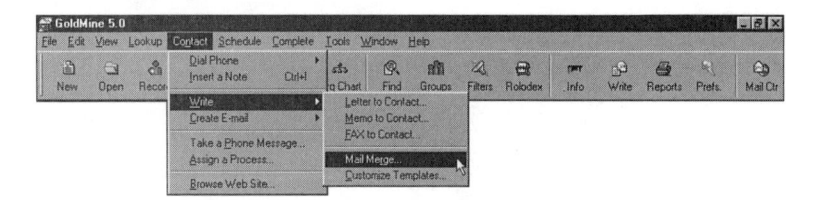

Figure 5.4
Writing or faxing to a host of contacts.

Starting an Email Merge

Apparently GoldMine people *write* letters and memos but they *create* emails! Figure 5.5 shows the way to create an email for a massive distribution.

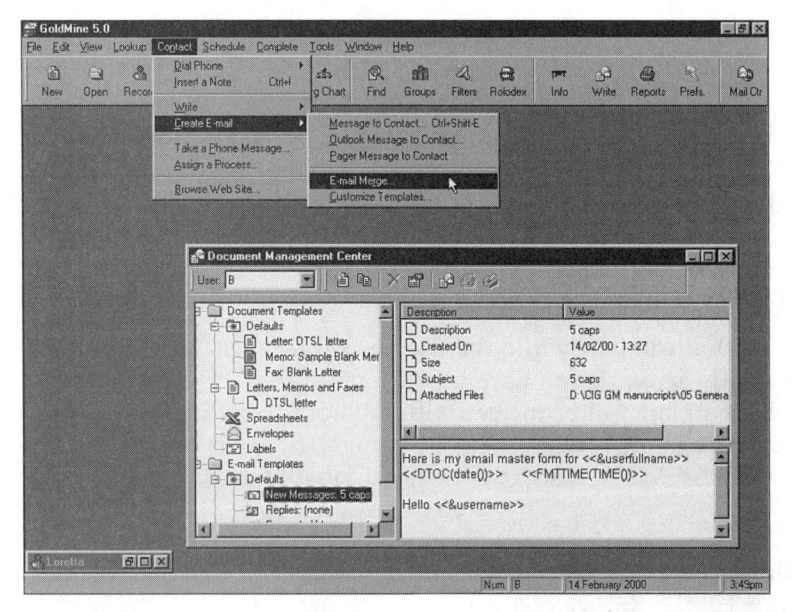

Figure 5.5
Creation is about to begin for an email merge.

The box in the lower-right pane of the DMC allows you to look over the text and fields of your template, but only if it is written in RTF (Rich Text Format). You can scroll and stretch the window if necessary.

75

The choice of targets for a mail merge, or even a clutch of pager messages, is a matter for shrewd judgement. GoldMine will accept a number of methods. What you have to do is to specify how the relevant contacts are to be chosen. Chapter 11, "Panning for Gold: Filtering Contacts from the Database," discusses the many ways of getting GoldMine to help find the right contacts for any activity you have in mind.

Figure 5.6 shows the Mail Merge Properties dialog box. It appears after you have selected the template to be used from the Document Management Center and clicked on the envelope-and-paper toolbar icon, which is labeled **Merge and Edit Template**.

Figure 5.6

Focusing mail merge properties on the target.

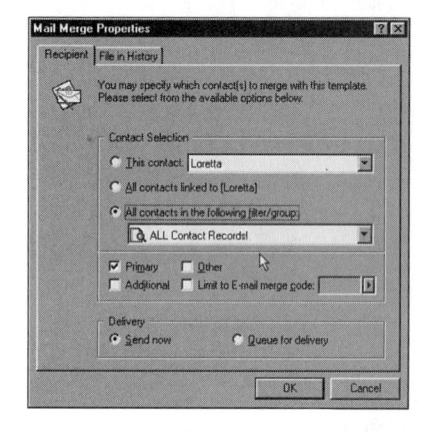

There are several ways to get to the Document Management Center. One way is to select **Contact** from the main menu. Highlight **Write** and click **Mail Merge**. This opens the Document Management Center. Click the type of template you intend to use for the merge and select a particular template from the listing—scroll the listing window if necessary. Now that you have highlighted the template, click the **Merge and Edit** button if you want to change anything in the document. Click **Print Template** if you are happy to have the existing template merged with contact data.

The default contact data that will be fed into the chosen template will be drawn from the contact that is currently active. If you have tagged a set of contacts or activated a group or filter, then the template will be merged with each of this set of contacts in turn. When you click **Print Template**, the Mail Merge Properties dialog box is opened and you can alter the default contact or contacts for your merge.

The Mail Merge Properties dialog box has two tabs:

- ➤ **Recipient**—Allows you to focus on particular contacts.
- ➤ **File in History**—Allows you to specify what records are to be kept after the merge.

Targeting is the same whatever the medium of the message. The main decision is whether to aim at all contact records or something less.

Chapter 12, "At the Corral: Building Contact Groups," discusses how to set up groups of contacts. You can tag them individually, or you can set up a filter that chooses according to the search pattern you define. Having picked out a set of contact records, you can designate them as a group.

Besides targeting a mailshot, the other decision to make about merging is whether to have GoldMine keep a detailed record of the full text of a mailshot for each contact. Or, just to make a note in the **History** tab of when it was sent and the name of the template used. Figure 5.7 shows the File in History tab of the Merge Properties dialog box.

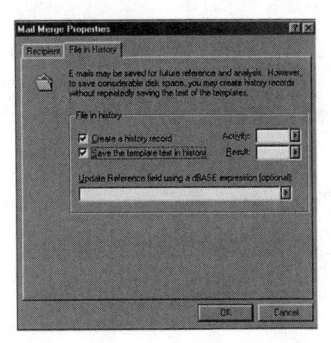

Figure 5.7

Arranging to leave records of a merge.

Recording a Document After Dispatch

Table 5.2 shows the options that appear in the File in History tab.

Table 5.2 Options for Archiving Mail Merge Documents

Option	Effect
Create a History Record	Saves information about the item sent but not the text of the template or form.
Save the Template Text in History	Saves the full text of what was sent.
Activity	Add or select an activity code or job code for later analysis or follow-up.
Result	Add or select a result code for later analysis or follow-up. The code for a queued email is not posted (saved) until the email is sent.

continues

Table 5.2 CONTINUED

Option	Effect
Update the Reference Field Using a dBASE Expression (optional)	Leaves the history entry Reference field with the result of a logical process that takes database informationand computes a result according to the expression entered or selected for this field. For example, &PARAM1 returns the path and filename of the merge form used.

Any of the File in History options might be set by default for a specific user or group of users.

Queued emails will appear in the Outbox of the E-mail Center. Print and fax queues are normally managed at the relevant devices or their servers.

Managing Form Printing

The Document Management tab contains the following check boxes for Document Management:

- ➤ **Link to Doc**—This will make a copy of any linked documents with every letter.
- ➤ **Save History**—This saves a brief entry in the contact record History tab for each mailshot.
- ➤ **Allow Hot Link**—This allows an optional link to a document to be added during final editing.

Document management assignments made in the Document Management tab will override the corresponding defaults set in the Save in History tab.

> **Mine Safety**
>
> **Mind Your Queues!**
>
> If you decide to Send Now, by email, for instance, you might miss an opportunity to send at a cheaper time. If you Queue for Delivery, perhaps for several days, you will at least have the chance to interrupt the process and perhaps make some improvements.
>
> If you have checked **Send Now**, your system might try to dispatch an email merge as soon as you close the Mail Merge Properties dialog box.

The Form Type section of the Document Management tab allows you to check the type and hence the printing format for the template:

- ➤ Document
- ➤ Spreadsheet
- ➤ Envelope
- ➤ Label

Setting Up Signature Bitmaps

A signature can be more than just a flourish—even in an electronic missive. You have to create a masterpiece and scan it into a bitmap file. Also you must tell your computer where to find this file.

After you have a lovely scrawl in the bitmap file, go to any document template and click the **Edit** menu. Point to where you want to sign, and select **GoldMine**, **Insert GoldMine Field**. Scroll until you can highlight and select the GoldMine field **&Signature**. You will not be allowed to leave without a reminder to save this alteration.

Only user B can have a template that will automatically insert the bitmap B.bmp. Another user can start a merge with the same template, and sign it if he has scanned and identified his own bitmap file.

Now you are able to send a mass mailing to a selection of your contacts. Select **Lookup** from the main menu and hold down **Ctrl** while you click each contact in the contact listing to tag it for the mailing. The title bar of the currently active contact record will keep a count of the number of records you have tagged.

Store Your Signature Bitmap Where GoldMine Can Find It

Use **Start, Find, Files or Folders** to highlight and open the GoldMine file GM.INI. Under the section headed [GoldMine], insert a line of text like this:

SigDir=*D*:\GoldMine\Signature

D stands for the name of the drive where GoldMine is located, and **Signature** is the name of a directory in which you have stored a scanned bitmap with the same name as you sign on with. Mine is B.bmp. The bitmap must be in a bmp file type.

Save the GM.INI file when you have altered it.

When you have tagged all your addressees, select **Contact**, **Write**, and then click **Mail Merge** in order to open the Document Management Center. Select the template you want to use. Click the **Print** icon and the Recipients dialog box will open where you should select **All contacts in the following filter or group**. Click the right arrow, if necessary, until you can see the funnel icon and the title **Active Contact Filter**, which you should click because it will use your tagged contact records as if they were selected by a filter.

You can click the **Printer** drop-down arrow and select **Fax** if you prefer this method. Select **Queue** and increase the number of days if you want the mailing to be delayed. Click **OK** when you are ready to launch the mailing or consign it to the queue. The process monitor will become active and show you how many contacts have been identified for the mailing.

If you have accepted the default destination as a printer, the mailing will go into the print queue. If you do not have a printer attached, you will be asked to type in the name of a prn file where the mailing will be kept until a printer becomes available.

Part 1 ➤ *GoldMining for Beginners*

> **The Least You Need to Know**
>
> ➤ GoldMine can call upon Word if the GMLink has been installed.
>
> ➤ Word can call upon GoldMine data fields if GoldMine is running at the same time.
>
> ➤ Templates can be created and edited to allow mass mailings without tears.
>
> ➤ Printing, faxing, and emailing can be just routine.

Part 2
Communicating Through the Internet

Two big explosions—cheap computers and the Internet. The dust is not yet settled—but get in there to see what is to be found amid the rubble. Email with the speed of light; don't spend all day chewing the end of your quill pen. There's a whopping wobbly wonderland of Web sites, sometimes junk with embedded gems. You can even get your working kit updated for free. What about a touch more style in your workplace? Go in for e-commerce and even c-commerce—keeping in touch with your customers.

The Internet can revolutionize the way you communicate. In these chapters, see how GoldMine can help.

Chapter 6

It Beats a Tin Can on a String: Managing Email

In This Chapter
➤ Adding GoldMine to the outside world

➤ Adding the outside world to GoldMine

➤ Being crafty with emails and other messages

Electronic mail goes down a wire and comes up the same wire. This wire might go directly to another computer, or it might pass through things. A modulator-demodulator, also called a *modem*, can be one of these things, in which case the modem has a telephone wire into your phone system. So does your handset. So does your fax.

Your computer has to take charge of the phone, fax, and anything else using the telephone cable. People who understand these things say that devices have to be installed. People who want to collect money say that installed devices need to be serviced by accounts.

There you have it. All you need is a wire, a device, and an account.

This chapter is mostly about making it work for you and your business when you have GoldMine installed. The phone and the phone account, you know about already. Same with the fax. So it is mostly about email.

Mastering Messages

GoldMine differentiates between the following types of messages:

GoldMine email	Must be to another GoldMine user.
Internet email	To anyone with a suitable address.
Telephone	Might be from a script or from notes. Might be improvised. Ought to be noted in a History record. Probably should have been scheduled beforehand.
Pager	To anyone with a known pager number, contact, or GoldMine user.
Internet email via Microsoft Outlook	Uses the same connections as the Outlook email manager software.
Shouting across the office	Needs no apparatus, but could often be usefully noted in a History record belonging to one or more contacts and users.
Whispering on a social occasion	Probably best not recorded at all.
Conversation during a visit to a contact	Should be noted as soon as possible on the contact record.
GoldMine Service and Support message	Provides links for updating and improving your installation. See Chapter 23, "Getting Tricky: Installing to a Network and Troubleshooting."

Emailing Another GoldMine User

GoldMine assumes you will need to transmit via the Internet, even to another GoldMine user. Figure 6.1 shows the mailto message form that is displayed when you select **Schedule**, **GoldMine E-mail**.

After you have created an email to one or more other users or user groups, you can specify additional recipients that you choose from the Contact Listing. This means you can send the same message to selected users and contacts.

If you start creating an email to a contact and then decide to send it to other selected users as well, there is a dialog box in which you can add more recipients to what started out as an email to one contact.

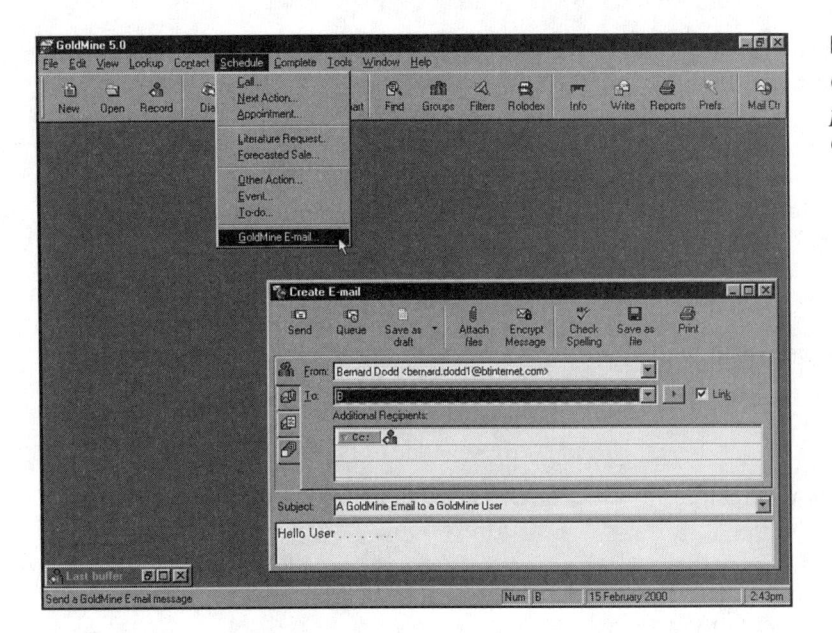

Chapter 6 ➤ *It Beats a Tin Can on a String: Managing Email*

Figure 6.1

Creating an email is supported by many helpful command buttons.

Emailing Contacts

If you want to send an email to the currently active contact, or to a group of contacts, select **Contact**, **Create E-mail**, **Message to contact** from the main menu, or press **Ctrl+Shift+E**.

Click the down arrow to see the addressees you have recently sent email to—click one of these to have it entered in the **To** entry window. Click the right arrow to see a drop-down menu that allows you to select from the following types of recipient: Contact, Manual Recipient, GoldMine User or Group, or Outlook (MAPI) Recipient. If you click one of these options, you will be taken through a sequence of dialog boxes until you have chosen the recipients of your message.

When you have written your message, click the **Send** envelope icon to send the message.

You can direct an email to many different recipients—contacts, users, and addresses that are neither. There are several ways of controlling your target address:

➤ Accept the default address taken from the currently active record.

➤ Type the target email address.

➤ Click the down arrow to show the list of your most recent addressees and choose a different address for this email.

➤ Click the right arrow and choose from the **To** drop-down menu to specify a different type of addressee.

85

The right arrow button displays the **To** drop-down menu over the Create E-mail window. This menu contains the following options:

To: Contact	Offers you the Contact Listing in which to identify your target.
To: Manual recipient	Invites you to type the email address of your target and to save it in the Manual Recipients Entry—a browse list for use on another occasion.
To: GoldMine User or Group	Offers the GoldMine User Recipient dialog box in which you can identify a user or user group. You also can elect to identify several users, one by one.
To: Outlook (MAPI) recipient	Offers the addresses in your Outlook address book.

When you select a method and make a choice of target, the To panel in the Create E-mail window will be suitably updated.

In the Additional Recipients panel of the Create E-mail window, there is a Cc button and a Contact icon. The Cc button offers a choice of being replaced by another addressee type—To or Bcc. Click the **Contact** icon to display the Contact Listing when you have decided which type of addressee you are identifying. When you double-click, or press **Enter**, on a contact highlighted in the listing, another addressee type button, of the same type, will appear in the Additional Recipients panel. You can mix and match addressee types.

The Subject field of the email can be filled by typing or by selecting from the browse list. One of the items on the browse list will be Select Template User. Choose this if you want to access the templates of another user. Otherwise, select an email template from your own list.

The Attach Files button opens the Attached Documents panel. You can drag and drop document icons into this panel if you want them to be attached to the email.

Right-click for the local menu anywhere in the Attached Documents panel, and then click **Attach** if you want to browse for your documents to be attached to this email. This local menu also allows you to open any of your attachments or change your choice of attachments.

Setting Options for Email

The Options tab button overlays a tab panel on the Create E-mail window. Figure 6.2 shows this overlay in place. The figure also shows that I have clicked the button labeled **Queue**, **Calendar and History Options**, which is located in the Options tab overlay panel.

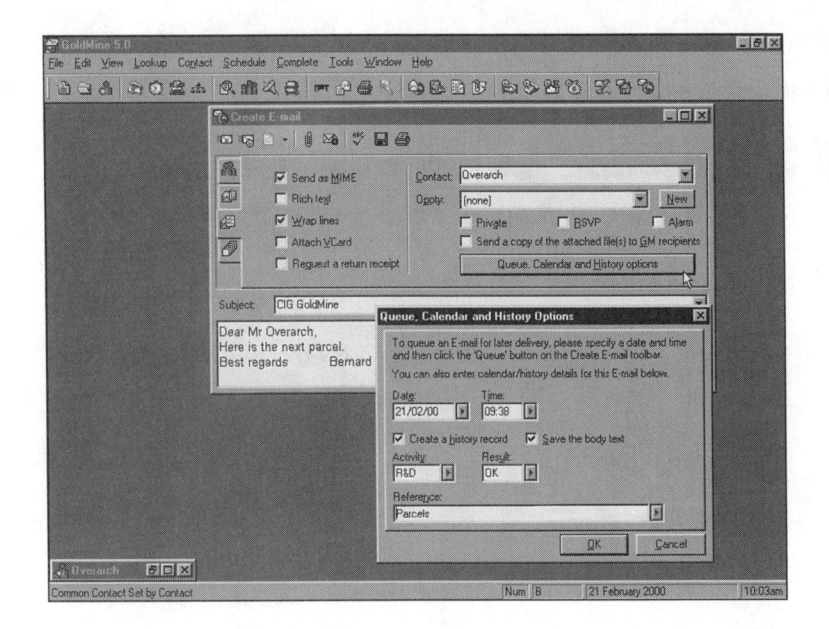

Chapter 6 ➤ *It Beats a Tin Can on a String: Managing Email*

Figure 6.2
Email can be told exactly how to behave in the Options tab of the Create E-mail window.

The following formatting check boxes are available in the Options tab:

➤ Send as MIME
➤ Rich Text
➤ Wrap Lines
➤ Attach VCard
➤ Request a Return Receipt

The Options tab offers a dialog box for specifying how the email shall be processed:

➤ **Contact**—A field window. Defaults to the active contact. Change by typing or selecting from the browse list. This window is grayed if the addressee is to be a GoldMine user.
➤ **Oppty**—A field window. Defaults to the Sales Opportunity associated with the active contact. You can select from the browse list if there is more than one. The New button opens the New Opportunity dialog box (see Chapter 15, "Looking for the Real Seams: Using the Opportunity Manager").
➤ **New**—A button that starts a new message.
➤ **Queue, Calendar and History Options**—A button that opens a dialog box of the same name, as shown in Figure 6.2.

The following check boxes are also available:

➤ Private
➤ RSVP

87

- Alarm
- Send a Copy of the Attached File(s) to GM Recipients

Specifying Queue, Calendar, and History Options

If you do not want your current email to be dispatched as soon as you have finished creating it, you can send it to a queue. In particular, you can say exactly when you want it to be sent and what kind of records you want to have saved in the contact record history.

The Queue, Calendar and History Options dialog box provides the following facilities:

- Date
- Time
- Create a History Record
- Save the Body Text
- Activity
- Result
- Reference

When you click **OK** to save these settings, you are returned to the Create E-mail dialog box. Here you have the choice of selecting the toolbar envelope icon to send the email, or the envelope-with-clock icon to have it queued for delivery, using the setting you have just established.

Targeting a Mail Merge

From the Create E-mail window, select the **Mail Merge** tab button if you want to send a similar message to many contacts. Figure 6.3 shows the dialog box for defining who shall receive your message.

If you select the check box **Merge this E-mail to a group of contacts**, the field below it will brighten and you can define how contacts are to be selected. If you also select the check box **Confirm each recipient**, you will have the chance to go through the filtered Contact Listing and confirm or reject any individuals.

The Mail Merge icon (a cascade of pages) in a Create E-mail window acquires a red band when a merge has been specified. Figure 6.3 shows that the targeted recipients for this mail, at the moment, are defined by a filter called "Contacts that are Customers." This is a filter belonging to user B. For more about filters and groups, see Chapter 11, "Panning for Gold: Filtering Contacts from the Database."

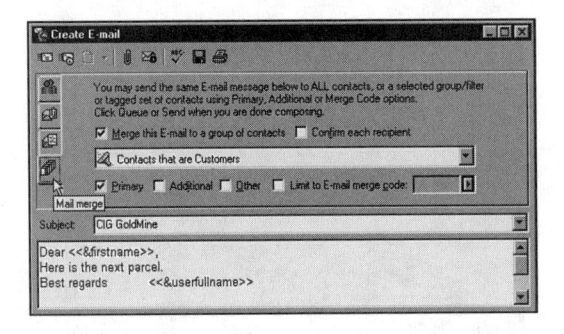

Figure 6.3
I can send my mail to a set of contacts that I have defined earlier by a filter or by assigning them to a group.

Each type of mail can be assigned a default template into which GoldMine will feed the appropriate details during the merge process. The name of the default template will appear in the Subject field. If you have been using another template, its name will appear instead of the default. Templates were discussed in Chapter 5, "24-Karat Printouts: Generating Paper by Printing and Faxing." The browse list for the Subject field includes an option to select from the templates of another user if you cannot find what you need among the public templates or those you created for yourself.

Refocus Your Merge Target

You can change the selection of recipients by picking another filter or group from the browse list, which will pop up or drop down if you click in the filter window.

If you do not want to specify the subject of your email by adopting the name of the template you are using, the Subject field will accept any text you type as the subject for the merged email.

Setting Up Internet Email Accounts

The mailto dialog box presumes that you have an email account through an Internet service provider (ISP) or through your company network.

If you need to set up or change an Internet account, select **Edit**, **Preferences** from the main menu. Check that your personal details are what you would want the world to know, and then select the **Internet** tab. Figure 6.4 shows my Internet account details as they are specified in my Internet Preferences.

89

Part 2 ➤ *Communicating Through the Internet*

Figure 6.4

Internet email needs a well-documented account with a mail server.

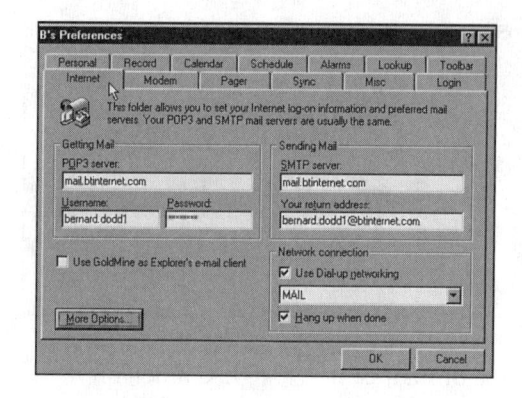

Your email preferences are further controlled by your choices on the tabs shown after clicking the **More Options** button:

Composing	Allows you to wrap, attach a VCard, add a signature file, and wrap lines to a specified length. Offers various ways of replying with or without quoting the original message. Controls the default email template.
Retrieval	Defines what shall be accepted and how often, and where it is to be archived.
Accounts	Allows you to define settings for more than one account.
E-mail Center	Sets the destiny of trash and some of the center's display features.
Advanced	Sets the manner in which incoming Internet and Web traffic will be processed.

Operating from the E-mail Center

The E-mail Center provides facilities for sending and receiving messages. Select **View**, **E-mail Center** or press **F5**. These function key routes are new with GoldMine 5.0. Just press the key for the function you need from anywhere in GoldMine. Figure 6.5 shows what invoking the E-mail Center reveals.

Figure 6.5

GoldMine accesses your mail in the E-mail Center.

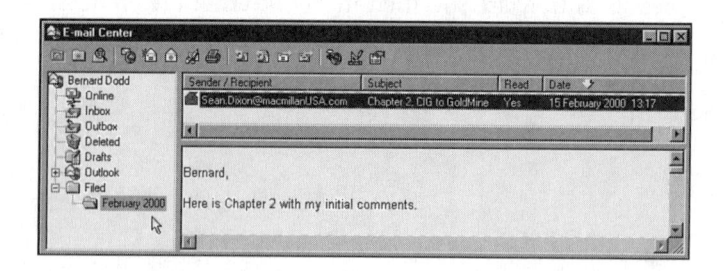

The E-mail Center toolbar has the following icons:

Create Folder	Creates a new folder as a subfolder of the highlighted item, unless this is a folder created automatically by GoldMine, such as the month of filed messages.
Delete Folder	You have to confirm a deletion.
Find Messages	Offers a search in selected folders over a date range for text strings in particular fields of a message, with or without case sensitivity.
Create New Mail Message	Offers your default email template in a Create E-mail window.
Delete Selected Message	There is no confirmation!
Open Selected Message	Shows the full message with attachment icons.
Mark Message as Unread	Toggles with Mark Message as Read.
Print Selected Message	Uses the default printer.
Reply	Replies to the selected message
Reply to All Recipients of the Selected Message	Replies to both contacts and users as appropriate.
Forward the Selected Message	Forwards a copy of the selected message to contacts or users that you identify from the listings.
Redirect the Selected Message	Redirects a copy of the selected message to contacts or users that you identify from the listings.
Edit E-mail Rules	Displays the E-mail Rules Center where the E-mail Rules Wizard helps you define trigger conditions and actions for the handling of incoming emails.
Edit E-mail Templates	Displays the Document Management Center.
Internet E-mail Preferences	Displays your Internet Preferences window.

Sending an Outlook Message to a Contact

To send an Outlook message to a contact, you have to have Microsoft Outlook 98/2000 installed in your system.

> **Outlook and Viruses**
>
> The Melissa and Love Bug viruses are script viruses that can work their way into your computer through the Microsoft Outlook address book.
>
> I strongly advise you to have your Outlook setup scanned for viruses before setting up a connection to GoldMine.

Select **Contact** from the main menu, and then select **Create E-mail**, **Outlook Message to Contact**. This command accesses Microsoft Outlook and allows GoldMine to read from the address book of that application. The communication is written and edited in Word 97 and then, if required, saved as a GoldMine template. The rest of the mailto procedure is comparable to the method for sending an email to a GoldMine contact.

Sending a Pager Message

To send a pager message, select **Contact**, **Create E-mail**, **Pager Message to Contact** from the main menu.

This will display the Send a Pager Message dialog box with the following options on the top tab, which is Page Message:

Page <<ContactName>>	Check box to direct this message to the pager of the currently active contact.
Page GoldMine User(s)	Field in which to type or select from a browse list of usernames and user groups.
Save in History	Check box to leave an entry in the History tabs of the contact(s) and an entry in the Activity List E-mail tab of the user(s).

The Reference or Subject of this entry will be Pager Msg:<<text of message>>, and the Activity type will be Other. The Result will be PG.

Schedule a Message — Schedules the pager message in the Activity List Open tab of the User(s).

Contact Info — A button to append the contents of the Pager Number and Contact Name fields to whatever has been typed in the message field. You might continue typing.

Type Message to Send to the Pager — Unlimited free text message field, although the pager will have been specified with a limited number of viewable characters.

The Send a Pager Message dialog box has a second tab titled Pager Info. This tab offers the following settings, which also are offered in the Pager tab of your Preferences dialog box:

Pager ID (PIN) — An entry field with a browse list button and a Save Settings check box.

Page by Sending an Internet E-mail to Address — A check box to brighten an entry field and display the browse list button.

Page by Dialing a Terminal Phone Number — A check box to brighten an entry field and display the browse list button.

Terminal's Maximum Character Width — A spin button window to specify the number of viewable characters in the pager.

The Send a Pager Message dialog box has a third tab titled Modem Setup containing two field windows with browse list buttons. These fields default to Modem COM Port COM2 and Modem Settings 300,e,7,1. If you normally send to pagers that operate at 1200 or 2400 baud, click the window over the default value of 300 and edit it to the higher rate used by your pagers. Click **OK** to save your alterations. The Modem Setup tab also contains some suggested modem commands and a Modem Initialization field window in which to enter such a command if your modem is failing to connect.

The Least You Need to Know

- ➤ Many messages and emails can be largely written beforehand as templates that need only slight adjustments, if any.
- ➤ You can mass mail to contacts and users.
- ➤ Messages can be passed to Outlook addressees and pagers.
- ➤ Messages can be queued until defined times and dates.
- ➤ All messages can leave history records.

Chapter 7

Are There Spiders in the Mine? Using the Web

In This Chapter

➤ Using Web search engines

➤ Receiving emails from your Web site

➤ Understanding a little about importing data from the Web

The World Wide Web has made the Internet so easy to use it's become a worldwide phenomenon. Many applications, including GoldMine, offer some kind of Web enhancement. Since the Internet is all about communication, it just makes sense that GoldMine contains some useful Web functions. In this chapter, you'll learn about GoldMine's Web abilities.

Contacting the World Wide Web

The World Wide Web is a connected set of Internet addresses that host graphics and text in layouts called *pages*. You view these pages with a special piece of software called a *browser*, such as Microsoft Internet Explorer. For example, http://www.goldmine.com/ is the address of the official GoldMine Web site. The Technical pages of this Web site begin at http://www.goldmine.com/newsgroups. From these locations, you can get GoldMine information and support.

> **Learn the Lingo**
>
> **Uniform Resource Locator**
>
> URL is the technical name for an Internet address that is written in a particular format. An Internet browser can recognize a properly formed URL, and can use it to attempt to link your computer to another computer in which the resource, such as a file containing a Web site, is located. A Web site has to have a URL. So does a search engine, like Yahoo!.
>
> Longer URLs usually include information pointing to a particular section of the resource, such as the first page belonging to the technical support department of GoldMine.

Finding What You Need

There's a great deal of information on the Web—not all of it useful. There is a smart way to focus on what you really need. This is called a *search* and it depends on you typing a search specification in a window belonging to a search engine.

A search on the Internet is conducted using a string of characters. Strings might be logically combined to focus the search, and some search engine software will invite the user to successively refine the search specification to reduce the number of hits. The data panel in Figure 7.1 shows how the AltaVista URL has a tail of codes that include commands to use a GoldMine field value as part of the search specification.

A *hit* is an Internet address (URL) that satisfies the search specification.

GoldMine approaches an Internet search using the data available from the active contact record. This information is selectively assembled in the format required of one or more search engines. Figure 7.1 shows the array of search engines that are delivered in GoldMine 5.0.

Select **Lookup** from the main menu, and then select **Internet Search** to display the Internet Search window. Highlight the service you want to use and then select one of the toolbar icons:

Search now	Begin the search using the chosen service and the data as it appears in the data view panel.
Toggle data view	Hide or reveal the data view panel at the foot of the Internet Search window.

Chapter 7 ➤ *Are There Spiders in the Mine? Using the Web*

`ISearch.ini` properties	Open Notepad with the `ISearch.ini` file displayed for editing, if necessary.
Reload	Display the search services again after the `ISearch.ini` file has been edited, or after the active record has been changed.

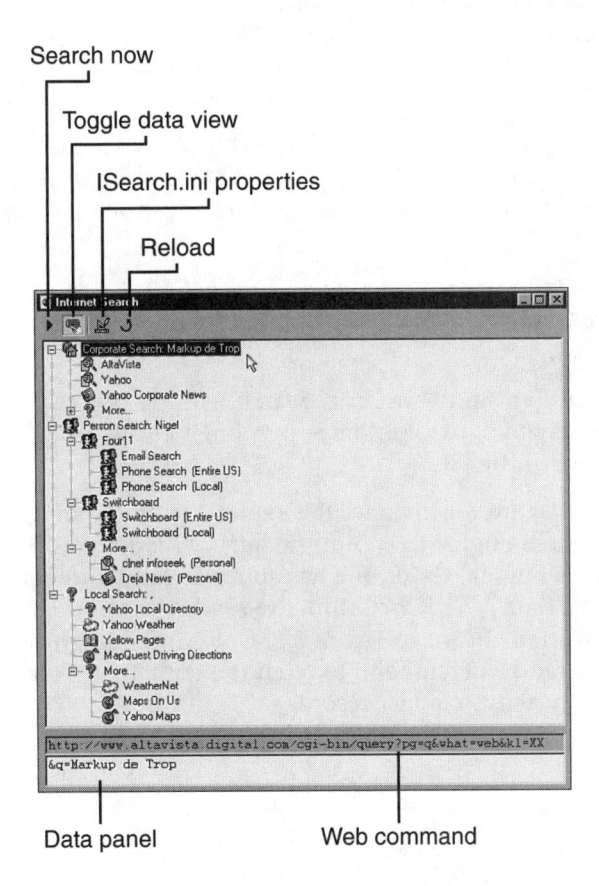

Figure 7.1
GoldMine will be ready to search the World Wide Web for company, contact, or any other field you have specified.

Callouts: Search now, Toggle data view, ISearch.ini properties, Reload, Data panel, Web command

Mine Safety

Notice GoldMine Version Differences

If your version of GoldMine 5.0 does not have the subtitle Sales and Marketing, your Lookup drop-down menu will have the options labeled Search, Toggle data view, Reload, and Properties.

97

If you want to edit the array of search engines used by GoldMine, you have to edit the initialization file that controls the GoldMine Search Engine.

Exploring the GoldMine Search Engine

Highlight the **Properties** option from the **Lookup** drop-down menu and select **Internet Search**. Then, select the `ISearch.ini properties` icon that appears in the Internet Search window. Now you will see a Notepad window containing the `ISearch.ini` file.

The `ISearch.ini` file comprises a set of commands in the Hypertext Markup Language (HTML) that will initialize the GoldMine Internet Search Engine and generate the items displayed in the Internet Search window. Figure 7.2 shows an extract from the initialization file.

Your GoldMine might be permanently connected to an Internet service provider (ISP). Alternatively, your system might be configured to dial up an ISP as soon as you try to access an Internet address.

The search service that you highlight in the Internet Search window will respond to the associated HTML commands in your GoldMine Search Engine initialization file as soon as a connection is made with the ISP.

The data panel that you saw in Figure 7.1 includes the expression &q=Markup de Trop. This tells the AltaVista search engine to accept the query "Markup de Trop." In the text of the GoldMine Search Engine, GoldMine has automatically formulated this query because of the command Data = &q = <<Company>>, which is in the AltaVista part of the Corporate Search section shown in Figure 7.2. GoldMine recognizes that <<Company>> is to be interpreted as a command to fetch the contents of the &Company field of the currently active contact record.

Figure 7.2

My GoldMine 5.0 Internet Search Engine knows how to get AltaVista to search for the company name on my currently active contact record.

```
; ISearch.ini
; GoldMine 5.0 Internet search engine
; Copyright (c) 1999 GoldMine Software Corp. All
rights reserved.
; Icons:
; isiCorporate=1, isiPersonal, isiLocal, isiLink,
isiSearch,
; isiNews=5, isiMaps, isiWeather, isiYellowPages,
isiDriving,
; isiStocks=10, isiInfo

[Section: Corporate Search: <<Company>>]
Icon= 1
[AltaVista]
URL1= http://www.altavista.digital.com/cgi-
bin/query?pg=q&what=web&kl=XX
Data= &q=<<Company>>
Icon= 5
```

If you have a GoldMine Internet Search Engine that has been initialized to offer a search using another contact record field, or a logical combination of fields, then this possibility will appear as a line entry in the Internet Search window. For example, you can conduct a search for a telephone number, a ZIP code, or even a last name plus a city.

When a search engine Web site finds a suitable address, you can click it to access the corresponding Web site. If you want to refine your search specification, the search engine will have the instructions and facilities to do so. For example, if you are asking the MapQuest Driving Directions search engine for a trip map for a journey between the address where your GoldMine system is registered and the address of the active contact, you might decide to simply have a city-to-city route, rather than door-to-door.

Alternatively, you can click the **Internet Search data** panel and edit the search specification directly. For example, you might want to plan a journey from a location different from the registered address of your GoldMine system. Any changes you make will be valid for just one search. The values in the contact record fields will not be changed by any alterations made in the Internet Search data panel.

Managing Web Site Addresses

The Web site addresses associated with the active contact can be edited by clicking the **Web Site** field in the contact record. You will be shown the Web Sites dialog box. Figure 7.3 shows that this contact has several Web sites.

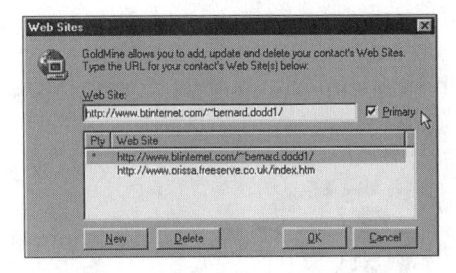

Figure 7.3

One of the contact's Web sites has to be checked as Primary and so becomes the default URL.

The Web Sites dialog box allows you to add, delete, or edit Web site URLs. When you have clicked the site to be used by GoldMine as the default, select the **Primary** check box. This address will be immediately written in the Web Site field of the active contact record. This field appears in the top right panel of the contact window.

All the Web sites and email addresses for the contact are recorded as line entries in the Details tab, along with the date on which they were entered or most recently edited. Emails take the URL as the Reference; you highlight and right-click a Web site line entry in the Details tab to display the local menu. Then add or change a reference text by choosing **Edit** from the local menu.

The Details local menu includes the Launch Web Site command. This will dial up or otherwise connect you to the Web site, which will appear in your Internet Explorer browser.

Making Contacts Through Your Web Site

You or your company might well have a Web site to advertise your goods and services, or simply to act as a focal point for collecting information from people who might turn out to be useful contacts.

You can place a standard **Mailto** command on a Web site page that will display a Mailto message form as soon as a viewer clicks an icon, a picture, or a word that you have defined as a hyperlink. When you are defining this hyperlink, you will have to supply an email address to appear in the Mailto form. If the viewer types a message and sends the form through his or her browser, this message will arrive in the mailbox of the addressee, as specified in the hyperlink.

If the addressee is running GoldMine, an email message arriving from a Mailto message generated on a Web site can be automatically directed to create a new contact record. Alternatively, the addressee can elect to have all such messages simply wait for individual attention in the E-mail Center.

Collecting Data from the Web

If you want to get more extensive data from a Web page than a freestyle email message, you have to establish a data-collecting form attached to that page. There must be facilities for a viewer of the Web site page to fill in this form, edit it, and submit it. The host system of the Web site will then send the completed form back to you as an attachment to an email.

> **Learn the Lingo**
>
> **Open the Gateway to Web Information**
>
> Information captured from the World Wide Web is known as Web Import Data. It is handled through software called the Web Import Gateway, using the Common Gateway Interface (CGI). The CGI can be written in a compiled language, such as C++, or in an executable script language, such as Perl.

When the completed and submitted email form arrives in your E-mail Center, GoldMine will offer to create a new contact record for it or associate it with an existing contact. If you have arranged for an automated process to trigger, GoldMine can take whatever actions you have specified. For instance, you can arrange for an email to be sent automatically in response to any form submitted from a Web site. Chapter 20, "A GoldMine Assembly Line: Automating Processes," discusses how these automatic responses can be prearranged.

Controlling Web Import

There is a special function key (F5) for you to press to call out the E-mail Center. Alternatively, from the GoldMine main menu, select **View**, **E-mail Center**, and then click **Preferences**, or select **Edit**, **Preferences**. Either action displays the Preferences window for your username. Click the **Internet** tab to show the Internet Preferences window. Then click the **Advanced** tab.

Figure 7.4 shows the Internet Preferences dialog box with the More Options, Advanced tab selected.

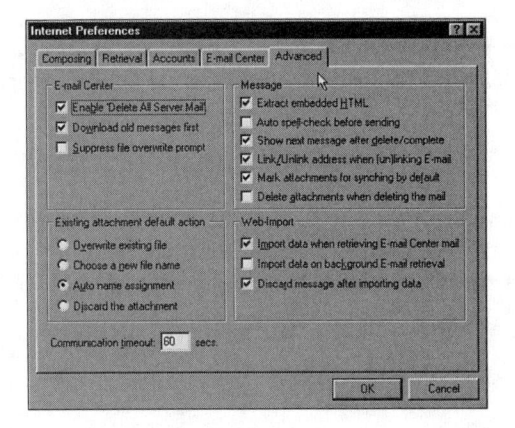

Figure 7.4

You can set your Internet Preferences to direct how GoldMine shall handle Web Import emails bringing data from your Web site.

The Web-Import panel of the Internet Preferences Advanced tab offers three check boxes:

Import Data When Retrieving E-mail Center Mail	Initiates Web import every time email is retrieved.
Import Data on Background E-mail Retrieval	Initiates Web import every time email is retrieved in the background.
Discard Message After Importing Data	Deletes the Web Import message after GoldMine has retrieved the information.

The advanced email preferences remain in force until you change them.

Prospecting with Web Site Messaging

The easy way to collect potential contact data from a Web site is to use a template prepared by an expert. The next best method is to progressively edit the source text of a Web page that you know is already working. For this you should be prepared with a little theory, which begins thus.

GoldMine's Web Import Gateway is a predefined sequence of software that uses three components:

➤ A Web form that can be viewed in a Web browser and be completed by a prospective contact.

➤ A Web server script to control what happens to the data collected by the form.

➤ GoldMine's Internet email reader to get the information into contact record format in your database.

What is needed is a script written in Hypertext Markup Language (HTML) and Perl. The following HTML call initiates a CGI Perl script held in a file named web7.pl in the Web site belonging to dtsl:

```
<FORM METHOD=POST ACTION ="http://www.dtsl.com/cgi/web7.pl">
```

When the Web site server gets this command, it fetches the web7 script and starts following it. This displays the form in the browser and handles the business of allowing the prospect to edit and correct entries before submitting the completed form.

The HTML call has to live in a server file with the suffix HTML; such as webimport.html, for example.

End of lecture—action to follow.

Creating the Web Form

A form to collect information from the Web has to end up in the HTML language and reside in the HTML directory on the Web site server. However, there are several methods of creating what you need in one format and have your system convert it to HTML. One way is to write the whole file in Word or Notepad and put in all the markers that HTML needs to be interpreted by an Internet browser. That's fine if you're already adept with HTML, but you don't have to learn to write all that arcane code. A quicker way is to create the form in Word and use the main menu command sequence **File**, **Save as HTML**. You will be warned that some Word formatting might be lost by converting to HTML. You can still edit the source HTML to improve the form.

Figure 7.5 shows a scrap of HTML obtained by selecting the **View**, **Source** command when the page is visible in the Internet Explorer Web browser.

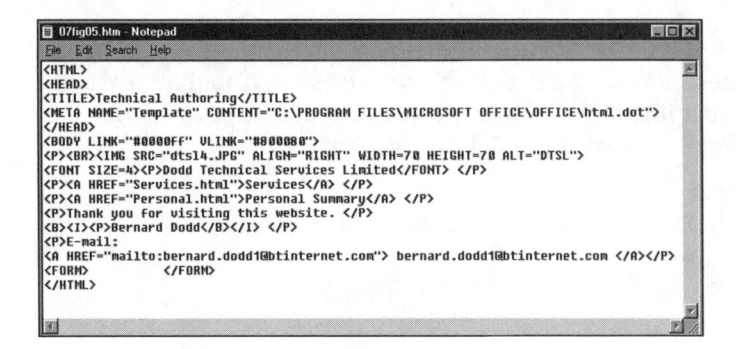

Chapter 7 ➤ *Are There Spiders in the Mine? Using the Web*

Figure 7.5
You can view the HTML code that underlies any Web page.

Here's the code from Figure 7.5:

```
<HTML>

<HEAD>
<TITLE>Technical Authoring</TITLE>
<META NAME="Template" CONTENT="C:\PROGRAM FILES\MICROSOFT
OFFICE\OFFICE\html.dot">
</HEAD>

<BODY LINK="#0000ff" VLINK="#800080">
<P><BR><IMG SRC="dts14.JPG" ALIGN="RIGHT" WIDTH=70 HEIGHT=70
ALT="DTSL"> </P>
<FONT SIZE=4><P>Dodd Technical Services Limited</FONT> </P>

<P><A HREF="Services.html">Services</A> </P>

<P><A HREF="Personal.html">Personal Summary</A> </P>

<P>Thank you for visiting this website. </P>
<B><I> <P>Bernard Dodd</B></I> </P>
<P>E-mail:
<A HREF="mailto:bernard.dodd1@btinternet.com">
bernard.dodd1@btinternet.com </A></P>

<FORM>           </FORM>

</HTML>
```

The way to scan a text in HTML is to match the pairs of bracket codes, such as <P> and </P>, that mark out the beginning and end of a logical section.

This example has a mailto command, although there is no form for collecting structured information and no special instructions to GoldMine about handling the email that might be generated by an interested visitor to the Web site.

103

Interpreting an HTML Form

The following HTML lines show how a data input field can be created for a Web page. Figure 7.6 shows that a text line forms the field title and a data input window of 10 characters and is to be associated with the field name "Zip."

```
<DT>Zip/Postal Code
<DD><INPUT SIZE="10" MAXLENGTH="10" NAME="Zip">
```

Figure 7.6
A Web site data entry field has to be given a name to pass the data to GoldMine.

The script will include directions to process the data labeled "Zip" and eventually this will end up in the Zip field of a GoldMine contact record. Other Web site form fields are handled similarly.

Understanding the Web Import File

Web import files can be written for many applications. Each application has to be able to execute a suitable file. The usual location for a GoldMine Web import file is in the GoldMine directory. This file contains a script written in Perl, or an equivalent gateway script language. This script assembles a mail message, line by line, that will be acceptable to the GoldMine E-mail Center. The message can include instructions for handling the data imported from the Web.

Triggers can be defined in this script that will initiate actions when interpreted by GoldMine. For example, if a contact is not already in the database, notify a particular user, and if this contact is located in a certain city, also notify the user who is responsible for prospecting this city.

Formatting the Web Import File

The special handling instructions plus the contact data collected from the Web are formatted as a Web Import File that optionally contains three sections separated by the following headers:

[Instructions]	Includes duplicate checking, sending email messages to GoldMine users, attaching Automated Processes, and running external applications if they are needed for further processing of the incoming contact data.
[Data]	Specifies the data fields in terms of the primary field names in a GoldMine database.
[ContSupp]	Specifies which Contact Supplementary information items are to be assigned to fields in the Details tab.

Interpreting the Instructions Section

You will probably look at an existing Web import script in Notepad. If you make any alterations, you must save the text. If you do your editing in Word, save the finished result as a Web page or HTML document type.

Checking for duplicate contact records is controlled by commands following the [Instructions] header, for example, DupCheck1=AccountNo. The first field to be checked must be one of the 10 indexed fields:

> Contact, Company
>
> Phone1, Zip
>
> AccountNo
>
> Key1, Key2, Key3, Key4, Key5

You also can specify additional DupCheck# instructions that test more than one field to determine if the incoming contact data is a duplicate.

Another technique for duplicate checking is based on ContSupp data by specifying the ContSupp record prefix, for example, cs1. When GoldMine determines that a record is a duplicate, but the contact name does not match the existing name, an Additional Contact is created to hold the incoming data under the existing contact record.

Consequent actions are specified in the Instructions section, such as OnNewSendEmail=contactName, NEW, Prospect to receive information. This will send the particular named contact, who will probably be a GoldMine user, an email based on the template called NEW with a message reference as defined in the instruction.

If you name a contact to receive an email who is not on your GoldMine network, you have to include the necessary addressing information in the data section of the Web import file. You can send notifications to more than one destination by specifying **OnNewSendEmail2**, **OnNewSendEmail3**, and so on.

Interpreting the Data Sections

The format of a Web import file following the [Data] header is designed to associate the named values with specific GoldMine fields. The Web import file will only identify data fields for the values that are to be imported. The format is fieldName=value. The actual entry has Value replaced by the name of the field that was assigned in the Web site form.

Figure 7.4 showed how whatever the prospect typed into the Zip field would be imported into GoldMine as a value named "Zip." It would be placed in the ZIP field of the contact record. This technique can be repeated for each of the field names as they appear in the GoldMine database files CONTACT1 or CONTACT2. A special item, email=value, is provided to capture the email address of the prospective contact.

The data processing instructions following the [ContSupp] header have to allow for the fact that supplementary contact details might comprise many additional fields. There can be up to nine ContSupp records, each with a dozen or so additional fields. Each Web import instruction will refer to the name of a particular field, but the names will be prefixed by the characters cs1, cs2... cs9, according to the detail field name to which they belong. This ensures that the values arrive in the correct places in the detail records of the relevant GoldMine contact record.

OnNewAttachTrack= is the format for attaching a named or numbered automated process track to a "New Contact" trigger event detected in the Web import processing. Chapter 20 discusses how to set up and use these tracks.

Run=<exefile> is the format for an instruction to launch an application, other than GoldMine, to process the incoming data. GoldMine will stop importing fresh data until the external application has finished processing and returned the results in a form acceptable to GoldMine.

Most of these instructions might be repeated if they are differentiated by including a numbered suffix.

Matching a Password for Web Imports

When you are editing a script for your Web import file, you can have an entry of the form Password=value, in the [Instruction] section. If you want your GoldMine to refuse any Web import files that do not contain the correct value for this password, you have to create a [WebImpPassword] section in your GM.INI file. There can be several passwords defined in this section, using the form Password#=value. The acceptable passwords are defined as Password1, Password2,...Password999.

A password can comprise a string of up to 20 characters. An instruction file can include only one Password=value entry.

Here is a sequence of operations that you might try as a review of the Web import technique. Open Word and write a Web site page.

Highlight a phrase such as "Send me a message" that you have typed in the page. Click the **hyperlink** icon and follow the prompts by typing in or browsing to another document in your computer. For example, you could create a document called My Email Center as a target for your hyperlink.

If you are on the Internet, you can create a hyperlink to your own email address.

Save your Web site page as a document of type HTML, or Web Page if you have Windows 2000.

Chapter 7 ➤ *Are There Spiders in the Mine? Using the Web*

Open Internet Explorer and type in the address of your HTML file. Press **Enter** or **Go** to view your draft Web site. Click any of the hyperlinks to move to their targets.

From your Internet Explorer, view a Web page and select **View**, **Source**. Use the spacebar and enter key to separate the pairs of codes, such as <TITLE> and </TITLE>.

Consider what lies within.

> **The Least You Need to Know**
>
> ➤ Some search engines can be set in motion via Lookup, Internet Search, and will seek the active contact.
>
> ➤ GoldMine can collect information that Web site visitors type into forms. Don't edit something that is working already!
>
> ➤ You can specify how GoldMine handles incoming Web information.
>
> ➤ Actions can be triggered by Web data.
>
> ➤ Web Imports can be protected by passwords.

Chapter 8

Remote Control: Updating GoldMine from the Web

In This Chapter

➤ Distributing your license

➤ Registering your installation

➤ Updating your GoldMine to the latest version

➤ Updating a GoldMine network

When you first install GoldMine, the program creates a single user called MASTER with Master rights that include creating other users. However, this Master is not all-powerful. There is a limit to how many users can be created, and this limit is defined in the license. In this chapter, I'll describe how you can upgrade your license online, allowing you to add more users and otherwise enhance your capability.

Exploring the Licensing System

The Master License that you or your company purchased along with GoldMine has a unique serial number. Various types of sublicenses can be created from this master, and each will have a serial number that is prefixed by the Master number.

This Master number is shared by all users and it is consulted when anyone attempts to synchronize data. You cannot synchronize with any GoldMine user who is operating with a different Master number.

The cost of a GoldMine Master License depends on how many users it supports. The welcome screen that appears when you launch GoldMine shows the license number. You also can view your license by selecting **Help**, **About** from the main menu.

Part 2 ➤ *Communicating Through the Internet*

Configuring Your GoldMine License

You will not be able to configure a GoldMine license unless you have Master rights. As I've said, these are assigned to a user called MASTER when GoldMine is first installed on a standalone system. With a network to look after, the network administrator will assume Master rights, probably to the exclusion of all other users.

If you are a standalone user, you will need to use your Master rights if you want to set up a portable GoldMine that will be able to synchronize with your base system.

The control over sublicenses is exercised from the License Manager window. From the main menu select **File**, **Configure**, **License Manager**. Figure 8.1 shows my GoldMine License Manager.

I have blanked out my real license number. It will be the same number for all the users on my team—including any remote or undocked users—so that we can all synchronize our databases.

Figure 8.1

Auntie Alice has a remote site license for two users. B and the MASTER can get undocked. Four of the five user licenses have been distributed.

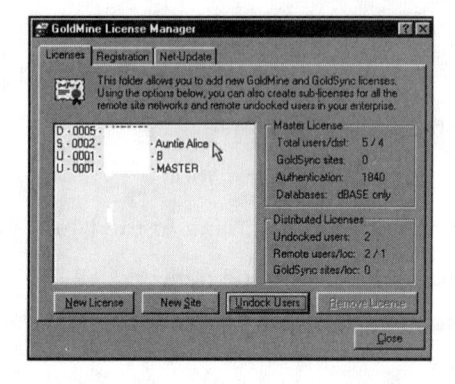

My Master License is type D-0005, which shows that it is for a dBASE system with up to five users. A single-user GoldMine 5.0 license, installation disc, and basic manual pack are retailed at about $150. Multi-user packages are sold through GoldMine Solutions Partners who will price them according to the additional services they provide.

The License Manager dialog box offers the following buttons:

New License	Used when you have purchased a new license that you want to combine with the existing license. You need to know the new license number and key code.
New Site	Offers to create a sublicense from your existing license for a remote site with a specified number of users—up to the limit set by your Master License.
Undock Users	Offers to create an undocked license for an existing user.
Remove License	Deletes, after a warning, the license number you have highlighted.

The procedure for creating a distributed license from an installed Master License, whether for a remote site or for an undocked user, entails reading and agreeing with a panel of conditions and restrictions. For example, a user might only have one license for an undocked installation of GoldMine. A remote site license might not be used to install GoldMine at more than one other location, although the remote license might allow for a specified number of users there. If you click **I AGREE**, GoldMine will generate a license number and key code that begins with the ID of the Master License.

Take Note of Your Remote or Undocked License ID

You have to make a note of a newly generated sublicense number and key code because you will need it when you install GoldMine in the remote site or on the portable computers that your undocked users will work at.

GoldSync is a GoldMine product that is controlled by a separate system of licenses, although these licenses might be managed from the GoldMine License Manager. The GoldSync distributed licensing options will not be active unless you have already installed GoldSync. With a small number of users, GoldSync is not needed. It has a section in the License Manager because it has to share the license number with GoldMine.

Registering GoldMine Licenses

If you have used the GoldMine License Manager to add—or in any way change—your arrangement of distributed licenses, you have to go through the registration procedure.

When the distributed licenses have been set up in the License Manager, click the **Registration** tab. This will display the details of the person or company to whom the original Master License was sold. Check the spelling, the numbers, and the email address, because this information gets used in templates and other automatic procedures.

If you need to make any alterations, click the **Net-Update** tab, and then click the check box labeled **Update registration information**. If you now click the **Registration** tab again, you will be able to edit the information. Back to the **Net-Update** tab—this time click the **Net-Update Now** button and wait for GoldMine to get in touch with the update Web server.

If you are already running the most up-to-date versions of GoldMine and GoldSync, you will get a cheerful message. Otherwise, the Web server will start to download the complete set of files needed to bring your system up to scratch. There is no charge for this service!

Whatever happens, your registration details will have been passed to the GoldMine Corporation database.

You might have been upgrading your GoldMine license to increase the number of sites or users. In this case, you will be offered the choice of automatic registration as soon as you identify the new license number and key code. This will link you to the GoldMine update server and pass over your details. However, you can leave blank the Automatic Registration check box and possibly edit your particulars and change your license distributions before you go for the Net-Update Now procedure.

All users who expect to synchronize must be running the same version of GoldMine.

Licenses Suffer from Typology

A Master License beginning **E-** (for Enterprise) is for a GoldMine running dBASE and/or a client/server configuration with a specified number of GoldSync users and sites.

D- signifies a GoldMine dBASE with a specified number of users.

G- indicates a GoldSync license for a specified number of sites.

U-0001 is for an undocked GoldMine user.

S-xxxx is for a remote site with *xxxx* GoldMine users.

Y-xxxx is for *xxxx* remote GoldSync sites.

B-xxxx signifies an increase of *xxxx* users to a GoldMine Enterprise or Standard dBASE license.

Never Tamper with LICENSE.DBF

The LICENSE.DBF file exists only in the GoldMine root directory in each installation. This file should not be edited because it provides a unique authentication seed, shared with all sublicenses, that is essential when synchronizing.

Understanding Net-Update Now

When the update server detects that you are not running the latest version of GoldMine, it downloads the necessary files into a subdirectory of the GoldMine root directory. This might take some time, but your existing GoldMine will keep on running. Eventually you will be asked if you want the update to be put in place.

What happens next depends on whether you are installing the download to a standalone PC or to a network. If you are on a standalone PC, and you select **Update your GoldMine System Now**, your GoldMine will shut down gracefully while the updating takes place.

Installing the File Download on a Network

If you are running GoldMine on a Windows NT 4.0 or Windows 95/98 network, you might have your GOLDMINE.EXE files installed locally, one set at each workstation. This can speed up processing considerably. In these circumstances, you must finish updating your Master system and then visit each workstation in the network and go through the Net-Update procedure at each.

Updating by Hand

You can update GoldMine workstations by copying files selected by *.EXE and *.DLL from a system that has already installed the latest Net-Update to the GoldMine directory. Obviously you should overwrite the files associated with the previous version at each workstation.

113

During the Net-Update sequence you are able to defer installing the update to a later time. The downloaded update files will remain passively in the directory to which you consigned them. When you are ready to activate them, go to your Windows Taskbar and select **Start**, **Run**.

In the Open Field window, type the path and name of the update file, for example, `D:\GOLDMINE\SETUP\GOLDMINE\GM5SETUP.EXE`. When you select **OK**, the updating will occur automatically.

Installing a Network Update Locally

The License Manager window acquires a new tab when you have completed your first Net-Update process and the GoldMine Corporation is aware of your status as a legal license holder. The Install Locally tab has the following options:

Install GoldMine in Local Path	You tell the update where to put the new files in the local workstation by selecting from a browser or by typing the path. The program files are updated, but the database files remain on the network server.
Create a GoldMine Shortcut on the Desktop	Adds a GoldMine icon to the desktop of your local system.
Automatically Update the Local GoldMine Program Files	Updates the GoldMine program files on your local hard drive whenever you install a new version on the network.
Install GoldMine Locally	Starts installing the update.

Do We All Speak the Same Language?

To confirm that each workstation on a network is running the same revision of GoldMine, select **Help**, **About** from the main menu. Check the version number.

Checking Your Details

If you're a little confused about your license status, don't fret. It's easy to check your details by accessing the Registration dialog box.

If you are a standalone user, log on to your GoldMine, check that you have a modem plugged in and powered up, and then select **Help**. If you then click **GoldMine Net Update**, you will be connected to the GoldMine update server. This will read your GoldMine license details and check to see if you already have the latest version. If you do not, the server will start downloading the entire GoldMine software.

Chapter 8 ➤ *Remote Control: Updating GoldMine from the Web*

There is no charge from GoldMine—but be prepared for the download to take a long time. And just when you think that the GoldMine update server must have gone off to another planet, a happy little dialog box will invite you to have your GoldMine automatically shut down and updated. The option is to leave the update to another time.

All this excitement might be too much for you. In my case, the downloaded box of software could not find enough disk space to unpack itself. "Free off 15MB and try again," it said.

If You Misplace Your GoldMine Update

When you connect to the GoldMine update server and are found to be less than fully up to date, a compressed new copy of GoldMine will be downloaded to a subdirectory of your current GoldMine program.

My downloaded update put itself in D:/GOLDMINE/SETUP/GOLDMINE with a box icon. Because I had to free space to let it out of the box, I had to click the box icon when I was ready. My existing GoldMine in D:\GOLDMINE was then overwritten. My login banner now shows the new version number and date.

The Least You Need to Know

➤ GoldMine is delivered with a license that can be distributed to a specified number of remote sites and users.

➤ A user might be given an "undocked" license to set up one portable workstation.

➤ Licenses ensure that different users can synchronize their data.

➤ Networks can have GoldMine programs on each workstation but share a database on the server.

115

Chapter 9

Prettying Up the Place: Customizing Startup and Settings

In This Chapter

➤ Adjusting how GoldMine starts up

➤ Arranging users in groups

➤ The art of adding fresh fields

➤ Building the contact record screens you really want

GoldMine is nothing if not flexible. You can rearrange just about everything. Some users just like to have things different from everyone else. Some like to have things as slick as possible. Some just leave things as they were when they found them. Perhaps you should go for the arrangement that minimizes your opportunities for making mistakes. Taking away any bits and bobs you are unlikely to use and putting your come-in-handy items out front can maximize your efficiency. This chapter shows you how to customize how GoldMine appears at startup.

Tightening Your Records

A user with Master rights can do things that will affect the database—get rid of some of those fields that your people never use. You could set up some fields to hold the data you really ought to collect for most of your contacts.

This section hopes to persuade you to review the fields provided by GoldMine and how they are used. You also are introduced to the art of adding fresh fields.

Reviewing How Your Fields Are Used

Does this problem seem familiar? You seem to spend so much time writing in your diary that there is no time left to do anything interesting. And if you're doing interesting stuff, you don't have time to keep a diary. I would rather fiddle with GoldMine than get to grips with what has to be done in the matter of real work. Yet tidying one's workshop is a surefire way of starting up a new project that makes it untidy again.

The casual approach is to look around your screens and see where the empty fields are. Do these spaces represent missing data that could be important? Have they fallen into disuse because you keep everything important in your head? Do you note everything in cryptic text or long essays in the note panels? Should you be looking to set up a field or two with really useful browse lists of standard items that between them will just about totally encapsulate what it is that you want to remember electronically about your contact persons? Answer this multiple choice for every entry: missing/useless/key point/supporting point.

> **Strike It Rich**
>
> **Punctuate Your Look-ups**
>
> The clever thing about a browse list item is that you can signal whether it should replace or supplement the entry already in the field. When you select a browse list item with no punctuation marks, it will replace whatever is already in the field, if anything. If you select a browse list item that is immediately followed by a semicolon (;), this item will be added to whatever is already in the field, separated from what is already there by a comma (,). The semicolon will not be entered. If your lookup entry is followed by the percentage sign (%), the entry (without the %) will be inserted directly in front of whatever is already in the field.

If you have installed any of the Industry Templates delivered with GoldMine 5.0, you will have some splendid browse lists, like the Commercial Real Estate options in Figure 9.1.

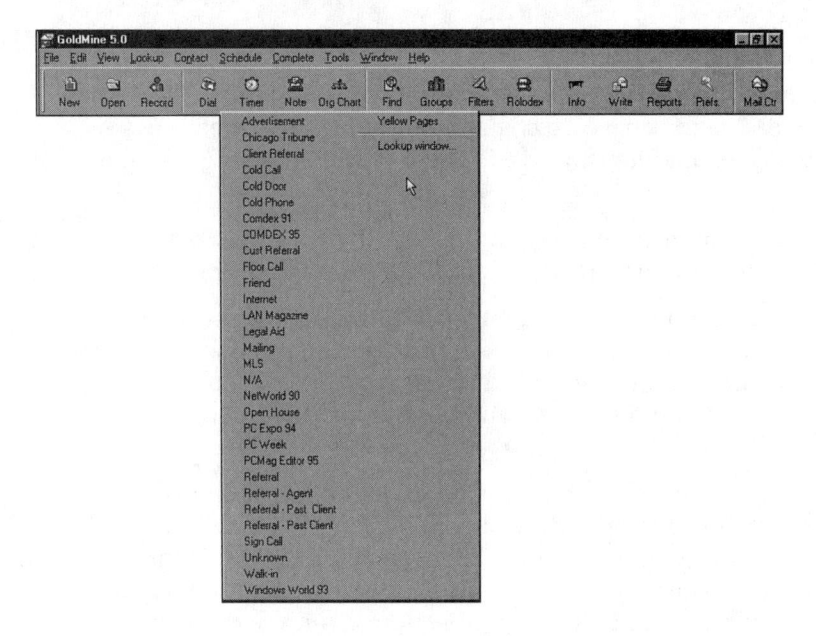

Figure 9.1
Have you really identified all the interesting sources of prospective customers?

Some industry templates will have useful browse lists that they will add to whatever items are already in place. Never mind. If you get too many, you can right-click in a field to edit the browse list and then press the **Delete** button when you have highlighted one you don't like.

Administering a GoldMine System

A GoldMine system is very well behaved. But it does need an administrative person who occasionally gives it a tweak, in a professional sort of a way, of course. The administrator has to see that the system runs properly and that the databases are maintained. He or she must see that the procedures are as efficient and effective as possible when they are properly followed by the users. Sometimes it might be necessary to clean up the contact record fields and their titles.

Suppose you are a standalone user. Guess who will have to be the administrator?

The administrator also might manage the users and control what menus they are allowed to access and what functions they might initiate. Somebody has to train new users and perhaps upgrade existing users so that they are aware of improved ways of working. Then there is the key issue of being able to exploit the wisdom held in the experience of the employees and in the various documents that have been produced from time to time, perhaps in a variety of systems. Chapter 18, "Share the Wealth: Distributing Nuggets of Information," discusses some of the ways in which GoldMine can bring existing wisdom into current circulation.

Customizing Processes

Virtually any of the GoldMine processes can be assigned custom settings. The easiest method of getting GoldMine to behave exactly as you want it to is by editing your preferences, or by having your administrator edit them when registering you as a GoldMine user.

For example, you can edit the Internet email connections by selecting **Edit**, **Preferences**, and then clicking the **Internet** tab in the resulting dialog box.

However, the administrator, or a user with suitable authorization, can set up initialization settings that assign suitable values to the control parameters that direct how GoldMine will start up. The administrator could set up your Internet connections and take away the possibility that you might get connected to another Internet service provider.

Your initialization settings are consulted when you sign in, although on first installation you will be operating under the default GoldMine settings. The rights and privileges are discussed in Chapter 1, "Staking Your Claim: Opening Up the GoldMine." The first person to open the GoldMine box and install it gets the best deal because that person automatically gets Master rights and therefore can make everyone else slaves, or at least workers. This can include putting limits on which preferences are adjustable by the user and which are assigned by the Master.

What happens when you click the GoldMine program icon is determined by the default settings in the system, perhaps influenced by customizing activities by the supervisor or individual users. For example, a user with Master rights can allow another user to bypass the sign-on screen and hence not need a password. A stand-alone user might operate in this way.

Managing the Users' Master File

The supervisor or administrator needs Master rights—like me! Therefore, I can decide who sees and does what when they log in.

To inspect and edit a user's permissions, select **File**, **Configure**, **Users' Settings** from the main menu. This action will display the Users' Master File dialog box. Highlight the user you are interested in and click one of the following options:

Properties	Displays the [Username]'s Properties window with tabs for Profile, Membership, Access, Menu, and Time Clock.
Preferences	Displays the [Username]'s Preferences window with tabs for Personal, Record, Calendar, Schedule, Alarms, Lookup, Toolbar, Internet, Modem, Pager, Sync, Misc, and Login.
Delete	Removes a username after a caution.

> **Strike It Rich**
>
> ### The First Master Has Access
>
> The first GoldMine user is assumed to have the username MASTER and the password access. The first Master is advised to change at least the password, if not the username as well.
>
> If you need to widen your permissions, you must select **File** from the main menu and then **Log in Another User**. This will show the login banner and you can sign in as the Master user if you know the username and password.

Click **New** to create a new user. Click **Close** to leave the Users' Master File dialog box.

Figure 9.2 shows the Login tab of B's Preferences. You use the browse buttons to select the type of GoldMine database and where the contact database is to be found. These choices are associated with the default username when you click **OK** to close this dialog box.

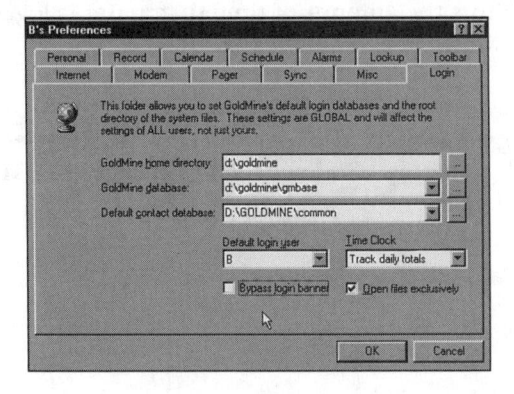

Figure 9.2

The supervisor with Master rights can set up the default databases for each user.

Selecting the GoldMine Home Directory

The login preferences include the path and name of the home directory that contains the GoldMine files that don't contain contact data. The non-data files include report and license files, forms, the InfoCenter, and filters. By default, GoldMine will enter the GoldMine directory where the program files are located.

If you are working in a network installation, all users must use the same home directory, and this must be on the network server. The home directory might not be located on an SQL database server, although an SQL server might store both the GoldMine database and one set of contact files to form the default contact database.

The default contact database contains the contact records, detail records, and history records that will automatically be loaded when this user signs on.

You can assign an optional password to the database entered in the Default Contact Database field by requiring the default user to encounter the login banner where a password is required. All users will have to enter this password.

The check box labeled Open Files Exclusively allows this user to open the selected database but excludes access by other users. This can speed up processing in a network. A database also can be restricted to users on the installation where it was first created. This is done during the File, New Database procedure.

Configuring a User's Time Clock

The Login tab of the Preferences dialog box offers three options for controlling GoldMine's monitoring of how long each user is logged in:

Disable time clock	Turns off login and time tracking.
Track daily totals	Default—records the cumulative amount of time logged in per day.
Track each login	Monitors the amount of time that a user is logged in to GoldMine for each login session.

To see a user's timekeeping habits, go to the **File** drop-down menu and highlight **Configure**. Click **User's Settings**. Highlight the user and click the **Properties** button. Now you see the [Username] properties window where you click the **Time Clock** tab to view the following details:

- Date
- Earliest login time
- Latest logout time
- Total logged time
- Number of logins
- Number of keys used
- Number of clicks
- CRC(X/ok)—an indicator for certain errors

Configuring User Groups

A user group is a collection of usernames. The name of a user group can be entered in most places where a username is called for. For example, you can send the same email template to all members of a user group.

To work with user group memberships, go to the **File** drop-down menu, highlight **Configure**, and select **User's Settings**. This opens the Users' Master File dialog box where you can highlight any of your users. Select the **Membership** tab of the **Properties** window when you have highlighted a particular user. Figure 9.3 shows this membership tab in action. Double-click any username to move it into or out of a group.

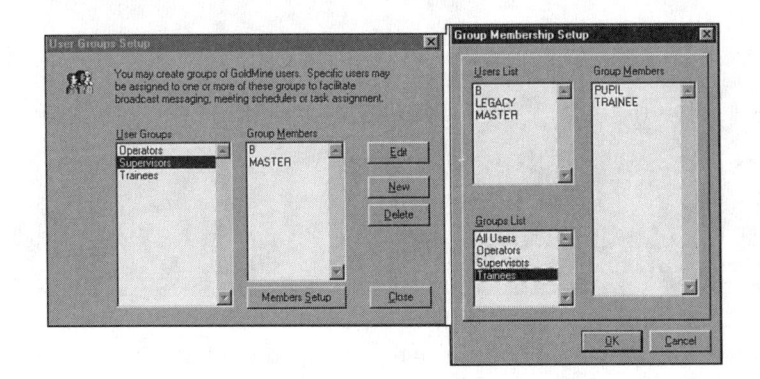

Figure 9.3
*While in the User Groups Setup, you can click the **Members Setup** button and rearrange the groups and their memberships in the Group Membership Setup dialog box.*

The Edit button in the User Groups Setup dialog lets you edit just the name of the group you have highlighted.

The group structure in Figure 9.3 is a simple one. The properties of each group can be defined in terms of the preferences and properties that describe the working environment of each user. New users can be rapidly created by assigning them to an existing group, such as TRAINEE. This will have the effect of setting their default properties and preferences to those assigned for the group. For example, you could establish that the TRAINEE group is not allowed to see or use menus that could disturb the configuration of the GoldMine installation.

Whether a newly created user will be able to alter any settings will depend on whether his or her group has been given permissions to do so.

Configuring Resources

A GoldMine resource is some kind of facility or equipment that can be booked for a definite period by only one user at a time. A meeting room would be a typical example. Before such a resource can be booked, it must be established in the GoldMine database by selecting **File**, **Configure**, **Resources**.

Figure 9.4 shows that some resources have been configured and the boardroom is booked for a meeting.

Figure 9.4

Resources are reserved when an activity is scheduled according to the choices you make at that time.

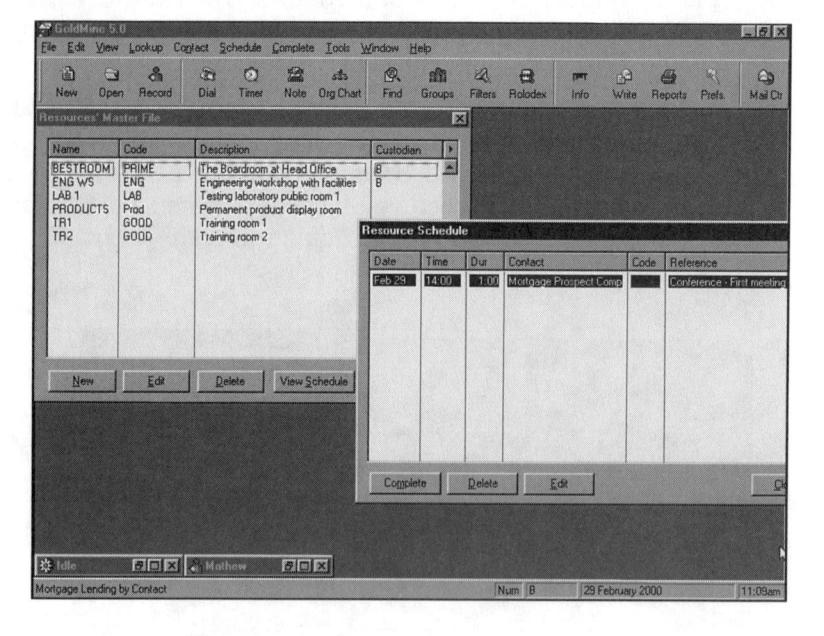

The booking of configured resources for a specific activity is discussed in Chapter 10, "Look, Then Leap: Scheduling Your Activities."

Rebuilding Your Screens

A field has three names:

- ➤ The global label that is determined by the GoldMine Corporation and displayed next to the data entry window in the contact record.
- ➤ An optional local label that can be changed by the user with Master rights and will replace the global label.
- ➤ The name assigned by the database to the data held in the field.

For example, point and click the space next to the Department field on a contact record. You see a data entry window. Click the right arrow and you will see the browse list for this field with the current value in bold, if there is a browse list entry already in this field. The field could be holding a typed-in entry that does not match anything in the browse list.

Point and right-click the space next to the Department field and you will see the local menu. If you click **Edit Dept**, you will get back to the data entry window. However, if you click **Properties**, you will see the Field Properties dialog box laid on top of the contact record in which the Dept field is the only area not shown in highlight. Figure 9.5 shows the Dept field, with the Field Properties dialog box open for business.

Figure 9.5

Every field can have a local label—but GoldMine gives it a global label and a field name.

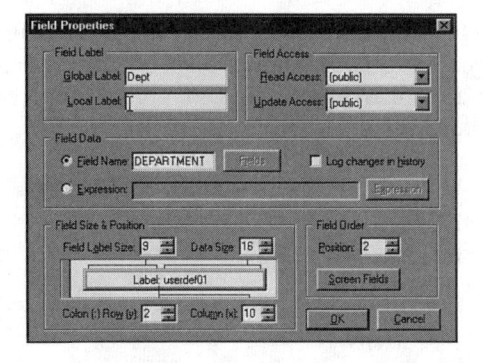

Suppose you want to change the label of the Dept field. When you have opened the Field properties box, you can just type the new local label and click **OK** to have it used throughout your database.

You can change the label of a field where it stands, or you can move a field to another position or to another tab.

You can have a field appear in more than one place, and have different labels although the data is always synchronized. You can invent new fields and add them to any "user" screen that has space. For instance, your Field tab will probably have been delivered with two examples of user screens: Technical Support and Customer/Prospect, for example. You can re-title these screens and repopulate them with existing fields of your own choosing. You also can create new fields to sprinkle about your user screens.

Scrutinize Your Industry Templates

Select **File**, **New Database**, and follow the instructions to create a database with the name of your creation, filed with blank records. Select **File**, **Open Database**, and click the database name you created. From your GoldMine installation disk, select **Install Industry Templates**. Choose one of the templates and follow the installation instructions.

Notice the many tabs and extra fields. Click some fields and consult their browse lists.

125

Right-click while pointing anywhere in the **Fields** tab to see what user-defined screens are available. Standard GoldMine as delivered has just two screens—End User Screen and Tech Support Screen. Figure 9.6 shows the Tech Support Screen in the Fields tab.

Figure 9.6
Although this is a commercial real estate template database with no records, I can still edit the fields and the screens they inhabit.

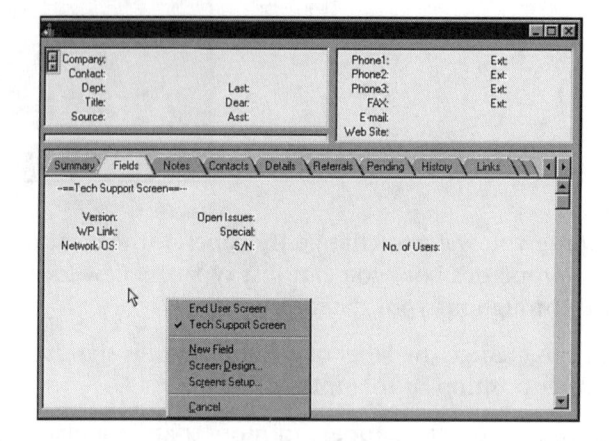

I have opened the local menu by right-clicking in the **Fields** tab so that I can add more fields in the empty spaces. If you feel you need a brand new screen, you can build it and add it to the screens available via the Fields tab. Your new screens can be given their own tabs so that you can have them displayed without going through the list in the Fields tab.

To begin creating a new field, select **File**, **Configure**, **Custom Fields**. Alternatively, right-click in the **Fields** tab of any contact record to get the local menu, which you saw in Figure 9.6. It contains the options shown here:

End User Screen	Displays the screen (supplied with GoldMine 5.0) of this name.
Tech Support Screen	Displays the screen of this name.
New Field	Creates a new field. Opens the Screen Designer toolbar and the Place Field dialog box (see Figure 9.7).
Screen Design	Allows you to identify an existing field, or create a new field, and drag it to a free space in the Fields tab. You will be invited to have the database rebuilt if you create a new field.
Screens Setup	Lists the existing screens and their fields. Allows you to clone a screen in preparation for editing it. You can edit any field in any user-defined screen.
Cancel	Closes the local menu.

The screen in view is ticked in the local menu. If other custom screens have been created or installed, their titles will appear in this local menu.

When GoldMine is delivered, there are two screens accessible from the Fields tab: End User Screen and Tech Support Screen. If you create new screens, or install an Industry Template, there will probably be many more screens available from the Fields local menu by right-clicking in the **Fields** tab.

Creating a New Field

The Place Field dialog box offers a drop-down menu of all the existing fields from which to choose. The New Field button allows you to define a field name. This must begin with U because it is a user-defined field. You must type in a short description that will become the Global Label of your new field. You then signify the field type as Character, Numeric, or Date. You specify the field length in characters and number of decimal places, if appropriate.

When you have defined the new field, you will be shown a highlighted version of the contact record, with your new field differently highlighted (mine is a red box) and temporarily located at the top-left corner of the Fields tab. You should drag the new field to a vacant space. When you drop it, the Field Properties dialog box will be displayed.

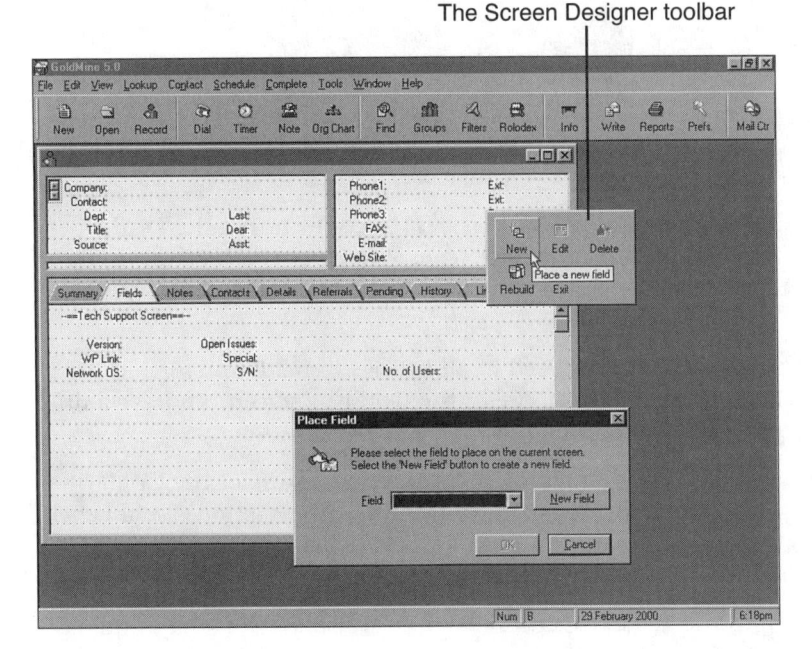

Figure 9.7

I can use the Screen Designer toolbar to place either an existing field, or one I shall create, in the open user-defined screen.

Part 2 ➤ *Communicating Through the Internet*

If you right-click in the **Fields** tab and select **Screen Design**, you will see the small untitled Screen Designer toolbar. If you had selected New Field, you also would see the New Field dialog box.

The Screen Designer toolbar offers the following command icons:

New	Creates a new field or places an existing field.
Edit	Edits a field that has been highlighted.
Delete	Removes the highlighted field.
Rebuild	Rebuilds the database to accommodate the new field(s).
Exit	Leaves the Screen Designer. Confirm rebuild if necessary.

My work with the Screen Designer includes defining a global label and a local label for a new field. Figure 9.8 shows that the new field name ULAPTOP begins with the letter U to signify that it is a user-defined field.

Figure 9.8

I have added a new field labeled Laptop using the Screen Designer and I am checking the Field Properties.

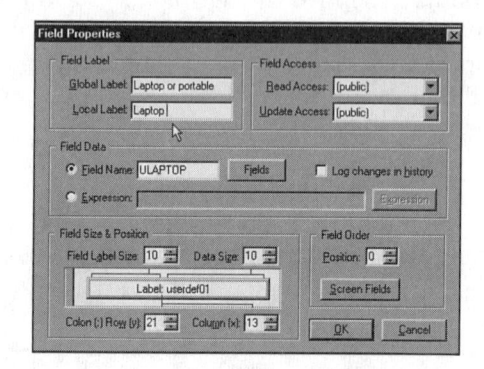

When you see the Field Properties dialog box, it is best to confirm that the local label of your new field is short enough to fit in your screen. Whatever you typed into the Description field will be taken as the global label and as the local label unless you edit the Field Properties.

The global label of your new field will be used in all listings of fields and screens. It will become the local label by default. Each use of the field in a screen can have a different local label if you edit the Field Properties.

The Fields button in the Field Properties dialog box displays a listing of the GoldMine and user-defined fields, with the following column headings: Description, Local Label, Name, Type, and Length. You can access the Field Properties dialog box, create a new field, or delete a user-defined field from this listing.

The Screen Fields button in the Field Properties dialog box displays a listing of the fields, their lengths, and their positions in the current screen. The listing title is formatted as Fields of Screen: [Screen name].

Creating a New Screen

A GoldMine contact record is a collection of panels or screens of information. A panel is designed to focus your attention on fields that contain personal details, phones, address information, and business interest.

A screen for a contact record is a view of some fields that are put together because they belong together, and you will probably want to work on them as a bunch. For example, the Pending tab shows a screen listing all the activities with the currently active contact that is not yet finished.

GoldMine might not have defined the fields you need for your business. Sometimes you can take over an existing field, rename it, and use it for your own purposes. But many types of business need to store many items of data. Fresh fields have to be created.

Now you can just collect and add new fields to the Fields tab. If there are too many fields to see at once, use the scroll button in the tab window. If you need just a few collections of fields, you can define each collection as a screen. The Fields tab will show the screen used previously.

Point in the **Fields** tab and right-click to see the possibilities and select the screen you want.

You might have a screen full of fields that you often need. This screen can be given its own tab. Then you can display the fields by clicking the tab label. For example, if you have a particular set of information that you collect when prospecting over the telephone, it might be easiest if all these fields were shown together, in the right order, on a screen designed specifically for telephone prospecting and given its own tab label.

If you put a field in more than one screen, any alteration you make in one place will be updated immediately in all the other locations of that field.

To begin creating a new screen, select **File**, **Configure**, **Custom Screens**. Alternatively, right-click when pointing in the **Fields** tab of any contact record.

The Fields tab local menu will list the screens that do not have their own tabs. GoldMine is delivered with two such screens:

> Tech Support Screen
>
> End User Screen

You can select either of these to become the default display for the Fields tab. If you select **Screen Setup**, you will see the Custom Screen Setup listing from which you can create new custom screens. Clicking the pop-up arrow invokes the local menu, which has the following commands:

129

Fields	Lists the fields of the selected screen.
Find	Searches for a screen on the basis of words or characters in the field names.
Output To	Copies the listing to Printer, Word, Excel, or Clipboard.
New	Begins creating a new screen with the Custom Screen Profile dialog box.
Clone	Creates a new screen as a clone of the selected user screen, beginning with the Custom Screen Profile dialog box.
Delete	Deletes the selected screen after a caution. You cannot delete either of the sample user screens provided by GoldMine.
Properties	Displays the Custom Screen Profile dialog box where access to the screen can be controlled. You can assign a tab name here if you want the screen to be available under its own tab.

Populating a new user screen with selected GoldMine and user-defined fields begins by selecting the new screen from the Fields tab local menu, or by clicking its tab, if it has one. Then you must use the screen designer to create or select each field and place it in your new screen. You will be prompted to agree to a database rebuild before leaving the screen creation procedure.

Cloning is a handy technique. Click a tab you like. If your open contact file was not built on this tab, all the fields will contain the value n/a. Suppose you find a tab that does match the database. I've got Buyer. I know it is compatible because all the fields in this tab have data entry windows. Click the space next to the field label to see if you can enter data. You might get a window with an empty browse list. You might find a good list of possible entries.

I've got a Property Type field that has a list of different types that a buyer might be looking for—farm, ranch, hut, palace, and so on.

My Buyer screen has loads of useful fields, such as Maximum Price, Minimum Price, Built Before, Built After. I'll clone this screen to become a Seller tab.

Right-click in the **Buyer** tab—or any tab will do—and select **Screens Setup**. Now you see the Custom Screens Setup dialog box where you highlight the screen to be your model and press the **Clone** button.

Clones need a new screen name—how about Seller Requirements?—and something short to fit in as the tab name. Press **OK** to see the Custom Screens Setup dialog box with your new screen in place. It will have the same fields as your model but a new screen name and tab name.

Chapter 9 ➤ *Prettying Up the Place: Customizing Startup and Settings*

> **The Least You Need to Know**
>
> ➤ An administrator can make GoldMine set itself to work in almost any manner.
>
> ➤ Screens can have surgery done to their layouts and content.
>
> ➤ Your installation of GoldMine can have screens that are unique to your business.

Part 3
Managing Contacts Efficiently

Let's get our act together. You don't want to just rummage about in your contact database. Your outfit makes magnificent strategic plans, terrifying tactical maneuvers, and tidy little reminders for the important things in life, work, and the universe.

Have we got something going together? In this section, it's a sure thing.

… **Chapter 10**

Look, Then Leap: Scheduling Your Activities

> **In This Chapter**
> ➤ Reviewing what is pending
> ➤ Finding time to do what has to be done
> ➤ Completing planned activities

Some authorities talk about managing time, but I find that time just goes on no matter what I try to do about it. However, there are days when I feel that I am going to exert complete control over what I do. GoldMine has some handy helpers so that you can at least plan what you intend to do and record how things have gone when it is all over.

Planning Things to Be Done

Some people say that you should make time for everything—set aside specific time slots on particular days of the week for your planning horizon. My planning horizon is about the middle of next week! You could spend ages using GoldMine simply to schedule activities and have no time to actually do them. On the other hand, where contacts of importance are concerned—and aren't they all?—it would be unwise to rely on your memory to tell you when a further action should occur.

As I mentioned in Chapter 2, "Scratching the Surface: Setting GoldMine to Work," GoldMine has a Personal Rolodex for keeping names and phone numbers that can be auto-dialed. There is also a To-do list function that will stack your entries in order of

Part 3 ➤ *Managing Contacts Efficiently*

the priorities you have assigned to whatever you've got to do, as you can see in Figure 10.1. A To-do list item can be linked to a contact record if you have something planned, but not in terms of specific start and finish times.

Figure 10.1

There is something of a private nature that I must do. It needs a priority but not necessarily an appointment.

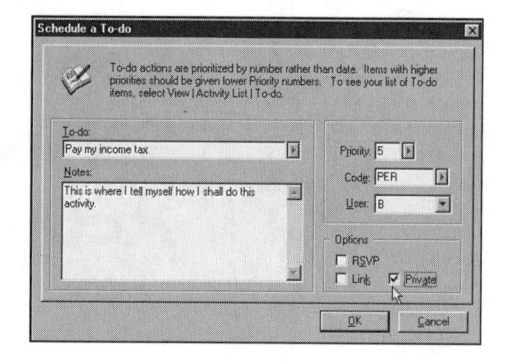

If you want to add something to your list of things to be done, go to the **Schedule** drop-down menu and click **To-do**. If you want to see what is already on your list, go to the **View** drop-down menu and click **Activity List**. If your list is not already on the top, click the **To-do** tab. Press the **F6** key to go directly to your Activity List window at any time.

When you tell GoldMine that you have completed one of these tasks, it's taken off the list. Alternatively, you can just delete it.

Strike It Rich

Keeping Some Things Private

If you click the **Private** check box when scheduling an activity, the code and reference fields will not be accessible to other users. They will be able to inspect the Real-Time Completed Activities Log for all users, but the code will be blank and the reference marked "[Private]" for the activities of other users. In short, other users can tell you did something during the time you scheduled a private event, but not what it was.

136

If you have something to do that is definitely related to one or more contacts, then this activity should be linked to the relevant contact records. A serious time manager also would at least pencil in a date and time of day for each of the intended activities.

> **Learn the Lingo**
>
> ### GoldMine Accepts No Pencilled-in Dates
>
> A scheduled activity will be accepted by GoldMine if there is shared free space on the calendars of all the users and configured resources involved.
>
> There are no tentative or pencilled-in bookings—but events can be rolled over into a subsequent period and rescheduled.

Contemplating Your Activities

Scheduling events just isn't enough—you need a way to check your Activity List. For one thing, other users might schedule events for you. It might even come to pass that something slips your mind and you need a reminder. Therefore you need to have a method of inspecting your impending activities. Select **View**, **Activity List**. You'll see a dialog box like the one in Figure 10.2.

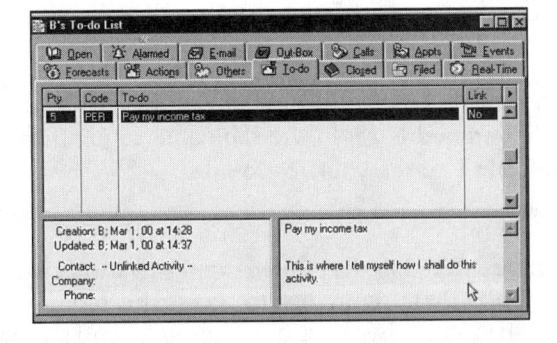

Figure 10.2

My planned but not scheduled activity appears in the To-do tab of my Activity List.

You also can press the **F6** key to go directly to your Activity List window from anywhere in GoldMine. Each time you access an Activity List, it'll display the tab you were viewing when you last closed the list. If you're viewing a list for the first time, the Open tab appears by default.

Your Activity List has the tabs shown in Table 10.1.

Table 10.1 Activity List Tabs

Tab	Function
Open	View all the scheduled and To-do activities that are pending because they have not been formally completed.
Alarmed	View pending activities for which an alarm has been set.
E-mail	View pending GoldMine and Internet email.
Out-Box	View created but not yet sent Internet email messages.
Calls	View pending scheduled calls.
Appts	View pending scheduled appointments.
Events	View pending events.
Forecasts	View pending sales.
Actions	View pending next actions.
Others	View pending other actions.
To-do	View my activities with a priority but no planned date or time.
Closed	View all completed activities.
Filed	View all sent and completed email.
Real-Time	View all completed activities for all users as logged in real-time.

Strike It Rich

Hot Keys for Your Activities

Press the **F6** key to open your Activity List window. When you have the Activity List open, press **Ctrl** and the underlined letter in the tab name to jump to that tab. For example, you'd press **Ctrl+T** to see your To-do list.

The display of your activities can be filtered and supplemented in various ways from the Activity List local menu (remember, you right-click to access this menu when you have highlighted an entry). Table 10.2 contains a list of these filters and supplements.

Table 10.2 Activity List Filters

Local Menu Item	Result
Zoom	Shows additional information about the highlighted item.
Complete	Completes the selected activity.
Reply	Starts composing an email reply to the activity contact or user.

Options	**Date Range**—Selects or enters limits to the date range.
	
	User—Selects a user to see her Activity List.
	
	Activities—Selects all activities or a combination of activity types to view.
	
	View
	    Detailed View—Toggles the activity window detailed view panel.
	    Sync Contact—Keeps the active contact record in synchrony with the activity highlighted.
	    Show Contact—Displays the contact name in the Contact column of the Activity List.
	    Show Company—Displays the company name in the Contact column of the Activity List.
	
	Link—Links the highlighted activity to the active contact record; re-links after a warning.
	
	Roll-over—Allows you to roll over all or some of your activities to another user or to another date, or to roll over each of the selected activities by a specified number of days—to yourself or another user.
	
	Filter—Opens the Activity Filter dialog box where you can set up a temporary filter over the Activity List display. This filter can be based on a selected user, activity type, activity codes, date range, or reference text assigned to the activity.
	
	Release Filter—Cancels the temporary filter and displays all the activities.

Find	Searches the Activity List with a character string.
Output To	Sends the Activity List to a printer, Word, Excel, or the Clipboard.
Delete	Deletes the selected activity, after a caution.
Edit	Edits the selected activity.

Figure 10.3 shows the Activity List local menu and some of its submenus.

Figure 10.3

There are many things I can do with the selected activity by right-clicking for the local menu.

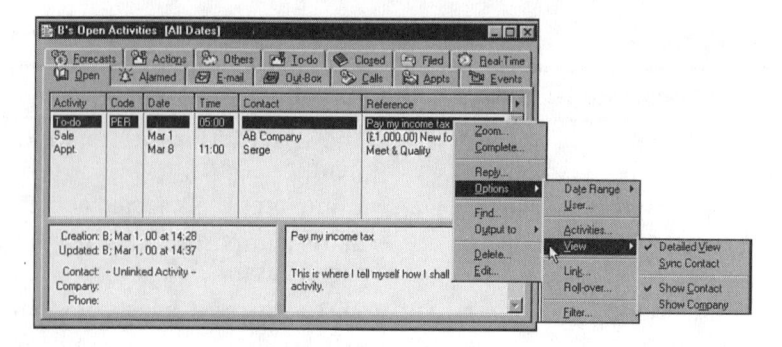

The Activity List in Figure 10.3 is displayed in the detailed view that includes two lower panels of information relevant to the selected activity. To access this display, go to the **Schedule** drop-down menu and click **To-do** if you are interested in your private list. Go to the **View** drop-down menu and click **Activity List** to see your work activities.

If you would prefer to see more activities in the listing, you can remove the lower panels. Right-click in the Activity List panel to get the local menu. Select **Options**, **View**. Click **Detailed View** to uncheck this setting. This will get rid of the lower panels and make room for more activities. To restore the panels and their contents, check **Detailed View**. Your view setting will apply to all the tabs in the Activities List window.

When you are looking at an Activity List that has been filtered, either by default specifications or by applying a filter, the title of the display window will usually give some indication. For example, in Figure 10.3, the Activity List window's title bar reads B's Open Activities [All Dates], indicating it's displaying open activities only.

Reviewing Your Past

The Activity List window has three tabs that essentially look at the past, although you might well find that there are lessons to be learned from history. Again, you can set a limit by defining a date range and perhaps a filter to limit the history records in which you have an interest.

The Closed tab details all the activities that you have completed—phone calls, for instance.

The Filed tab shows all the completed messages that you have sent. The details include the date and time the message was sent.

The Real-Time tab gives access to a log of all the completed activities, whatever their type, and also records the duration of each activity as it was logged at the time. If you click any column heading, the display will be sorted according to the values in that column.

Completing an Activity

If you are diligent, you will probably complete as many open activities as you can, and you'll want GoldMine to indicate as such. Its easy—highlight the activity you're working on and select **Complete** from your local menu.

This action will invoke a dialog box in which you can fill in a form to record how successful you have been. Posting this form by selecting **OK** gives you the bonus of clearing this particular item from your open Activities List and from your Calendar. It will be credited to you in the History tab of the contact concerned and in your Real-Time Complete Activities Log.

> **Strike It Rich**
>
> **Mystery Date**
>
> If you think you have lost some scheduled activities, check your current date range. You might be looking in the wrong part of your calendar.

You might want to consult your manager, or your conscience, about the choice of entry you should select for the following fields when you are completing an activity:

➤ **Code**—Does your company have a set of codes that differentiate between activities on the basis of what is happening or according to how the time is billed?

➤ **Result**—There is one nice entry here—Sale—but the lookup window allows you to set up a variety of other options, if they would be helpful.

➤ **Success**—GoldMine allows only two choices: Successful and Unsuccessful. I hope all your entries belong to the former!

Remember, the context in which you use the classifications is up to you. A friendly chat with a contact might be classified as successful if you remain friends, or only if you definitely move towards a forecasted sale.

Replying to Another User

You might find yourself obliged to offer some remarks to another user who has scheduled some activity on to your Calendar and hence to your open Activities List.

Pick an activity and right-click for your local menu. Choose **Reply**. Up will come a partly written email based on your default email template. The good news is that your log will show that you at least replied to the other user who offloaded it.

Linking to the Active Contact

Linking should happen all the time in true contact management. Every action and action plan should refer to the specific contact or company that is targeted. In many instances, your system will have been set up to create this linkage automatically. As you move through an Activity List display, your workspace of contact records will probably be shuffling itself to bring forward the relevant contact record. Select **Sync Record** in the Activity submenu.

Furthermore, GoldMine will offer you the data taken from this linked contact record whenever you attempt to generate a message or leave some notes or other records about your work.

However, there might be occasions when you have to create or change this linkage to a particular contact record. Perhaps one of your contact persons has changed companies. You might be working on a task or project that has previously not been targeted at any contacts.

Suppose you have scheduled a call and you decide to link it to a different contact. Your Activity List local menu has the item **Link**, which you can select to create a connection to whichever contact record is active at the time.

> **Strike It Rich**
>
> **An Activity Record Might Have a Secret Link!**
>
> You can link any activity record to any contact—but the name of the original contact will not be changed. All you will notice is that the active record is not the same as the name in the contact field of the activity line entry of your Activity List.

The advantage of a valid link is that the scheduled activity will include information such as the company name and telephone number taken up from the linked contact record, together with any notes recorded in the Activity List dialog box. This extra information is displayed when you highlight an activity in one of the Activity tabs, if you have selected the **Detailed View**. Although you can see the information, you can't alter it unless you right-click the highlighted activity and select **Edit** from the local menu.

Dating an Activity

Pressing **F7** or choosing **View**, **Calendar** will display your calendar. It appears in the layout you were using previously; the Day calendar layout is the default. You can click any calendar tab to change this layout. You also can press **Ctrl+Shift+** the underlined letter on the tabs to move your display between calendar layouts.

Chapter 10 ➤ *Look, Then Leap: Scheduling Your Activities*

Recording Activity Details

An activity needs a date. Go to the **View** drop-down menu and select **Calendar**. Alternatively, you can press the **F7** key. This displays the Calendar window. Right-click the date you have chosen for the activity. Choose **Schedule** and click the type of activity you are planning.

You will have to fill a form to specify the details of a new appointment, as shown in Figure 10.4. One of the fields on this form offers a drop-down menu so that you can still change the title of the form from Schedule an Appointment to whatever type of activity you select from the following list:

Call

Next Action

Appointment

Other (Action)

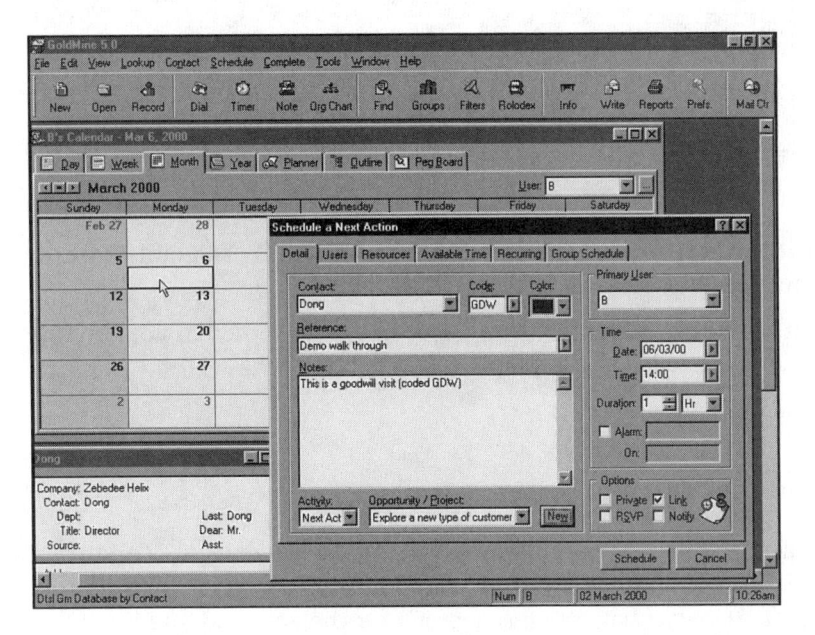

Figure 10.4

I have filled in some details about my appointment with Mr. Dong and I am about to click Schedule to record it as one of my planned and timetabled activities.

One way to schedule an activity is to go to the **Lookup** drop-down menu and click **Contact**. The currently active contact will be already highlighted, but you can click another contact in the contact listing. If you now click and drag this highlight, a "little person" icon will follow your cursor to your calendar, where you drop it into a date or time slot in one of the tabs: Day, Week, Month, Year. Figure 10.5 shows this process in action.

143

While you are dragging, you cannot change the calendar layout, but some layouts have extra calendar displays into which you can drop your appointment if you do not want to schedule it for the date currently displayed.

Figure 10.5

Mr. Dong from Zebedee Helix is being dropped into my calendar to make an appointment.

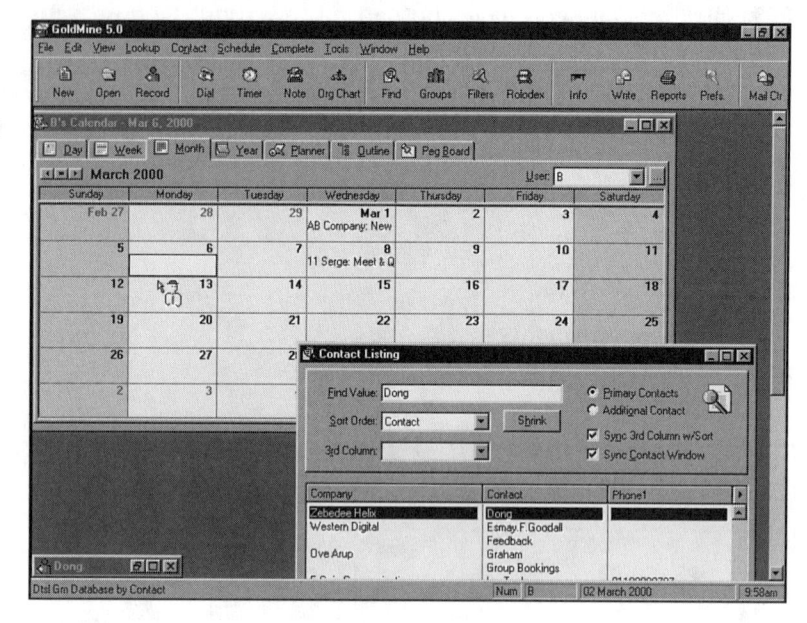

If the time slot you drop into is defined, such as 2 p.m. on March 2, 2000, this time will appear in the scheduling dialog box. You can edit it here if necessary.

Planned activities that have been scheduled into GoldMine, or recorded in your To-do list, will appear in each of the following displays:

- Calendar(s) of the user(s) involved
- Activity List(s) of the user(s) involved
- Pending tab of the contact(s) involved

You can access and edit the activity records from any of these screens. For example, in your calendar Day tab will appear all your tasks—your To-do actions plus whatever appointments, actions, and events have been scheduled for the date that you have highlighted in the calendar.

If you have associated an activity with a sales opportunity or a project that is not directly connected with a forecasted sale, the details of this activity also will appear in the records of this opportunity or project. Chapter 15, "Looking for the Real Seams: Using the Opportunity Manager," discusses this facility.

Scrutinizing Other People's Diaries

If you have been given permission, you can select any user from the **User** drop-down menu and examine his or her calendar. If you select the menu item **(Multiple Users)**, you can specify any users or user groups. Their combined timetables will be displayed in the calendar. Each scheduled activity will be labeled with the usernames or group names of those taking part.

Press **F7** to see your calendar. Right-click the calendar window to get the local menu. Select **Activities** to decide what you want to see in your calendar. Figure 10.6 shows the Select Activities to View dialog box where you can choose which types of activity to have displayed in your calendar.

Figure 10.6

I am prepared to see absolutely all scheduled activities in my calendar display.

Allocating Time to an Activity

Experts in squeezing more useful endeavor into the flexible working day advise you to assign specific moments in your future for absolutely everything. GoldMine is party to this wicked plot. Scheduled activities have to have at least a default starting time—this very moment—and a sensible duration.

To do this, you must right-click the date in one of the calendar layouts. This brings up the local menu. Select **Schedule** and click the type of activity you are scheduling. Now you will have a form with plenty of fields waiting to receive data.

145

If you want to change the date or time of a scheduled activity, click it in one of the calendar layouts and drag it to where you want it to be scheduled. You also can right-click an activity in a calendar, an Activity Listing, or in the Pending tab of the relevant contact record. The local menu will display and you click **Edit** to access the schedule details and change the appointed date and time in the dialog box. If you do not add either *a* (for a.m.) or *p* (for p.m.) after typing in a figure, GoldMine will assign morning or afternoon according to the most likely position in the working day. You might find that your system has been set up to schedule calls to start, as a reminder, five minutes before the time you enter. Pressing the up arrow key will advance the time by increments of five minutes. The down arrow will subtract five minutes.

GoldMine needs to know how long you expect a scheduled call to last. It's going to mark off the appropriate duration in your calendar, or in somebody else's calendar, if you are not going to make the call yourself. You can just put a figure into the Duration field, and GoldMine will assign a reasonable unit of time. For example, 8 is assumed to be eight minutes, 2 is taken as two hours. You can always select the units deliberately in the drop-down list.

Using Your Calendar

I'm a big calendar person. This section will show you how useful the Calendar can be. For starters, click the **Maximize** button in your calendar window and then click and drag the vertical borders to adjust the relative size of the panels and, for example, the number of monthly calendars in view.

To schedule a birthday party for yourself, first decide which contacts are to be invited. Go to the **Lookup** drop-down menu and select **Contact** to display the Contact Listing dialog box. Hold down **Ctrl** while you click the contacts you want to invite. Click again on any chosen contact that you want to drop from your list.

These highlighted contacts in the listing are now referred to as tagged contacts. There's more about tagging in Chapter 11, "Panning for Gold: Filtering Contacts from the Database." Tags remain in place until you either exit GoldMine or close the Contact Listing window. Any action you schedule will be directed at all the tagged contacts.

When you have tagged the contacts who are to be invited to your party, right-click a suitable date in your calendar and select **Schedule**. Click the type of activity, such as **Other Action**. You will see the Schedule an Other Action dialog box, or the corresponding dialog box for the type of activity you are planning.

The Schedule dialog box has several tabs. It defaults to the Details tab. Enter or select the starting time and the duration. Type a helpful phrase in the reference panel so that you will recognize this event when it appears in your Activity List and in the Pending tabs of any contacts who are to be involved. Check **Notify** if you want GoldMine to send reminder messages to participating contacts and users.

To invite any user friends, if you have any, click the **Users** tab and check **Additional Users**. Double-click particular users or user groups, such as **All Users**, to add them to the users who will be taking part in the scheduled activity. Double-click any user you want to remove from the list. Users will have the scheduled activity automatically entered in their Calendars and Activities Lists.

Your own username is assigned as Primary User by default—but you can click the down arrow to select another user as the Primary User. For example, you might want to have the notifications sent from a different user. The Primary User has full rights over the activity record. Others can view it but not alter it.

Rescheduling an Activity

Tragedy! Your goldfish tank has leaked and ruined your carpet. Postpone your birthday party for a week. Press **F6** for your Activity List and use the down arrow to scroll down until your party is highlighted. Right-click it for the local menu and click **Edit**. This brings up the activity record where you can type a fresh date or click the right arrow to bring up the calendar where you can click a suitable date. Press the **Select** button and you will be back in the activity record window. Select **OK** when you are satisfied—oh yes, check the **Notify** box so that everyone will know what is happening.

Deleting an Activity

Whoops! Sometimes a scheduled activity gets timetabled by mistake—or perhaps you have a better use for that block of time. You could change things and let GoldMine record what you have done automatically, just like it always does. However, if you don't want to leave any traces of your error or overtaken ideas, choose **Delete** from the local menu while you are pointing at the offending entry. For example, press **F6** to see your calendar if you are not already looking at it. Click the left or right arrows until you see the scheduled activity. Right-click the item in your calendar to get the local menu, and choose **Delete**.

You will get a warning message in case this is not exactly what you intended. GoldMine will remove this highlighted activity from the Calendar without recording anything in the history file.

Muddling Your Schedule

You could be forgiven if you scheduled two phone calls to start at the same moment. You also might schedule a long call that could overlap another appointment. Such rare (hopefully!) events are known as *scheduling conflicts*. Unfortunately, GoldMine will have none of them!

If you try to schedule an event that overlaps something already on your calendar, GoldMine will present a warning box. You will get the chance to ignore the potential conflict with an existing entry, or you can edit your schedule to avoid the conflict.

Locating Another User

The Peg Board tab of the Calendar shows which users are currently logged in to your GoldMine system. You might possibly be able to judge how busy they have been recently.

You can use this ability to notify other GoldMine users when you are out of the office. To do so, select **File**, **Log Away**. Doing so displays the dialog box called I'm Away from My Desk, as shown in Figure 10.7. You can choose the option button that best indicates your whereabouts (or where you want people to think you are, anyway).

Figure 10.7

A user who is active on the GoldMine system will leave records on the Peg Board, especially if he says when he is absent from his desk.

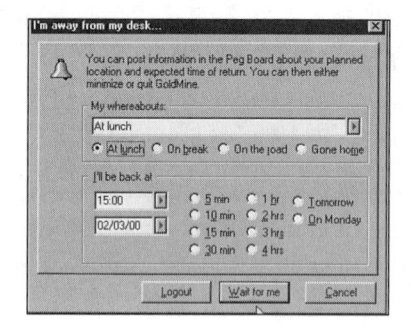

Alarming Activities

The Alarm check box in the Activity Scheduling dialog box will have GoldMine display a warning panel on your screen 10 minutes before the scheduled moment for the call or other activity. You can type a different alarm time, or use the spin buttons. You can right-click in a field to work with the graphical calendar and clock.

Strike It Rich

You Can Set the Warning Time

GoldMine shows you when an activity is due by displaying a warning panel some time beforehand. You can adjust how much time is allowed by choosing **Edit**, **Preferences** from the main menu, and then clicking the **Alarms** tab.

148

There is an Alarmed tab in your Activity List that specializes in collecting all activities for which an alarm has been scheduled.

Making a Private Call

In the world of an active GoldMine system, a private call is defined as any call that is not automatically linked to the currently active contact record or to some other contact that you specify. You must deliberately uncheck the **Link** box before you click the **Schedule** button to book yourself a time slot for this private call.

If you have unlinked the scheduled call from the currently active record, the reference to it will appear in your user Calendar and in your Activity List. When you have made your private call, and told GoldMine that you have completed this scheduled item, the existence of the private call will be recorded only in the Closed tab of your Activity List.

Restricting a Private Entry

If you check the **Private** check box, when scheduling or completing an activity, the contents of the following fields will not be displayed to anyone except the designated User, the recipient, and any specially authorized users:

- (Activity) Code
- Reference
- Notes

If any other users inspect your calendar, they will see that you have reserved a time slot for a private activity, but they will not be able to read the reference entry nor any notes you might have saved.

The Least You Need to Know

- A To-do activity is with you until you complete it.
- A scheduled activity can be rescheduled and changed from one type to another, or even assigned to another user.
- Completing an activity is the businesslike way of removing it from your pending lists.

Chapter 11

Panning for Gold: Filtering Contacts from the Database

> **In This Chapter**
> - Looking up contacts using basic information
> - Digging up details
> - Tagging records for the time being
> - Making a filter to single out some people but not others
> - Saving a filter for use on another occasion

When your system gets going, it will accumulate loads of contact records. You must be prepared to keep them under control. You could potentially have them all on your work top, cluttering things up and overwhelming you. Hey, a contact manager is supposed to make your life easier, not harder!

You can't reduce the number of things waiting to be done by hiding the contact records to which they are linked—but you can pick certain records to work on next. In this chapter, you'll learn how.

Finding Particular Contact Records

Your currently active contact has a Summary tab in which the Record field will show you the order number of this record and the number of contacts you have in your workspace. This set of contacts will be taken from the database currently open—you might have the entire database potentially available, or you might have filtered out a lesser number for a particular purpose. If a filter is currently active, the name of this filter will appear in the title bar of every record selected by it.

Part 3 ➤ *Managing Contacts Efficiently*

Learn the Lingo

There Is Always an Active Contact Record

GoldMine will not let you close all contact records. If you want to clear you workspace, the best you can do is click the Close button of each open window. When you get to the last open contact record window, this attempt to close it will merely minimize it at the foot of your workspace. The contact to which it referred is still the active contact.

Searching on Basic Information

To fetch a particular contact record from your database, select **Lookup** from the main menu, and then select one of the first four searching methods:

- ➤ **Company**
- ➤ **Contact**
- ➤ **Last (name)**
- ➤ **Phone1**

These options refer to indexed fields in the contact record that can be used for rapid searching. When you click one of these indexed field–searching methods, the Contact Listing dialog box will appear on top of your workspace, as shown in Figure 11.1.

Figure 11.1

The Contact Listing dialog box shows the 3rd Column field box, and the list is sorted in alphabetical order in this column.

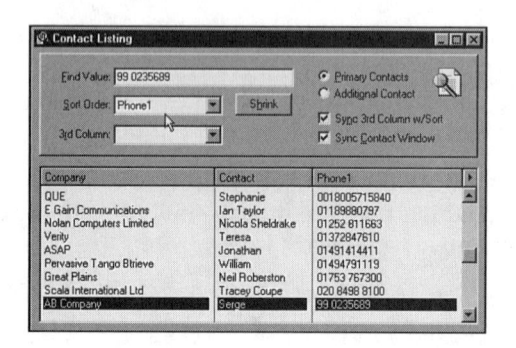

The Contact Listing dialog box allows you to control the display by entries in the data entry windows described in Table 11.1.

152

Table 11.1   Contact Listing Dialog Box Options

Option	Description
Find Value	As you start typing a name or other value, the contact listing will roll up to match your partial entry with the values in the field you selected as the basis for sorting.
Sort Order	Type or select a field as the basis for the sort order of the contact listing display. This will default to the field you selected as a Lookup option, but you can change it.
3rd Column	The contact listing has a Company column, a Contact column, and a third column that contains the values in whatever field you enter or select from the browse list.
Primary Contacts	Default option button. Search is focussed on the primary contact.
Additional Contact	Option button. Search will look only for additional or secondary contacts as listed in the contact record Contacts tab.
Sync 3rd Column w/Sort	Check box. Checked by default. Ensures that contents of the 3rd column correspond to the field name in the Sort Order box.
Sync Contact Window	Check box. Checked by default. Ensures that the active contact record corresponds to the contact selected in the contact listing.

Searching on Indexed Fields

If you want to refine your search for a contact, use one of GoldMine's fields that are automatically indexed. Select **Lookup**, **Indexed Fields**. Doing so will drop out a further range of search fields from which to select:

- Zip, City, State, Country, Account No.
- Key 1, Key 2, Key 3, Key 4, Key 5

The labels of the fields in a contact record can be configured to suit your requirements. For example, the GoldMine Demo database has the following labels for keys 1–5:

- Contact Type
- Business
- Interest
- Accnt Mngr
- Open

Any field lookup table that you consult using F2, for example, will contain the field labels that you see on your normal record screen. You can start a search by double-clicking the field label (not the entered value) of any of these indexed fields where they are displayed in the drop-down menus.

The sort order of the Contact Listing will correspond to the indexed field that you chose for the search.

Narrowing a Search for Contacts

When you have a reasonable number of contacts listed before you, the one you are looking for might be visible, so you can click it. Otherwise, you can start typing a value in the **Find Value** box. As you type, the listing will move so as to find a record with a search field that starts to match what you have entered. GoldMine's search is not case sensitive.

If you press **Enter**, the contact record you have chosen will hide the listing. If you right-click, the resulting local menu will give you the following options:

Show Record

Find

Output To

You might well be in sync with your contact records, so the active contact record will be nearby on your workspace.

Calling for Another Record Window

There are as many different ways of working with GoldMine as there are users. However, you might find it useful to have more than one contact record window open in your workspace, perhaps for comparison.

Press the **Record** icon, or select **View, New Contact Window**. You get another contact record window, complete with spinner buttons. The contact encapsulated in your new window will be the one that follows your currently active contact in your most recent Contact Listing. The lucky beneficiary of this new window will become the new active contact.

You have to make do with a single Contact Listing, however. If you click into a different contact window, the person surrounded by a dotted box in the Contact Listing will be the one in your active contact window.

Chapter 11 ➤ *Panning for Gold: Filtering Contacts from the Database*

Strike It Rich

Truncate Your Record Panels

Provided there are no open field windows on your active record, repeated use of Ctrl+W will cycle through various contact record displays, losing or gaining a panel of fields each time.

It might be useful to have minimal contact record fields in view if you have several contact windows open.

Spinning for a Record

Spin buttons in a contact window give you access to the next and previous contact record in the ordering you established last time you structured the Contact Listing. For example, if you choose Last (Name) as the query method to find the contact record for a particular person, GoldMine displays the contact record that alphabetically follows or precedes the last name of this person, like Hardly Ableman follows Trobe Aardvaark, for instance.

The marker in this listing does not move when you spin the contact record window and so change the active contact.

You can use the **Window** option from the main menu to choose one of the windows already open in your workspace. These windows are listed as 1, 2, 3, and so on, with the name of the window or the contact/company alongside.

You can operate the spin buttons on your active record window to replace this record with any other contact record in your open database. This will not affect any other contact records you have in your workspace. You could even end up with two copies of the same record! Any changes you make to one copy will be promulgated to the other as soon as you finish working with it as the active record.

Finding Records Using Their Details

You can find a record by looking for information in a field that might be hidden in a tab, for example. This search can extend to fields that are not automatically indexed by GoldMine and so are not normally offered for searching.

From the main menu, select **Lookup**, **Detail Records**. Figure 11.2 shows that you can select a type of detail and then choose one of the possible values for that detail.

Figure 11.2

Looking up detailed records helps you find contacts that have the same entry in a particular field, even if that field is not one indexed for rapid searching.

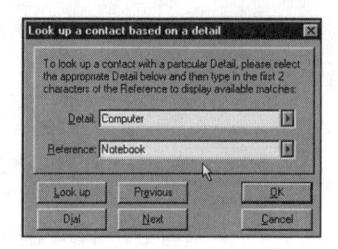

The Look Up a Contact Based on a Detail dialog box allows you to scroll to the **Previous** and **Next** record in the set of records that have the detail you are looking for. If you click the **Look up** button, you will see a listing of all the records that have some kind of entry in the Detail field that you have specified. The Look Up Detail dialog box also offers you the chance to dial Phone1 from the record that has become active as the result of your search.

Exploring Filters

A *filter* is a selection process that can be applied to your current database to reduce the number of records to a smaller set that is easier to work with. For example, you might set up a filter that selects only records of companies located in a specific geographical area. The filter might be a complicated search based on a logical combination of the values taken from several specified fields in your contact records. You can assign a name to a filter and save it for use on another occasion.

When you have filtered your database, you can assign a group name to the set of chosen contact records. This allows you to quickly access the same records another time. There are various ways you can add to or remove the records in your group. These are discussed in Chapter 12, "At the Corral: Building Contact Groups."

Tagging Contacts for Immediate Use

Tagging is a process of clicking records in the Contact Listing so as to pick them to form a temporary set that will remain together just for the current working session. You can, if you want, save a tagged set of records as a named contact record group so that you can get hold of them again at a future work session.

The way to tag a record is to highlight it from the Contact Listing. The standard Windows techniques apply. For instance, you can tag a block of contacts by highlighting the first and then pressing **Shift** while you click the last. If you are holding down **Ctrl**, your clicks will highlight or release individual records.

The highlighted records are all tagged until you either close the Contact Listing or exit GoldMine.

Chapter 11 ➤ *Panning for Gold: Filtering Contacts from the Database*

As you build up a set of tagged records, your open contact window will have a title that reports what you have done, as a preamble to the title of the active record—for example, 11 Tagged Records; Contact Percy.

The tagged contacts become the set of records in your workspace. You can spin between them or use any of the Lookup functions on this set.

Strike It Rich

Open an Extra Contact Window to Add to Your Taggies

From the main menu, select **View**, **New Contact Window**. This new contact window will spin through the entire contact listing. If you select **Lookup**, **Contact**, or **Lookup**, **Company**, for instance, the Contact Listing will still display highlights on the members of your tagged contact set.

Additional highlights will not affect your original tagged group unless its contact window was active when you opened the Contact Listing. However, any changes you have made to the highlights in the Contact Listing will be reflected in your tagged records window as soon as it next becomes your active window.

A window of tagged records can be saved as a named group for use in a future session, or you can simply work on them and have their set membership forgotten when you either close the Contact Listing or log off.

To save a collection of tagged records as a group, go to the **View** drop-down menu and select **Contact Groups**. You see the Filters and Groups dialog box, which is illustrated in Figure 11.3. Point to a space in the Filter Name panel and right-click for the local menu. Select **New** to get the Group Profile dialog box. Type in a suitable name for your group of tagged records. Click **OK**.

Now you will see the Group Building Wizard welcome screen. Click **Tagged records** as the method for building the group. Click **Next**, **Next**, **Finish**. Each page of the wizard offers interesting options—but they can be safely ignored if you just want to keep your tagged records together as a named group. There's more about groups in Chapter 12.

If your selected records have been saved as a group, the name of the group will appear as part of the title bar in the active contact record window. This title bar also will acquire the names of any filters that you might subsequently impose.

Figure 11.3

Look for a suitable filter to identify a particular set of contacts.

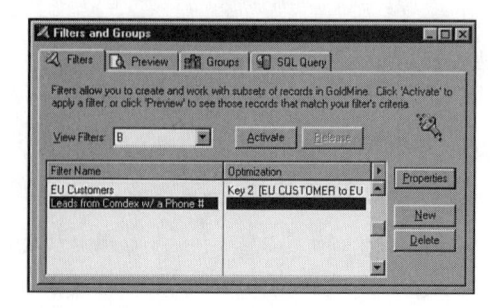

Any GoldMine function that can be applied to a contact record can be automatically carried out on a set of tagged records, a filtered set, or a contact record group.

For example, if you select **Contact**, **Create E-mail**, **Message to Contact**, or better still, press **Ctrl+Shift+E**, you will open the Create E-mail dialog box. You will be invited to have your message sent to each of your tagged records, or to some other target, perhaps defined by a different group or filter.

> **Strike It Rich**
>
> **Untag a Record If You Don't Want It in Your Set**
>
> In the Contact Listing display, hold down **Ctrl** while you click any highlighted (tagged) contact that you want to drop from this set.

Building a Filter

Before you build a new filter, you might like to see if there are any filters already available that might be copied and edited. Select **Lookup**, **Filters**. Figure 11.3 showed the Filters and Groups dialog box.

Filters can be public or owned by a specific user or user group. You might need permission to use the filter of another user. Any new filter that you build will be owned by you unless you select another user or [public] as the owner. GoldMine might be delivered with examples of filters, and the installation of an Industry Template might add some more (see Chapter 22, "Boom Town: Extending GoldMine by Adding on Software").

Building a Filter Expression

The Preview tab of the Filters and Groups dialog box shows you the details of the filter you have selected (see Figure 11.4).

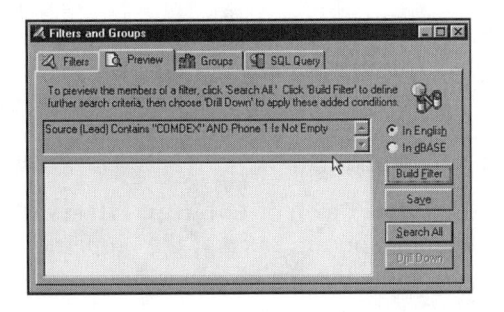

Chapter 11 ▸ *Panning for Gold: Filtering Contacts from the Database*

Figure 11.4

The Preview tab of this filter shows that it will pick out all contacts that have COMDEX in the Source field and a Phone1 field that is not empty.

When you click the **Search All** button, the Filters and Groups dialog box will list all the records in the open database file that pass this filter.

The **Drill Down** button commands the filter to search through the records already identified to pick out those that satisfy some extra or different search expression that you have specified in the Build dialog box. You can keep on drilling down using different filters until you have identified exactly those contacts you want to work with.

Editing a Filter

The filter expression might be edited from the Preview tab. You normally need to click the **In dBASE** option button to have the expression displayed in the dBASE language before attempting to edit it. Figure 11.5 shows this translation for the filter shown in English in Figure 11.4.

In practice, rather than attempt to edit a complex filter expression, you might find it easier to have a collection of simple filters that you apply in succession, if necessary, with the Drill Down function.

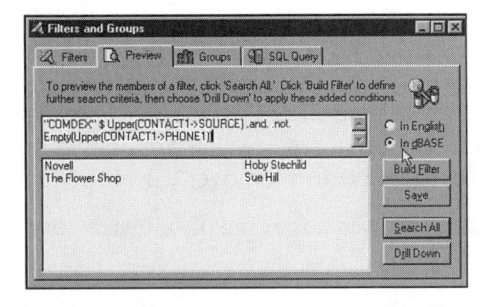

Figure 11.5

This filter expression can be edited or copied to the Clipboard and used elsewhere.

If you point to the filter expression and right-click for the local menu, you will be offered the following standard Windows commands with which to edit the filter expression: Undo, Cut, Copy, Paste, Delete, and Select All.

To inspect or edit an existing filter, select the **Filters** icon or **Lookup**, **Filters**. Highlight the existing filter. Then select the **Properties** button. You see the Filter: [filter name] dialog box, open at the Properties tab where you can edit the name, if necessary. Assign ownership of this filter to another user at this stage, or leave it by default as owned by you. Then select the **Build** tab.

To start building a new filter, select the **Filters** icon or **Lookup**, **Filters**. Then select the **New** button. The New Filter dialog box appears, open at the Properties tab. Here type the name for your new filter. Then select the **Build** tab.

A Build Filter button also is available in the Preview tab so that you can improve the expression used in an existing filter or in a new filter still under development. Figure 11.6 shows the building process in action.

Figure 11.6
This filter is focusing on a combination of field values and something yet to be defined about the previous result.

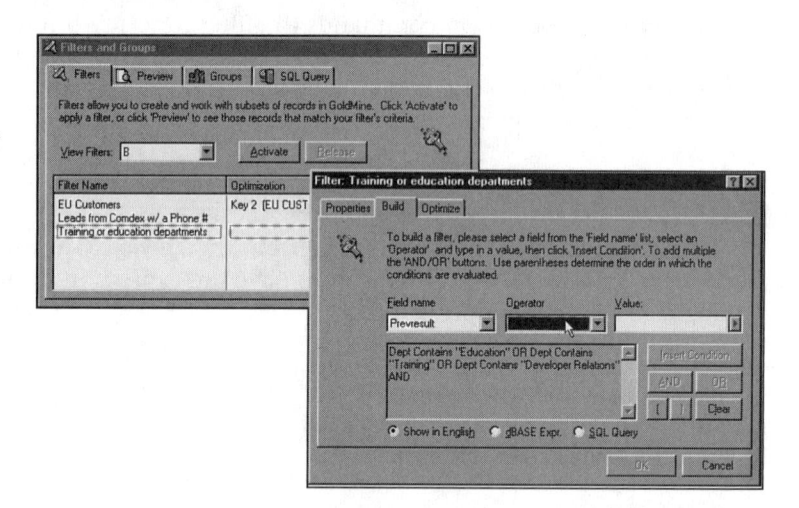

The process of building a filter comprises cycles of selecting a GoldMine indexed record field, a logical operator, and then a value. These three terms constitute an expression. The Build tab offers buttons to insert a three-term expression followed by a connective AND or OR. Open brackets and closed brackets are offered at appropriate stages in the expression building. The Clear button removes the entire expression.

The values in filter expressions are not case sensitive. Telephone area codes should be entered in parentheses.

Option buttons are provided so that you can choose the language in which the filter expression is displayed. English is easy to follow, dBASE allows you to cut and paste terms, and SQL is only appropriate if you are working with an SQL database server.

Using a Filter

A filter is really useful if you want to have a method of picking out contacts on the basis of something obscure or if you want to apply a search that will include any new or altered contact records in your database. By contrast, a group is a fixed set of contacts that will not include any new arrivals unless you deliberately add to the group.

For example, a sensible filter to have on hand is a search for any contact records that do not have any entry in a specific field—Address and Phone1 are rather important.

Go to the **Lookup** drop-down menu and select **Filters** to get the Filters and Groups dialog box. Press the **New** button to get the New Filter dialog box and type in the name of your sensible filter. How about "No phone or no address" as a sensible name?

Click the **Build** tab. Go to the **Field Name** drop-down menu and select **Phone1**. Scroll up or down if you cannot see the field name you need. Go to the **Operator** drop-down menu and select **Is Empty**. Click the **Insert Condition** button and you will see GoldMine has accepted the logical search specification Phone1 Is Empty. Now you must get your OR in. Click the **OR** button. This will type in the OR qualifier and highlight the Field Name box ready for you to choose another field. Select **Address**. Select the operator **Is Empty**. Click the **Insert Condition** button. Click **OK** to preserve your sensible filter.

Optimizing Record Selection

The Optimize tab of the Filter dialog box is used to set up searching conditions that will speed up the processing when the filter is active. Figure 11.7 shows the Optimize tab.

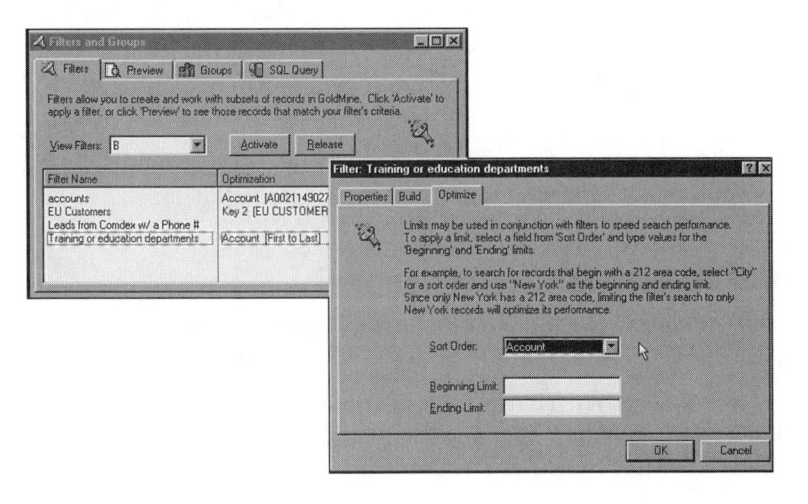

Figure 11.7

My filter is optimized to sort my records by account number.

161

You can specify the sort field to be used as a basis for ordering the search and then set upper and lower limits to the field values. The restricted subset of the database defined by the optimizing criteria is used in a preliminary filtering so as to speed up the processing of what might be a lengthy filter expression.

Reviewing the Scope of a Filter

If you have chosen to activate a particular filter, many GoldMine commands will apply only to those contact records that have passed through your filter. The working set of contacts will be available from the contact record window that was active when you activated the filter.

If you are looking at a contact record that will fail the filter you have just activated, it will remain in view until you seek another. Thereafter, only filtered records will be accessible from the window in which the filter was activated.

The following commands and command groups will apply to the filtered set of contact records:

- Next Record [Page Down]
- Previous Record [Page Up]
- Merge Forms or Write Letter
- Delete Old History of ALL Contact Records
- Delete ALL Contact Records
- Global Replace commands
- Synchronization commands
- Export Data commands

The filtering expression will be applied throughout the database until the filter is released. Therefore, scanning a large database might be slowed down by a complex activated filter.

To release a filter, select **Lookup**, **Filters**. This displays the Filters and Groups dialog box, in which the active filter will be highlighted. Click the **Release** button.

Previewing Filtered Records

If you want to see what result your filtering would achieve, select the **Preview** tab in the Filters and Groups dialog box. Then click the **Search All** button.

You might find that you have too many records in your filtered set. Click the **Build Filter** button and add another expression to your filter using AND or OR. Alternatively, you can clear the filter expression and select or build a different filter.

If you now click **Drill Down**, GoldMine will apply your extended or replaced filter expression to just those contacts that were selected previously.

If you extended your filter, the same result will be achieved if you choose **Search All**, but it could take much longer, because GoldMine will go through the entire database applying your extended filter.

If you selected or built a different filter before choosing **Drill Down**, the new filter might miss some records in the database because it will be applied to the subset of records chosen by the first filter you activated.

The Least You Need to Know

- Highlighting a record in the Contact Listing will tag it.
- Click with Ctrl held down to build up a collection of tagged records.
- Don't close the Contact Listing window until you have finished with your tagged records.
- Any action you take while you have a set of tagged records open might well be carried out on every one of them.

Chapter 12

At the Corral: Building Contact Groups

> **In This Chapter**
> - Assigning a set of contacts as members of a named group
> - Adding members to a group
> - Using a filter to build a group

You can make a contact group by putting like with like—even though they don't have to like each other—but they have something in common. Do you operate in geographical regions? Have you contacts of special priority? After you define a contact group, it is easy to send a similar message to each one, for example. This chapter covers how you can work more efficiently by grouping your contacts.

Working with Contact Groups

A *contact record group* is a way of dealing with many contacts by separating them temporarily from the open database. Many groups can be defined—but no more than one of them can be activated at one time.

A group has a Group Profile comprising a name, an owner, and perhaps a user-assigned code. The user who creates a group will be assumed to be the owner unless the group is declared Public or assigned to a different user.

The Filters and Groups window appears if you select **View**, **Contact Groups** from the main menu. The Groups tab will be on top, as shown in Figure 12.1. Highlight the group name, then right-click it to bring out the drop-down menu shown in the figure.

Part 3 ➤ *Managing Contacts Efficiently*

Figure 12.1

The Education and Training Group has only three members in the current database. They are sorted by Title. I'm going to recruit more members.

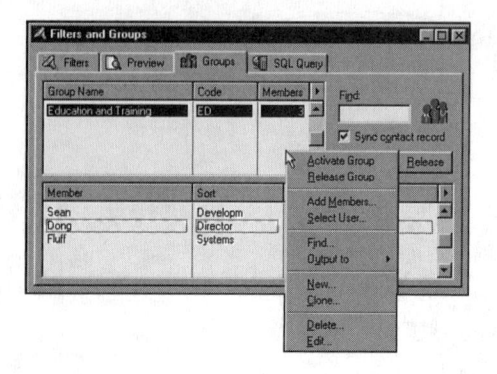

Tagging Your Gang

A *tag* is a temporary mark placed on a contact in the contact listing. You know you have tagged a contact when the line entry is highlighted.

Pull out your possible targets by selecting **Lookup** from the main menu and then clicking **Contact**. This will show you the contact listing.

Click the down arrow to see the drop-down menu where you can choose how you want your list of contacts to be sorted. Any one of these fields can be used for sorting:

Company	Phone1
Contact	Contact Typ
Last	Account
City	Industry
State	Interest
ZIP	Accnt Mngr
Country	Open

Your installation might have been customized to give other names to these fields—but your drop-down menu will show you what choices are available.

When you have your contacts listed in a convenient order, highlight those you want in your gang. Click and drag down the list if your targets are next to each other. Hold **Ctrl** and click individual line entries if you don't want a whole batch. Click again on a contact that is highlighted if you want to remove its tag.

The contact listing is a window, so you can see how many contacts you have tagged by clicking **Window** in the main menu. The drop-down list will include an entry that tells you how many tagged records you have and which record is the active one. The title of the record window also notes how many tagged records you are working with.

Your tagged records window might start by showing as the active record a contact who is not tagged. However, if you use the spin buttons to change the active record, you will find that you can click through only the tagged contacts.

This set of tagged records will stay highlighted while the contact listing window is open—but you will lose the membership unless you make them join a group. Click **View** from the main menu and select **Contact Groups**. Now you will see the Filters and Groups window. Click the **Groups** tab. Point within the Group Name and right-click. This displays the local menu in which you can select **New** so that the dialog box will open. Here you type in the name of your new group—**The Gang**—and select **OK**.

All you have done so far is tell GoldMine that you have a group called "The Gang." As yet, there are no members. Right-click **The Gang** in the Groups tab to get the local menu where you will be offered **Add Members**. Select this to open the Group Building Wizard. Select **Tagged Records** as the method for building the group and then press **Next**.

The Group Building Wizard now allows you three optional entries. You can have the membership sorted in a particular order, and you can assign a reference value to a particular field in their contact records. You also can set a limit to the number of records to be allowed into the group. Press **Next** to get past the optional entries and reach the Finish screen. If you press **Finish**, you will launch the process monitor and its screen will keep you posted on the various operations that have to take place to form your group.

Your Groups tab will show that "The Gang" has members—in fact, those contacts that you tagged in the first place. Now you can tag other contacts to form different groups because you can always reassemble "The Gang" by activating the group of this name.

Building a Group with a Filter

A filter is a logical formula for picking out some contacts from a database. A simple filter will search out all contacts where the value in a specified field equals a given value; for example, where the Source field value equals "Comdex2000."

To see what filters have already been set up in your system, click **Lookup** from the main menu, and select **Filters** to bring up the Filters and Groups window. Select **(public)** from the **View Filters** drop-down menu, unless you want to look at filters that you reserved for your own use.

To see the logical formula assigned to a filter, highlight the filter name and select **Properties**.

Activating a Group

When you have highlighted one of the contact groups listed in the upper panel, and while you are still pointing within the upper panel of the Groups tab, right-click. The Groups (upper panel) local menu appears, which you saw in Figure 12.1, and provides the options shown in Table 12.1. If you already have an active group or filter, or if you have tagged some records, the contacts displayed in your record window will be the result of applying each of these search specifications in order. The record window title will show you what methods have been used to select the records. For example, **Filter: Experts; 6 Tagged Records; Active Record: Professor Carat** shows that the Experts filter was applied to the whole database, and from the resulting subset, six contacts were tagged. Just from the title, we do not know whether Professor Carat is a member of this subset, or was selected as the active record by some other means.

If you want to add the active record to a group, select **Add Members** from the local menu in the Groups tab of the Filters and Groups window and launch the Group Building Wizard. If you want Professor Carat to be identified by the Experts filter, you have to make sure that the field used by this filter contains the critical value in Professor Carat's contact record.

> **Strike It Rich**
>
> ### A Dedicated Key for the Local Menu?
>
> Some keyboards have a key with an arrowed menu icon on it. The manufacturers might refer to it as the *application key.* To get the local menu that suits where you most recently clicked, press this key.
>
> This key works in GoldMine, Microsoft Word, and a number of other applications.

Table 12.1 Contact Group Options

Option	Description
Activate Group	Ensures that the active record window will display only those records that are members of the selected group. Displays the group name in the title of each contact record.
Release Group	Allows the active record window to display all the records in the database.
Add Members	Launches the Group Building Wizard to begin assigning new members to an existing group.

Option	Description
Select User	Offers the Select a User dialog box to allow a different user to be selected and so gain access to different filters and groups.
Find	Specifies and launches a character string search in the list of group names, or in hidden fields of the Group Profiles, such as Code.
	The Direction panel contains four option buttons that allow you to direct the search: Up, Down, Top, Bottom.
	These option buttons will automatically show a black dot to report the progress of your search as you click the **Find Next** button.

Output To	Prepares to send the list of group names to:
	    Printer
	    Word
	    Excel
	    Clipboard

New	Prepares to build a new group by completing the Group Profile dialog box (see Figure 12.2).
Clone	Saves a copy of the active group under a different name. You must edit or replace the existing name. If no group is active, clone the group highlighted in the Groups tab of the Filters and Groups window.
Delete	Removes, after a caution, the definition (Group Profile) of the highlighted group—but leaves the contact records intact in the database.

Edit	Edits one or more fields in the Group Profile:
	    Group Name
	    Code
	    User

See Figure 12.2 for a look at the Group Profile dialog box in action.

Part 3 ➤ *Managing Contacts Efficiently*

Figure 12.2

I am going to build a new group coded as Exp for Experimental in the Group Profile.

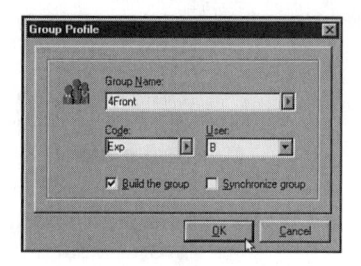

When you click **OK** to accept the Group Profile, you might see the Group Building Wizard, shown in Figure 12.3. If the default Build the Group check box was still checked when you closed the Group Profile, GoldMine will launch the Group Building Wizard and you will be invited to specify how the members are to be chosen. Otherwise, GoldMine will create a Group Profile without identifying any members.

Figure 12.3

The Group Building Wizard offers various methods for generating lists of contacts—some are only available when you have already tagged or filtered out some potential members.

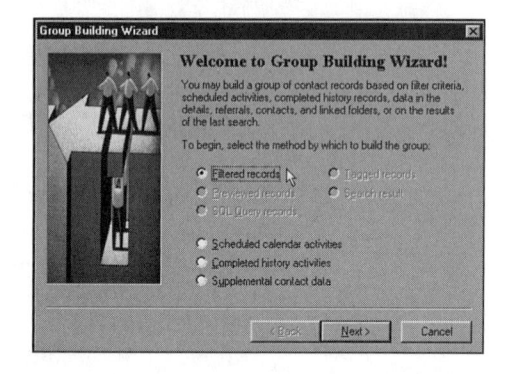

If you selected **Synchronize Group** in the Group Profile dialog box, GoldMine will track all the information necessary to bring all the contact records in the group up to date while the group is being built. By default, GoldMine does not synchronize the group because doing so would require a large amount of processing.

After a Group Profile has been created, you can alter the membership, but synchronization is no longer a possible option.

Using the Membership Local Menu

To work with a group, select **View**, **Contact Groups** from the main menu. The Filters and Groups window appears. The Groups tab will be on top.

If you select a group and click the **Activate** button, the lower panel of the Groups tab will show brief details of the membership. The local menu of this lower panel, obtained by right-clicking while you are pointing within it, offers the commands shown in Table 12.2.

170

Table 12.2   Activate Groups Local Menu Options

Option	Description
Sort Members	Sorts the members list: **Clear All Sorts** **Sort by a Field**—Lets you enter or select a GoldMine field name. **Sort by an Expression**—Lets you enter or select an expression to control the sort. **Reference Expression**—Lets you enter or select an expression to control what will appear in the Reference field of the Group Member Profile. The sort field value appears in the Sort column of the member listing.
Sync Contact	Default setting to synchronize the active contact record with the member highlighted in the listing.
View	Controls what is displayed in the Member column: View Contact View Company View Both
Find	Offers a search to locate a member on any character string embedded in the contents of the Member column.
Output To	Outputs the list of members to Printer, Word, Excel, and Clipboard.
New	Adds the contact in the active contact window to the group. Optionally, you can add an explanatory reference or sort code. If the group is currently activated, you can open another contact record window in which to display any contact you want to add to the group.
Delete	Allows you to remove a highlighted member from the list, after a caution.
Edit	Allows you to edit the Group Member Profile of any member you have selected: **Reference**—An explanation or automatically inserted GoldMine field **Sort**—A sort code Your changes appear in the Groups tab Member listing and as a new or edited line entry in the Members tab of the contact record to which they refer.

Adding Group Members

From the Filters and Groups dialog box, select the **Groups** tab. Highlight the group to receive new members.

The upper-panel local menu offers the Add Members command. This will launch the Group Building Wizard so that you can select many contacts to become new members.

The lower-panel local menu offers the New command, which will assign the active contact to the group, offering you the chance to enter a reference, a sort code, or both.

You can use the upper- and lower-panel local menus to work on the group specifications, profiles, and memberships without actually accessing the contact records. However, if you change the group memberships of any contact in one of your open contact record windows, or if you alter the Group Member Profile, the effects will be visible in the Members tab of the contacts concerned.

Controlling the Group Building Wizard

When you are creating a new group, the default settings in the Group Profile will direct you into the Group Building Wizard. You also will arrive at this wizard if you select **Add Members** from the local menu for the group name listing in the upper-panel of the Filters and Groups dialog box.

The options available for controlling the Group Building Wizard vary according to whether you have already selected a set of records by tagging or by activating a filter or a group. The Back button allows you to go back and perhaps make a tagged or filtered selection before you create the group.

Table 12.3 shows the group building methods available when you have not already identified any records.

Table 12.3 Group Building Methods for Unidentified Records

Method	Description
Filtered records	Clicking **Next** will invite you to select an existing filter from your own list or from another user to be used to build this group or add members to it.
	Alternatively, you can click the **Build Filter** button and create a new filter expression. See Chapter 11, "Panning for Gold: Filtering Contacts from the Database."

Method	Description
Scheduled calendar activities	Clicking **Next** will invite you to define which types of scheduled activities you want to use, the user or user group, the date range, and the activity code.
Completed history activities	Clicking **Next** will invite you to define which types of completed activities you want to use, the user or user group, the date range, the activity code, and the result. The options for choosing completed activities are the same as for scheduled activities.
Supplemental contact data	Clicking **Next** will allow you to specify which type of supplemental contact data record is to be searched to select the group member:
	Details—Enter or select a Detail field name and a keyword or character string to identify the contact by a search in the Reference field of the chosen Detail.
	Document Links—Enter or select a keyword or character string to identify the link by a search in the Reference field or fields seen in the Links tab of the contact record.
	Additional Contact—Enter or select a keyword or character string to identify the primary contact by a search in the Reference field or fields seen in the (Additional) Contact tab of the contact record.
	Referrals—Enter or select a keyword or character string to identify the primary contact by a search in the Reference field or fields seen in the Referrals tab of the contact record.

Using the Optional Settings

Each of the group building methods offers a first dialog box to define how the group will be built. See Figure 12.4 for an example; it shows a group for activities in the coming month. A second dialog box allows you to add further instructions, as shown in Figure 12.5.

When you are creating a new group or when adding members, the Optional Settings dialog box supports the following kinds of facility:

➤ Have the members assigned a sort code or a GoldMine field name.

➤ Add the value of a GoldMine field to the Group Member Profile in the Reference field.

➤ Have a filter expression applied to the group to, for instance, limit the number of contact records assigned to the group or field value(s) to be accepted.

Part 3 ➤ *Managing Contacts Efficiently*

Figure 12.4

I am defining a group based on all scheduled activities for one month ahead.

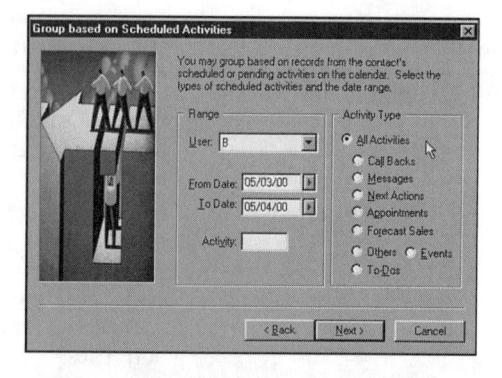

Figure 12.5

Optional settings can automatically make your group easier to use by adding important connecting information, such as the reference in the calendar entry that has caused each member to be selected.

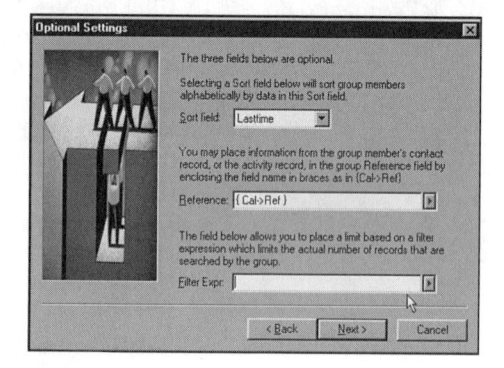

Building from a Set of Contacts

The group building methods, shown in Table 12.4, depend on a set of records having been assembled in an active record window before you launch the Group Building Wizard to create a group or add members to it.

Table 12.4   Group Building Options for an Active Set of Records

Option	Description
Previewed records	Allows you to build a group on the basis of a set of records that you have selected by activating a filter. You must click the **Preview** tab of the Filters and Groups window to ensure that GoldMine locates the records and presents them in an active record window. They also will be listed in the Preview tab.
SQL Query records	If you are running a database system that accepts SQL (Structured Query Language), you can perform an SQL query to assemble a set of contact records. You must leave open the SQL Query Result window to allow GoldMine to automatically add the contacts found by the query to the membership list of the group you are building.

Chapter 12 ➤ *At the Corral: Building Contact Groups*

Option	Description
Tagged records	The tagging procedure must be completed before you try to build a group from these records. You must leave the tagged records window open while using the Group Building Wizard.
Search result	Builds a group or adds members to an existing group if you have already conducted a Text Search. You must leave open the Searching [fieldname] window.

The Group Building Wizard will not offer any of these methods unless you have already assembled the set of records by tagging or some kind of search. A filtered set must be previewed before it can be used to build a group.

SQL—The Structured Query Language

GoldMine uses databases for its programs and for the records associated with your users, their activities, and their contacts. Two database languages are available: dBASE and SQL. The GoldMine contact files in both of these database languages have the same structure, although the filenames will be different. Your GoldMine license controls which language or languages you can use. SQL is preferred if your contact files are held and managed from a dedicated contact file server. This allows rapid searching.

SQL queries are a logical combination of expressions that can be stored in the SQL tab of the Filters and Groups window. You might be able to access the SQL expressions of another user to assemble a complex query, which you can then save for future use.

175

> **The Least You Need to Know**
>
> ➤ There are many different ways of assembling a group of contact records. You can save the membership list under a group name.
>
> ➤ When you activate a group, the contact records of all the members will appear in an active contact window, with the name of the group in the title.
>
> ➤ You can perform operations on the whole of an active group by a single command.
>
> ➤ A contact can be a member of more than one group—the details are displayed in the Members tab of the contact record.

Part 4
GoldMine in Business

Put down that blunderbuss—we want no blunders here. Be selective and focus on contacts for a particular purpose: high potential; previous neglect; located in a part of the territory that is easily visited. Sample your contacts and your team members as if they were fine wines: Compare and contrast the qualities; give them all the attention they deserve. What would bring out the best flavor?

If this is a gold mine, you don't want to spend all your effort on chasing fool's gold. Read on to see how GoldMine can make your operations more efficient and pay off better.

Chapter 13

At the Mill: Generating the Reports You Like

In This Chapter

- Finding a suitable pre-configured report
- Preparing the data for a report
- Previewing a report
- Refining the presentation of a report
- Customizing a report

There are many reasons why you might need to run a report on your database. A report can allow you to view your data selectively and organized according to your interest. Although there are many reports already designed and readily available from GoldMine, you can edit and customize any of them to suit your purpose. This gives you a powerful and flexible way of organizing and viewing data.

Introducing the Report Generator

The purpose of the GoldMine Report Generator is to make it easy to produce a report from the current database. The technique is to access a report template and merge with it the GoldMine records that will provide the data. A report template is often referred to as simply a report, it being taken for granted that suitable data will be merged when the template is run or compiled.

Part 4 ➤ *GoldMine in Business*

There are several questions you need to ask yourself before launching the Report Generator:

➤ Why do I need a report?

➤ What selection of data would need to be processed to give me what I need?

➤ What elements do I need to see in the report?

➤ How shall the report be formatted for screen presentation?

➤ How shall the report be formatted for printed output?

A useful place to start is with the reports that are delivered with GoldMine. You can see their titles by clicking the **Reports** icon or selecting **File**, **Print Reports** from the main menu. Figure 13.1 shows the Reports Menu.

Figure 13.1
The Reports Menu is a gateway to dozens of reports designed earlier for you to preview, edit, and generate. The profile of this report template contains notes on how it is constructed.

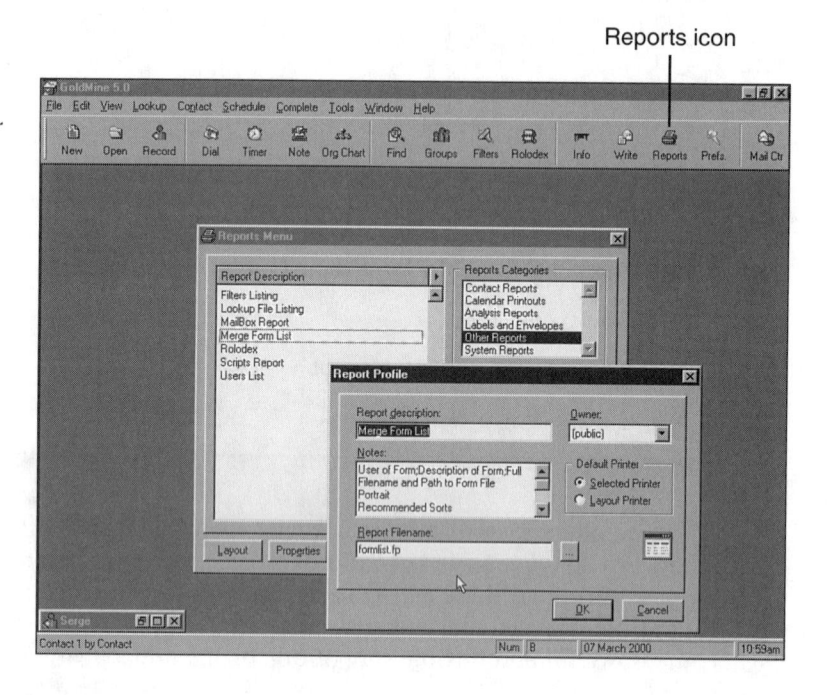

Choosing a Report Category

Select a category from the Reports Categories browse window in the Reports Menu dialog box, and then select the report title that you are interested in. The default output is to the screen, so you are in no danger—yet—of wasting paper.

The following report categories are delivered as standard:

- **Contact Reports**—Contact listings
- **Calendar Printouts**—Activity List reports
- **Analysis Reports**—Analyses of sales, opportunities, and phone calls, for example
- **Labels and Envelopes**—Templates for special paper sizes
- **Other Reports**—Various report templates
- **System Reports**—Tabulations of the elements of the GoldMine system and the uses that have been made of it

Your installation might have some additional categories, so you might have to scroll to find them.

Scrutinizing a Report Template

When you have clicked a report title, the Properties button in the Reports Menu dialog box will show you the Report Profile display window. The Record Profile can be altered in this display, to change the report title, for instance.

The fields in the Report Profile window often contain very useful information:

Report Description	The name of the report as listed in the Reports Menu.
Notes	Terse, but informative, notes about the GoldMine fields and other contents of the report in a scrollable window.
Report Filename	Do not alter this except to replace it with another GoldMine form file.
Browse for File button	Click this button if you want to browse the directory of GoldMine form files in order to choose a different template to be associated with this report profile.
Owner	Standard reports are (public). New reports default to the user who created them.
Default Printer	Option buttons: Selected Printer Layout Printer

You can edit any of these fields without disturbing the report template, although GoldMine will not expect you to invent a new filename for the standard report template.

Don't Tamper with GoldMine Report Templates!

It would be prudent to copy a report template and save it under another filename before altering the GoldMine original. The Report Profile does not affect the way the report is compiled, although it does say which form file contains the template.

When you click **OK**, the Report Profile window will close and return you to the Reports Menu.

Looking at a Report's Layout

The Layout button of the Reports Menu window opens a schematic display of the report's layout. No actual contact data is included. At the top of the window, the Form Designer toolbar will be presented.

Form Designer has a Preview icon that shows what the report will look like using whatever data is currently accessible. A contact report, for example, will use the active contact record or set of records, as appropriate.

The preview display has a Layout icon to revert to the schematic version.

Double-Click a Report to See What You Would Get

The Reports Menu allows you to choose a report category and then shows you what preconfigured reports are available in that category.

If you see something interesting, double-click its title to see a preview of what you would get using your open database file and contact record or records (filtered).

Although you can use the Preview and Layout displays to see what each standard report is going to look like, the toolbars in these windows are primarily used by report and form designers to modify and create templates.

You might find that most reports you need are already available in preconfigured report templates that you can inspect and run from the Reports Menu.

Suppose you want to print a screen version of a set of name and address cards for some tagged or filtered contacts. Go to the **Lookup** drop-down menu and select **Contact**. Scroll through the Contact Listing holding down **Ctrl** and clicking any contacts you want to print. Release Ctrl and you have a highlighted set of tagged contacts.

Alternatively, if you have a suitable filter, go to the **View** drop-down menu and select **Contact Groups** to open the Filters and Groups dialog box. Click the **Filters** tab. Highlight the filter you want and click the **Activate** button.

Whether you have tagged the contacts or selected them by a filter, what you will now have is a subset of contact records from the database—and GoldMine will assume that any command you issue will be applied to all the contacts in this subset.

Now is the moment to go to the **File** drop-down menu and select **Print Reports**. Don't worry—you won't waste paper, because the Reports Menu dialog box will open where you can click **Window** or **Printer** before you create the report. If you want to see your contact information in the name and address format, select the **Address & Phone Report**.

Before you click the **Print** button to create the report and send it to your chosen destination, select the right option in the Contacts panel of the Reports Menu dialog box:

- **All**—Prints for every contact in your database
- **Current**—Prints for just the currently active contact
- **Filter or Group**—Prints for the currently activated filter or group, which includes a set of tagged records

When you choose to print a report to the window, you get the Report Preview toolbar in which there is a Jump button that will allow you to look at different parts of the report.

Using the Report Generator

Select **File**, **Print Reports**, or click the **Reports** icon, to view the Reports Menu dialog box. Click the category of report and then the title you need.

Consider the reports of another user if you cannot find what you need. The User default is (public).

The Type field defaults to GoldMine. Other options might be available in your installation; Crystal Reports, for instance.

GoldMine will adopt the defaults or accept your specifications in the following report parameters where they are relevant:

> **Contacts**—All (default), Current, Filter, or Group
> **Output to Window (default) or Printer**—Individual pages can be printed from the window display.

Parameter options that are not relevant to the report you have chosen will be faded. Some system reports might not be available in your installation. In these cases you can inspect the layout but the Sort and Print command buttons will not be operational.

Parameters that you set in a report profile will be retained for future use with this template.

The Reports Menu contains the following buttons:

Layout	Accesses the form designer.
Properties	Displays the Report Profile dialog box.
Sorts	Displays the Report Sorting dialog box. This option is not available if you select Calendar Printouts.
Options	Offers either the Contact Report Options dialog box, or the Calendar Report Options dialog box.
Print	Sends the report to the selected output device.
Close	Exits the Reports Menu and returns to the GoldMine work area.

The Report Options dialog boxes, for Contact or Calendar Reports, allow you to specify user, date range, data, and layout options for the report selected.

Using the Reports Local Menu

Select a type of report and then scroll down the list of reports until you have highlighted one you are interested in. As always, right-click to access GoldMine's local menu. The local menu for the Reports Menu dialog box replicates some of the buttons—but some of these choices will not be in bold to show they are available if the report you've chosen does not need them:

> **Print**—Sends the report to the selected output device.
> **Layout**—Accesses the Form Designer.
> **Options**—Offers either the Contact Report Options dialog box, or the calendar Report Options dialog box.

- **Sorts**—Offers the Report Sorting dialog box, about which you'll learn more in a moment.
- **View Saved**—Offers the Select Report File to View dialog box. Report files have the .FRC extension.
- **Find**—Initiates a text search in the report list.
- **Output to**—Sends the report template list to Printer, Word, Excel, or the Clipboard.
- **New**—Offers the Report Profile dialog box for completion.
- **Clone**—Offers the Report Profile dialog box for editing to create a copy of an existing report template.
- **Delete**—Removes the selected report from the listing and deletes the template file, after a caution.
- **Properties**—Offers the Report Profile dialog box for editing.

The Report Sorting dialog box has the following options:

Primary Sort Secondary Sort Tertiary Sort	Option buttons. The dialog box reports the database files and fields used by default and a range requirement, if any (see Figure 13.2). You can select different database files and fields from the browse lists.
Sort Database	Enter or select a different database, if necessary.
Field Name	Enter or select a different field, if necessary.
Start at	Enter the lowest value for the range according to the field used for the selected sort.
End at	Enter the highest value for the range according to the field used for the selected sort.

Some reports depend on the data being sorted before you call for the report. In such cases you will see a cautionary message.

The Report Sorting dialog box includes a Save as Defaults button. If you click this button, your sorting specification will be saved and will appear by default next time you use this report.

Choosing What to Report About

The Contact Report Options dialog box prepares a Contact Report or an Analysis Report by allowing you to select which types of data record will be scanned for the report, as you can see in Figure 13.2.

Figure 13.2
You can be very selective when setting up the Contact Report Options.

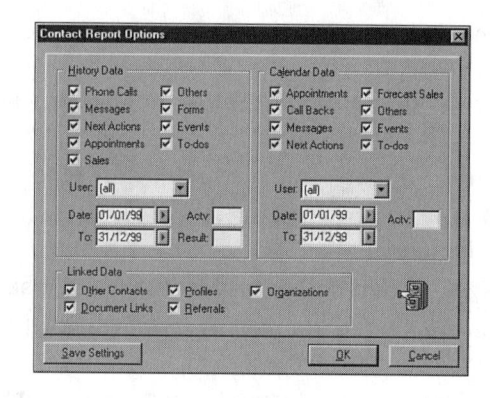

Reporting History Data

A history record includes the date, time, and user. There also should be an explanatory reference text for each activity. Any or all of the following choices can be selected in the History Data panel of the Contact Report Options dialog box you saw in Figure 13.2:

- Phone Calls—Including Call Back and Phone Message data
- Messages—Including Phone Messages, Email Messages, and MS Outlook Messages
- Next Actions
- Appointments
- Sales
- Others
- Forms—Lists data about forms that GoldMine generated for the contact
- Events
- To-dos

The History Data panel of the Contact Report Options dialog box includes data entry fields to refine the scope of the report in the following ways:

- **User**—Defaults to (all)—select a user if you want to concentrate the report, perhaps on yourself.
- **Date**—Sets the earliest date on which a history record must have been created to be considered for the report. GoldMine, as delivered, defaults to the first day of the previous calendar year.
- **To**—sets the latest date on a history record for it to be considered for the report. GoldMine as delivered defaults to the last day of the previous calendar year.

- **Actv**—Allows you to enter a three-character (maximum) activity code with which a history record must be marked to be in the report.
- **Result**—Allows you to enter a three-character (maximum) result code with which a history record must be marked to be in the report. If you specify both an activity code and a result, both of these codes must be entered for a history record to be considered for the report.

The History section of a contact report will be omitted if there is no data in any of the History types you have checked.

Reporting Calendar Data

A calendar record includes the date, time, and user who created the entry. There also should be an explanatory reference text for each activity. Any or all of the following choices can be selected in the Calendar Data panel of the Contact Report Options dialog box:

- Appointments
- Call Backs
- Messages—Includes Phone Messages, Email Messages, and MS Outlook Messages
- Next Actions
- Forecast Sales
- Others
- Events
- To-dos

The Calendar Data panel of the Contact Report Options dialog box includes data entry fields to refine the scope of the report in the following ways:

- **User**—Defaults to (all)—select a user if you want to concentrate the report.
- **Date**—Sets the earliest date on which a calendar record must have been created in order to be considered for the report. GoldMine, as delivered, defaults to the first day of the previous calendar year.
- **To**—Sets the latest date on a calendar record for it to be considered for the report. GoldMine, as delivered, defaults to the last day of the previous calendar year.
- **Actv**—Allows you to enter a three-character (maximum) activity code with which a calendar record must be marked to be in the report.

The Scheduled Activity section of a contact report will be omitted if there is no data in any of the Calendar types you have checked.

Saving Report Options

The Contact Report Options dialog box includes a Save Settings button. If you click this, the choices and data in the dialog box will be retained and will appear by default next time you use this report.

Sorting Report Data

The presentation of a report might be much improved by having the data sorted. The trick is to get the sort to improve the clarity and emphasize the important elements. Although they are classified as reports, no sorting is carried out on Report Categories Calendar Printouts or Envelopes and Labels.

The Report Sorting dialog box allows you to set up one, two, or three levels of sorting. For example, you can have a Primary Sort alphabetically by Company and the Secondary Sort to be Contact. By this means, records will be reported in company groups differentiated by contact name.

The Tertiary Sort field is used only where two records match in their Primary and Secondary sort field values.

If you have not specified fields for Secondary and Tertiary Sorts, records with the same Primary Sort field values will be sorted according to their date and time of entry in the database.

The GoldMine database files to which sorting commands are addressed are identified in the browse list as follows:

- Contact1
- Contact2
- ContHist
- ContSupp
- Cal
- OpMgr
- OpMgrFld

When a sort has been specified by the report template, or determined by your entries in the Report Sorting dialog box, the search scheme is displayed beside the appropriate sort level name. For example, Primary Sort Contact1->Lastname (range), is interpreted as indicating that the report will be generated from contact records that include values in their Lastname fields that fall within a range that has been specified by entries for Start At, End At, or both.

These entries need not be the entire values, provided the beginning characters are specified. GoldMine will infer missing start and end values. For example, if you enter just a start date, the end date will be taken as today. Your system will have been delivered with a default start date several years earlier.

If the field is alphabetical, and you enter a letter in the Start At field, GoldMine will assume that you want all the letters from your start to the end of the alphabet.

Printing a Report

The Reports Menu (which you saw in Figure 13.1) includes a pair of option buttons to direct the report output to Window or to Printer. The default is to Window, where the display will look as if it had been printed on the selected printer. From the main menu, select **File**, **Setup Printer** to confirm or adjust the printer settings.

To initiate a print to the default printer, select from the main menu **File**, **Print Reports**. The Reports Menu will be displayed. Highlight the required report, select **Printer**, and click the **Print** button.

> **Strike It Rich**
>
> **Take a Look at the Report Before Printing**
>
> If you have selected **Window** as the output destination for your report, when you click the **Print** button, the first page of the report will be displayed on the screen.
>
> The status bar will show a message like this: Report created successful: Total of 14 records. Page 1 of 3.

Inspecting a Report Onscreen

If you have directed a report to print in the window, GoldMine will adopt the printer parameters already set up and display the first page of your report with the Print Preview toolbar along the top of your screen.

189

The Print Preview toolbar contains the following command icons:

Close	Cancel the preview and return to your GoldMine workspace.
Open	Open the Reports Menu ready to select a report.
Save	Save the report based on the current records to a disk file selected by browsing or entered by path and filename.
Layout	Display the schematic layout of the report with the toolbars to edit it, if necessary.
Preview	Display pages as if on the selected printer.
Print	Select which pages to print in the Print Pages dialog box.
Printer	Confirm or change the printer and page settings.
First	View the first page of the onscreen preview.
Previous	View the previous page of the onscreen preview.
Next	View the next page of the onscreen preview.
Last	View the last page of the onscreen preview.
Jump	Position the preview at a page number that you enter.

The Least You Need to Know

- ➤ GoldMine probably has the very report you need already designed.
- ➤ Many pre-configured report templates allow you to make considerable alterations and save your designs for use in the future.
- ➤ You can print a report to the Window to see what it will look like before wasting paper on it.

Chapter 14

Round Up a Posse: Building a Sales Team

> **In This Chapter**
> - Putting users into groups
> - Setting up work spaces
> - Timekeeping
> - Controlling who sees what

A team or a group of users can be recognized by GoldMine and then any action directed at the user group will be carried out automatically for every member. One useful kind of group is for new GoldMine users—people you perhaps want to help by allowing them only a limited range of software functions. When they have become skilled at the beginners group work, they can be reassigned to a group at the next level, or to a group that works only on a particular type of business operation—telemarketing, for instance. This chapter tells you how to define such groups.

Pressing a Posse

When there's something big to be done, you might have to pick out your best team and give them what they need to do the job. But you have to be careful not to let everyone do just whatever they want to.

> ### Learn the Lingo
>
> ### The Master Can Have a Helper
>
> The user who sets up working groups is normally one of the few users given Master rights to GoldMine. However, the Master can decide to give certain users permission to assign users to groups.
>
> The user with Master rights selects **File** from the main menu, and then highlights **Configure** and clicks **Users' Settings**. This opens the Users' Master File dialog box where the users are listed.
>
> The Master selects a user and then clicks **Properties** to get the [username] Properties dialog box. Clicking the **Access** tab opens the permissions. One of these is titled Build User Groups. This should be checked if this user is to be given permission to create user groups and assign users to them.

Suppose it's up to you to decide what kinds of people you are going to have on your team. There are various ways of differentiating user groups:

- By type of work done
- By the knowledge and experience of the person
- By the geographical location of the team member—the user
- By the geographical or company-defined region of the contacts
- By the products or services being purchased or sold

There is no reason why a particular user should not have membership of several user groups—Expert and California and Aerated Widget Sales and Servicing, for example.

Assigning Users

Nobody gets in the team unless he is an official GoldMine user. This means that he must have been assigned a username, and that the total number of users in the system is within the conditions of the GoldMine license.

If you have Master rights, or if you have been given permission to build user groups, choose from the main menu **File**, **Configure**, **Users' Settings**. This will display the Users' Master File in which the users are listed (see Figure 14.1).

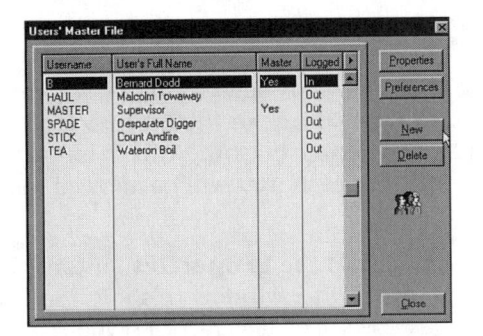

Chapter 14 ➤ *Round Up a Posse: Building a Sales Team*

Figure 14.1

These are the possible users, although most of them are logged out right now.

Not a very promising collection of talent—but they will have to be assigned to user groups. Choose **File**, **Configure**, **Users Groups**. Now you can see how the talent is deployed in the User Groups Setup window, as shown in Figure 14.2.

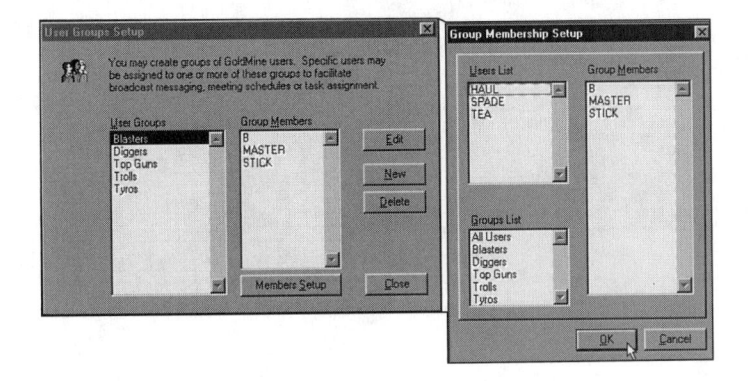

Figure 14.2

The Blasters are a select few.

Highlight a group name and the members will be shown on the right. If you now click the **Members Setup** button, you will open the Group Membership Setup window, also shown in Figure 14.2.

Assigning Group Membership to a User

Now is the moment to toggle your people in, or out, of the group on which you are working—Blasters, in this instance. Point to a username, double-click, and it will jump across to the adjacent panel—Users List to Group Members, or the other way around.

If you want to look at another list of candidates, All Users, for example, click an entry in the Groups List display window—scroll if you have to—and toggle away.

When you click **OK** in the Group Membership Setup dialog box, the membership of just the one group will be assigned. You will be returned to the User Groups Setup dialog box, where you can highlight another group if you want to enroll new members or throw some out.

193

Controlling User Access

Who gets the keys to the GoldMine? The answer is determined by whomever has access to the Users' Master File (refer to Figure 14.1). In the Users' Master File dialog box there is a Properties button and a Preferences button. With these two buttons, the user with Master rights can control what each user will be allowed to do with, or to, GoldMine.

Figure 14.3 shows that I selected a user, clicked the **Properties** button, clicked the **Ownership** tab, and scrolled through the Owner window to show Top Guns—one of the user groups. Individual users can also be selected as record owners.

Figure 14.3

User B has Master rights, and any new records he creates will be owned jointly by the Top Guns user group.

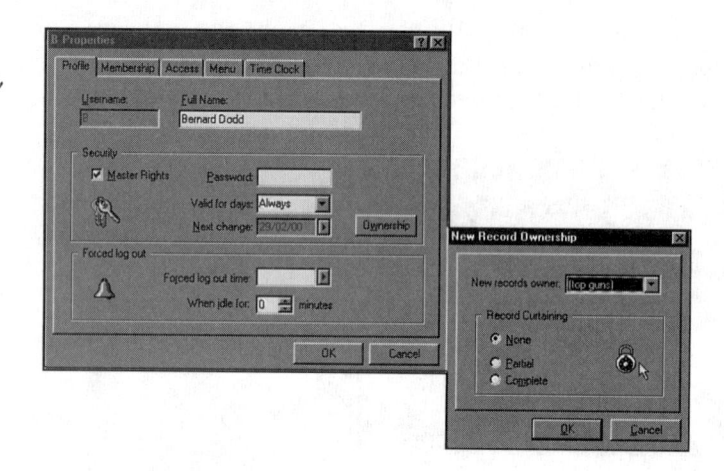

Owning a Record

The owner of a contact record has the joy of being able to hide or curtain all or parts of the data from other users. If a user group is the owner, any member of that group can play about with the curtains. The lower part of a contact record, including the tabs, has a curtain. So does the upper part.

If a record is assigned Partial curtaining, only the basic contact and company information is displayed to any user who's not the owner.

If the owner of a record has decreed Complete curtaining, all that an outsider could see, apart from the message Private to [username], would be the Record title bar with the contact name, plus the spin buttons to open a more interesting contact record.

If the owner assigns Complete curtaining to a record, users who are not in the owner's group will find that this record is counted in the Summary field as a member of the database, but they will see nothing—not even the basic contact information.

When a new record is created, GoldMine assumes that it will be in public ownership, or at least owned according to the specification set up for the logged in user in the New Record Ownership dialog box that you saw in Figure 14.3. The default curtaining is None.

If you want to assign a new contact record to another user, or if you want to have it wholly or partially curtained from anybody but yourself, select **Edit**, **Record Properties**. Then, click the **Ownership** tab and choose a new user or user group to be the owner. At the same time, you can choose which type of curtaining shall be applied if anyone else should be so bold as to make this record her active contact.

> **Strike It Rich**
>
> **Private Records Are Delete-Proof**
>
> If you have assigned Complete curtaining to a record for your eyes only, any busybody trying to perform a global delete—of record data, not the planet—will be thwarted. Whatever you put behind the complete curtain is retained completely.

You might well want to schedule some activities for yourself in connection with one of your favorite curtained records. Such activities will be necessarily linked to this contact record. However, anyone outside the ownership cabal will not be aware of this linkage.

Checking on Memberships

If you want to see which user groups include a particular user, go to the main menu and click **File**. Highlight **Configure** and click **Users' Settings**. This opens the Users' Master File dialog box where you can highlight the user you are interested in. Click the **Properties** button to open the [username] Properties dialog box, and then click the **Membership** tab.

The Membership tab of a user's Properties window shows to which group or groups that member belongs. One list is titled Member of Groups, the other Excluded From. You can double-click group names to make them jump out of one list into the other. Okay the change and you have put the highlighted user into a new group, or excluded him from one.

If you are primarily interested in the membership of a group, click **User Groups** go to the main menu and click **File**. Highlight **Configure** and click **Users' Settings**. This opens the User Groups dialog box, in which you can flip users in and out of user groups by double-clicking each username.

195

Letting Users Operate Particular Functions

Usernames—like most objects held in a GoldMine database—have properties that define something important. When you highlight a username in the Users' Master File, for example, there is a Properties button to click if you want to examine the information held about that user, including what permissions have been assigned.

The Properties dialog box of a particular user has the following tabs:

➤ **Profile**—Particulars of that user, including such important matters as whether the user has Master rights.

➤ **Membership**—Lists of groups to which the user belongs and is excluded from, displayed in the User Groups Setup dialog box.

➤ **Access**—Controls what the user is allowed to see and do.

➤ **Menu**—Controls which GoldMine menu commands will be available to the user, and which options in the submenus will be operative (green spot) or forbidden (red spot).

➤ **Time Clock**—Displays the times this user is logged in or out over past days, as set in the Login tab of the user's Preferences.

Granting User Access to Records

An important tab of a user's properties is Access because it is where the supervisor can control which types of GoldMine records are to be available to that user. The Access tab of the [username] Properties dialog box, shown in Figure 14.4, has three panels, each containing several data entry windows:

➤ Contact Record
➤ General Access
➤ Access to Others

Figure 14.4

This user has access to just about everything.

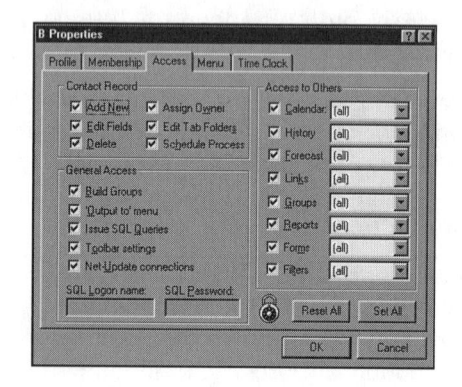

Access permissions regarding a Contact Record can be granted or withheld individually in the following categories:

- **Add New**—This user is allowed to add a new contact record to the database.
- **Edit Fields**—User can change the values in any of the fields.
- **Delete**—User can remove a contact record, and/or the scheduled activities associated with it, from the database.
- **Global**—Delete is available only to users with Master rights.
- **Assign Owner**—User can assign a different record owner to public records or to records she owns. A user who is a member of a user group cannot change the ownership of records owned by that group.

  The default owner is (public)—but a user with this permission could set up a private record accessible to no other user. A user with Master rights could delete such a record.
- **Edit Tab Folders**—User can add fields and field views to the Contact Record Tabs window and edit their contents.
- **Schedule Process**—User can set a runtime and date for an automated process.

Permitting Special Functions

General Access permissions are granted or withheld as shown in Table 14.1.

Table 14.1 A User Can Be Permitted to Perform Any of These Actions

Check Box Title	Permitted Action
Build Groups	User can create contact group names and assign contact records as members of these groups.
'Output To' Menu	User can make copies of contact and other data in formats that can be accessed by other systems:
	Printer
	Word
	Excel
	Clipboard
Issue SQL Queries	User can search the SQL database using commands in the query language.
Toolbar Settings	User can move and create toolbars. User can control whether temporary bubble texts or icon labels are displayed.
Net-Update Connections	User can initiate GoldMine system net update.
SQL Logon Name	This name is automatically entered when accessing the SQL database.
SQL Password	This password is automatically entered with the SQL Logon name.

Seeing What Others Are Doing

A user's permissions to view and edit the contact and other records owned by other users are controlled from the Access to Others panel in the Access tab, described in Table 14.2.

Table 14.2 A User Can Be Permitted to View Data Owned by Another User

Data Record Type	Permitted Action
Calendar	User can view the calendars of members of the user group named in the drop-down window.
History	User can view the history records of members of the named user group.
Forecast	User can view the forecasted sales of members of the named user group.
Links	User can view the linked documents of members of the named user group.
Groups	User can access the contact groups belonging to members of the named user group.
Reports	User can merge contact records with the report templates of members of the named user group.
Forms	User can merge data or enter information into the document, email, fax, and form templates of members of the named user group.
Filters	User can activate the filters of members of the named user group.

Table 4.3 describes the four buttons found on the Access tab of the User's Properties dialog box.

Table 4.3 A User's Properties Dialog Box Has Setting Buttons on the Access Tab

Button	Action
Reset All	Blanks out all the check boxes so that the user will have no access.
Set All	Ticks all the check boxes so that the user will have access to all types of records.
OK	Applies and saves the patterns of access permissions for this user. Closes the Access tab.
Cancel	Closes the Access tab without making any changes to the user's access permissions.

The commands used for the functions to which a user is denied access will not be active in the relevant toolbars or menus. For instance, if a user is not allowed to create records, the New Record command will be grayed out in the File menu. The New icon will be visible in various toolbars, but will not execute any command.

Controlling Users' Menus

The Menu tab of the User's Properties dialog box displays a set of menus arranged in Windows Explorer format. You can click a plus sign or double-click an icon to see the menu expanded, as shown in Figure 14.5. Alternatively, you can click the **Expand** button to see all the menus expanded. By clicking any expanded menu item, you toggle access to it. A green spot indicates permission to access; a red spot indicates permission is denied.

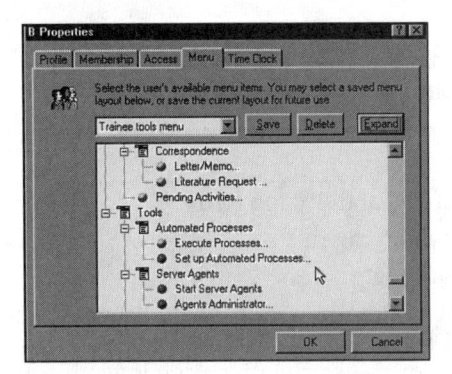

Figure 14.5

The Menu tab of a User's Properties dialog box shows which commands are going to be available and which are not.

If a menu command is only available to a user with Master rights, you will not be able to assign permission for its use to someone who does not have Master rights.

Saving a Menu Template

Figure 14.5 shows the pattern of permissions that has been saved under the user-defined name "Trainee tools menu." You can set up a pattern—if you have Master rights—and click the **Save** button. You will be invited to type in or edit the name of the Save Menu template.

The menu templates that are already available are listed in the drop-down menu of the Template Name type-in field. If your system has no menu templates, there will be no down arrow to show the drop-down menu.

Inspecting a User's Timekeeping

The Time Clock tab of the User's Properties dialog box shows the User Log—the timekeeping records that have been stored for the user (see Figure 14.6).

Figure 14.6
Work, work, work—every day, from morning till night.

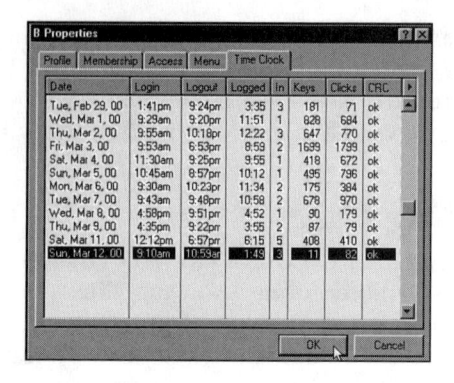

The User Log shown in the Time Clock tab is described in Table 14.4.

Table 14.4 Information Stored in the Time Clock Records

Column Heading	Entry
Date	Date of the activity log entry.
Login	Time of logging in.
Logout	Time of logging out.
Logged	Length of time logged in, including any time spent logged away. Either the time logged in at one work session, or the cumulative time logged in for that date—as set up in the user's Login Preferences.
In	Number of tracked sessions that day. If your preferences have been set to cumulate the time logged in for the day, the value will be 1.
Keys	Number of keystrokes performed while using GoldMine.
Clicks	Number of mouse button clicks performed while using GoldMine.
CRC	Displays ok only if there has been no tampering with the log entry by a system outside of GoldMine.

Each user has a set of records that are used to generate the [username] Preferences dialog box. To see your own preferences, select **Edit** from the main menu and click **Preferences**. To see the preferences of another user, if you have permission to do this, select **File** from the main menu and highlight **Configure**. Click **Users' Settings** and highlight the username you are interested in. Click **Preferences** and then click the tab you need—there are 13 tabs.

When you have navigated to a [username] Preferences dialog box, click the **Login** tab. Here you will find the **Time Clock** data entry window. Click the down arrow to see the timing options. Choose another if you have permission.

Table 14.5 shows the timing options available in the [user name] Preferences dialog box at the Login tab in the Time Clock data entry window.

Table 14.5 The Time Clock Can Be Set or Disabled

Time Clock Option	Action
Track Daily Totals	Record the cumulative login time for each day.
Track Each Login	Record the timing of each work session.
Disable Time Clock	No time information logged.

Whether an individual user can adjust or switch off the Time Clock will depend on the permissions assigned by the supervisor with Master rights.

Controlling Access to a Contact Database

Although each contact database is designated public by default, you can restrict access to a specific database file to a single user or user group. Choose **File**, **Open Database**. This will display the Contact Set Databases dialog box. Highlight the line entry for the contact set database you are interested in. Click the **Properties** button to reveal the Contact Set Profile dialog box. Type in or edit the following fields, as required:

- ➤ **Description**—Give the database a different title if you don't want to use the title it has already.
- ➤ **File Code**—A unique value assigned to this database to ensure correct synchronization with remote databases that may have been given different local names.
- ➤ **Path (Alias)**—The location of the contact set.
- ➤ **Database Type**—Limited to the types set up with ODBC drivers through the Borland Database Engine (BDE), or through the SQL server if your system is using this to manage the databases, for example, dBASE, ORACLE, SYBASE, MSSQL, DB2, INTRBASE, INFORMIX. Microsoft Access (drivers *.mdb) and Microsoft Paradox (drivers *.db) are also supported by GoldMine.
- ➤ **Grant Access to This File For**—Default is (public). Type in or select the database owner—a user or user group. Only a designated owner can open this database file and access the contact set.
- ➤ **Grant Access from This GoldMine License Only**—Check this option if access is to be allowed only to the holder of the licensed copy of GoldMine in which the user with Master rights is operating.

Part 4 ➤ *GoldMine in Business*

- ➤ **Logon Name**—Automatically use this entry to access the SQL server (15 characters maximum).
- ➤ **Password**—Automatically use this password with the SQL Logon Name (15 characters maximum).

A user with Master rights can access all contact sets.

Hiding User Screens

A user-defined screen can be a set of fields created in the Fields tab of the contact record. Standard GoldMine is delivered with two such screens:

- ➤ End User screen
- ➤ Technical Support screen

Different screens can be set up by installing an industry template and by designing them yourself if you have permission. A user-defined screen is also referred to as a *field view*. A field view can exist as a view that is displayed in the Fields tab. If there is more than one, the local menu will allow you to select which field view shall be displayed. To see what screens are available in your implementation, click the **Fields** tab and right-click a blank space in the tab. Click any of the field view titles to bring the screen to the front of the Fields tab.

Learn the Lingo

Get Tabs on Your Best Views

A field view can be given a user-defined tab name, in which case the field view will be displayed in its own tab and not as one of the options in the Fields tab.

Right-click a space in the **Fields** tab and select **Screens setup** from the local menu that will be displayed. This opens the Custom Screens Setup dialog box. A field view that is available in the current database will be marked Yes.

Right-click when pointing in the **Fields** tab to display the local menu (see Table 14.6).

Table 14.6 The Fields Tab Local Menu Opens the Screen Designer

Menu Option	Action
[Screen name]	The name of the currently open screen is ticked in a list of the available field views.
New Field	Launches the Screen Designer and displays the toolbar ready to choose an existing field to place in the screen, or to create a new field to place there.
Screen Design	Launches the Screen Designer to work on the current field view.
Screens Setup	Displays the Custom Screens Setup dialog box in which are listed all the user-defined screens and the number of fields they contain. The Fields button allows you to edit or delete individual fields in the Fields of Screen:[screen name] dialog box.
	You can use the Properties button to access the Custom Screen Profile dialog box in which you can create or edit a tab name for a selected custom screen. This dialog box also allows you to determine whether any of your screens should not be assigned (public) ownership and therefore access. You can enter or select a username or user group name as the screen owner. This Screen Is Available in the Current Contact Set is the label on a check box. You can toggle this check mark if you want to restrict your custom screen to a particular contact set (database file). The adjacent padlock icon will show "open" if the screen is not locked to the current database.
	A New button allows you to create a new field view using the Screen Designer.
	A Clone button allows you to copy an existing screen in order to redesign and rename it before saving it as another tab or one of the views available in the Fields tab.
Cancel	Closes the local menu. The Screen Designer has its own Exit icon.

You can get to the Custom Screens Setup dialog box by selecting its icon or by choosing **File**, **Configure**, **Custom Screens**. Alternatively, you can right-click any open toolbar and click **Setup**. This will display the Setup toolbar in which you will find icons for Fields and Screens that take you to the Screen Designer.

Part 4 ➤ *GoldMine in Business*

Custom Field Views Need Short Names

When you are assigning a frightfully helpful name to a new or cloned custom screen, you are allowed space for 20 characters. However, there is room for no more than about seven characters in the tab bar—it's best to begin your name with something obvious.

For example, suppose you need a special tab for a job you are doing. Click the **Fields** tab. Right-click in a space. Click **Screens Setup** to get the Custom Screens Setup dialog box where you can type in a name for your new screen. If you type a name in the **Tab Name** data entry window, this name will appear on a new tab. If you leave the tab name field empty, your new screen will be added to the list of screens that can be shown—one at a time—in the Fields tab.

Now set up access by an entry in the **User Access** data entry window. Leave as the default entry [public] to make it available to all users, or click the drop-down button to see a list of all the user groups and individual users on your GoldMine system.

Click **OK** and you will see your new screen, with its own tab name if you have given it one, as a highlighted line entry in the Custom Screens Setup dialog box. At this stage you could carry on and create another screen. Don't bother to click Fields because you have not yet assigned any fields to this screen. Clone is a button to make a copy of an existing screen that you will edit and save under a new name.

Click **Close** to shut down the Custom Screens Setup dialog box. Click the tab you have just created—or right-click the **Fields** tab and select it if you didn't give your new screen a tab name.

Keep Tabs on Your Tabs

Can't see your new tab? Did you give it a tab name of its own? Click any tab and press the right or left arrow to move along your set of tabs. Alternatively, click the left or right arrows in the tab title bar until you find your new tab title.

204

Now you have a blank tab space. Point in it and right-click. Select **Screen Design**—because that is what you are going to do. Up comes the Screen Designer toolbar. You won't believe how easy it is.

Select **New** from the Screen Designer toolbar to open the Place Field dialog box. Click the down arrow to get the lookup list of fields that have already been defined and set up in the database. Scroll down until you can highlight the field you want to place in your new tab, or in the Fields tab if you did not create a new tab.

When you click **OK**, your highlighted field will be shown in the top-left corner of the tab. Click it and drag it to where you want it to be. Click and drag any other fields that you want to move. Click **Rebuild** in the Screen Designer toolbar before you exit. Click **Exit** in the Screen Designer toolbar to leave your screen view designing session.

If you made changes to your new view, and selected Exit before selecting Rebuild, GoldMine will remind you that the database must be rebuilt before the new field becomes active. When you have finished customizing your screens and fields, go to **File** and select **Maintain Databases**. To maintain the current contact set database, click **Next**. Check the **Rebuild and Pack** option and then click **Next** again. If there are other users on the system, select the option to warn them to log off in the next few minutes. Finally, click **Finish** to start the rebuild operation.

The Least You Need to Know

- ➤ If you can see a menu option in bold type, you probably have permission to use it.
- ➤ Any part of your display windows can be customized to suit the way you would like to work.
- ➤ It is possible to have records and parts of records for your eyes only—nearly.

Chapter 15

Looking for the Real Seams: Using the Opportunity Manager

In This Chapter

➤ Giving a future sale a date, a value, and a probability of success

➤ Developing plans for an opportunity or project

➤ Building a team and documenting what might affect the outcomes

➤ Analyzing team performance

A complex sale could entail a group working as a team with several organizations, contacts, products, and services. As the relationships between the contacts develop, new contacts will be made and some existing contacts may change their roles in the team. GoldMine has a project manager for tracking a complex project that does not directly have a specific sale in mind. If the team is working towards a scheduled sale, then the project manager becomes an opportunity manager by allowing the team to focus on the hoped-for financial results.

Forecasting the Odds

You might have a personal way of managing sales—but GoldMine has a method of supporting you. Some discipline is involved. You have to put a date on a future sale, and you have to assign a value to whatever you expect to sell. Yet even GoldMine knows that the future is not totally predictable. So you will be invited to assign a probability percentage to your forecast. Then, by arithmetic, the potential value in your sales pipeline becomes the expected sale revenue times the probability of the sale being won.

Part 4 ➤ GoldMine in Business

Betting on Making a Successful Sale

One-hundred percent is a foolish value to bet because it does not allow that the sale could go wrong. Zero is also rather an odd probability because it seems to suggest that a sale is impossible.

Situations change. You can change the forecast date, the probability, even the products and values. The point of all this is that the members of your company sales team can focus their efforts on achieving good sales results if they all know what is in the pipeline—GoldMine likes to have a sales funnel.

GoldMine suggests a scheme that uses the steps, more or less, of a sales process as the markers for assigning the probability of a successful sale (see Table 15.1).

Table 15.1 Suggested Interpretations of Sales Probabilities

Probability	Interpretation
20%	Interest in the product(s) but as yet unconfirmed
30%	Confirmed interest
40%	The proposal has been selected for evaluation
50%	Evaluation of the product(s) in progress
60%	Evaluation looking good
70%	Passed evaluation
80%	Final approval in progress
90%	Purchase order in progress

Curiously, there is no probability attached to a confirmed purchase order. You can develop your own scheme to suit your line of business.

GoldMine can help you manage sales in three ways:

- ➤ Look at Forecasted Sales.
- ➤ Use the (sales) Opportunity Manager.
- ➤ Use the Project Manager to prepare a campaign and later have GoldMine convert the project into an opportunity.

Chapter 15 ➤ *Looking for the Real Seams: Using the Opportunity Manager*

The basis of the Opportunity Manager is the forecasted sale, which is an activity that you can schedule.

> **Learn the Lingo**
>
> ### Work with Opportunities or Projects
>
> In the Opportunities Manager, you can switch between Opportunities and Projects by clicking the **View** drop-down menu. What's the difference? A GoldMine project is a team effort entailing many tasks. A GoldMine opportunity is a project that has a specific sale as its objective.
>
> A project does not have a forecast value nor a probability of being successful. Otherwise, the Project Manager functions are the same as for the Opportunity Manager.
>
> GoldMine has a handy toggle that will convert a project into an opportunity if you are prepared to assign revenue and probability. It can just as easily toggle an opportunity into a project.

Scheduling a Forecasted Sale

From your dealings with a contact, now active in your workspace, you have an inkling that a sale is possible. When? What? How much? How do you prepare?

Select the **Schedule** icon or choose **Schedule, Forecasted Sale**. This displays the Opportunity Properties dialog box, with the particulars of your active contact already entered—if you have a good contact record (see Figure 15.1).

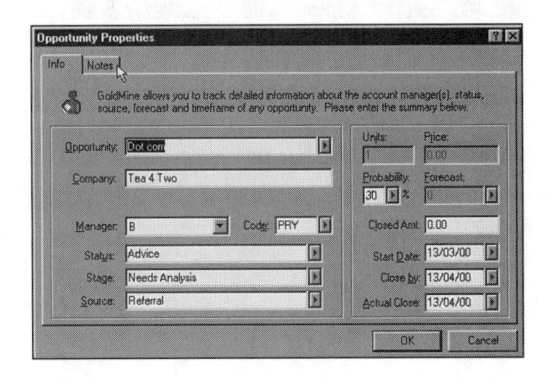

Figure 15.1

This could be the beginning of something big. I have scheduled a forecasted sale. My contact "Caddy," with the Tea 4 Two company, is interested in three product units that would be required a month from now—if the sales order gets confirmed.

209

Part 4 ➤ *GoldMine in Business*

Figure 15.1 shows a forecasted sales activity that is being associated with a new sales opportunity in the Opportunity Properties dialog box. Select **Schedule** from the main menu. Choose **Schedule a Forecasted Sale** to get the dialog box. The Opportunity/Project data entry window has a drop-down menu so that you can decide whether to create a new Opportunity—with a sales amount and probability—or a new project, which will have the similar processes to an opportunity—but no forecasted sale amount, and no probability. After the opportunity has been created, it will be available in the drop-down menu for use in scheduling other forecasted sales.

When you click **OK**, the forecasted sale is added to the Pending tab of the contact record. As an activity waiting to be completed, it will also be mentioned in your activity list.

Inspecting Forecasted Sales

As a user, you can press the **F6** key to open your activity list and see what sales are in your pipeline by clicking on the **Forecasts** tab.

As a sales manager, you could call up a standard or customized report. Refer to Chapter 13, "At the Mill: Generating the Reports You Like." For a rapid look-see at your team, choose **View**, **Analysis**, **Forecast Analysis**. Select which member(s) of your team you are interested in and click on the **Analyze** button (see Figure 15.2).

Figure 15.2

These two members of the team have very little sales potential.

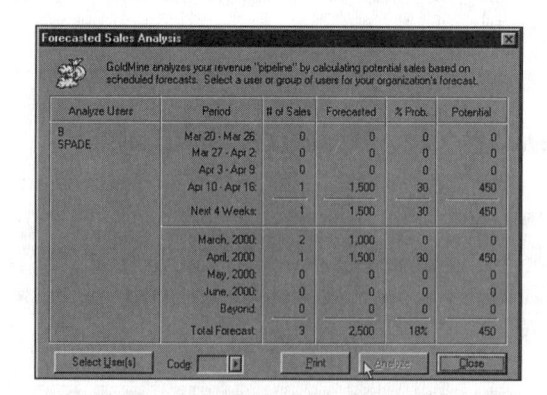

You may be interested only in the active contact—look at the Pending tab to see what sales have been forecasted.

The quick way to the Opportunity Manager is to press **F9**. Alternatively, choose **View**, **Sales Tools**, **Opportunities**. Figure 15.3 shows that the new opportunity has been added to the listing.

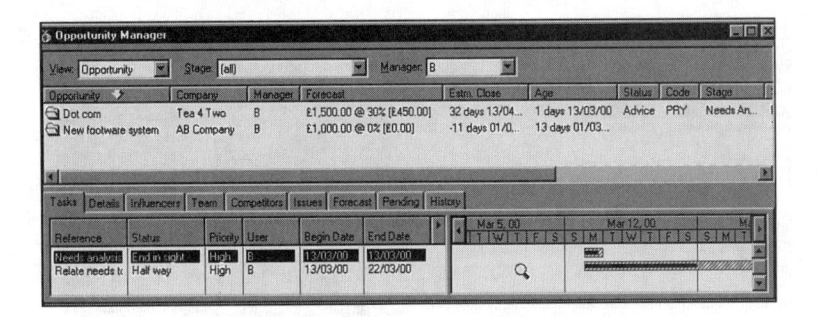

Chapter 15 ➤ *Looking for the Real Seams: Using the Opportunity Manager*

Figure 15.3
This sales opportunity has two tasks scheduled. I have a spyglass ready to zoom out to the monthly schedule calendar.

> **Strike It Rich**
>
> ### Opportunities Have Sliding Column Windows
>
> All the columns in the Opportunity/Project Manager have adjustable widths—except in the calendar window. Click and drag the vertical column boundaries. Use the left and right arrow buttons to shift the calendar window.
>
> This will help you read any long entries or columns that are out of your window.

The Opportunity Manager opens with the Tasks tab on top. Figure 15.3 showed how two tasks have been scheduled and black-lined to indicate that they are partially completed.

There is clearly a great deal of work to be done to bring the sales opportunity to a successful result—creating some more tasks and assigning people to perform those tasks would seem sensible.

Dealing with an Entire Opportunity

The upper part of the Opportunity/Project Manager lists either projects or opportunities, according to your choice in the View field of the manager. The upper panel has a different local menu from the lower panel. The upper panel controls the entire highlighted project—the lower panel contains the tabs, which refer to individual tasks and other factors affecting the outcome.

Figure 15.4 shows the upper panel local menu about to be used on the Dot com opportunity.

211

Figure 15.4

This opportunity is about to be accessed, cloned, converted, given a new companion, or even deleted.

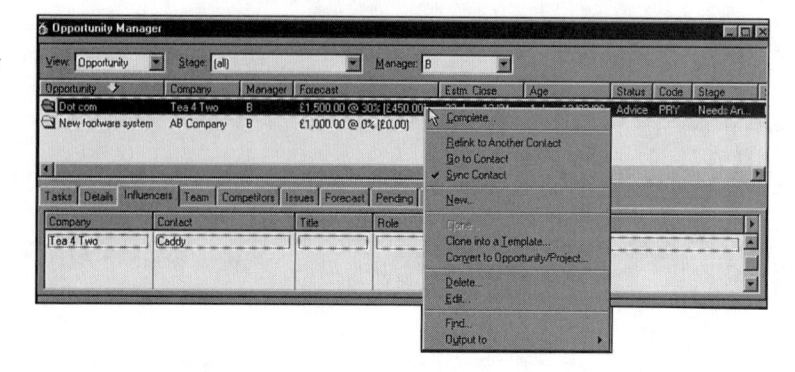

To view the Opportunity Manager, press the **F9** key or select **View**, **Sales Tools**, **Opportunities**. This opens the Opportunity Manager window, where the existing opportunities are listed. The upper panel of the local menu for the Opportunity Listing window of the Opportunity Manager contains the following options:

- **Complete**—Immediately records that the opportunity has been completed.
- **Relink to Another Contact**—Displays the Contact Listing to chose a contact other than the active contact.
- **Go to Contact Record**—Displays the contact record that is currently active.
- **Sync Contact**—Toggles to change the active contact record in synchrony.
- **New**—Opens the New Opportunity dialog box.
- **Clone**—Active only if the opportunity is based on a template. Creates an identical copy of the current opportunity that has to be saved under a different name.
- **Clone into a Template**—Saves a copy of the opportunity as a new template.
- **Convert To**—Converts, with a caution, Opportunity/Project—the current opportunity into a project, or the current project into an opportunity.
- **Delete**—Deletes the opportunity, with a caution.
- **Edit**—Displays the Opportunity Properties dialog box for editing.
- **Find**—Initiates a character string search in the list of opportunities.
- **Output To**—Copies the Opportunity list to your choice of output medium between Printer, Word, Excel, or the Clipboard.

Tasking an Opportunity

The way to update a task for an opportunity or a project is to right-click, or press the **local menu** key when your cursor is pointing in the Task Listing window and you have highlighted the task entry line.

The Tasks local menu offers the following choices:

- **Go to Task**—Move the highlight to another task.
- **Complete**—Black-line the whole of the task in the calendar window. Change the status to (Completed).

- **Find**—Initiate a character string search in the Task Listing window.
- **Output To**—Send a copy of the task listing to Printer, Word, Excel, or the Clipboard.
- **New**—Display the Task dialog box to create a new task for the current opportunity or project.
- **Delete**—Delete the highlighted task, with a caution.
- **Edit**—Display the Task dialog box for the highlighted task.

New tasks are added to an opportunity using the Task dialog box, shown in Figure 15.5. This is also shown in response to the Edit command from the local menu.

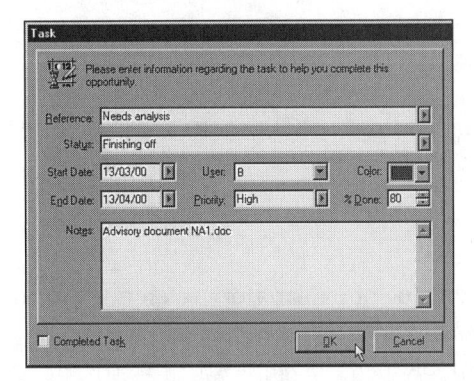

Figure 15.5

This Needs Analysis task is being edited for Status.

In Figure 15.5, the task Start and End Dates are specified. The Priority is High. Eighty percent of the work is done. The default Color code for the calendar display is blue. A Notes entry reminds you that there is an advisory document on how to do a Needs Analysis.

A quick way to finish a task is to check the **Completed Task** check box in the Task dialog box.

Viewing the Opportunity Calendar

The scheduling or calendar window of the Opportunity Manager has left and right arrow buttons to shift the span of the calendar displayed. The shift will be one time unit per button click. For instance, the default calendar display indicates days grouped in units of one week.

Point in the calendar window and your cursor will change to a spyglass. Click when the spyglass is visible to zoom. Each click increases the length of the timetable bars and hence decreases the scope of the calendar display window. The first zoom on the calendar shows the dates of the Sundays, and the day the week begins, grouped into units of one month. The left and right arrow buttons will shift the span by one month per click.

Right-click to decrease the length of the task timetable bars and hence increase the scope of the calendar window—out to the limit of about eight years. The visible span of the calendar also depends on how much space you have allocated to the calendar in the line window that is shared with the task listing.

Providing Opportunity or Project Details

If you want to create a detail in an opportunity or project, press **F9** for the opportunity manager and click the **Details** tab. Details are listed using the following column headings:

- Item
- Reference
- Linked Document

Point to the space in the lower panel and right-click for the local menu. Select **New** to open the Detail Properties dialog box.

A detail in GoldMine is defined by the following field values:

- **Item**—Name or type of the detail.
- **Reference**—Typed or selected value or explanatory reference for this detail.
- **Associated Document File Name**—The path and name of an optional linked document, of any type, that should be associated with this detail. There is a File Browse button adjacent to this field that launches Windows Explorer.
- **Allow File to Synchronize**—A check box, ticked by default, that ensures that any changes to the associated document will be reflected in the copy that is presented if the linked application is launched.

There is no limit to the number and variety of Opportunity/Project details that can be entered into the Details tab. Relevant Web sites are conveniently stored as Details.

Differentiating Projects and Opportunities

The main differences between the presentation of a project and sales opportunities are in the number of tab views available.

Table 15.2 shows the tabs of a project and an opportunity.

Table 15.2   Project and Opportunity Tabs

Project	Opportunity
Tasks	Tasks
Details	Details

Project	Opportunity
Contacts	Influencers
Team	Team
	Competitors
Issues	Issues
Pending	Pending
History	History

Most GoldMine functions apply to both projects and opportunities.

Identifying Influencers

An influencer is a contact person who could make a positive or negative difference to the outcome of a project or sales opportunity. When an opportunity is created, the active contact is automatically entered as an influencer. Other influencers would be the decision-makers in the target company or their advisors. In a project, the key people are known simply as contacts.

As an activity progresses, it may become clearer just what role each person is playing in relation to the possible outcome, its probability, and its likely date of completion. Therefore the Influencer dialog box provides the following fields:

- **Company**—Company of the influencer.
- **Contact**—Name of the contact.
- **Title**—Company title.
- **Role**—Role or function thought to be exercised by the influencer on this occasion.
- **Response Mode**—The name of the predicted manner of response or attitude of the influencer towards the product or service you are trying to sell, for example, Supportive, Neutral, Hostile.
- **Notes**—Free text.

To edit the information you are storing about an influencer, press **F9** for the Opportunity Manager and highlight the opportunity. Click the **Influencer** tab. Highlight the influencer you want to edit and right-click for the local menu. The local menu to the Influencer tab provides the following options:

- **New Linked Contact**—Displays the Contact Listing ready to select an existing contact for the link.
- **New Unlinked Contact**—Displays the Influencer dialog box to create a contact not already in the database.
- **Relink to Another Contact**—Displays the Contact Listing to chose a contact other than the active contact.

- **Go to Contact Record**—Displays the contact record that is currently active.
- **Delete**—Removes the highlighted influencer record, with a caution.
- **Edit**—Displays the Influencer dialog box.

Assembling a Team

Press **F9** for the Opportunity Manager and highlight the opportunity your team is going to work on. Click the **Team** tab. Your own user information will appear as a team member by default. The sales or project team is listed under the headings of Member, Title, Department, and Role. Highlight the member of your team you want to edit and right-click for the local menu. The Team tab of the Opportunity Manager has a local menu with the following options:

- **New**—Displays the Sales Team Member dialog box in which you can enter information about a GoldMine user or another contact who is to be a member of the team.
- **New Linked Contact**—Displays the Contact Listing from which you can double-click on the contact who is to be a member of the team. The Sales Team Member dialog box is displayed for you to enter the Role and optional Notes.
- **Go to Contact Record**—Displays the contact record of this team member.
- **Delete**—Removes the contact from the team.
- **Edit**—Displays the Sales Team Member dialog box for editing.

The building of a team could start with the team leader—you, probably. Select **Schedule** from the main menu and highlight **Schedule a To-do**. In your Schedule a To-do dialog box, click the right arrow and click **Lookup** window so that you can press **New** and make the To-do entry "Tidy my desk." Press **Select** to have this lookup entry automatically inserted in your Schedule as To-do dialog box. Edit the priority for this task to 1 for highest. Do you really need notes on how to tidy your desk?

Some users give themselves a contact record. If you do this, you can link an activity to your own contact record by selecting the **Link** check box before you click **OK** to finish scheduling this activity. Get the key contact record on top of your workspace as the active record by selecting **Lookup**, **Contact**, and then highlighting a contact from the Contact Listing. Alternatively, spin through your open contact records, if there are not too many.

Now to begin a new project: Press **F9** for the Opportunity Manager. Change the default Opportunity to Project if you don't want to speculate about sales revenues and the probability of a successful completion. You can allow GoldMine to generate a sales opportunity with a zero sales revenue—but you will be cautioned to check that this is not just a mistake on your part.

Point to a space in the upper panel of the Opportunity Manager and right-click for the local menu so that you can click **New**. In the New Opportunity dialog box, type in a memorable name for your new Opportunity. You are not allowed to have nameless projects or opportunities. Click **OK** when you are finished with the dialog box—you can edit this information later on if necessary.

GoldMine now fills up a fresh line in your Opportunity Manager. From now on you can select this opportunity by selecting its name from the Project/Opportunity drop-down list when you are working on any activity connected with it.

> **Mine Safety / DANGER**
>
> ### When Should a Type-In Become a Lookup?
>
> You could just type a task in the data entry window—but it might be one of those activities that ought to be scheduled again in other projects or opportunities, and so it will be simpler to have it in the lookup list. Some editions of GoldMine even have a default to-do list that includes phoning your mother!

Feeling lonely? Press **F9** for the Opportunity Manager and highlight the opportunity you are working on. Click the **Team** tab and point to a space on it. Right-click and select **New** to get the Sales Team Member dialog box. Choose **User** or **Other Contact** from the **Member** drop-down menu. Next to this box is a data entry window with a drop-down arrow that will offer you either a list of users and user groups, or the name of the active contact, depending on what kind of team member you are co-opting. Click the chosen user or chosen user group.

Documenting the Competitors

Press **F9** for the Opportunity Manager and highlight the opportunity you are working on. Click the **Competitors** tab and right-click for the local menu if you are creating a new competitor record. The Competitors tab of the Opportunity Manager displays line entries created by selecting **New Linked Contact** or **New Unlinked Contact** from the local menu. If you select **New Linked Contact** you will see the Contact Listing where you click the contact to be linked as a competitor. This contact becomes the active contact.

If you select **New Unlinked Contact** you do not see the Contact Listing. In both cases, you are shown the Competitor dialog box in which you can enter or select details as follows:

> Competitor   Rating
> Contact   Status
> Product
> Strengths
> Weaknesses
> Notes

If your new competitor is linked to a contact record, GoldMine enters the Company name and Contact name automatically.

Documenting Issues

An *issue record* documents issues that are important to the customer so that a user can be assigned responsibility for ensuring that the customer's needs are addressed.

The Issues tab of the Opportunity Manager displays line entries created by selecting **New** from the local menu. You are shown the Issue dialog box in which you can enter or select details as follows:

> Issue
> Status
> Priority   Date   User
> Notes

The entry in the User field normally indicates the user team member who is responsible for dealing with the issue.

Learn the Lingo

Opportunities Have a Past, Present, and Future

The Forecast, Pending, and History tabs for an opportunity contain entries similar to those in a contact record.

Analyzing the Sales Pipeline

Figure 15.2 showed one of the Analysis functions being used for a quick look at the sales forecasts of selected users. There are two routes to this analysis:

➤ Choose **View**, **Analysis**, **Forecast Analysis**.

➤ Press **F6** or choose **View**, **Activity List**. Then click the **Forecasts** tab. You will see only the forecasted sales of the user who is logged in. However, if you right-click for the local menu, the **Analyze** option will display the Forecasted Sales Analysis report window, in which you can select user(s) and click the **Analyze** button to get the calculated potentials.

You will need permissions to view the sales of other users—unless you have Master rights.

The options shown in Table 15.3 are available from the View, Analysis submenu.

Table 15.3 Activity Analysis Options

Type of Analysis	Purpose
Sales Analysis	Allows you to specify a date range and choose users, activity code, and result code for a report under the following headings: User Forecast (Potential) Closed Sales Quota Difference Forecast Difference
Statistical Analysis	Allows you to specify a date range and choose users, activity code, and result code. Displays the Statistical Analysis of the Completed Activities report.
Forecast Analysis	Allows you to specify a date range and choose users and activity code. Displays the Forecasted Sales Analysis report (refer to Figure 15.2).
Graphical Analysis	Offers the Graphical Analysis Options dialog box in which you can select the types of activities, the date and time of day spans, the type of graph, and the users before the graph is displayed onscreen or printed.
Leads Analysis	Allows you to open a Leads Analysis file and have it analyzed by source or another parameter. See Chapter 16, "At the Assayer's Lab: Analyzing Leads."
Quota Analysis	Prepares to analyze Forecasted, Closed, and Lost sales against quotas for selected users (see Chapter 16).

The statistical analysis of completed activities shows just how much work you have done and just how effective it has been. Any of the onscreen analysis displays can be printed or dispatched as an attachment to an email message.

Assigning and Analyzing Quotas

One of the reasons for assigning sales quotas per period is to allow GoldMine to report the performance of a user over a number of periods. You have the choice of how these reports are compiled—for example, sales (forecasted, completed, lost) can be compiled as a percentage of the quota or as a percentage of the forecast sales.

From the main menu, select **View**, **Analysis**, **Quota Analysis**. Figure 15.6 shows the Quota Listing dialog box in which I have clicked on the **Edit** button to see the details of B's quota, shown in the Quota Profile dialog box.

Figure 15.6

Give quotas to sales team members—different periods and different amounts, according to experience.

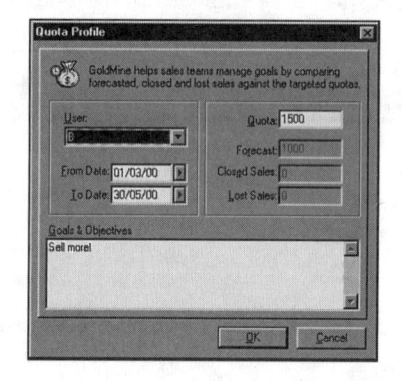

The user named Haul has been given two quotas for successive months, so I have clicked the option button to have the display sorted by user. The default sort is by period.

There is a motivating slogan in the Quota Profile Goals and Objectives window. You can place up to 64,000 characters in this field. Users who are viewing the quota and the consequential performance report can inspect these goals.

The sales figures are based on the recorded amounts entered when a forecast sale is completed. A closed sale entry in the quota analysis report will be the total dollar amount recorded in the sales activities completed in the period. Lost sales are similarly identified when a forecasted sales activity is completed.

When a user schedules a forecast sale with an expected close date that falls within a quota period, the Forecast Sales entry will be updated. The percentage of Forecast Sales against sales already completed in the period is the value presented in the Closed Sales column.

GoldMine's default quota period is a calendar month. You can assign different periods in the Quota Profile dialog box.

Chapter 15 ➤ *Looking for the Real Seams: Using the Opportunity Manager*

> **The Least You Need to Know**
>
> ➤ Sales can and should be forecasted with a date, a value, and a probability of success.
>
> ➤ Projects are team or multitasked activities that do not necessarily lead to a forecasted sale.
>
> ➤ Projects can be converted to opportunities—and back again.
>
> ➤ GoldMine can tell how hard and how well you have been working.

Chapter 16

At the Assayer's Lab: Analyzing Leads

In This Chapter

- ➤ Tracing the origins of good business
- ➤ Who is bringing in the business?
- ➤ Which sources yield the most leads?
- ➤ Which sources are the most profitable?
- ➤ Using leads analysis to add values to a field lookup table

Sales people sometimes talk about a sales pipeline—GoldMine calls it a *sales funnel*. At the narrow end of the funnel is the achievement of revenue after a successful sale. Into the wide end of the funnel goes a mixture of ideas that could lead to contacts. These ideas can be taken from lists of various kinds, from previous customers, from inquirers, or from purchasers of related products and services. This chapter shows how to use the powerful database analyzing functions to sort out the best sources of leads and which users in your team are generating most business.

Preparing to Analyze Leads

How to get some people actively working towards a sales opportunity was discussed in Chapter 15, "Looking for the Real Seams: Using the Opportunity Manager." This chapter concentrates on processing what will hopefully be a large number of genuine prospect leads. The problem might be to decide how much work to put in before sidelining a contact. The Source field of a contact record is provided for the purpose of tracing where contacts came from, when, and how well your company treated them.

Click **View** from the main menu, and then from the drop-down menu highlight **Analysis** and click **Leads Analysis**.

Figure 16.1 shows the Leads Analysis [Last Run] dialog box. It shows that the current contact set contains 27 records in which the Source field has not been assigned a value. There were four contacts arising from an advertisement in the *Conspectus* magazine.

Figure 16.1

Somebody has been careless about assigning a value to the Source field. How can we advertise properly, if we don't know how our contacts learned of us?

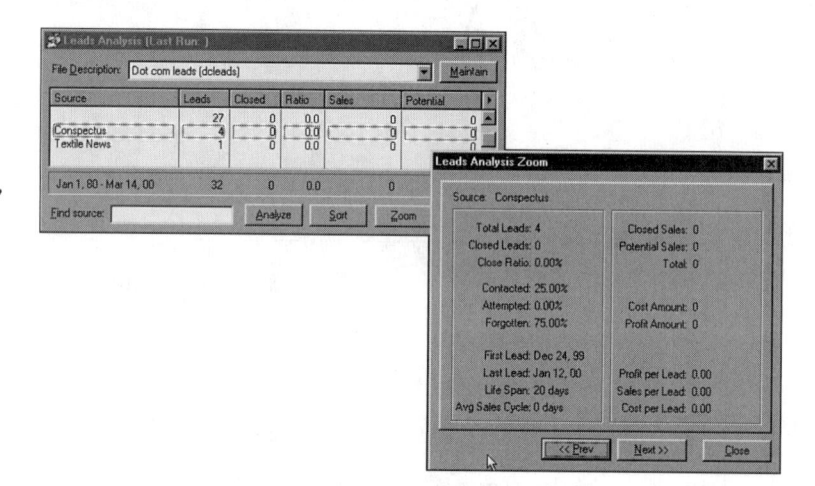

The **Zoom** button has been clicked to display the Leads Analysis Zoom report, which can be shifted between sources by the **Prev** and **Next** buttons.

Interpreting Lead Analysis

The Leads Analysis Zoom report you saw in Figure 16.1 shows that there were four leads from this source. None of these leads has been closed, which requires at least one completed sales activity. None of them has generated sales revenue, or even a potential sale. This is not surprising because only 25% of the leads has enjoyed a callback or indeed any kind of contact. There were no unsuccessful attempts to make contact, so 75% seem to have been forgotten.

What is the explanation? These leads from this source arrived in GoldMine between December 24, 1999, and January 12, 2000. Was the firm all on holiday, or something?

This source seemed to have a life span of 20 days—but because there were no sales arising, we don't know what the average sales cycle would have been.

Did this advertisement cost anything? You bet it did. This analysis clearly needs better data.

Costing the Source of a Lead

Click **View** from the main menu, and then from the drop-down menu highlight **Analysis** and click **Leads Analysis**. You will see the Leads Analysis [Last Run] dialog box with the File description entry box already showing the name of the leads analysis file that you specified as the archive for the results of the previous run. Mine was creatively called Leads One. The results of your previous run are listed in the dialog box. If you have never performed a leads analysis, or if you deleted the file after reading the results, you will see the Open Leads Analysis File dialog box in which you are invited to select an existing leads analysis file or create a new one.

If you choose to create a new leads analysis file, you are asked for a file description and a filename, both of which are displayed in the listing of leads analysis files. What a good idea it is to be clear and precise when describing a leads analysis file! It makes it so much easier to find again.

Click **OK** when you have created a new file or selected an existing file. Now you will see something like Leads Analysis [Leads One] as the file description in the Leads Analysis [Last Run] dialog box. That dialog box will be empty if this is a new file or full of the previous result if you have selected an existing file.

Leads Analysis Has Been Improved

GoldMine 5.0 has been improved by making the Leads Analysis dialog boxes easier to use. If you have not yet updated your version, you might find that the sequence of dialog boxes is slightly different, although your options and their results will be similar.

Point in the listing area of the Leads Analysis dialog box and right-click for the local menu. The local menu to the Leads Analysis [Last Run] dialog box has the following options:

Analyze	Confirm or edit the basis for the leads analysis:
	    Field (defaults to Source)
	    Optional Field
	    Date Range
	    Check box: Add New Sources to Lookup

Sort	Select the column upon which to sort the sources:
	    Source
	    Total Leads
	    Leads Closed
	    Closed Ratio
	    Closed Sales
	    Potential Sales
	    Closed + Potential
	    Cost per Lead
	    Sales per Lead
	    Profit per Lead
	    Cost Amount
	    Profit Amount

Zoom	Display the Lead Analysis Zoom report (refer to Figure 16.1).

View	Alter the pattern of fields displayed in the Lead Analysis window:
	    Sales and Profit
	    Cost and Profit
	    Cost and Profit per Lead

Edit Source Cost	Change the cost assigned to the highlighted source.
Maintain Source Cost File	Open for editing the Source Cost File, in which are held the source names and their associated costs.
Find	Initiate a character string search in the source profile fields.
Output To	Copy the display window contents to Printer, Word, Excel, or Clipboard.
Delete	Delete from the analysis all inactive sources: fewer than a specified number of leads (the default is 2), no costs, or no forecasted potential sales associated with them. A caution is provided.

Clearly, my leads analysis would make a lot more sense if I were to assign some costs to the various sources.

Get More Information About Leads

The default field for Leads Analysis is Source. You can select **Company**, for example, if you have many blank source entries, to provide the Optional Field and to generate more line entries in the Lead Analysis report.

Using Leads Analysis in Cunning Ways

You know it makes sense—analyze your sales performance. From the **View** drop-down menu, select **Analysis.** Highlight **Sales Analysis** to get the Select User dialog box. Choose **OK** because you will be already selected by default as the user.

You will now be looking at the Sales Analysis window. Type in or click the right arrow to select a **From** date and a **To** date that will show your performance in the best possible light. If you are inquisitive you could try selecting another user. However, unless you have Master rights, you might not be allowed to see the performance of other users. You might be a great sales person. You might have to restrict the display by selecting an activity code or a result code to focus the report of your achievements. When your ego is satisfied, click **Analyze** to view the results.

Your results are tabulated as line entries under the following column headings, which are abbreviated on the report screen:

 User

 Quota

 Forecast [Potential]

 Closed Sales

 Quota, Difference as a percentage

 Forecast, Difference as a percentage

But suppose you have no sales performance to analyze. Perhaps you should find out what entries have been typed in the Source field to see where your leads are coming from.

GoldMine compiles a list of all the values in your open contact set that appear in the Source field. When you click the **Analyze** button, you are invited to confirm that the Source field is to be used. You can select another field from the lookup table. Thus you can generate a listing of all the values that have been entered in this particular field. The analysis also will show how many contact records contain each value that has been detected in the chosen field.

> ### Strike It Rich
>
> ### Pop Up Your Lookups
>
> You will remember that GoldMine uses the word *lookup* as the label on a button in the main menu and as the name of those handy tables that pop up when you right-click in the space on a contact record where you would like to put some data. If you have clicked a field entry space, a data entry window will appear there with a right arrow for you to click to drop down the lookup list, if there is one.
>
> This is power. The administrator with Master rights can control which users are allowed to invent new items for a Lookup, and which users must choose one of those there already. Lazy administrators—not you, of course—just let the first few users type anything. Then later on they run a report on any important field to see what entries should be set up as a multi-choice—and perhaps compulsory—lookup table. The F2 function key will display a lookup table if your cursor was pointing to a field data space when last you clicked.

The Add New Sources to Lookup check box is part of the Lead Analysis dialog box. If you have checked it, any typed-in entries to the Source field that were not already in the F2 lookup for that field will be automatically added to the lookup list.

You can use the same technique to expand the lookup table of other fields—just name the field as the basis for a Leads Analysis, and ensure that the check box is checked so that all the existing entries become options in the lookup for that field.

The automatically added lookup values are always entered in uppercase letters. This follows the convention that other case patterns will be considered as matches for the entries.

Maintaining Leads Analysis Files

The specification for any leads analysis is stored in a file for which you can create a title in the **File Description** field and a **File Name**. These two values are listed in the Open Leads Analysis File dialog box that is displayed if you click the **Maintain** button in the Leads Analysis window that you saw in Figure 16.1. This is where you can select a leads analysis file or create a new one.

Deleting a Leads Analysis

The **Maintain** button in the Leads Analysis [Last Run] window gives access.

When you attempt to delete a leads analysis file, the Delete Leads Analysis Profile dialog box is displayed. By default, GoldMine will delete both the leads analysis profile record and the attached analysis file created when the profile was last run.

If you want to keep the last analysis data, clear the check box before clicking **Delete**.

The Least You Need to Know

- ➤ Leads analysis uses the values in the Source fields, by default, to trace the profitability of each source.

- ➤ A source should be assigned an amount that equals the cost of getting leads there over the reporting period.

- ➤ It is easy to compare the yield and the profitability of different sources of sales leads.

Part 5
Administering a GoldMine Installation

Somebody has to look after the winding gear—else you'll never get anything to the surface. Do you know where to find everything quickly if there's an emergency—or a lucky strike?

Those old-timers had loads of know-how. They kept it secret, mostly. But in our outfit we can let people in on our secrets because we are all going to share in the profits.

Some of the old skills are wondrous to watch. Now there are some clever ways to set up automatic skills that whiz through the preliminaries and the follow-up paperwork so that you get more time to think and to speak to your people and their contacts.

Even those newcomers can be helped with a handy prompting script with data being captured all the while.

There are salespersons seeking to extend their territory by selling us devices to extend ours. One or two nice add-ons could make a world of difference. You might be able to stake out more claims.

Chapter 17

Be the Boss of the Territory: Maintaining Databases

In This Chapter

➤ Looking after GoldMine and its files

➤ Merging duplicate contact records

➤ Doing something to every contact record in a chosen batch

➤ Deleting unwanted contact records

Most of GoldMine's internal activities are carried out automatically—you hardly ever notice them, especially if you have a fast workstation. However, there is inevitably a great deal of traffic. Records of appointments and calls, plans and follow-ups, have to be moved and updated. This leaves spaces in your database that ought to be consolidated to make the best use of the files and stop unnecessary searching. This chapter is about what you ought to do to keep GoldMine in the best of health.

Maintaining GoldMine

GoldMine housekeeping includes frequently sorting data and throwing out the rubbish. There is a tiny discrimination to make: updating GoldMine versus maintaining GoldMine. Updating GoldMine is done by selecting **Help**, **Update GoldMine**, and involves downloading the latest software from the GoldMine Web site. Maintaining GoldMine is a matter of carrying out housekeeping procedures for which GoldMine provides wizards and such.

Maintaining the database files includes performing procedures, such as indexing, that improve the performance of your GoldMine system.

Part 5 ➤ *Administering a GoldMine Installation*

To measure the present speed of your system, choose **Tools**, **System Performance**. GoldMine runs a test that can be used to create a benchmark standard against which to measure the effects of any improvements or data cleansing you might carry out. If you have the Tools toolbar in view, there is a rocket icon button that launches the test.

While the test is running, the speed of your installation will be displayed in the status bar with a message such as "621 records/second on 39,456 of 29." This shows that my computer is processing an average of 621 records per second, that the test has handled 39,456 records up to now, and that my database contains only 29 contacts. If there were more contacts, or if my screen display were set differently, then these figures would be different. The central processor speed and the video subsystem speed are critical factors, as is the rate at which your system can handle file input and output through the network if your database is held on a server. If you are running other tasks during the performance test, such as a print run, then the record handling speed will be lower.

While the test is running make a note of the speed so that you can test the effect of your database maintenance by running the performance test again when you have finished. To stop the performance test, click the same **Tools** option you used to start it, or click the rocket icon.

> **Mine Safety**
>
> **Backup Before Building**
>
> Files that are destined to be rebuilt and repacked by the Maintenance Wizard should be first backed up in case it makes a mess of things.

There are many good things you can do to GoldMine files—but first you have to check that your system, including GoldMine, is backed up to a professional standard.

Backing Up

All GoldMine files should be backed up according to a regular schedule using an adequate supply of backup tapes or other media to cover the eventuality that corrupted files remain unnoticed for several days. The following types of files contribute to the GoldMine system:

➤ Contact data files
➤ Setup data files
➤ Program files

A full backup would include all types of files. An intermediate backup would cover the contact data and setup data files. A minimal backup would include only setup files and subdirectories. The absolute minimal backup would include only the contact data files.

Identifying GoldMine Files

The following types of files are distinguished by their suffixes:

- Program files: *.EXE
- Setup files and subdirectories: *.D*
- Reports: *.FP

These suffixes apply only to a dBASE system.

An index file contains pointers to the contents of data files. The index files can be manipulated rapidly and presented in convenient ways so that you, or the system, can locate the data and process it.

For various reasons, index files can become corrupt. The effect is suspected if contacts cannot be located, or if some of the fields are not displayed. Perhaps a user is refused login even though he presents the correct password. The drill is to have other GoldMine users log out, and then maintain the database.

If you change the arrangement of fields in a contact record, or add fields to the tabs, the database has to be rebuilt. This is clearly in the province of the network administrator or system manager. All other users have to log off while the databases are being maintained.

The good news is that there is a Maintenance Wizard.

Preventing Corrupt Indexes

SQL databases are rather good at keeping themselves pure—but dBASE systems should really be re-indexed fairly frequently. The message from those who know is to always exit GoldMine gracefully before you attempt to power down your terminal. Alt+F4 will do nicely. A failure of power while GoldMine is writing to disk will be likely to leave corrupt indexes.

Network users should log out of the file server before shutting down.

Single PC users should run SCANDISK.EXE from time to time. This won't stop them from being single users, but might obviate future distress.

Copying and Moving Records

Your company may be maintaining separate database files for different territories. And who knows, a new sales manager may mean a rearrangement of territories. There may have to be a movement of contact records from one database to another.

Open the database containing the records you intend to copy or move. Select the records to be copied or moved by tagging or through a filter or group. Choose **File**, **Synchronize**, **Copy/Move Records**.

Use the lookup to identify the destination database. Click to process either the **Current Record** or a **Group of Contact Records**. Choose a filter or group to define the records to be processed.

Identify the **Transfer** method as either **Copy Records** or **Move Records**. If you want these records marked as deleted, you have to select **Sync Deletions** so as to prevent them being synchronized by any other GoldMine system.

When you click the **Go** button, the process monitor will track the progress of the copy or move operation. You will not see the effect on the receiving database until you open it.

Directing the Maintenance Wizard

The main job of the Maintenance Wizard is to re-index certain files so that GoldMine can get hold of their contents quickly. To get the wizard out of his den, select **File**, **Maintain Databases**. Next, you have to select one of the following options:

- Current Contact Set Files
- Individual Files
- All Database Files
- Automatic Maintenance

The default choice is to maintain the current contact set. You can pick which files to maintain—or fix the lot. If these files are leaning towards large, perhaps an overnight arrangement for automatic maintenance is indicated.

Rebuilding...Packing...Sorting

This sounds like someone is moving house. In fact it is the subject of the next dialog box of the Maintenance Wizard. If you check **Rebuild and Pack the Database Files**, you will be offered check boxes to Sort the Database Files or Verify the Data and Synchronization Information. All these are good things to have—if your database is not too large for the time you are prepared to have it out of action.

The sorting will arrange the database files according to the indexes most often used.

The **Next** button may deliver a warning about language drivers and accented characters. This you can ignore if your data does not contain any such characters. Otherwise, you will have to get the correct language driver installed.

> **Learn the Lingo**
>
> **Verify the Data and Synchronization Information**
>
> This is a good option to choose because it performs three tests:
>
> ➤ Is the data readable?
> ➤ Are all sync fields in the synchronization records of the database file(s) populated?
> ➤ Is there is any duplication of unique fields?

Now you can see the **Finish** button—but there is a check box that will force any other users out of GoldMine before you begin.

GoldMine will show you the wizard's progress as it flies about tidying up everything before returning you to a serene work space with no fuss at all. Do you have a large set of contacts? Loads of appointments? I suggest you put the wizard on night shift.

Arranging Automatic Maintenance

Your choice in the directions to the Maintenance Wizard may have generated a display of the Automatic Maintenance dialog box.

You will be asked to select the logged user—who must have Master rights—who will be responsible. This user must be logged in over the period when the maintenance is scheduled.

Then you have to enter or select a clock time at which the automatic maintenance should start. The Maintain Files dialog box requires you to tick at least one of the following:

Calendar File

Sync Log Files

GoldMine Files

Current Contact Set

All Contact Set Files

System Logs

For the group of file types you have ticked, you can elect to **Pack**, **Rebuild and Index** or to **Index Only**. You must also select the frequency from the following drop-down list:

Every Day

Every Other Day

Twice a Week

Every Week

Every Other Week

Once a Month

The next stage in preparing automatic maintenance is to identify what shall happen to the system logs. You can enter the number of days that logs should be kept, and you must select one or more of the following types of system logs:

Process Monitor Logs

Maintenance Logs

Users Login Logs

Error Logs

Sync Logs (Session & Details)

You must check if you want deletions to be synchronized.

Finally, you must check that all remote users are currently in sync if you want to purge any old sync log entries. You can tick one or both of **Contact Set Logs** and **GoldMine Files Logs**. If you intend to purge any Contact Set Logs, you will be asked to confirm that you really do want to deal with the contact set you chose earlier.

Convert *All* Databases to the New RECID Format

This is a message that appears just once when you first index a database after installing GoldMine 5.0/GoldMine Sales and Marketing. The new record ID format is designed to be compatible with a wide range of add-on systems. See Chapter 22, "Boom Town: Extending GoldMine by Adding on Software."

Now you can click **Finish** to put the Automatic Maintenance package to sleep until the due time.

Administering Records

Although there is a jolly wizard to maintain databases, it is still just possible that some of the records, although perfectly maintained in the database, contain nonsense.

In order to keep the contact records in good working order, the noble system administrator will have a hygienic system of GoldMine housekeeping. This will include frequently sorting the data and throwing out the rubbish.

Consolidating Duplicate Records

One kind of rubbish is a duplicate record. The following methods are provided to merge duplicates:

- **Merge/Purge Wizard**—Launches the wizard that will ask you to specify how you want to combine (merge) similar records, and what to do about records that seem to be duplicated.
- **Merge Visible Records**—Updates the one contact record that has input focus by merging information from all other contact records that are currently visible in their separate record windows in GoldMine's work area. This is often used to combine duplicates. The contributing duplicate records are identified as additional contacts in the Contacts tab of the top record, where they are automatically given the reference value Duplicate Record.
- **Merge Tagged Records**—Creates one contact record by merging information from all the records that have been tagged by highlighting them in the Contact Listing. All contributing records are deleted, after a caution, leaving their data in the active record.

Plan out your method and choose **Tools, Merge/Purge Records** to arrive at the submenu containing the three options.

If you don't have any extra record windows in your work area, you will not be offered the Merge Visible Records method. If you have not tagged any records in the Contact Listing, you will not be able to merge them. This leaves only the…

Driving the Merge/Purge Wizard

This wizard starts with an implied question that is almost unintelligible. You have to tick one of these check boxes:

- Merge/Purge Using a Predefined Profile
- Merge/Purge Using New Criteria

You can leave it at the default predefined profile and click on the **Next** button if you know you have one or more such things prepared earlier. You will be able to select the profile to be applied and go on to the next window, where you will be able to target your selected profile at **All Contact Records!**, or at any of the contact filters or groups you may have defined or stolen from another user (see Chapter 11, "Panning for Gold: Filtering Contacts from the Database").

But if you don't have any useful predefined profile for merging and purging, you have to tick the check box **Merge/Purge Using New Criteria**. You still have to select the target filter or group of contact records.

Figure 17.1 shows what GoldMine means by a predefined Merge/Purge profile. This display will be empty if you have not been able to select a predefined profile. You can now specify new criteria or edit the existing profile of criteria.

Figure 17.1

This is how GoldMine is going to know if two contact records should be treated as duplicates and therefore subjected to a painless merge.

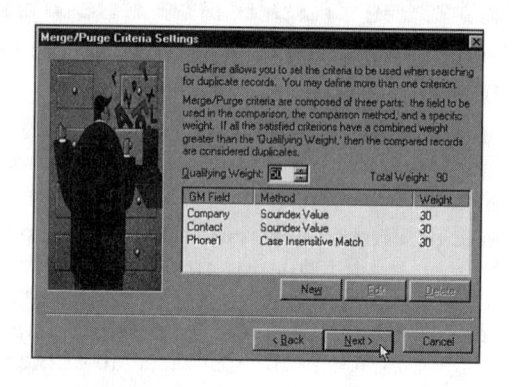

Setting Up Merge Criteria

Two contact records that have all the same field values are obviously duplicates. But what if some fields are different—or some empty? Suppose the creator or updater of these records could not spell very well? Suppose some of the data is not correctly presented?

Somebody has to set up a *profile*—a list of attributes and their critical values—that can be used to arbitrate supposed duplicates. Figure 17.1 shows the following Merge/Purge profile:

GoldMine Field	Method	Weight
Company	Soundex Value	30
Contact	Soundex Value	30
Phone1	Case Insensitive Match	30

This profile also has spin buttons to adjust the total weight that will qualify. If the total of method weights reaches the critical value, GoldMine will declare that the two records match.

Selecting Field Comparison Methods

If you decide to add a criterion to a Merge/Purge Profile, you will be offered the Merge/Purge Criteria Setting dialog box. Here you select the GoldMine field to be compared across any two records. Then you must choose one of the following comparison methods:

- Soundex Value (sounds like)
- Exact Match
- First Word
- 1st n-Characters (entry window with spin buttons)

You have a check box that is active for the character-based methods and allows you to insist on case-sensitive comparison or to ignore case.

> **Mine Safety**
>
> **Zounds!**
>
> The Soundex Value, when comparing two fields, is calculated from the beginnings of the two field values. However, some reasonable mistakes in listening to a name over the phone, or in spelling, may not be picked up.
>
> For example, Azel is not matched with Hazel.
>
> And which regional accent was used to create the Soundex masters?
>
> However, it works fairly well on the whole, hole, ole, owle.

Whichever method you have chosen, it has to be assigned a numerical weight that will be added to the total if the match criterion is satisfied. There is an entry window with spin buttons to set this number.

When you have settled on a method of telling which nearly matching records are to be combined, click the **Next** button to move on through the Merge/Purge Wizard.

> ### Strike It Rich
>
> **Sweeping Gently so as Not to Lose Gems**
>
> Merging and purging can be conducted in stages, using filtered sets as necessary, and applying different profiles so as to consolidate the good stuff and remove the rubbish. If you add criteria, the maximum total weight will increase. You can adjust the individual method weights or adjust the Qualifying Weight.

Whisking Away the Dross

When you merge visible records or tagged records, the matching records are merged together into a new record in which they will be referenced as Duplicate Record in the (Additional) Contacts tab. Their old records are purged from the database—useless shells that they are.

The Merge/Purge Wizard has more disposal methods up his sleeve. These are known as Merge Methods:

- **Keep the Record That Was Created First** (default)—Consults the value in the Creation field on the Summary tab of the contact record.

- **Keep the Record That Was Last Updated**—Most recent edition of this contact's information. Consults the Last Update field on the Summary tab.

- **Create Linked Additional Contacts in Each Record**—All the matching records will be inter-linked and cross-referenced as Duplicate Record in their (Additional) Contacts tabs.

- **Create Additional Contact of Non-surviving Record** (default)—The primary contact is taken from the deleted duplicate record and becomes an additional contact in the Contacts tab of the surviving record.

- **Prompt Me Before Merging Records**—Leaves all the decisions until a set of duplicates is discovered. You have to select everything for each set in turn.

- **Dry Run: Only Show Duplicates—Do Not Merge or Purge**—Nice idea, especially if you have just created an unusual profile. You will be prompted to save the profile under a Profile Name.

Chapter 17 ➤ *Be the Boss of the Territory: Maintaining Databases*

> **Mine Safety**
>
> **Will Everything Be All Right on the Night?**
>
> GoldMine literature suggests that you never do a Merge/Purge unless you have previously backed up the original database and had a dry run on the profile you intend to use.

Just when you think the wizard is ready to run, up comes another dialog box. This time it's about Purge Method—what GoldMine is to do when a duplicate record is found:

➤ Delete the Duplicate Record
➤ Update a Field with a Value to Indicate Record Deletion

If you take the second choice, you are asked to select which field you want to update, and what value you want to be placed there to testify that a duplicate to this record has been deleted. It may be the case that your duplicate non-survivor contains useful Calendar, History, or ContSupp (supplementary contact data) records. You can tick a check box to have such information merged to the surviving record.

At this point you are invited to save the Merge/Purge profile under a Profile Name—you don't have to.

If you click **Next**, you'll be warned that a Merge/Purge run can take some time—but you can stop it by clicking **Cancel**. The **Finish** button launches the run and displays the GoldMine Process Monitor window until the work is over.

Making Global Changes to Contact Records

A global change is not effective across the whole planet—only across the contact set delimited by the currently open database. The Global Replace Wizard is competent in this area. It can replace one or more field values in each contact record.

As you would expect with such a big job as global replacement, there are many options:

➤ Replace a field entry, whatever it is, with a particular value, across all records in the database or in the filtered set if one is activated.
➤ Update a field using an amazingly advanced option.
➤ Exchange the values of two fields.

Back Up Before Global Surgery

It is most strongly recommended that you back up your database before attempting to globally replace anything. Not that it would—but if anything should go wrong, there is no way of recovering after a global replace has had its dastardly way. Except, that is, by restoring your prudent backup.

Don't Globally Replace the Account Number

The account number is not a pretty sight. Happily it usually stays in the background. If you globally replace the values in this field with a single value—hey presto—you have reduced your database to a single meaningless record.

What could you usefully replace? How about the value in the Source field? Replace nothing or rubbish with the name of an advertising campaign, for instance.

This is a job for the Global Replace Wizard. Choose **Tools**, **Global Replace**. The default choice is **Replace a Field with a Value**, so you can click on the **Next** button to get two entry fields:

> **Replace Field**—Select one from the drop-down list.
> **With Value**—Type in, or select from the lookup window, whatever you want to appear in the selected field in all the contact records in your database, or in the filtered set that you may soon define.

The **Next** button gives you a chance to check the field chosen and the value intended to fill it. You might like to do some other field fillings in the same run. Select **Back** and repeat the field and value business as often as you want. The **Next** button now offers you a chance to stay with **All Contact Records!**, or to single out one of your filters or contact groups so as to refine the target for your global replace.

Extending Global Replacements

The Global Replace dialog box includes three check box lines that only become active if there is something for them to work on:

- **Expand Partial Contact Records**—If some of your records are partial, they will contain only fields held in the file CONTACT1. This saves space.

  If you want to work on other fields, GoldMine will automatically expand the partial records. Uncheck this if you want the partial records to miss out on this global update and remain unexpanded.

- **Update Linked Fields (Based on lookup.ini)**—A field can be linked by an AutoUpdate instruction held in the LOOKUP.INI file. Uncheck this box if GoldMine has found such updates but you don't want them to be active.

- **Log Updates in History**—Global changes to fields can, and perhaps should, be logged in case it is necessary to unravel a global update.

Logging Updates in History

If you elect to record global changes to field(s) in history, the following System Logs will be updated:

- **Process Monitor Log**—Displays the date, time, user, and number of records changed by the global replacement. This monitor is displayed while the global update is in progress. You can save or inspect the details.

- **Contact Files Log**—Displays the date, time, user, field name, and the value inserted by the global replacement.

Viewing the Contact Files Logs

The CONTTLOG file records all changes to contact records.

These are the contact set files:

Contact1.dbf

Contact2.dbf

ContSupp.dbf

ContHist.dbf

ContGrps.dbf

ContUDef.dbf

Select **View**, **GoldMine Logs**. This displays the System Logs window (see Figure 17.2).

Figure 17.2

My maintenance log shows that I had a successful database run only yesterday.

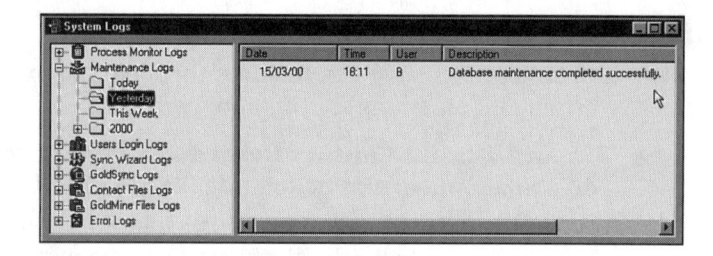

The System Logs window is in Windows Explorer format, so you can expand any item until you find what you are looking for. Each file has a listing of all the events that altered a field value. If you look at a file log, the column headings should be interpreted as follows:

- **Sync Stamp**—Date and time that the record was added to the contact set.
- **Log Stamp**—Date and time that GoldMine recorded the activity.
- **User**—User who created or last modified a field in the record.
- **Field Name**—GoldMine field affected.
- **Current Field Value**—The current contents of the field.
- **RecID**—GoldMine-assigned unique record identifier. The first seven characters code the creation time of the record.
- **Company**—The value in the Company field of the contact record, or the contact record linked with this record if it is not itself a contact record—calendar, history, and so on.
- **Contact**—Name in the Contact field of the linked contact record.

Similar contact headings are used in the listings from all the contact file logs.

Viewing the GoldMine Files Logs

The GMTLOG file records updating events that affect all the GoldMine files apart from the contact files.

To view updates to these files, select **View, GoldMine Logs**. This displays the System Logs window in which the logs are named in the Microsoft Explorer layout. Highlight and expand the chosen item by clicking the plus sign.

The column headings are similar to those used for the contact file logs, which are listed in the previous section.

Substituting a Value from Another Field

The Global Replace Wizard can take a value from one field in a contact record and substitute it for the value now in the target field. Alternatively, you can have the two fields exchange values.

Is this a good idea? One reason for shifting all the field entries in a host of contact records is to get the entries into a field that GoldMine automatically indexes. This makes it easier and quicker to use a field in accessing contacts and information about them.

Open your active record and maximize the window. These are the Indexed Fields:

- Company, Contact, Last (name), Phone1, City, Zip, Account No.
- The five user-defined Key fields—Key1, Key2, Key3, Key4, Key5. They live in the lower right panel of the contact record above the tab bar.
- Any fields identified in the Detail tab.

These fields may have had their field labels customized.

Account Number Is Special

The Account No. is automatically generated by GoldMine when a contact record is added to the database. This field cannot be relabeled or edited—even by a creature with Master rights. The first six characters are interpreted as the date in YYMMDD format.

You can use these characters to pick out records created on a specific date.

When you have worked out what you want to go where, choose **Tools**, **Global Replace** to launch the Global Replace Wizard. Tick the check box **Exchange the Values of Two Fields**. The nice wizard will ask you to feed it the details, bit by bit.

Updating a Field with Advanced Options

The bold record administrator can tick the check box titled **Update a Field Using Advanced Options**. The global replacement options offered are as follows:

- Replace the Entire Field with Value
- Replace Text with Value (entry window)
- Insert Value at Position (spin button window)
- Evaluate Value as dBASE Expression

In each case, the value is what you have entered in the Replace field.

247

A choice from the second panel of Convert To options can be combined with the first, or used on its own:

- Proper Case
- Upper Case
- Lower Case
- Phone Format

Replacing with a dBASE Expression

The target for a replacement is a GoldMine field that you select under directions from the Global Replacement Wizard. You have to enter or select text or another value to form the Replace field. If you have elected to interpret this Replace entry as a dBASE expression, you can arrange for data from one or more GoldMine fields to be processed before being entered into the target field as a replacement.

This technique can be used, for instance, if you have imported data from another application into various GoldMine fields. You can combine these field values and put the result in the single target field. For example, you could import separate first and last name fields from an address book application and locate them in two GoldMine fields—CONTACT and LASTNAME would do nicely. They both live in the CONTACT1 database file. A dBASE expression could be entered as the replace field value and evaluated during a global replace run.

> **Learn the Lingo**
>
> **Trim the Trailing Spaces and Join First and Last Names**
>
> The dBASE expression for this operation is as follows:
>
> ```
> LTrim(Trim(CONTACT1->CONTACT)+ " " + CONTACT1->LASTNAME)
> ```
>
> The destination field for the concatenation would probably be CONTACT, so that your records would always be titled with the full name of your contact.
>
> This expression even works if your contact has no first name.

The global replace evaluation of dBASE expressions only works if the imported data is already located in GoldMine fields. However, there are methods of importing data and processing it on the way (see Chapter 18, "Share the Wealth: Distributing Nuggets of Information").

Deleting Records

Deleting is the process of setting aside records so that they are not accessed. Their space is not actually freed. They still slow down processing. Rebuilding and repacking frees off space and speeds up processing.

Select **Edit**, **Delete Contact** if you want to remove the currently active contact record from the database. You will be first invited to confirm just how much deleting you had in mind. The following options are all selected by default, but you can uncheck any of them:

- Delete This Contact Record
- Delete Contact's Scheduled Activities
- Delete Contact's History Records
- Delete Contact's Opportunity/Project Records
- Synchronize This Record's Deletions

The deletion goes ahead when you click the **Delete** button.

Deleting All (Filtered) Contact Records

As you would expect, you need to have Master rights to delete quantities of records. Normally you would use this command only on a filtered set or group of contact records. From the main menu, select **Tools**, **Delete Records Wizard**. You will have the following choices:

- ➤ Delete Old History Records
- ➤ Delete ALL (Filtered) Contact Records
- ➤ Delete This Contact Record

Removing Old History

If you are removing history records, clicking the **Next** button allows you to select a filter or group. If you already have an active filter or group, you can still select a different one. GoldMine will ask you to specify the cut-off date. Before anything serious happens you must respond to the prompt to type in **Delete All History Records**. Capitalization does not matter here, but spelling does. Clicking **Next** brings you in sight of the **Finish** button, although you can still check or uncheck the box. This will ensure that all remote users have the deleted records removed from their databases.

If you are removing all filtered records, you also have to select the filter or group. Then you have to select which other associated record types are to go. Before action begins you must enter the magic words **Delete ALL Contact Records**. Check that the filter is the one you intended before you click on the **Next** button. If necessary, deselect the **Synchronize Deletions** option before clicking on the **Finish** button.

If you are using the wizard to delete a single contact record, you will get a chance to say what associated records are to be deleted at the same time, but there is no magic sentence and no warning before the currently active record vanishes without trace. You can see why they say you should back up a database before dabbling in deletions.

Using the Record Wizards

Suppose you want to create some new contacts, perform some activities on them, and then consign the historical evidence of these activities, but not the contact records themselves, to the bin—rubbish, not binary.

From the **File** menu, select **New Record** and type some details in the Add a New Record dialog box. For practice, make the company names all include a particular sequence of characters so that you can use a character search later on. Press **OK**. Repeat this process until you have created a few new records, all with a certain string of characters embedded somewhere in their company name fields.

Spin your active contact or select **Lookup** and highlight a suitable contact—one of those you have just created. Click **Schedule** and then select **Call**. Fill in the details required by the Schedule a Call dialog box. Press **Schedule**. Repeat this scheduling on some of the other new contacts.

Select, for practice, **Complete**, **Scheduled Call**. Then make the necessary entries in the Complete a Call Back dialog box. Press **OK**. Repeat this process for some other new contacts, perhaps scheduling and completing other types of activity.

Suppose all the history records of completed activities on the filtered contacts had to be deleted up to, but not including, a particular date. Select **Lookup** and choose **Filters**. If you have a suitable filter, select it. If you want to create a filter, click **New** and give your filter a name such as "My new filter." Click the **Build** tab and follow the instructions in the dialog box to build the logic of the new filter. For example, you could select the Company field and the Operator "Contains" and type in, as the Value, the characters you previously embedded in the imaginary contacts you created for practice. Click **OK** when your filter is ready.

The name of your new filter will now appear in the Filters dialog box, which will still be open. Select it and press **Properties** if you want to alter the logic. Click the **Preview** tab to see the logic and press **Search All** to see which contacts will be selected when you activate this filter.

If you are happy about this selection preview result, click the **Filters** tab and press **Activate** to have the filter operate on your currently open records. Each of these records will now have the name of the filter in their title bar as well as the contact name.

To strip off the histories from the filtered records you need a wizard. Select **Tools**, **Delete Records Wizard**. Check **Delete Old History Records**. Press **Next** and see the Delete Wizard dialog box where the data entry window will be showing Active Contact Filter because you have a filter active. You could choose a different filter from the drop-down menu.

Press **Next** when you are satisfied that the scope of the delete wizard is going to be defined correctly by the filter you have active and which is named in the title bar of your active contact record.

Edit the cutoff date if necessary. If you leave it as today's date and you have just completed some activities for today, then they will not be deleted. As instructed by the wizard, type in `Delete Old History Records`. When the typing is correct, the **Next** button will become active. Push it. This opens the About to Delete Records dialog box. You can deselect the **Synchronize Deletions** if you don't want GoldMine to go through all the related records that are affected by your deleting. Press **Finish** when you are ready to delete the history records belonging to the filtered contacts up to but not including the specified cutoff date.

Before you release the active filter, choose **Tools, Global Replace Wizard**. In the dialog box, accept the default option **Replace a Field with a Value** and press **Next**. You can now select the field and type in the value to be placed in it instead of whatever is there now. For example, click the drop-down arrow and select the field **Comments**. Type in a message such as `Cleared history`. Press **Next**. You will see the field name and the value you have just typed in. As the wizard tells you in this dialog box, you can press **Back** if you want to set up some additional global replacements in the contact records that have been selected by your active filter.

The Expand Partial Records option will be checked by default because you are going to replace a field that is not going to be visible if you have been creating records with a limited display of fields.

When your global replace is assembled, press **Next** to confirm or change the active filter. Press **Next** again and read the warning that you should not launch a global replace unless you have recently backed up your files because there is no way to recover the information over-written by your replacements.

Press **Finish** and watch the Process Monitor record your Global Replace; then see how your filtered records have identical entries in their Comments fields.

The Least You Need to Know

- GoldMine needs rubbish to be cleared out.
- Merge, Purge, and Delete are for wizards.
- The rubbish must be recycled by rebuilding and repacking the files before you will notice much increase in speed.
- Sets of contact records can be uniformly updated on a field-by-field basis.
- Database Maintenance works nights if you leave on the Master's terminal.

Chapter 18

Share the Wealth: Distributing Nuggets of Information

In This Chapter

➤ Linking contact records to data files

➤ Keeping track of contacts in their organization charts

➤ Organizing important company information

➤ Arranging sales literature for automatic dispatch

The most important repository of shared information in a GoldMine user community is the InfoCenter where any type of information can be stored for consultation by all the users and then selectively copied to customers. Like a conventional library of books, the InfoCenter needs stocking with items that are truly useful. Product information must be accurate. Policies and procedures must be up to date. Like a library, the InfoCenter has to have a way of cataloging the contents so that users can find what they need. This chapter is about building such a repository, using it, and keeping it alive and well.

Linking to Another Data File

Your installation may need to store more information than can be conveniently entered into the contact record fields. You may have a body of information that is likely to be needed by many users working on different contacts. In such circumstances it may be convenient to create a file in a word processor, spreadsheet, or other application, and then have it linked to one or more GoldMine contact records.

Linking from the Links Tab

To create a link, first you must highlight the contact entry in the Contact Listing by selecting **Lookup**, **Contact**. You may already have the relevant contact active on your workspace, in which case you can click on the **Links** tab. In the browse window below the tab title, right-click for the local menu and select **New**.

This will open the Linked Document dialog box. Type in the filename you want, or select it by browsing your computer for the document or spreadsheet you want to link.

You are invited to enter a descriptive **Document Name**, and you may decide to leave some notes to explain what you are doing and why you have decided to link this document to your active contact record.

Linked documents can be restricted to the username or user group name selected at this stage. If you do nothing, this document will be treated as a public document that can be linked freely by any user.

If you did not browse for a target file, now is the moment to type in the path and filename. In any case, check that GoldMine has got hold of the right target.

If I want to read or edit a linked document, I can select the local menu when I am pointing in the **Links** tab. The local menu options are as follows:

➤ **Launch**—View the target document, spreadsheet, or other application
➤ **Move**—Move the target to another folder
➤ **E-mail Document**—Send the target by email
➤ **Find**—Find something within the target
➤ **Output To**—Send the target to the Printer, Word, Excel, or the Clipboard
➤ **New**—Link to another target
➤ **Delete**—Remove this link
➤ **Edit**—Edit the details of this link

These options apply only to the link that has been highlighted in the Links tab of the currently active contact record.

Beware the Default Document Link

Unless you deliberately uncheck the box **Allow File to Synchronize**, GoldMine will transfer the target file to each remote database during synchronization.

You can link a file by drag-and-drop. First you have to open both GoldMine and Windows Explorer so that you can see the opened folder holding the target file. When you can see at least part of your active contact record and the icon representing the target file, drag this file icon and drop it into GoldMine, anywhere in the contact record window.

> **Strike It Rich**
>
> **Link a Folder of Files to a Contact Record**
>
> To link the entire contents of a folder, proceed as for file linking, but ensure that the linked filename is in fact the name of the target folder. Drag-and-drop works on folders as well as individual files.

The drop action will open the Link dialog box so that you can enter the descriptive Document Name that will appear in the Links tab line entry. Before selecting **OK** to finish the dialog box, you can set the synchronize check box, determine the document owner, and enter any explanatory notes needed.

Removing a document link is simply a matter of highlighting the line in the Links tab and then pressing the **Delete** key on your keyboard. You can also use the local menu to delete a document link. You have to confirm your intention to delete.

Editing a Linked Document

You can access a linked document outside of GoldMine and edit it with your word processor or other relevant application. You would then save the altered document. Alternatively, from the active contact record in GoldMine, you can highlight the link and select **Launch** in the local menu.

If you have launched an application from GoldMine, you will be asked to confirm saving any changes you have made before you can close the application. Of course, GoldMine will not be able to use a link to any edited document until it has been saved to the same filename and path as appear in the Links tab on the contact record.

Nurturing Organizational Trees

An organizational tree, like a family tree, is made up of parents and children, grandchildren, and so on. GoldMine has a tree-building function that uses the Windows

Explorer icons, and a toolbar command icon named Org Chart. The toolbar icon toggles on and off the organizational chart window panel to the left of the contact record window. The tree-building function is energized by pointing to the Org Chart panel and right-clicking for the local menu, which contains the following options:

> **Link to Organization**—Opens the Contact Listing. You double-click on the target contact to which you want to create a link. GoldMine adds your active contact as a new link, with the document icon, to the organization chart of the target contact.
>
> If necessary, GoldMine creates an organization chart comprising the target company name with the target contact name plus the new contact name you have just linked to it.
>
> **Create a New Organization**—Uses the active contact record to make an organization chart comprising the Company with one link to the primary Contact.

There is a scrolling search window above the main panel in which you can type or paste the beginnings of a company name. This search window behaves exactly like the search window in the Contact Listings. The first match found with a company name selects the active record automatically. The organization chart for this company is displayed, with the contact link highlighted in Figure 18.1.

Figure 18.1

The organization chart depicts relationships—could be within the corporate group, could be among the competition.

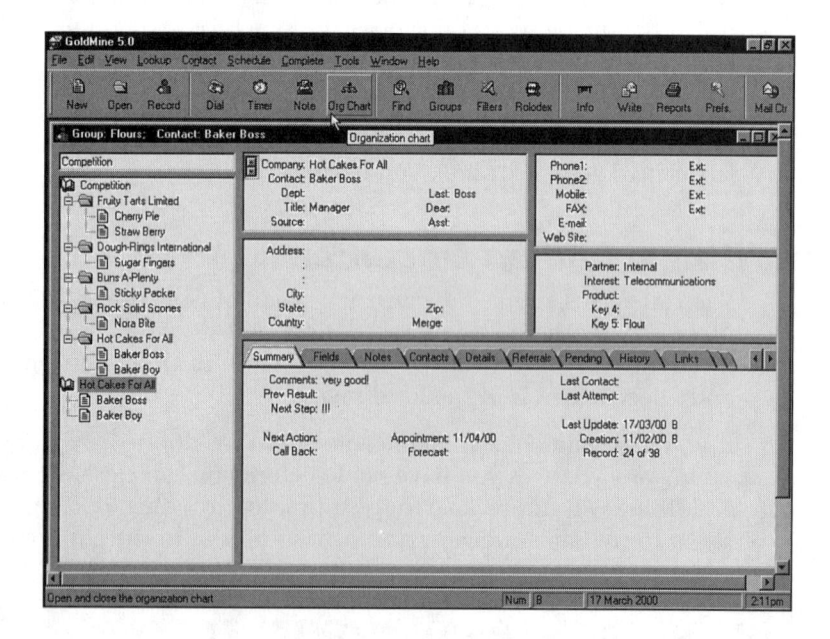

Double-click to open a book or folder. Click a document link and the corresponding contact record will become the active record on the top of your currently open contact window. Spin or otherwise change the active contact, and the corresponding organization chart will be displayed—if there is one.

If there is no link between an item in the organization chart and a contact, the active contact will remain unchanged if you click on that item.

Adding Branches

After you have created a new organization, right-click any icon in it, and the following local menu appears:

- **New Link**—Offers the Contact Listing so that you can double-click on the contact that you want to place in the chart under the same section and at the same level as the item you highlighted. Contacts at the same level are arranged in alphabetical order.

- **New Section**—Places a new section closed-folder icon under or below the highlighted item. Choose **Under** to create a lower-level folder to the right. Choose **Below** to create a folder at the same level.

- **New Organization**—Assumes the company name of the active contact. Places the closed-book icon at the highest level (to the left). Click on the book to open it and show that the new organization includes the contact that was active when it was created.

    There is no visible connection to any other organizations in the organization chart.

    However, if any linked contact is highlighted or activated as part of a section that is activated, all other organizations to which that contact belongs will reappear in the chart as closed books.

- **Activate Section**—Removes from the organization chart display panel all entries not connected with the highlighted item. Filter the records in the record window to exclude those not linked to this section.

- **Release Section**—Returns the records in the record window to the full contact set.

- **Replicate Data**—Offers to copy data from the field(s) you select to each of the other contacts at the same organizational level as the contact highlighted in the organization chart when you opened this local menu. A dialog box reminds you of the scope of this replication and offers the following options:

    Address

    Phone numbers

    Key fields

    User defined fields

    Field [select from lookup]

257

> **Options** —The following actions refer to the item highlighted in the organization chart:

> > **Link to Contact**—Shifts the link from the contact active when this item in the organization chart was created to the contact record you now choose from the Contact Listing. The linked contact record becomes active when you click on the chart item.

> > **Unlink from Contact**—Removes any link to a contact record so that you can view the contact records of other members of the organization, perhaps prior to linking to one of them.

> > **Convert Entry to Section**—Changes the highlighted document icon to a closed-folder icon with the same name. You are cautioned before this happens.

> > **Link Group/Filter Members**—Adds all members of the activated group or filter to the section highlighted in the organization chart. You are cautioned before this happens.

> > **New Contact Record**—Creates a contact record, which can be a duplicate, for which you complete an Add a New Record dialog box. This new contact is added to the same section as the highlighted contact.

> **Delete**—Removes the highlighted member from the organization, after a caution.

> **Properties**—Offers the Section Properties dialog box in which you can edit the section name and clear a check box to release the link between this section and a contact record. This dialog box also appears if you are working on a document item representing a contact.

Trees are for linking existing records to show where the individual contacts stand in relation to each other and to their parent companies, head office, affiliates, even rivals. When you link several contacts to an organization chart, a copy of this chart is added to the organization charts of each of these linked contacts.

Looking Up a Referral Connection

If two contacts are connected by mutual referrals, clicking on a contact line entry in the **Referral** tab will display its contact record and organization chart. The Referral tab will be open, and so you can initiate the reverse process by clicking on the appropriate referral entry.

The Organization Chart icon in a toolbar toggles the chart display panel in the currently open record window. Alternatively, press **Ctrl+Q** to toggle the organization chart.

Depicting the Competition

Up to five generations can be organized under one book icon. Each generation or level is represented by a folder icon indented successively.

You can have one book to represent your corporate identity, and separate books to represent each of the competitors. Figure 18.1 shows a set of competitors that is displayed when any contact or section in that chart is highlighted. Every contact has the same Competitors organization chart because it represents a competitive network.

Each competitor can also have a separate book to represent his own organization. This will not be linked to any contact outside his own company, and so will not be displayed as part of the chart of any outsider.

Rearranging the Furniture

You can click and drag any link or section and drop it on the organization or section that is to become its parent. There is no facility for copying a piece of an organization chart, but you can duplicate record details and create a new name, if necessary.

Using the InfoCenter

The InfoCenter is a collection of documents that are linked using the same Windows Explorer display icons as an organization chart. Click the academic mortarboard icon or choose **View**, **InfoCenter**.

> **Strike It Rich**
>
> **Knowledge Is All in Books**
>
> You have guessed that the academic mortarboard icon can open the InfoCenter. When the center is open, the mortarboard sits up on the left of the main menu, where you can click on it to send off the professors or control their display window.

GoldMine is delivered with a useful set of documents arranged under three tabs; two are editable, one is read-only:

- **KnowledgeBase**—Basic GoldMine know-how.
- **Personal Base**—Empty space for privates.
- **What's New?**—Features of GoldMine 5.0.

The What's New? tab contains only document-level items. It is not organized into sections, nor can you directly add pages or sections. You can search it but not edit anything. However, any new pages you create in the KnowledgeBase will be automatically copied to the What's New tab.

If you have highlighted a page in the What's New tab that is also discussed in the main tab, a Show Topic in KnowledgeBase icon button is active.

Authoring a Book

Each editable tab has the following toolbar icons, although they will not be active unless there is something for them to work on:

- **New Book**—Create a book item for which you must supply a name.
- **New Folder**—Create a folder beneath the highlighted item. You must supply a name.
- **New Topic Page**—Create a page beneath the highlighted item. You must supply a name.
- **Edit**—Highlight a book, and you will be allowed to rename it or add a section. The renaming is promulgated through all references to it. You can also attach a file and control access to the book.

    Highlight a section, and you will be able to rename it or add a page. The renaming is promulgated through all references to it. You can also attach a file and control access to the section.

    Highlight a page, and you can edit the topic title of the page and supply key words for searching the table of contents. Page names automatically include the book and section names as prefixes. You can also attach a file and control access to the page. You can see when a page was last updated and which user wrote it from the title bar of that page. The page title bar is visible only while you are highlighting the page title in the Explorer-type InfoCenter display panel. The page title is replaced by an editing toolbar, if you click in the page itself, because GoldMine is expecting you to start editing it—if you have permission to do so.

- **Attach a File**—Allows you to enter or browse for a file, and to signify whether it shall be synchronized to ensure that changes to the source file are reflected in the results presented to GoldMine. Covers all types of files supported by your system.

> **Delete**—Offers to delete the highlighted item and its sub-items.
> **Create a Table of Contents**—This is best used only on folders or books because it writes the table of contents in place of any text already associated with the highlighted item in the book organization chart. Selects the titles of the folders and pages.
> **Search**—Find an item in the InfoCenter.
> **Launch Attached File**—For example, open a Word document or an Excel spreadsheet.

Any new page that you create is automatically displayed in the What's New? tab. You can read it but not edit it. However, there is a Show Topic in KnowledgeBase icon button to get you back to the original in the KnowledgeBase, where you can edit it. GoldMine will automatically update the version accessed from the What's New? tab.

> **Beware the Auto-Alphabeticizer**
>
> When you assign a name to a book, a folder, or a page, GoldMine will always tidy things up by displaying your masterpieces in alphabetical order of their titles, thankfully within sections—no thought at all for the freely flowing progression of meaning and the unfolding of understanding. For example, Chapter 1 comes before Introduction.

Although you probably won't want to remove the GoldMine advice—just yet—it is perfectly possible to annotate it. Just click the space in a page you want to work on and the basic editing toolbar appears in place of the title (see Figure 18.2).

Saving edited pages is expected—and prompted if necessary.

Searching the InfoCenter

If you click on the binoculars icon, you are offered a search dialog box to indicate what you want to search for. The GoldMine search engine can be fired up to leave no stone unturned in the InfoCenter.

Part 5 ➤ *Administering a GoldMine Installation*

Figure 18.2

I am editing a page in the KnowledgeBase. When I save this page, my user ID and the date will appear in the title bar that replaces the editing toolbar.

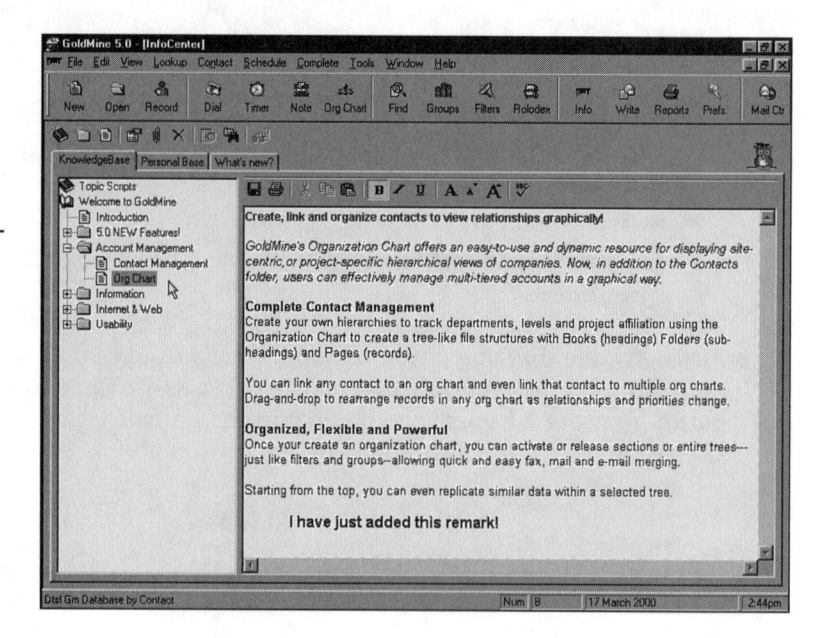

The basis for the search is a word, phrase, or character string that you enter in the Search dialog box. The Search Scope of the survey is delimited by choosing one of the following:

- ➤ Entire contents.
- ➤ Name of the highlighted book, section or page.
- ➤ Last pages found—these are displayed in the Search Results tab.

The Search Area is further delimited by selecting some or all of the following:

- ➤ **Keywords**—As supplied by the author per page.
- ➤ **Topic Name**—As displayed in the organization chart of the InfoCenter at the book level.
- ➤ **Folder Name**—As displayed in the organization chart of the InfoCenter at the folder level.
- ➤ **File Names**—As supplied when documents are attached to pages, sections, or books.

The search can be made even more picky by checking **Match Whole Words** or **Match Case**.

Search displays the findings as clickable document icons in a separate Search Results tab. A search again icon is provided to locate the search string in each of the documents found. The text in which the search was successful is displayed in the page window, with the search string highlighted.

Extracting Information

Of course, it depends what you have in your InfoCenter. Sooner or later you will not need any of the GoldMine introductory publicity. What you might have there are all the come-in-handy lists and drawings that would be so useful to your customers when they are contemplating becoming even better customers.

Let us suppose that you have engaged a good technical author. The key documents are in place or at least linked to pages in the InfoCenter KnowledgeBase.

Printing and Faxing a Topic

Figure 18.3 shows the local menu available to handle a topic from the InfoCenter.

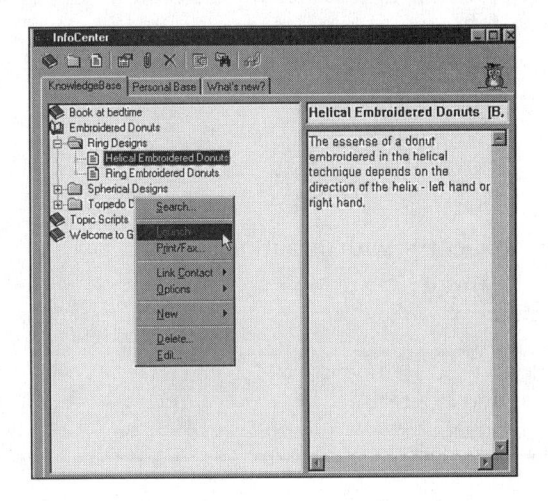

Figure 18.3

A topic can be printed or faxed. You could even highlight some or all of it and copy it to the Clipboard to insert in an email.

The local menu duplicates some of the toolbar functions (see Table 18.1).

Table 18.1 Local Menu Options for Printing and Faxing

Option	Function
Search	Opens the Search dialog box
Launch	Launches the application that runs an attached file, such as Word or Excel
Print/Fax	Sends the highlighted book, section, or topic to the default printer or fax
Link Contact	**Show Contact**—Shows the contact record of the linked contact, if there is one

continues

263

Table 18.1 Continued

Option	Function
Search	**Link Contact**—Links the active contact to this topic
	Unlink Contact—Removes link between a contact and this topic, if there is one
	Sync Linked Contact—Changes the active contact record to correspond with the highlighted topic
Options	**Create Table of Contents**—If the highlighted item is not a document
	Delete Folder—If the highlighted item is a folder
	Import—Imports an InfoCenter topic from another GoldMine system
	Export—Exports an InfoCenter topic to another GoldMine system
New	Book
	Folder
	Page
Delete	Delete the topic entry, with a caution
Edit	Edit the topic profile:
	Topic
	Keywords
	Folder
	Attached file tab
	Access tab

Fulfilling Literature

Using the Literature Fulfillment Center is a matter of choosing which literature items—sales or cultural—you want to send to the active contact, to some tagged contacts, or to a filtered set, perhaps a group. But first you must have some literature available to send—I will gloss over that.

From the main menu, select **View**, **Literature Fulfillment**. This displays the Literature Fulfillment Center. Suppose you want to make arrangements to send some of your company's literature to the active contact. Select **Schedule**, **Literature Request**, which invokes the Schedule a Literature Request dialog box shown in Figure 18.4.

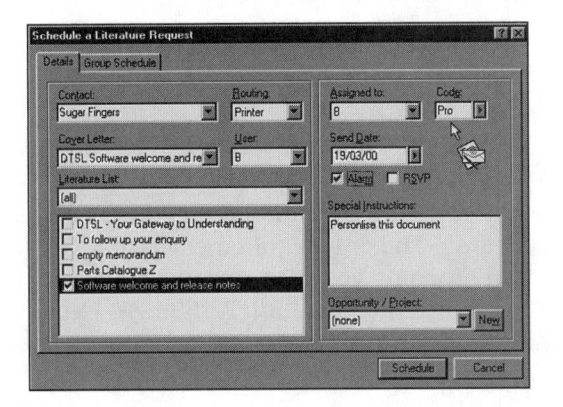

Chapter 18 ➤ *Share the Wealth: Distributing Nuggets of Information*

Figure 18.4

Scheduling a dispatch from the Literature Fulfillment Center.

The Literature Fulfillment Center has to be primed with at least the names of your sales literature items. When you have opened the center, select **Literature List**, and select **New** from the local menu or click on the **New Literature** icon to display the Literature dialog box.

Mine Safety

GoldMine Assumes Your Literature Is in Stock

The Literature dialog box defaults to Stock in the Output To field so that any literature reference record you create will be supplied—hopefully—from stock. Use the field drop-down to select either **Fax** or **Printer**, if you are going to register a new item in the Literature List.

When you have chosen either Printer or Fax as the output routing for a new literature item, you will be offered the following input fields:

- ➤ **Type**—You can invent a set of literature types or perhaps adopt a company scheme that has been set up in the lookup table for this field.
- ➤ **Description**—This title text should enable you to recognize which item is about to be dispatched.
- ➤ **Filename**—Browse or enter the full path and filename of your literature item (not required for items to be dispatched from stock).
- ➤ **Allow File to Synchronize**—This means that you will always send off the latest version of your literature item (not, regrettably, applicable to items to be dispatched from stock).

> **Edit**—Launches the application in which the literature was created or one that has been designated for editing it.

Creating a Contribution to Literature

There are no limitations on how you first create your literature—Word, Excel, HTML Web page, or some other medium editor. The only requirement is that you know where it is, or can recognize it when browsing your directories. What GoldMine expects is that you register your tome with the Literature Fulfillment Center. Highlight the **Literature List**, right-click for the local menu, and complete the Literature dialog box, as shown in Figure 18.5.

Figure 18.5

I'm adding a new opus to the available literature.

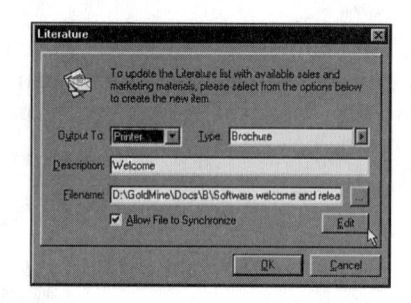

Memos and faxes are often written in .TXT—Text—format (Microsoft Notepad) or in .RTF—Rich Text Format—(WordPad). You can also save documents in these formats from Word. Literature items stored as *.TXT files or *.RTF files will have their first few lines displayed in the lower-right pane of the Literature Fulfillment Center window. You can scroll over text documents that are too large to fit into the pane. Items held in other formats and applications are not visible in this pane.

Reviewing Literature Requests

Requests for literature fulfillment are posted by users who are logged on. The user responsible for dispatching these items is selectable at the time. Literature fulfillment requests can be inspected by clicking on the relevant time period icon in the Literature Fulfillment Center:

- Requester
- Cover Letter
- Contact
- Routing
- Date

Click the **+** sign of any of the monthly displays to see the number of requests per day.

Reviewing Queued Documents

Queued documents are displayed in a time period layout similar to the literature requests. The following columns are displayed in the daily listings:

- User
- Template
- Contact
- Zip Code
- Output (print or fax)
- Track (if an automated process)

Click the + sign of any of the monthly displays to see the number of requests per day.

Reviewing Recently Printed Documents

Printed Documents are displayed under the following time period headings:

- Today
- Yesterday
- + This Week
- + This Month

The following columns are displayed:

- User
- Template
- Contact
- Zip Code
- Output (print or fax)
- Track (if an automated process)

Click on the + sign of the This Month time period to see the number of requests per day.

Working with the Information Facilities

The whole of GoldMine is an information center—but the organization charts, the InfoCenter, and the Literature Fulfillment Center are related because they use the Explorer hierarchical family tree display layout and functions. The Literature

Fulfillment Center uses the family tree layout to get to the scheduled operations for editing.

The operations on an organization chart are very similar to operations on a book in the InfoCenter. For example, to generate a company family tree for the currently active contact, click the **Maximize** button to get the largest contact record display, which will include the Organization Chart panel. Alternatively press **Ctrl+Q** to see this panel in the contact record window you have open already.

If you have recently used Ctrl+C to copy a highlighted phrase to the Clipboard, you can point to the top-left panel of the organization chart display and right-click for the local menu where the **Paste** option will be active. Paste in your phrase if you want it to be the title of your chart.

If you right-click in a lower panel of the organization chart area that is empty, your local menu will offer the following options:

- **Link to an Organization**—Select this if your active contact belongs to an organization chart you have already created in another contact. You will be offered the Contact Listing where you can double-click the contact that has the organization chart you have in mind. This will be copied to your current contact who will appear at the lowest level of the organization chart.

- **Create a New Organization**—Choose this to build a new family tree for the current contact.

GoldMine automatically generates a new organization chart by putting the Company field value at the open-book icon level and the Contact field value at the document-page icon level. If either of these fields is blank, GoldMine just uses the value in the other. If both Company and Contact are empty—perhaps you have created a new record just because you have a telephone number that you want to investigate—then the organization chart will have the open-book and document icons but they will not have any text labels.

You can apply a very similar technique in the InfoCenter. Choose **View**, **InfoCenter**. Click the book icon and type in the title or stay with the default <New Book>. Press **Enter**. Point to the text panel and make notes about your new book. Click the diskette icon to save your notes. Point to the hierarchical display and right-click your book to get the local menu when you are ready to create a new book, folder, or page.

Highlight a book, folder, or section in the InfoCenter and right-click for the local menu. Click **Edit** to get the Section Properties dialog box. Click the **Attached File** tab to see the path to the file currently attached, if any, and press the browse button if you want to attach a different file to the highlighted section.

When you start using the Organization Chart and the InfoCenter functions, you will find that there are many levels of submenus that allow you to control access to the

Chapter 18 ➤ *Share the Wealth: Distributing Nuggets of Information*

information and to manipulate its structure. Any of the items in either of these information repositories can be attached to a contact record or, with permission, sent to one or more contacts.

> **The Least You Need to Know**
>
> ➤ Contacts can be linked to organizational charts.
>
> ➤ Useful information can be managed in structures like organization charts.
>
> ➤ Sales material and other documents can be prepared as a literature list, from which selections can be requested for automatic dispatch on specified dates to selected contacts.

Chapter 19

High Noon: Synchronizing Records

In This Chapter
- What to do if you want two computers to each update their GoldMine databases so that they are identical
- How to share with an Outlook contact database
- How to synchronize with your Palm Pilot
- How to post prospects to your portables

If you work in a sales team, you must be able to let the others know any new information you have about your shared contacts in case they can make use of it. And you would like them to return the favor. This chapter shows you how to use GoldMine's procedure for this called synchronizing records.

Synchronizing with GoldMine

The process of synchronizing data is designed to harmonize the data records of two or more GoldMine installations that share the same license. The I.D. of the license is used to make sure that no stranger can access the data.

The method is to define a transfer set of changes in each installation, and then arrange sessions at which each remote workstation submits a transfer set and receives the most up-to-date transfer set from the Master installation. In each of the installations,

GoldMine compares the two transfer sets to evaluate the following conditions for each record field that has changed since the previous synchronization:

- If the retrieved field information is more recent than what exists already, accept it and update the field concerned.
- If the receiving field contains information that is more recent than what is being retrieved, make no changes.
- If the two fields were last modified on the same date, make no changes.

Both the Master GoldMine and the remote GoldMine carry out all these checks—so, by the end of a bidirectional session, both their local databases will contain the same information.

Setting Up a Session

A synchronizing session can be set up in various ways, according to the facilities available:

- Modem connection
- Direct Internet connection
- Internet email
- Wide Area Network (WAN)
- Remote Access Server (RAS)

The session can begin by waiting for a remote system to call in, or by calling out. The remote system can be a GoldMine or a GoldSync system. A GoldSync system makes it easier to manage a large number of remotes.

GoldMine provides a Synchronization Wizard to manage the whole process. In particular, the wizard helps you define a profile of settings that you save for future use.

Figure 19.1 shows that I have already defined a session profile called "Everything both ways." I have launched this profile to create a session. At the moment, the GoldMine Process Monitor is reporting that there is only one automated process running—my synchronization session—and GoldMine is "Listening for an Internet Protocol (IP)," which is a signal to make a connection from a remote user.

Figure 19.1

I have defined a synchronization profile called "Everything both ways" so I can keep in touch with my remote sites. My process monitor is waiting for one of them to dial in to my modem.

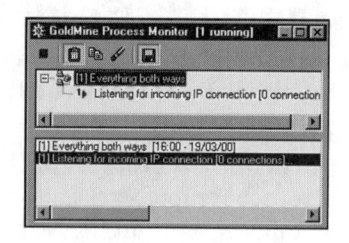

> ### Hello GoldSync
>
> GoldMine 5.0 by itself easily looks after the mutual exchange of transfer sets of synchronization information between two GoldMine installations. However, you might need to have several sites all in harmony.
>
> This multisite synchronization is best managed automatically by GoldSync, a specialized enhancement of GoldMine, that runs on one of your workstations dedicated as a GoldSync server. This would not normally be the same workstation that runs as the GoldMine file server. There might be several GoldSync servers in the network. GoldMine sites and GoldSync servers can synchronize with each other.
>
> If you purchased the basic version of GoldMine 5.0, then GoldSync is not included. If you have GoldMine 5.0 Enterprise Edition or GoldMine 5.0 Sales and Marketing, then GoldSync is included in the package.
>
> There is a GoldSync Administration Center that allows each site to have its own profile that defines what kinds of data are to be updated. If your installation has one, you can access it by selecting **File, Synchronize, GoldSync Administration Center** from the main menu.

You might want to send a new contact record to a member of your sales team while you are still in touch over the phone. This process is called synchronization in one direction. Bidirectional synchronization is what I have prepared for in my current session.

> ### Dynamic IP or Static?
>
> A dynamic Internet protocol is an electronic address that an Internet service provider assigns to your modem as necessary. A static IP address is a permanent arrangement for networks that need to be frequently synchronizing their data.

It is very convenient to define your synchronization settings as a profile for repeated and timetabled use in the future—but, supposing you get some important new information, you also can start a session immediately.

Rousing the Synchronization Wizard

From the main menu, select **File**, **Synchronize**, **Synchronization Wizard**, or click the **Synchronization** icon. Your first entry will default to a session Sync Profile you defined previously, if you have one. GoldMine will check the check box **Sync using the settings of a Sync Profile**.

If you have more than one profile, you can select from the lookup table.

The other options are to start defining a new session or to use a sync profile belonging to a GoldSync site. You can define a session for immediate use and save it as a Sync Profile—or, you can just start up the session without saving the profile.

With a profile selected, clicking **Next** takes you to another dialog box where you have to specify how this session is to be managed:

Connection Method	Drop-down menu:
	Internet (Direct)—You dial the connection.
	Modem—Connection dialed by the modem.
	Network—Permanent connection.
Answer an incoming connection	You get the message, "Listening for an Internet Protocol(IP)[0 connections]," in your process monitor.
Connect to remote	You can choose to wait or initiate a session.

Synchronizing When Disconnected

If you have decided not to run a connected session, you can choose one of the following:

- **Send a transfer set to remote by email**—You have to enter or select the email address and an optional password.
- **Create a transfer set**—You have to browse for or enter the path for the transfer file. You can optionally supply a password.
- **Retrieve a transfer set**—You have to browse for or enter the path to an empty directory folder for the transfer file. You supply an optional password, and direct whether the records are to be retrieved as well as the transfer set. You also can elect to dispose of the transfer set or archive it.

Each method has the appropriate follow-up sequence of dialog boxes in the Synchronization Wizard. The same connection password has to be used at each terminal of a synchronization session.

TCP Port

This is a default number like an extension to the IP address. GoldSync uses 5993. You are advised not to change this. The same port has to be used at the remote GoldMine.

If you have several Internet providers for synchronizing using the Internet (Direct) connection method, GoldMine will try each in turn until successful. You can use the local menu to move an address up or down the list.

Synchronizing by Sneaker Net

Yet another method of synchronizing is to have the transfer sets sent as files on portable disks or tapes.

If you are going to use a floppy disk or other portable medium, create a subdirectory to hold them, because GoldMine will not store files in a root directory. If the named subdirectory exists, it should be empty. If it does not exist, GoldMine will create it.

Figure 19.2 shows how to tell GoldMine what you want to transfer and which users are to be in the exchange.

Sneaker Net

The term Sneaker Net evolved when networking PCs with technology like EtherNet was still relatively uncommon. It implies that you share files by walking from one standalone machine to another carrying a floppy disk.

As you progress through the wizard, you will be asked to target your contact records from the following drop-down menu:

➤ Only the current contact record.
➤ All changed contact records (default).
➤ Contact records linked to the Send user's calendar list.
➤ All filtered records and user-scheduled activities records.

In the same dialog box is a display of your contact sets from which the default is your Current Contact Set.

Figure 19.2
The Send Options define what shall and shall not take part in the transfer—types of records, users, and user groups.

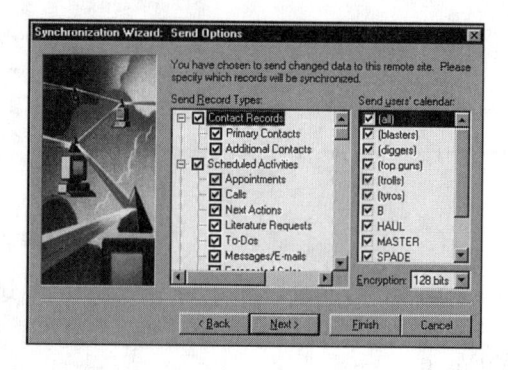

Filtering for the Transfer Set

The next dialog box offers you the chance to select an existing filter or group from which GoldMine or GoldSync will build the transfer set. There is an Options button for dBASE systems only, which offers you the choice of either of the following so as to use the optimum searching method:

Search for changed records by the TLog records.	Select this method if almost all the records in your filtered contact set have changes that need to be promulgated. GoldMine first finds all changed records—then it applies the filter to identify the ones you want to transfer.
Search for changed records by the Filtered records.	Select this method if: Number of filtered records is small compared to number in the database. or Most of the changed records in the database are not going to be identified by the selected filter because you do not need to include them in the transfer set.

At this stage, there is still a chance to build a new filter or define a group that can then be used to delimit the transfer set.

Browsing a Transfer Set

When you are defining a session that includes retrieving a transfer set, you are offered a check box labeled Unpack Transfer Set Only—Do Not Retrieve Records.

GoldMine will decompress the transfer set and place it in the directory you designated in the Path for transfer set field. The set also will be decrypted using the password.

However, under this option, none of your contact records will be updated. What you can do, however, is inspect the contents of the transfer set with a database-browsing utility.

Defining a Transfer Cutoff Moment

A transfer profile includes a date and time at which further changes are not considered for a transfer set. You can choose to ignore a cutoff and send all contact records. If you are transferring records linked to activities, you will have defined which users or user groups you are interested in. The Cutoff Date/Time dialog box has two date and time entry panels so that you can accept or change the cutoffs separately for each subset of records.

The cutoff dates and times will be suggested by GoldMine automatically from records kept since the previous transfer. This ensures that the synchronization will include no gaps and no redundant or overlapping transfers. However, you can enter different dates and times, if necessary.

Defining Send Options

The Transfer Set Send Options dialog box allows you to identify one or more contact sets and database files from which GoldMine will develop the transfer sets.

A database file might contain a unique collection of record types. When you select a database file in the Send Record Types panel, you also can use the check boxes to control which record types are to be considered for transfer. As an example, the supplementary contact records are stored in the CONTSUPP database file. The following record types are only found in a CONTSUPP file:

- Deletions
- Organization records
- Additional records
- Detail records
- Extended profile headers
- Referral records
- Linked records
- Linked documents

The default is for GoldMine to select all record types for all the database files.

Learn the Lingo

Encryption

128 bits—Only available for U.S. installations of GoldMine and GoldSync.

32 bits—The rest of the world.

128 bits can also decode 32-bit transfer sets.

Transfer sets passing through a GoldSync server can be edited there because a set of permissions is consulted before allowing retrievals.

If you are retrieving a transfer set and choose **Request data from a GoldSync server**, you will be offered the following possibilities:

➤ I am picking up waiting transfer set.

➤ I will wait online while GoldSync creates the transfer set.

➤ I will pick up the transfer set later.

Defining Retrieval Options

The Transfer Set Retrieve Options dialog box allows you to specify the Retrieve Options in the same way you would define a transfer set you are sending. You can choose to create a filter to apply to the incoming transfer set. You can select from available contact sets and database files, with their included record types. The contact set might be circumscribed by the transfer set, but if there is more than one, you can choose which to focus on.

As with sending, you can elect to retrieve calendar activities belonging to select users or user groups, all users, or no calendar activities at all.

Synchronizing with Microsoft Outlook

One of the advantages of being able to synchronize records is that you can link up with various services or devices and their resident applications. Wizards are available for Outlook 98/2000, Palm Pilot, and Windows CE PDA. In this section, I'll cover Outlook, and discuss the others in a moment.

To get to grips with the GoldMine Outlook Synchronization Wizard, select **File**, **Synchronize**, **Sync with Outlook** from the main menu.

A session profile is selected or defined in the wizard to control single or bidirectional data transfer. You can save this profile for use in the future. If the default profile is what you want, select **Finish** to initiate the session. As with GoldMine to GoldMine sessions, the actual data transfer can await the establishment of a suitable connection.

Defining Options for Outlook Synchronization

The first Wizard window is the Outlook Synchronization Options dialog box. It provides the following options:

➤ **Send and Retrieve: To/From Outlook**—Presents the Record Selections dialog box.

➤ **Send Only: To Outlook from GoldMine**—Presents the Record Selections dialog box.

➤ **Retrieve Only: To GoldMine from Outlook**—Presents the Ready to Synchronize dialog box.
➤ **Fresh Sync (Delete GoldMine Data in Outlook)**—If you uncheck this option, you might get duplicate records in Outlook.
➤ **Advanced**—Presents the Advanced Options window.

Setting Advanced Options for Outlook

The General tab of the Advanced Options window is the default. You use it to define a date range for Outlook records from which transfer data is to be drawn. You also can set other parameters, such as the separator for designating telephone extensions—the default is (,). The number of characters of notes sent to Outlook defaults to 2048. You can change this limit.

> **Learn the Lingo**
>
> ### How Many Notes?
>
> You can speed up the synchronizing process by limiting the size of the notes text that you are prepared to transfer. If your people write only a few sentences, then a maximum of 256 will do, which is just enough for this paragraph including spaces.
>
> You've guessed that multiples of 2—such as 4096, 2048, 1024, 512, and 256—are best if you want to waste as little space as possible.

The General tab of the Advanced Options window also allows you to select the following options:

➤ Sync deletions from Outlook to GoldMine
➤ Sync deletions from GoldMine to Outlook
➤ Retrieve all data from Outlook regardless of last sync date
➤ Synchronize RSVP

These options allow you to specify how your Outlook and GoldMine are to operate together.

279

You can click **OK** to accept the defaults or after completing the options in the General tab. However, there are four more tabs that offer ways of making GoldMine synchronize to suit your business: Field Mapping, Contacts, Calendar, and Task.

The Field Mapping tab is used to define how GoldMine field data is to be placed in Outlook fields. The dialog box lists pairs of corresponding field names in GoldMine and Outlook. Options allow you to view the correspondence in either direction. Editing can destroy existing data when the next transfer takes place. Facilities are provided to add new mappings and delete existing mappings.

The Contacts tab specifies where GoldMine is to place contact information in the Outlook folders. You have the following options:

- Send/Retrieve GoldMine Contacts Using Outlook's Default Contact Folder (the default option)
- Send/Retrieve GoldMine Contacts Using the Contact Folder Selected Below (a data entry window becomes active in which you can type the path to the folder or click a browse button to find it)
- Empty the Contact Folder in Next Synchronization

The Calendar tab specifies the Outlook folder used for scheduled activity information. The same options appear—only the word Calendar replaces Contact.

The Task tab specifies the Outlook folder used for To-do activity information ordered by priority rather than date. The same options appear yet again—only the word Task replaces Contact.

Click **OK** when you've finished with the Advanced Options tabs and you'll arrive back at the Outlook Synchronization Options dialog box. Click **Next** to get to the Outlook Synchronization: Record Selections dialog box. This is where you choose which GoldMine contact records to send to Outlook by choosing among the following options:

- Contact Records Selection—current contact only
- Cutoff [date entry window][time entry window]
- All Contact Records Changed Since Cutoff
- Contacts in Current Active Filter/Group Changed Since Cutoff
- Contacts in Group Changed Since Cutoff [entry window for a scheduled event][entry window for choice of user or user group]
- Contacts with Calendar Activities From [date entry window] To [date entry window]

These options can be combined in limited ways—data entry is automatically controlled according to the selections you make.

Click **Next** when you have specified how contact records are to be selected for sending to Outlook. This displays the Outlook Synchronization: User's Calendar Selection dialog box. Select **My Calendar** if you want to send the selected records from your calendar alone. Select **Others' Calendar** to use the dialog box to select one or more user groups or individual users, including yourself.

Click **Next** to display the Ready to Synchronize dialog box. If you are creating or editing a profile, you will be invited to save it under a profile name before clicking **Finish** to leave the wizard and initiate the synchronization session.

The Process Monitor will display the progress of the synchronization and report the numbers of records transferred.

Synchronizing with Palm Pilot

Suppose you have arranged some activities while on the road with your Palm Pilot. Not a moment should be lost before you get those activities into the contact records in the shared database where they belong. Even your To-do planned activities should be copied to your activity list so that other users can arrange appointments with you.

When you create an activity in Pilot, the cursor appears on a line next to the starting time. Write a forward slash (/) in the graffiti section to tell the Pilot that you are going to issue a command. Write **L** to get the phone number lookup. Select the contact who should be linked with the activity and then select **Add**. You will get a Pilot display containing the following fields:

- First name
- Last name
- Default phone number
- Default field type—select **W** for work

If you now write a colon (:) in the graffiti section, any text that you now add will become the reference text when the activity is copied to GoldMine.

Mine Safety

Don't Mess with Pilot

Do not alter the line that appears in the Pilot notes screen. Doing so could seriously damage your sync.

Palm Pilot has a software disk that has to be installed in your desktop computer so that it will be able to communicate. Follow the Palm Pilot installation instructions.

> **Strike It Rich**
>
> **Install Conduit**
>
> The first time you perform this procedure, GoldMine will ask you to install a Pilot conduit. See the next section for details.

Mapping Pilot fields into GoldMine fields follows the procedure already described for Outlook. From GoldMine select **File**, **Synchronize**, **Sync with Pilot** from the main menu. This displays the Goldmine Pilot Synchronization Wizard dialog box. If you are lucky, you will be able to select **Sync using the settings in the following Profile**. There may be several profiles that you can choose from by clicking the drop-down menu down arrow button.

If you need to create a profile, then you have to select **Start a new session**. Then follow the procedure already described for synchronizing with Outlook.

To lay hands on the GoldMine Pilot Synchronization Wizard, select **File**, **Synchronize**, **Sync with Pilot** from the main menu.

Most of the wizard is the same as that for synchronizing with Outlook. The difference comes in the conduit and the purge. The conduit defines which Pilot record categories are to be updated; the purge defines which data types are to be deleted before synchronization.

> **Strike It Rich**
>
> **Show the HotSync Dialog Box**
>
> GoldMine has a HotSync dialog box that can be used to start a synchronization with Pilot. You can choose to have it appear before synchronizing starts. It also can access the Custom dialog box that will change the synchronization settings in the remote Pilot.

The Palm Desktop is a software application that sets up a default Palm conduit, which is essential to allow GoldMine to synchronize with Palm Pilot.

Installing the GoldMine Pilot Conduit

The first time you try **File**, **Synchronize**, **Sync with Pilot**, GoldMine will complain that it cannot detect an installed GoldMine Pilot conduit. It will ask if you want to install a conduit. If you select **Yes**, the conduit settings will be activated.

The Advanced Options window of the wizard includes a Conduit tab:

Install Conduit	Defines the Pilot record categories to be updated during synchronization.
Uninstall Conduit	Removes the conduit.
Priority	Sets the order of priority between the Pilot conduit and the Palm Desktop conduit. Select **0** or **1** if the Pilot conduit runs first, **3** or **4** if Palm Pilot runs first.

Selecting Data Categories to Purge

The Advanced Options window Purge tab offers a range of settings for purging data in the following categories:

- Address book
- Date book
- To-do list

Purging Pilot data cannot be undone—the prudent GoldMiners backup data before embarking.

Here are some more advanced options:

- Always delete the Pilot Address book/Date book/To-do list before synchronizing. This option is sometimes used by road warriors who maintain contact data in GoldMine but take selections from it when they travel with a Palm Pilot.
- Delete the Pilot Address book/Date book/To-do list in the next synchronization. This option just marks the chosen records for deletion but they remain in place until the next update. This option is used when a user takes over a Palm Pilot used by another and intends to have a clear out at the next synchronization.
- Only delete Pilot Address book/To-do list in selected Categories. You can select which categories are to be deleted in each item—not applicable to the Pilot Date book.
- Synchronize new Pilot items from all categories. Updated or new Pilot data is all sent to GoldMine. You also can select particular categories, such as Unfiled, Business, and Personal. User-defined categories appear after the next synchronization.

Pilot allows you to store address, To-do, and activity information in various categories. The Defaults tab of the Advanced Options window allows you to choose which of these categories are to be synchronized with GoldMine. The default category is Business address.

Selecting Contact Records for Pilot

Records are selected for Pilot by checking either:

- Current contact only includes linked calendar activities.
- All contact records changed since cutoff date and time.

The remaining record selection options allow you to specify the contact transfer set creation method and to select or create a filter or group to delimit the scope of the transfer. Contacts also can be selected on the basis of their connected calendar activities falling within a specified date range.

Pilot can be sent the calendar section activity records of selected users.

Your created transfer profile can be named and saved, or you can go ahead and synchronize without saving it.

Confirming HotSync Settings

The General tab of the Advanced Options of the Pilot Synchronization Wizard includes the Show HotSync option. This displays the profile that is currently selected for synchronizing with Pilot. This display will always appear unless you select **Don't show this dialog again**. You could alternatively uncheck **Show HotSync** in the Advanced Options General tab.

The remaining options are Continue, Change or Edit sync Profile, Stop, or View Summary (of the settings for the current transfer profile).

Synchronizing with a Windows CE Device

The Windows CE operating software is used in the following types of workstation:

- HPCs—Hand-held Personal Computers
- PDAs—Personal Digital Assistants

GoldMine can synchronize with such devices, except for the Notes data.

From the main menu select **File**, **Synchronize**, **Sync with Windows CE PDA**. This elicits the GoldMine WinCE device Synchronization Wizard. The dialog boxes are similar to those for other synchronization wizards. You are invited to select or define a transfer profile, and either save it as a named profile, or synchronize immediately.

Chapter 19 ➤ *High Noon: Synchronizing Records*

The Least You Need to Know

➤ GoldMine has wizards to prepare you for synchronization with anyone who will take you on.

➤ You can share as much or as little information with your colleagues as you care to define in your profile.

➤ After you've got a good transfer profile, sharing the records of your team is absolutely simple.

➤ Microsoft Outlook, Palm Pilot, and anything that runs Windows CE is within synchrony.

Chapter 20

A GoldMine Assembly Line: Automating Processes

In This Chapter

➤ Templates are models or patterns to get things ready for work or for sending off to contacts

➤ Macros are handy helpers triggered from the keyboard or a toolbar icon

➤ Tasks are things you do—perhaps GoldMine could do some of them on your behalf

The very essence of GoldMine is automatic work that helps you keep in touch with your most valued contacts. There are many such automatic processes working behind the scenes. Your scheduled appointments get written to your calendar, for instance. This chapter is about setting up extra automatic mechanisms to help you do business exactly the way you want to.

Making GoldMine Work for You

You must discern where your best business efforts are to be found and make sure you set up polished routines that allow you to do well every time. The experts call them *templates*.

Chapter 5, "24-Karat Printouts: Generating Paper by Printing and Faxing," discussed templates or models for documents such as letters, faxes, emails, and spreadsheets.

Templates are also created in order to have routine typing performed during complex procedures such as constructing a sales opportunity. This was touched on in Chapter 15, "Looking for the Real Seams: Using the Opportunity Manager." Now is the moment to look at Project templates again.

> ### Strike It Rich
>
> ### Projects or Opportunities?
>
> A *project* is a collection of tasks that have to be done to achieve the intended result. GoldMine has a project manager to document this kind of activity, and, in particular, allow many users and perhaps contacts to cooperate. An *opportunity* is a project with an anticipated financial outcome on the positive side—a sales value, which also has a probability. Sales value times probability equals potential.
>
> Now GoldMine has introduced an option to allow sales opportunities to be created without going firm on an expected sales revenue. You could save such things as templates.

So a template is a piece of work that is started but not quite completed. The message template is waiting for the addressee and the date—at least. The project template is waiting to be told what the nonstandard tasks are to be and if any new members are to be added to the team.

How do you use a template? You get hold of a set of contacts and select the template. GoldMine throws the contact data into the template, or copies of it, making each version particular to the individual contact. Then, with your permission, it sends off the letters, or notifies the project team members what they are going to have to do by certain dates.

A template is the basis for a one-step Automated Process: Add contact records to the template and dispatch.

There are already many automatic processes in GoldMine. They are all very sensible and will often keep you out of trouble. Contact management itself is sensible because it encourages you to attach most of your work to particular contact persons and their unique records. GoldMine automatically puts your scheduled actions into your personal activity list and your diary. The same actions appear automatically in the Pending tab of the contact record to which they are pertinent.

The standard automatic procedures of GoldMine are those that are likely to be needed by almost every user, no matter what their business. Customizing is the process of setting up software to suit a particular industry and perhaps a particular company in that industry.

Recording a macro is the process of telling that software what to do in order to suit a particular individual or departmental function in a specific company. Some macros are very elaborate routines that carry out a complex series of actions, making decisions as necessary on the way.

By contrast, I've got a macro that lives in my word processor to type my postal address, telephone number, and email address—in a flash, triggered by an icon that looks like a fish. I shall not speak of the many weird macros that I have had to construct to get this book into the devious formats required by the publisher!

Chapter 4, "The Right Look: Making Things Happen," described how to record a macro in GoldMine. The procedure is very similar to the recording of a macro in Microsoft Word.

The idea of a macro is to perform a useful task that has been developed by GoldMine. This task is put into a sophisticated system for setting up procedures that can be triggered by events defined in various ways. A triggered macro is referred to as an *Automated Process* in GoldMine.

Identifying Useful Processes

GoldMine's concept of automated processes has been developed so as to allow you to set up a series of predefined actions. Each of these actions, called software agents, has enough information to call on the computer to perform a task on each of the contacts, or groups of contacts, in the database.

Each software agent needs to be able to detect whether the moment has come for it to leap into action. It must have a trigger condition defined. For example, if a contact record has just been created, send the contact a specific welcome letter. The trigger is the fact that a new record has been created for which the welcome letter has not yet been dispatched. The action is to dig out the template for the welcome letter and spread over it the details of the contact as defined in the template—address, date, Dear [*Contact Name*], and so on.

An Automated Process could do more. It could use the geographical location of the contact's company to decide which sales representative should pay a visit. The software agent could consult the calendar of the representative and make an appointment. An internal email could be sent to confirm that the representative was going to be able to keep the appointment. When this had been confirmed, the welcome letter could be completed with the name and proposed date of a visit from the representative.

Performing Administrative Tasks

Another little job for an Automated Process is to keep looking over history records to see if any contacts are being neglected. If so, the user responsible can get an automatic email.

Another type of administrative task was discussed in Chapter 19, "High Noon: Synchronizing Records." Here the updating of one database from another was carried out by a transfer profile that controlled the synchronizing software.

The following list gives an idea of the range of activities that can be built into Automated Processes:

- Handling workflow.
- Managing leads and directing them to the sales team.
- Keeping in touch with contacts, prospects, and former customers.
- Sending Warranty Renewal reminders.
- Direct mailing that is customized according to the interests and other details in each contact record.
- Validating newly entered contact data.
- Providing periodical training material to new GoldMine users.

One of the best ways of learning how to really drive down the GoldMine is to go along with someone who has been there before and left a trail in the form of an Automated Process or template.

Mine Safety

GoldMiners Needn't Invent a Pick or a Shovel

Many routine tasks have already been converted into standard GoldMine functions, reports, templates, or wizards.

Check that what you need is not already there before building a new Automated Process.

Working with Processes

To see what processes are available, click the cogwheel icon or choose **Tools**, **Automated Processes**, **Setup Automated Process**. This reveals the Automated Processes Setup dialog box. The process displayed will be the one you looked at previously.

Click the **Maintain** button to see the Processes Listing dialog box, shown in Figure 20.1.

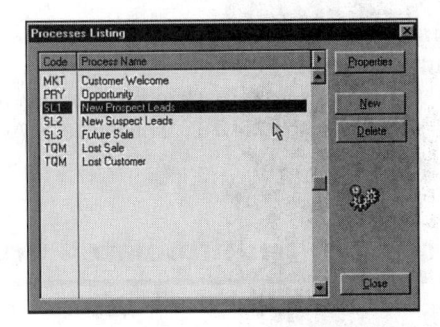

Chapter 20 ➤ *A GoldMine Assembly Line: Automating Processes*

Figure 20.1

When I look at the Processes Listing, I can see that GoldMine has already developed some very good model processes—New Prospect Leads, for example.

The Automated Processes in Table 20.1 are delivered as standard in GoldMine 5.0.

Table 20.1 Process Codes for Classifying Automated Processes

Code	Process Name
MKT	Customer Welcome
PRY	Opportunity
SL1	New Prospect Leads
SL2	New Suspect Leads
SL3	Future Sale
TQM	Lost Sale
TQM	Lost Customer

These process codes are examples provided by GoldMine. You can devise your own system as you create processes or edit their properties.

Interpreting a Process Listing

The illustration of an Automated Process in Figure 20.1 shows that the steps are numbered and presaged by a letter. The letters signify the type of step (see Table 20.2).

Table 20.2 Automate Process Task Codes

Code	Task Type	Conditions
P	Preemptive	Execute this task if and when the condition is satisfied. Evaluate the conditions in the numerical order.
S	Sequential	Execute this task when there are no other sequential steps of lower step number yet unperformed.

The numbers are used to sequence the steps. They are usually assigned in steps of 10 so that later additions may be inserted in the numbered sequence.

As an example, choose **Tools**, **Automated Processes**, **Setup Automated Processes**. You will see the Automated Processes Setup dialog box with a listing of the task steps for the first automated process already installed in your system. The following process listing (see Table 20.3) refers to the New Prospect Leads Automated Process.

Table 20.3 Process Listing of an Automated Process

Seq	Event	Trigger	Action
P10	If sale, attach to Customer Welcome	History	Attach Track
P20	If forecast, attach to Opportunity	Schedule	Attach Track
P30	If sale, remove from New Prospect	History	Remove Track
P40	If forecast, remove from New Prospect	Schedule	Remove Track
S100	Add Prospect to Group for Referral	Immediate	Add to Group
S110	Print Report: Contact for Referral	Immediate	Report Line
S120	Match Prospect Lead to Consultant	Immediate	Schedule
S130	Print FAX: You've Referred	3 Days	Print Been
S140	Print Letter: Check on Referral	4 Days	Print
S160	Schedule follow-up for Referral	Immediate	Schedule

The names of existing processes (tracks) appear with initial capitals in process listings.

Defining Track Properties

If a track has been attached, GoldMine will obey its commands when the time comes to execute Automated Processes during a scan. Just how a track is attached is partly determined in the Properties dialog box that belongs to the Automated Process in which it is used.

The properties of an Automated Process are revealed when you click on the **Properties** button after you have highlighted the process in the Processes Listing.

The Process Options in the Properties dialog box are as follows:

➤ **Allow Only One Attachment of This Process per Contact**—A good idea if the process is for new contacts!

➤ **Allow Users to Attach This Process**—This is not an automatic attachment. It has to be definitely and selectively assigned by a user.

➤ **Execute This Process Immediately When Attached by a User**—This is an extravagance. Normally, automated processes are executed in batches when a scan takes place.

➤ **Execute This Process Only on Complete Scans**—Is there no circumstance when you might want to execute immediately?

➤ **Restart This Process Automatically When It Ends**—This Automated Process is going into perpetual motion—okay for a checking routine.

➤ **Attach This Process to All New Contact Records**—This looks like serious follow-up business that is executed automatically for all new contacts.

> **Learn the Lingo**
>
> **Attaching a Track**
>
> The process listing in Table 20.3 records several uses of the word "attach," as in "attach to Customer Welcome" and "Attach Track."
>
> An Automated Process, or part of it, can be referred to as a track. A *track* may be of any length or complexity—it is the building block of office automation. You can attach several tracks to each other to form a larger unit, which you can then use to build even larger tracks, and so on.

Each process is given a three-character process code by which it can be classified and sorted. Processes can be publicly owned or owned by a particular user or user group that is identified when the process is created—and possibly modified thereafter.

Defining a Track

The GoldMine definition of a track is a sequence of one or more events. An event is an ordered set of step-by-step instructions for processing GoldMine data so as to arrive at a result. A result in this context is a logical outcome, such as Yes or No, and there may be a value as part of the result if the instructions entailed fetching the contents of a GoldMine field or performing a computation.

> **Strike It Rich**
>
> ### Events Are If-Then Combos
>
> You can interpret a GoldMine event as an if-then expansion. If this happens, then the stated consequences should happen also.

The really useful thing that you can do with a track is to attach it to one or more contact records. Then GoldMine will discover it the next time a scan takes place. And then the events in the track can take place—if the conditions are suitable.

Triggering Actions

An essential part of any event is its trigger. An event does not become interesting until and unless something pulls its trigger. Action follows only if the conditions defined in the trigger evaluate to the logical outcome True. A trigger, which may be of any complexity, stays at False unless all its component conditions combine to an overall evaluation of True.

The action part of an event can be of any complexity, and may include further events, each with their own triggers.

One of the useful triggers used in Automated Process management is the "Wait-a-bit" condition. After one event has finished, GoldMine waits for a specified number of days and then launches into the predestined action. After sending the literature, wait a week and then call back. Your calendar reminders are like this. They wait a bit and then send you a warning message.

Sequencing Events

The numbering of events in a process listing is used to determine the order in which GoldMine looks to see if trigger conditions have been met. Lower numbered events are processed before higher.

However, the P events (Preemptive Events) are given top priority. If GoldMine finds that a track has been attached to a contact record, it looks to see if this track contains any preemptive events. These have to be executed in numerical order without delay.

You could think of a preemptive event as an action that has a simple trigger. The event fires at the next scan after all other preemptives in the same track with lower sequence numbers have had their turn.

A contact record can acquire several tracks—so GoldMine will attend to them in order before looking at the next contact to be processed.

Attaching a Track to a Contact Record

You could have a whole garage full of tracks—but nothing would happen with them unless they became attached to a contact record. GoldMine keeps a record of all tracks that have been attached. For each track it notes the event number to be processed next. When an event is triggered, and therefore action occurs, GoldMine updates the number of the event to be processed next. Select **Contact**, **Assign a Process**. This will offer you a listing of the available Automated Processes from which to choose. The listing will be in the order of its user-defined process codes.

Your user ID will be the default entry as the Attaching User. You can select another user. Click **OK**.

Any track that you attach to a contact will appear in the Tracks tab of that contact record. You can attach as many tracks as necessary.

When an event in an attached track is processed, the Tracks tab line entry will be updated to show what the next event will be. The Tracks tab uses the following column headings for the tracks listing:

- **Process**—The name of the Automated Process.
- **Last Event**—The date of the last event, or the date the process was attached if no event has yet been processed.
- **Next Event**—The name and detail of the next event in the track.
- **Trigger**—The condition that will trigger the next event, such as Immediate or Wait 7 Days.
- **Action**—The type of action, such as Print.

If you right-click in the **Tracks** tab of a contact record, the local menu will contain the following options, although only the first option will be active if the Tracks tab is empty:

- **Attach Process**—Choose an Automated Process to attach to this contact record.
- **Remove Process**—Remove the highlighted attached process.
- **Branch to Event**—*Branch*, or skip without actions, to the event that you now select from a listing of all the events in the highlighted attached process.
- **Execute Processes**—Display the Automated Processes Execution dialog box in which you can choose to scan processes for this contact or for many contacts defined by a group or filter that you select (see Figure 20.2).

Executing Processes by a Scan

The Automated Processes Execution dialog box shown in Figure 20.2 is accessed from the local menu of the contact record Tracks tab, or by selecting the gear wheel icon, or by choosing **Tools**, **Automated Processes**, **Execute Processes**.

Figure 20.2

I am going to scan through my Customer contact group to execute all the Automated Processes that have pre-emptive or next events that can be triggered. I have also chosen to attach the Customer Welcome track to each one of them.

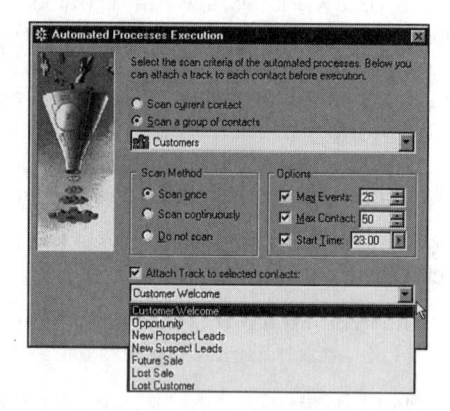

If you have arrived at the Automated Processes Execution dialog box via a contact record, the default choice will be Scan Current Contact.

If you have come via the Tools menu, the default choice will be Scan a Group of Contacts.

The following options can exercise further control over the scan method:

- **Scan Once**—Take one look and then become idle.
- **Scan Continuously**—Keep scanning in case new tracks are attached or the next event triggers become active.
- **Do Not Scan**—Record the entries but do not scan straight away.

The execution of the scan can also be limited by the following options:

- **Max Events**—Spin button entry window to limit the number of events processed.
- **Max Contact**—Spin button entry window to limit the number of contact records processed.
- **Start Time**—Type in, or press **F2** and select from the clock, the time of day for the scan to begin.
- **Attach Track to Selected Contacts**—Click the envelope icon to select an Automated Process from the lookup table.

Click on the **Process** button to launch the scan. As with all processes, the Automated Process Monitor window will roll up encouraging messages as the scan proceeds. You can halt a scan from this monitor and have it resume later.

Building an Automated Process

First you need to plan what you are going to automate. Then you must get to the Automated Processes Setup dialog box via the gear wheel icon or **Tools**, **Automated Processes**, **Set Up Automated Processes**. From the Automated Processes Setup dialog box, click the **Maintain** button to get to the Automated Processes Listing.

Alternatively, click the gear wheel icon labeled **Proc.** This is in the Setup toolbar (see Figure 20.3).

Figure 20.3

I have undocked the Setup toolbar to get to the Proc. icon. From the Automated Processes Setup dialog box, I clicked the Maintain button and created a new process, which I named Process 2000 in the Properties dialog box.

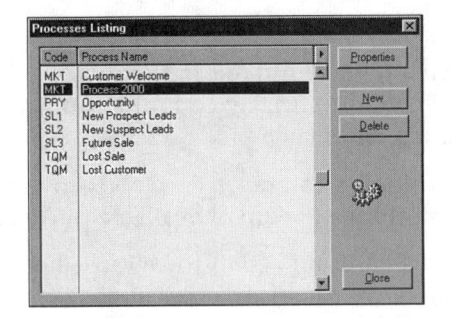

If you intend to alter an existing process, perhaps it would be wise to make a copy under a different name and work with that. Suppose you are creating a new process as shown in Figure 20.3.

Get to the Automated Process Setup dialog box via the gear wheel icon or by choosing **Tools**, **Automated Processes**, **Set Up Automated Processes**. In the Automated Processes Setup dialog box, use the **Process** drop-down menu to select the process you intend to modify. Scroll, if necessary, until you can highlight the event you want to alter. Press **Edit** and change the event by using the drop-down menus in the Event Properties dialog box. Press **OK** to have your alterations made permanent.

If you want to create a new event, press the **New** button to start generating a new event for it in the Event Properties dialog box. The event number you or GoldMine assign to this new event will determine where it will appear in the order of processing.

I have named the first event Test interest. I'll make it a preemptive event—GoldMine has assigned the sequence number 10 to it.

In the Trigger pane of the Event Properties dialog box, I have chosen a trigger type that uses a dBASE condition. Figure 20.4 shows that I have clicked the **Options** button to access the Expression Builder dialog box.

I have already generated the first condition, which is to test that the Interest field of a contact record is not empty. Now I must AND the condition that the Interest field value is equal to Authoring, which is one of the items on my lookup list for this field.

Figure 20.4

I am building the expression that will test whether the Interest of a contact "is not empty" AND "is equal to" the value "Authoring."

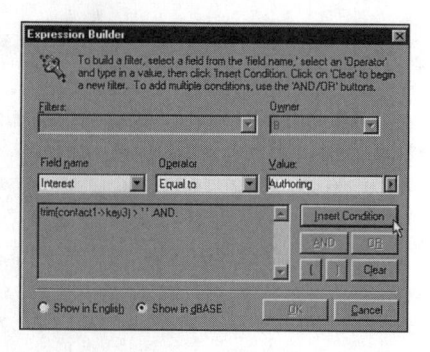

In summary, the first event in my Process 2000 track is an immediate test of whether my contact has expressed a positive interest in the subject of authoring. I add events comprising logical combinations of trigger conditions, operators, and field values, so the track is displayed in the Automated Processes Setup window.

As part of the trigger definition, I can tick a check box to trigger a filter. The **Filters** button allows me to select from a lookup of available filters and groups.

My next job is to attach a significant action to be carried out with every contact for which the trigger conditions are satisfied. I have already chosen to perform the action **Add to Group** by selecting this action from the lookup in the Event Properties dialog box. When I click the **Options** button I will be invited to complete the Add a Group Member dialog box as follows:

- **Group**—Select the name of an existing group belonging to the chosen user.
- **User**—Select the user if not the default logged on user.
- **Membership Reference**—Enter or select an explanatory text.
- **Sort Field**—Enter or select a GoldMine field for sorting contacts in this group.

The track building dialog boxes tend to offer you defaults based on what is possible and what you have chosen previously. There is almost no limit to the length of a track or to the complexity of the events within it.

Selecting What to Trigger On

The Event Properties dialog box has a Trigger panel containing a Trigger On field and other options that vary according to the entry in this field.

Any History Record Can Pull a Trigger

A history trigger can be based on any one of the following activity types:

Phone Calls	E-mails
Next Actions	Appointments
Sales	Others
Lit. Request	Event
To-dos	Forms

Trigger On entries are selected from the following lookup table (see Table 20.4).

Table 20.4 Types of Event Triggers for Automated Processes

Trigger Basis	Setup Method
Elapsed Days	Offers a spin button window for the number of days and a check box to call on a filter chosen from a lookup of filters and groups.
Immediate	Offers a check box to call on a filter chosen from a lookup of filters and groups.

Detail Record	Offers an Options button that displays a Detail Trigger dialog box in which you define the type of detail record:
	
	    Details—you choose which
	    Document Links
	    Additional Contact
	    Referral
	
	You select or type in keyword(s) for each type of record. You may optionally specify the maximum age in days of the record.
	
	Check boxes are provided for:
	
	    Attempt to trigger only once
	    Trigger filter [choose filter or group]

continues

Table 20.4 CONTINUED

Trigger Basis	Setup Method
History Activity	Offers an Options button that displays the possible activity types from which you must choose one, limited if necessary by maximum age, and selected by any of: 　Activity (code) 　Result (code) 　User 　Ref 　Outcome—Any Outcome 　Outcome—Successful 　Outcome—Unsuccessful
Scheduled Activity	Offers an Options button that displays the possible activity types from which you must choose one, limited if necessary by age (+/- days), and selected by any of: 　Activity (code) 　User 　Reference Contains
dBASE Condition	Offers an Options button that displays the Expression Builder dialog box (refer to Figure 20.4).
Disabled	Removes any dialog box to include a trigger in the event you are building.

Strike It Rich

Any Scheduled Activity Can Pull a Trigger

A scheduled trigger can be based on any one of the following activity types:

Call Back	E-mail Message
Next Action	Appointment
Forecast Sale	Other
Lit. Request	Event

If you create an event with a disabled trigger, the action you chose is carried out if the event has become the next action and a scan is taking place.

Choosing an Action for an Event

The **Action** panel of the Event Properties dialog box allows you to select a type of action and then click the **Options** button to specify the parameters of the action you have chosen.

The Perform Action field has the following lookup list:

- **Print Form**—Offers the available form templates and allows you to set up the printing or faxing arrangements.
- **E-mail Message**—Allows you to specify the parameters for email delivery, merge, and file in history.
- **Print Report**—Offers the available file list, divided into reports categories:

    Contact Reports

    Calendar Reports

    Analysis Reports

    Labels and Envelopes

    Other Reports

    You can also specify the contact(s) as All, Current, Filter, or Group.

- **Schedule Activity**—You can choose the scheduled activity type and also specify which user shall be identified with the action, when it takes place:

    Record owner

    Assigned user

    Attaching user

    Logged user

    User from field [field lookup]

    The Option panel has an Activity Details button that allows you to fill in the Schedule a(n)[activity type] dialog box.

    You can also schedule the activity a specified number of days:

    From Today

    From Trigger Date

- **Create History**—Offers a choice of which type of history record to create. You can check Attempt to Trigger Only Once and/or Trigger Filter [choose a filter or group].

- **Create Detail**—You specify the detail and a reference text with notes if you need them. There is an Info tab you can click to access eight numbered fields, each with a data-entry window and a lookup editing facility that you access by clicking the right arrow button on the data entry window.
- **Add to Group**—You select the group and specify the membership reference text.
- **Update Field**—You choose the field and specify a dBASE expression to update it with.
- **Remove Track**—Removes this track from the contact record so that it is not processed in the next scan.
- **Add a New Track**—You choose an existing track to be attached to this contact and check it if you want the track to be executed before carrying on with the parent process.
- **Branch to Event**—You choose an event in the current process for a Goto Event action.
- **Run Application**—Allows you to specify an executable application file with suitable parameters, or dBASE expression. You can also execute a Dynamic Data Exchange (DDE) command for which you supply the service name, topic, and DDE client command.

The Least You Need to Know

- Macros, templates, and Automated Processes (tracks) are pre-arranged pieces of work that save you time and reduce errors.
- Tracks can automatically perform tasks of any complexity if they are attached to a contact record from which they can draw the necessary information.
- You can set up Automated Processes that attach tracks to contacts in many different ways to work for you.

Chapter 21

Line Please: Creating Telemarketing Scripts

> **In This Chapter**
> ➤ Using a telemarketing script
> ➤ Editing an existing script
> ➤ Making a new script
> ➤ Using a script to direct the collection of basic data

There are two advantages to using a GoldMine script for telemarketing or other sales contacts—you are told what to say, and GoldMine automatically provides a way of entering your record of what was said in response. There is also the option of having a branching script that is adjusted as a result of the data you have just entered or information that was in the contact database already.

Selecting a Script

Talking to prospects is best done by real people online, if not face to face. But you can partially automate this process. GoldMine as delivered encourages you to manage your time and keep freshening contact information. A script can be written for those who have a repetitive kind of telephone interview to conduct. As the script unfolds, so GoldMine can be prompted to offer the screens for the user to enter relevant data. Each entry brings up the next element of script, and so on until the interview is concluded.

At any time during the running of a script, the **InfoCenter** button is sitting on the script window ready to open the stored information that could be so arranged as to be in the class of "Really Useful" (see Chapter 18, "Share the Wealth: Distributing Nuggets of Information").

To see the scripts available, select the **Scripts** icon on the toolbar or **View**, **Sales Tools**, **Scripts** from the main menu. Click the down arrow of the **Script** field for the lookup if you want to select another script.

Editing a Script

If you click the **Maintain Scripts** button, you will get the Branching Scripts Listing dialog box, in which you see the number of runs that each script has been through. If you select a script and click the **Edit** button, the Branching Script Profile dialog box will be displayed. Here you can select a question and click the **Edit** button to get the Branching Script Question dialog box.

Figure 21.1 shows how the introductory question of the sample script can be accessed for editing.

Figure 21.1

The answer to this question will be stored in the chosen field of the currently active contact record.

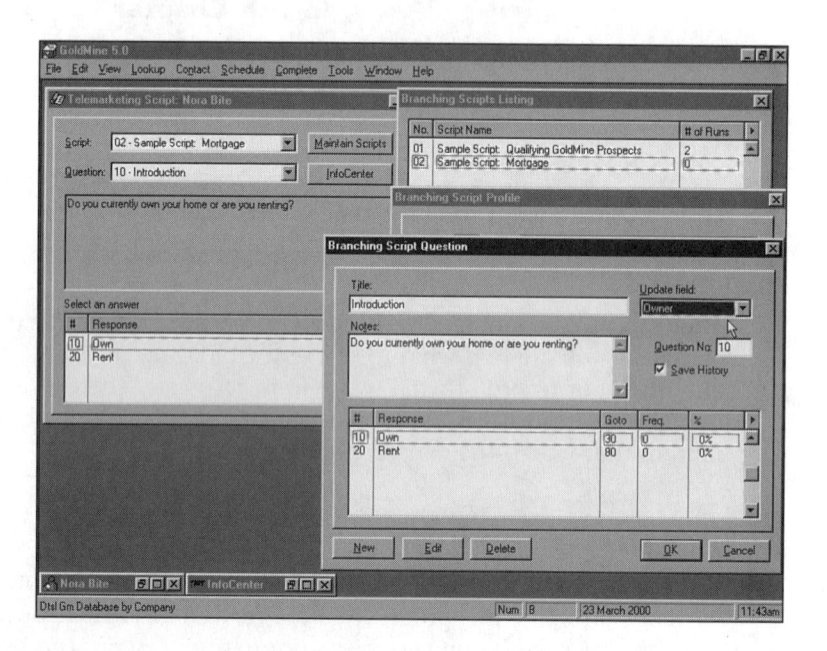

When a script is being used, the sales representative highlights one of the possible answers as being the nearest to the response made by the contact. If you double-click an answer, the script moves on to the next question. Questions also can be arranged to elicit information that is typed in. The chosen or prompted answer can be stored in a field in the contact record. If you single click a question while you are running a script, and right-click to get the local menu, you can choose to add a reference note or to review the dialog box.

If you choose **Enter Note** from the local menu, you will be shown the Reference Note dialog box in which you can type your remarks. Click **OK** to have them saved, and you will be returned to the script.

If you select **Review Dialog** from the local menu, you will see the Review Script display window. This shows the name of the script, the user who is or was running it, and the date and time the script was launched. Each question is reported as **Q** followed by the name of the question. The next line is marked **A** and reports the chosen or typed in answer.

> **Learn the Lingo**
>
> **Mark Up Your Script**
>
> You can freely edit and annotate the questions and answers in the Review Script window. There is a scroll button so that you can access any part of the recorded dialog box. Press **OK** when you want to return to the script. Your edits will be saved automatically until you reach the end of the script.

Each script question, the response, and any editing you did in the Review Script window will be temporarily saved unless the script maintainer has unchecked **Save History** for that question.

Saving the Questions and Answers

When you get to the end of script, the Save Script dialog box is displayed. Here you can elect to permanently save both the dialog and statistics, or one or the other. The statistics are used to compute the frequency and percentage for each answer to each question.

The dialog box reports the user, the time and date of starting and completing the script run, and all the questions and answers with their notes—if any. If you decide to save the dialog box alone, the only information saved will be those questions and answers to which you added a note. You will therefore be able to read your note alongside the question and answer to which it refers.

The dialog box and statistics are both displayed if you click the **Review** button. Before leaving the Save Script dialog box for this script you can enter or select an activity code (job code) and/or a result code.

The History tab of the active contact record will be automatically updated with a line entry showing the result code and a reference text comprising the name of the script. Running a script is classed as an Other action. Whatever detailed information the user chose to save at the end of running the script will be available if you select **Zoom** from the local menu while the History tab entry is highlighted.

Changing the Questions and Answers

If you are editing a question in the Branching Script Question dialog box, the Title field of the question can be directly edited. You also can work on the Notes field in which the speaking script for the user is suggested.

The Notes field also can include reminders to the user of what GoldMine actions should be carried out as a result of the contacts answers—such as scheduling a callback.

If you have highlighted an answer line, you can click the **Edit** button to change the answer or check **Prompt for response**. Check this check box if you want the sales representative to type in the response given by the contact. Questions of this type are flagged by Enter Response in the Response field.

At this stage you can edit the question number and the number to which the script will branch for each of the possible answers.

You might choose a contact record field in which to save the answer to this question by entering its name in the **Update** field, or by selecting a field from the lookup.

If you click the **New** button, you will be invited to type an additional answer possibility together with the number of the question to which the script will branch, if that response is entered.

Creating a New Script

If you select the **Scripts** icon or **View**, **Sales Tools**, **Scripts** from the main menu, you will be offered the Execute Script [contact name] window. This will default to the beginning of the lowest numbered script directed to the active contact. If you click the **Maintain Scripts** button, you will get the Branching Scripts Listing.

Click the **New** button to get the Branching Script Profile dialog box. This allows you to enter a number and title for the new script and to add questions to it using the **New** button.

Directing Data Entry

Your first contact with a contact can be critical. One scheme is to run a directed data entry script. Such a script has a series of questions with but a single answer each. The idea is to get a bunch of GoldMine fields primed with relevant data.

Each question is directed at one particular GoldMine field. And each question is checked as Prompt Response because you want the user to type the answer from the contact into the field that will become the corresponding field value in the contact record.

Put notes as necessary to persuade the user to ask the right questions so that the target field gets the data that is pertinent. As you would expect, you are going to save the text of the dialog box, perhaps the statistics as well, when the script has terminated.

> ### The Least You Need to Know
>
> ➤ A telemarketing script tells you what to say to a potential client so as to get hold of what you need to create a good contact record.
>
> ➤ Scripts can be easily adapted from existing models.
>
> ➤ A branching script asks different questions according to the answers received.
>
> ➤ GoldMine will keep track of the answers and put them in the contact records where this makes sense.
>
> ➤ You can refer to the InfoCenter while running a script.

Chapter 22

Boom Town: Extending GoldMine by Adding on Software

In This Chapter

➤ Installing a customization of GoldMine to suit your industry and your type of contact

➤ Looking for enhancements to GoldMine

➤ Sampling add-on software from the GoldMine Tools CD Catalog

Many GoldMine users will not need all the fields available in the standard contact record. Some users will use the customizing facilities to rename existing fields to suit their own business. This chapter introduces some of the ways in which software and hardware providers have sought to extend GoldMine.

Using GoldMine Industry Templates

There are two classes of add-on software:

- ➤ Templates
- ➤ Applications

A template can range from a partly finished document that needs only to be merged with a contact record to a complex report that entails considerable data processing. Some templates, such as GMLink, for example, set up a relationship between software applications—GoldMine and Word, in this example. GMLink rearranges the configuration of your system so that your word processor is all ready to create GoldMine templates—and GoldMine can easily call up Word to display and edit documents or templates for documents and reports.

> **Fax at Your Fingertips**
>
> For more information on using templates such as GMLink, refer to Chapter 5, "24-Karat Printouts: Generating Paper by Printing and Faxing."

Next in order of complexity come the Industry Templates. These are predefined templates that not only provide you with documents suited to your particular industry, but also redesign the contact and other records of GoldMine to fit in with the way you intend to work.

The standard software of GoldMine can deal with templates that have been saved as GoldMine templates because this process registers the location of a template so that any GoldMine function can find and use it.

If the standard GoldMine software cannot carry out the function you require, then you have to nominate the application that can. For example, the GMLink template nominates Microsoft Word as the processor for documents.

Many third-party manufacturers have developed hardware and software that is compatible with GoldMine. These additional functions are referred to as add-ons. Such an enhancement package might include document templates, modifications to the GoldMine record design, and integral application programs that control hardware and the processing needed to use it.

Choosing an Industry Template

An industry template typically provides a set of resources to customize GoldMine for a particular type of customer. The template might change the local labels on some of the contact record fields, although their global labels will remain as defined by GoldMine.

Having changed the label and hence the purpose of a field, it makes sense to provide a different lookup table for that field. Industry templates often install copious lists of industry-specific values for the important fields.

With a change of field usage, some customized reports might be needed. Again, these will be installed with the template.

GoldMine 5.0 is delivered with the following examples of industry templates:

- ➤ Commercial Real Estate
- ➤ Financial Services
- ➤ Legal Services
- ➤ Life Insurance
- ➤ Mortgage Lending
- ➤ Property and Casualty Insurance
- ➤ Residential Real Estate

Any one of these industry templates might be installed for a specific database. You can have more than one industry template installed—but you must maintain a separate database for each industry template.

Installing an Industry Template

The industry templates provided with GoldMine 5.0 are installed by selecting **Install Industry Templates** from the installation welcome screen that is displayed when the delivery disk is accessed. This displays the welcome screen of the Templates Installer. You are reminded that a target database must be open in GoldMine before you can install an industry template.

The template is likely to install some or all of the following features:

- Custom reports pertinent to the industry.
- Custom details, which are extra fields attached to contact records that can be updated and subsequently used in searches.
- Custom key fields, which are indexed key fields Key1–5 that can be relabeled.
- User-defined fields that can be assigned to information pertinent to the industry. The template will probably install an extensive relevant lookup list for each GoldMine standard and user-defined field.

Select **Next** to launch in installation dialog box. You are invited to select the industry template you want to install. Click **Next** and you will be shown a list of the possible options with the recommended default choices already ticked. This is a typical list:

- Fields
- Details
- F2 Lookups
- GoldMine Reports
- Automated Processes
- Filters
- Delete all existing F2 Lookups

All except the last item are suggested. This arrangement of options will add the industry template F2 choices to those already in your field lookup tables.

Select the **Next** button and you will be warned that the installation of the chosen industry template might take some time and cannot be cancelled after it begins. Then you select **Finish** to display the process monitor and complete the installation.

> **Restart After Installing**
>
> Changes to GoldMine do not take effect until you have shut down and restarted your computer.

Copying and Moving Records

Moving records between databases might be needed when rearranging sales territories, or when setting up databases for newcomers to use for practice. If a contact moves from one territory to another, you might want to move the contact record. A contact might move from one industry to another—from one database to another built under a different template.

Open the database containing the records you intend to copy or move. Select by tagging, or through a filter or group, the records to be copied or moved. Select from the main menu **File**, **Synchronize**, **Copy/Move Records**.

Use the lookup to identify the destination database. Click to process either the **Current Record** or a **Group of Contact Records**. Choose a filter or group to define the records to be processed.

Identify the **Transfer** method as either **Copy Records** or **Move Records**. If you intend to move the selected records, you have to select **Sync Deletions**. This marks these records as deleted so as to prevent them from being synchronized by any other GoldMine system.

When you click the **Go** button, the process monitor will track the progress of the copy or move operation. You will not see the effect on the receiving database until you open it.

> **Copying Records Between Industry Templates**
>
> If you copy one or more records from a database built using an industry template with extra tabs and fields, you will loose the data in these extra fields if the receiving database does not have corresponding fields. The fields do not have to share the same local name or label to correspond—only the same GoldMine global field name.
>
> If you copy a record from a standard GoldMine record to a database using an extended set of fields, the incoming record will be copied to the record format of the receiving database.

Exploring the Add-On Categories

The GoldMine Industry Templates and related products are classified according to the following Industry Solutions list:

Accounting
Auto Dealer
Banking
Business Services
Computer Solutions
Construction/Home Building
Financial Services
Government/Public Service
Health Care Solutions
Insurance
Legal Services
Manufacturing
Mortgage Lending
Non-Profit
Personnel
Professional Sports
Public Relations

Part 5 ➤ *Administering a GoldMine Installation*

Publishing
Real Estate
Security Services
Telecom
Trade Associations
Utilities
Wholesale Distribution

You can see this list by selecting **Help**, **GoldMine Web Site** from the main menu. At the Web site, click **Industry Solutions**. Alternatively use a Web browser to reach http://www.goldmine.com/care/isolutions/. Click any industry to see a selection of products that are compatible with GoldMine.

Sampling the GoldMine Tools Catalog

A selection of add-on products is demonstrated in the GoldMine Tools CD Catalog, which is delivered with GoldMine 5.0. Insert the CD and allow it to autorun.

Some CD-ROMs Play Themselves

Most software products that are delivered on a CD will start to run as soon as you put them in your computer. There is often an option to take a tour of the software as well as the option to go ahead with an installation.

Yet another possibility is for the CD to install—with your permission—a document reader if you do not already have it. The GoldMine Tools CD Catalog will install the Acrobat reader, which it needs to show you the products and play the commentary.

If you have disabled the Autorun feature, or if your system does not respond when you insert a CD, select the **Start** button and choose **Run**. Click the down arrow button for the drop-down menu to see if you have an entry like D:\AUTORUN.EXE. Type this in if you do not have one to select. If you have more than one hard disk, your CD drive letter might not be D.

Click the **OK** button to start the CD.

Chapter 22 ➤ *Boom Town: Extending GoldMine by Adding on Software*

You can review the Tools CD contents by Categories, Products, or Companies.

These are the Categories:

- Accounting Links
- Addressing
- Customer Management
- Data Utilities
- Faxing
- HelpDesk
- Internet Technology
- Label Printer
- Mailing/Shipping
- Mapping
- Order Entry
- PDA Integration
- Quoting
- Report Writing
- Sales Force Management
- Telephony
- Training

For each category, there is an annotated list, and for each item on this list there is an audiovisual introductory presentation and demonstration.

The Least You Need to Know

➤ GoldMine is compatible with a wide range of predesigned forms, documents, and spreadsheet templates.

➤ A template can contain software that rearranges the fields, their labels, and their lookup lists.

➤ Many industry templates are available—seven are included on the GoldMine 5.0 installation disk.

➤ A list of industry templates and associated products is on the GoldMine Web site at http://www.goldmine.com/care/isolutions/.

➤ You can see and hear a demonstration of many add-ons by running the GoldMine Tools CD Catalog delivered with GoldMine.

315

Chapter 23

Getting Tricky: Installing to a Network and Troubleshooting

In This Chapter

➤ Installing to a Windows 95/98/2000 or NT 4.0 Network

➤ Coping with common problems

➤ Seeking additional information

This chapter is for the more experienced user who has taken on the responsibility of installing GoldMine to a network. There are some suggestions for troubleshooting that apply to all GoldMine installations.

Installing to a Network

The following types of networks can be equipped with GoldMine 5.0:

➤ Windows 95/98/2000
➤ Windows NT 4.0

Part 5 ➤ *Administering a GoldMine Installation*

> **Strike It Rich**
>
> **NT Is Becoming More Important**
>
> The software of Windows 2000 and the GoldMine applications that are to work with it frequently use NT procedures. NT is not just for big systems.

Installing GoldMine 5.0 on either of the Windows network systems is carried out from a workstation that is not the network server. Peer-to-peer networks do not have a dedicated network server computer. Nevertheless, GoldMine requires that you choose one of the fastest workstations in your network to become the GoldMine server, even though it will not be wholly dedicated to this task alone.

Installing GoldMine 5.0 on a network server begins with you inserting the installation CD-ROM. Select **Install GoldMine 5.0** from the initial screen. Select **Next** to view the Software License Agreement. Select **Yes** if you agree with the terms.

Complete the Setup Type dialog box by checking **Custom** as the type of setup. Either select **Browse**, and type `C:\Apps\GoldMine`, or navigate to the location of your current GoldMine, if you have one. Select **OK**.

Select **Next** and check each of the following:

- Program Files
- Help Files
- Reports & Form Templates
- Workstation Setup Files
- Uncheck Database Engine

When you've done so, select **Next**.

The file types you have specified are now copied from the installation disk to the destination folder.

You are then required to type your registration information, with your serial number and key code taken from your License Certificate card.

Chapter 23 ➤ *Getting Tricky: Installing to a Network and Troubleshooting*

> **Learn the Lingo**
>
> **Database Engine?**
>
> The Borland Database Engine (BDE) is a piece of software that can be shared between several different applications and can access various databases. GoldMine automatically installs the BDE and configures it to suit most types of network use. Knowledgeable network supervisors can customize the settings.

Sharing the Directory

While you are at the network server workstation, right-click on **Start.** Select **Explore**. Navigate the C drive until you can select the **apps** directory folder, or whatever folder you installed GoldMine to. Right-click to display the local menu. Select the **Sharing** tab.

If your system is Windows 95 or 98, click **Shared As** and type the **Share Name** (such as `Program Files`). Enter an explanatory note in the **Comments** field to make it clear that this folder is shared for GoldMine. Select **Full** as the **Access Type**.

If your system is Window NT 4.0 or Windows 2000, click **Shared As** and type the **Share Name** (such as `Program Files`). Enter an explanatory note in the **Comment** field to make it clear that this folder is shared for GoldMine. Click **Permissions**. Select every GoldMine user, or a defined group that includes all GoldMine users. Select **Full Control**.

In both types of systems, Explorer will mark a directory that has been correctly shared with a hand icon.

Configuring the Workstations

Each individual workstation must be configured to communicate with the workstation you have designated as the GoldMine server.

Launch Windows Explorer. Select **Tools**, **Find**, **Computer** from the main menu. The display will include at least the GoldMine server computer in the location Network Neighborhood. Double-click the name of this computer in the listing. Doing so will display which resource folders on this computer are shared. Select the folder containing GoldMine, most likely Program Files. Right-click for the local menu and select **Map Network Drive** to display a dialog box of this name. Select an unused drive letter from the **Drive** drop-down list. This drive letter has to be one that can be designated the same on all GoldMine user computers in the network.

Select the check box **Reconnect at logon** to make sure that this workstation will have access to the GoldMine server under the drive letter designated—G, for example.

Personalize User GoldMine Icons?

Some users have more than one type of work they do. They could perhaps use GoldMine in quite different ways in each case. To ensure that a user chooses the right configuration for the work role, you could launch GoldMine from different icon buttons.

At each workstation, with all programs minimized, right-click and select **New**, **Shortcut**. In the **Command Line** field, type `G:\PROGRAM_FILES\GOLDMINE\GMW5.EXE /u:Panner`, or the corresponding path to your GMW5.EXE.

This is only applicable if the GoldMine user at the workstation really does want to sign on as Panner.

Make as many shortcuts as you need for each user or type of user.

With a GoldMine icon on the workstation desktop, you can double-click it to launch GoldMine. However, you must sign on as MASTER, and you must use the installation password ACCESS. Now hold down the **Ctrl** button while you click **OK**. Doing so reveals the Contact Set Databases window containing the names of all the available contact set databases.

Right-click for the local menu and select **Attach Database**. For the **Description** field, type in `Workstations map for Common`. The Path(Alias) field should receive your GoldMine location, such as `G:\PROGRAM_FILES\GOLDMINE\GMW5.EXE`. Select **OK**.

Highlight the new database line entry and select **Open**.

As the person with Master rights, you will have created a suitable population of users to inhabit your network outposts.

First-Level GoldMine Troubleshooting

The definition of a first-level problem is tied to what the normal GoldMine user or supervisor can expect to deal with using the standard functions provided. Errors can occur during installation and during normal operation. There is not always a clear distinction between the two sources of error—some error messages can appear during or after installation.

If GoldMine has been running and a problem occurs, assume first of all that it is due to a corrupt index. Consult Chapter 17, "Be the Boss of the Territory: Maintaining Databases." Then select the **Index** icon or **File**, **Maintain Databases** from the main menu. Rebuild and re-index the database you were using when the problem occurred.

Interpreting an Insufficient Memory Error

If you are in the process of installing GoldMine, the following message might appear: `Insufficient Memory to Run Application`. The same message can appear after a successful installation. There are two probable causes:

> Insufficient memory to start installing GoldMine. Free off at least 65,000KB of physical memory and try again.
> GMW5.EXE or one of the GoldMine DLL files has been corrupted. Replace GMW5 and files *.DLL in the directory to which you are trying to install GoldMine or in which it was running before the error message appeared.

Interpreting a BDE Error

Another problem that can appear during or after installation concerns the IDAPI32.DLL file or the configuration file IDAPI32.CNF that is needed to set it up. This driver file is needed for the Borland Database Engine (BDE), which GoldMine needs to access the databases.

> **Mine Safety**
>
> **Shun the BDE Administrator**
>
> Select **Tools**, **BDE Administrator** from the main menu only if you are sure you know what you are doing. This utility affects all programs in your computer that use the BDE to access databases, not only GoldMine.

It is possible that another application has been using the BDE or is still using it and has altered the BDE Registry entries from those needed by GoldMine. If you have installed GoldMine in a workstation that already has an incompatible or corrupted version of the BDE, this problem could occur. GoldMine requires BDE version 4.51 or higher.

Users on a Local Area Network (LAN) can call on a shared installation of the BDE. When a GoldMine on a workstation is launched, it will check the Registry for the location of the BDE, which GoldMine will then load from that location. If the BDE is not identified in the Registry, GoldMine will look in the Registry subdirectory \Setup\BDEShare. After the BDE has been located and loaded, GoldMine will update the Registry with a reference to its location.

If the BDE is still not found, the GoldMine: Find IDAPI32.DLL dialog box will be displayed in which you can type the path to this DLL file or browse for it. If you cannot find this file, you have to cancel the dialog box and reinstall the Borland Database Engine.

The remedy might be to exit from other programs that are using the BDE and try GoldMine again. The normal mode of operation is for each application to have a configuration registered in the BDE for each mode of database access and format that it requires. GoldMine installation sets this up for dBASE files by default.

If shutting down other programs does not work, then it might be necessary to remove the current BDE Registry entries using the BDE Administrator utility. Select **Tools**, **BDE Administrator** from the main menu. Do not change anything without professional advice.

Troubleshooting the Link to Word

There is a useful troubleshooting remedy in Microsoft Word, after you have installed the link from GoldMine. From the Word main menu, select **GoldMine**, **Uninstall GoldMine Link**. This will uninstall all the components of the link. If your link gives you any trouble, uninstall it and shut down your Word to save the Normal.dot template without any GoldMine frills. Then, reopen Word and reinstall the link by locating the GMLink.dot template and selecting **Open**.

Exploring GoldMine Support Services

The first line of support is the literature supplied with GoldMine and the installed help files. The second line is the GoldMine Web site. If you have GoldMine running, select **Help**, **GoldMine Web Site** from the main menu.

Support from GoldMine Software Corporation is provided for GoldMine 5.0 and GoldSync for matters that are strictly within the scope of GoldMine software. For example, problems arising in add-on software are the responsibility of the supplier of that software. You also can obtain advice on these matters from an Authorized GoldMine Solutions Partner. Consult the GoldMine Web Site at http://www.goldmine.com/.

Chapter 23 ➤ *Getting Tricky: Installing to a Network and Troubleshooting*

Consulting GoldMine Newsgroups

A Web browser or newsreader can get you into GoldMine technical support newsgroups. You can browse the messages there and other readers will offer their advice if you post a query of your own. GoldMine resellers and dedicated GoldMine Technical Support engineers also join in these newsgroups.

After you have GoldMine up and running, you can select **Help**, **GoldMine Newsgroups** from the main menu and choose your source of wisdom.

> **Learn the Lingo**
>
> **Get Your Internet Browser Primed with Newsgroups**
>
> In the newsgroups part of the GoldMine Web site, there are instructions for setting up Internet Explorer so that it might be primed with the current newsgroups and their locations.

You might find some of the existing messages interesting. They will tend to cover matters that are not explicitly discussed in the help files or in the GoldMine manuals. However, you sometimes find a beginner's plea for help—which might or might not elicit useful replies.

Emailing a query or request for help to a newsgroup is straightforward. Your Internet browser, such as Outlook Express, will allow you to select a news message and then make a New Post to it in the form of an email. Your outgoing news message will wait in your out tray until you next update your newsgroups.

> **The Least You Need to Know**
>
> ➤ Most problems arising after a successful installation can be solved by rebuilding database files.
>
> ➤ Almost all other problems are cured by shutting down GoldMine and starting up again.
>
> ➤ The manuals, the help files, and the GoldMine Web site are full of useful advice.

Glossary

action Task performed automatically in response to a trigger as part of an Automated Process.

active contact record The top contact record in an active contact record window. Functions normally apply to the active contact record. Also referred to as the record with input focus.

activity list A window comprising 14 tabs that list different types of scheduled and completed activity records.

add-on A package of software and/or data available as an optional enhancement to GoldMine.

additional contact Information about individuals associated with the primary contact stored in the Contacts tab.

application An independent program that can be called upon by GoldMine to perform a task and return the result—such as Microsoft Word.

Automated Process™ A track or sequence of two or more events. Each event interprets instructions to perform defined activities.

Boolean expression A logical statement that evaluates to either True or False.

Borland Database Engine (BDE) The software used by GoldMine and some other applications to access various databases.

branching script A question-and-answer framework through which the user can take different routes according to the responses of the contact.

browse window   A list of data items from which a selected item will be copied to the field to which the browse list or lookup table belongs. A browse list, lookup table, or drop-down menu can be accessed by pointing to a field space to display the field input window, and then clicking on the right arrow button to display a drop-down menu. Fields can be customized to display a lookup table or browse list automatically when selected. Point to the field input window and press the F2 key or right-click to access a dialog box to edit the browse list.

calendar   A window with six tabs showing scheduled activities and events from the activity lists of selected users in various calendar formats. The seventh Peg-Board tab displays which users are online or on different types of absence.

calendar file   Store of records of activities scheduled for a future date.

contact listing   A listing of the contacts in the open database file.

contact record   The standard unit of information in GoldMine. The contact is the focus of all records of pending and past activities.

control menu   The Windows menu of standard commands to manipulate the active window.

directed data entry   Allowing a field value to be entered rather than Yes or No during the running of a branching script.

docked user   A network or standalone user licensed to operate GoldMine in either the docked or undocked mode who has a sublicense for each mode.

document link   A recorded association between a particular document and a contact record. The document can be in any format accessible by the GoldMine installation or one of its associated applications.

Dynamic Data Exchange (DDE)   Windows functionality that allows Microsoft and compatible applications to exchange commands and information with each other and with GoldMine.

End User Screen   A predefined view containing 10 fields that appears in the Fields tab of the contact record if no other field view has been defined and/or selected. See also *Tech Support Screen*.

Event   1. A scheduled calendar activity defined by its duration and the users to be present, such as a conference.

Event   2. A step-by-step instruction comprising a trigger and an action. Part of an Automated Process or track.

F2 lookup   A browse window accessible by pressing the special function key F2.

field   A unit of information contained in a record.

Glossary

field view   A set of up to 999 user-defined fields maintained in the Fields tab folder of the contact record. A selection of these fields can be assigned a tab name and will appear as a separate tab.

filter   A sort specification applicable to the contact database.

forecasted sale   A potential or anticipated sale logged for tracking and planning purposes and associated with particular contacts and users.

form designer   A layout functionality for creating custom report templates that access the GoldMine contact database.

freeform data   Observational or subjective information recorded in freeform text.

GoldSync   An enhancement for GoldMine's method of automating the synchronizing of remote GoldMine systems over standard telephone lines, networks, or the Internet.

group   A subset of contact records.

history   A contact record tab that displays the chronological log of all completed activities related to that contact.

history file   A store of records of scheduled activities that have been completed. History records are removed from the calendar file.

indexed field   A contact record field for which GoldMine maintains an index file to facilitate rapid retrieval of the contact record on the basis of the field value: Company, Contact, Last (name), Phone1, City, Zip, Account No., Key 1, Key 2, Key 3, Key 4, Key 5.

InfoCenter   A GoldMine window arranged in Help file layout that includes functions to maintain and display any type or format of information useful to an organization or an individual user. The information items can be individually linked to a contact record.

.INI   The file suffix that denotes a special text file used to change functionality in GoldMine or GoldSync. Some entries are automatically generated; some .INI settings can be edited by the user, such as defining a bitmap signature file.

input focus   Directs commands or typed input to the currently selected record, or its entry, in a listing.

KnowledgeBase   A tabbed division of the InfoCenter that stores information shared by all users.

limit   A parameter used to constrain a Boolean expression to certain data types or range of values.

local menu   The set of commands available in some browse windows and window panels. Accessed by pointing and pressing the local menu key, or key F2, or by right-clicking in the panel. Many fields and panels have an arrow button that will display the local menu or lookup as appropriate. A window may have different local menus for different panels. See also *browse window*. The local menu commands affect only options or information in the currently selected browse window.

macro   A stored recording of a series of commands and/or keystrokes that can be replayed rapidly, or as recorded from either a toolbar icon or the command line.

Main Menu   The bar display located directly under the GoldMine title bar. Contains first level commands that open pull-down menus of lower level commands.

maintain   To edit or adjust one or more parameters of a record or set of records.

merge code   One or more special codes to identify additional contacts to be merged with a selected template document.

merge/purge   A method of consolidating information and deleting duplicate records from the open database under control of the Merge/Purge Wizard.

Multiple Document Interface (MDI)   Windows functionality that allows GoldMine to simultaneously display multiple dialog boxes or other information displays.

operand   Data upon which an operator determines the outcome of an expression, in a filter or trigger, for example.

operator   The symbol or term that specifies a function to be performed on data (the operand) during a search, such as equal to, greater than, or less than.

opportunity   An entity managed by the GoldMine Opportunity Manager, such as a complex sale that could entail a group working as a team with several organizations, contacts, products, and services as a package that could be renegotiated while in process.

organizational chart   A GoldMine function that portrays relationships between contacts in a tree-like structure displayed in a panel in each of the contact records associated with it.

partial contact record   The defined space used to store the primary information that is displayed in the upper portion of a contact record. Used automatically by GoldMine to conserve space when a new record is created. Expands to become a complete contact record as new information is entered.

pending activity list   A contact record tab titled Pending that displays a chronological log of all scheduled activities related to that particular contact that can be viewed in a contact record.

Glossary

PersonalBase A tabbed division in the InfoCenter that remains private to the user who created the items in it. An item in the PersonalBase can be linked by the owner to a contact record.

primary contact information Information in the upper portion of the contact record that displays the company name and the relevant particulars of the primary or most-used contact at that company.

project A complex team activity that is managed like a sales opportunity except that the probability of achieving a stated financial outcome is not part of the planning.

remote synchronization The process that transfers sets of data from one GoldMine or GoldSync system to and from other such systems in order to update the shared contact databases.

report generator A function that combines standard or customized report templates with information from a GoldMine database in order to display or print it. See also *form designer*.

selected record The record identified as active by a highlighted entry in a browse window with input focus. The target for any commands or typed input.

sort To arrange any type of record in order according to the values in the Sort field.

spin control Click on up or down arrows to scroll contact-by-contact through the contact records in an open record window. Each contact record window has its own spin control.

statistical data The type of stored information that does not depend on a subjective view or impression recorded in freeform text.

status bar The bar display located at the bottom of the GoldMine work area. Shows system-related information such as time, date, user, and the status of NUM lock and CAPS lock. If you have set this in your preferences the status bar can show a brief description of a highlighted menu command or a toolbar icon confronted by your mouse pointer.

tab folder A tab or tab folder is a view of information or a section of a dialog box. The titles of available tabs are arranged along the top of the tab folder panel as a tab bar. If there are many tabs, only part of a tab may be visible. Left arrow and right arrow buttons are provided, if necessary, to move along the titles. Clicking a tab brings it to the top as the open tab, and a local menu may become available. Large tabs may have vertical scroll bars. The space in the window available for the tab folders may be adjusted by clicking on the panel separating border and dragging.

Tech Support Screen A predefined field view containing seven fields. The title field of the Fields tab shows which predefined screen is open. The local menu allows you to select the End User Screen or any other user-defined screens that have been created.

telemarketing script See *branching script*.

template A model, pattern, or boilerplate that can be merged with contact data to create a document such as a printable document or a complex record entity such as a project or sales opportunity. A template can contain dynamic elements such as macros that initiate actions in addition to compiling a merged document.

title bar The top line of the GoldMine window, where the version number will be displayed. The title bar of another application, such as Microsoft Word, will be similarly labeled. A record title bar will include the company or contact used to identify the contact record plus any filter or group that is activated. Title bars typically displays the software name and the version number, such as GoldMine 5.0.

toolbar A set of mouse-sensitive icons providing one-click execution of selected commands. Toolbars may be moved, edited, and created. Predefined toolbar layouts may be displayed by selecting **Edit**, **Toolbars**. Form designer has a toolbar that is displayed as necessary.

track A sequence of defined workflow processes used to perform tedious, repetitive tasks. See also *Automated Process*.

trigger A predefined logical condition, based on GoldMine data, that initiates a particular action in an Automated Process.

undocked user A GoldMine user working on a remote or mobile GoldMine system. The user must have an undocked sublicense that corresponds with a docked license. Any user can have only one undocked sublicense.

VCR controls Three buttons located in the top-left corner of the Calendar that change the displayed time frame one time unit in the past, to the present, one unit in the future. The units will be day, week, month, or year, depending on the calendar tab view selected.

wizard A predefined sequence of windows and dialog boxes that guide the user through a complex task.

work area The part of the GoldMine window that displays the open windows and in which they can be moved or reshaped. Typical windows opened in the workspace or work area include one or more open contact record windows, the Calendar, the Activity List, and the Contact Listing. Only one open window can be active at a time.

Index

Symbols

: (colon), 281
, (comma), 118, 279
// (double slash marks), 41
... (ellipsis), 13, 29
% (percent sign), 41
; (semicolon), 41, 118
/ (slash), 281

A

About command (Help menu), 16, 109, 114
About to Delete Records dialog box, 251
absolute minimal backups, 235
academic mortarboard icon, 259
accepting Group Profiles, 170
access, controlling
   contact databases, 201-202
   menus, 199
   user, 194
access permissions, assigning to users, 196-197
Access tab, 192, 196-198
Access to Others panel, 198
access to others permissions, 198-199
Accessories command (Programs menu), 35
account numbers (global changes), 244
accounts (Internet email), setting up, 89-90
Action panel, 301
actions, 294
   selecting for events, 301-302
   triggering, 294
Actions tab, 138
Activate button, 170
Activate Group command (Contact Group menu), 168
Activate Groups local menu, 171
   Delete, 171
   Edit, 171
   Find, 171
   New, 171
   Output to, 171
   Sort Members, 171
   Sync Contact, 171
   View, 171
Activate Section command (organizational tree local menu), 257
activating
   groups, 167-168
   toggle options, 38-39
active contacts, 152
active records, 36
activities, 25. *See also* tasks
   completing, 57-58, 141
   dating, 143-145
   deleting (Calendar), 147
   linking to contacts, 141-142
   private, 136, 149
   replying, 141
   rescheduling, 147
   scheduling, 56-57, 137, 146-147
   time, setting, 145-146
   viewing
      details, 26
      history, 140
      uncompleted, 25
Activity Details button, 301
Activity List, 25
   filtering, 138-139
   tabs, 137-138
   viewing, 26, 137-140
Activity List command (View menu), 25-26, 52, 136-137, 140, 219

The Complete Idiot's Guide to GoldMine 5

Activity List window, 137
activity window, 26
Actv field, 187
Add a Group Member dialog box, 298
Add a New Record dialog box, 37, 250
Add Members command (Contact Group menu), 168
add-ons, 15, 309-310
    applications, 309
    templates, 309-310. *See also* Industry templates
adding
    fields, 129
    items to To-do list, 136
    licenses, 110
    members to groups, 168, 172
    notes to contact records, 39
Additional Contact option button, 153
(Additional) Contacts tab, 242
addresses (Web sites), editing, 99
administering GoldMine, 119
advanced options (Outlook), setting, 279-281
Advanced Options window, 279-281
Agents Administrator command (Server Agents menu), 58
Alarm check box, 88, 148
Alarm tab, 50
Alarmed tab, 138
alarms, setting, 148-149
Alerts tab, 43
Allow File to Synchronize check box, 214, 254
Allow File to Synchronize field, 265
Allow Hot Link check box, 78
alphabetizing
    books/folders/pages, 261
Always Auto Refresh Field List check box, 65

Analysis command (View menu), 52, 210, 219, 224
Analysis menu commands
    Forecast Analysis, 210, 219
    Graphical Analysis, 219
    Leads Analysis, 219, 224
    Quota Analysis, 219-220
    Sales Analysis, 219, 227
    Statistical Analysis, 219
Analysis report, 185
Analyze button, 210, 219, 228
Analyze option (Leads Analysis [Last Run] dialog box), 226
analyzing
    leads, 223-224
    quotas, 220
    sales performance, 227-228
    sales pipelines, 219-220
App Identifier field, 69
Application key, 40, 168
applications
    add-on software, 309
    launching, 106
Appts tab, 138
arranging windows, 46-47
assembling teams, 216-217
Assign a Process command (Contact menu), 295
assigning
    General Access permissions, 197
    icons to macros, 61
    memberships to users (user groups), 193
    probabilities (sales), 208
    quotas, 220
    user access permissions, 196-197
    users to user groups, 192-193
Associated Document File Name field, 214
Attach a File toolbar icon, 260
Attach VCard check box, 87
Attached Documents panel, 86
Attached File tab, 268

attaching
    descriptions, 41
    documents, 86
    explanation, 41
    tracks, 293-295
Attachments button, 86
Automated Process Monitor window, 296
Automated Processes, 58-59, 289-291
    creating, 297-298
    events (triggers), 299-301
    monitoring history records, 289
    process listings, 291-292
    selecting trigger, 298-299
    synchronizing records, 289
    task codes, 291
Automated Processes command (Tools menu), 58, 290-292, 296-297
Automated Processes Execution dialog box, 296
Automated Processes menu commands
    Execute Processes, 58, 296
    Set Up Automated Processes, 58, 290-292, 297
Automated Processes Setup dialog box, 290-292, 297
Automatic Maintenance dialog box, 237
automatic registration (licenses), 112
automatically updating GoldMine, 114
automating
    fields, 70
    maintenance, 237-239
Available Time tab, 57

B

backing up
    data, 234-235, 244
    GoldMine, 8

332

Index

backups, 235
Basic toolbar, 29, 39
BDE (Borland Database Engine), 319
BDE Administrator command (Tools menu), 59, 321-322
BDE errors, troubleshooting, 321-322
bi-directional synchronization, 273
binoculars icon, 261
books
    alphabetizing, 261
    creating, 260-261
Borland Database Engine (BDE), 319
Branching Script Profile dialog box, 304-306
Branching Script Question dialog box, 304-306
Browse List window, 41
browse lists, 41, 118-119
browsers, 95
browsing transfer sets, 276
Build button, 160
Build Filter button, 162, 172
Build Group check box, 170, 197
Build tab, 160, 250
building
    filter expressions, 158-159
    filters, 158-160
    organizational trees, 256-257
buttons
    Activate, 170
    Activity Details, 301
    Analyze, 210, 219, 228
    Attachments, 86
    Build, 160
    Build Filter, 162, 172
    Cancel, 198
    Cc, 86
    Clear, 160
    Clone, 130, 203
    Close, 184
    Contact, 54
    Contact Info, 93

Copy All, 16
Delete, 249
Drill Down, 159
Edit, 69, 123, 220, 304-306
Expand, 199
Fields, 128, 203
File Browse, 214
Filter, 298
Go, 312
GoldMine, 16
InfoCenter, 304
Insert Condition, 161
Jump, 183
Layout, 182-184
Look up, 156
Maintain, 229, 290, 297
Maintain Scripts, 304-306
Maximize, 146
Members Setup, 193
Merge and Edit, 76
More Options, 90
Net-Update Now, 111
New, 22, 48, 203, 306
New Field, 127
New License, 110
New Site, 110
OK, 198
Options, 86, 184, 297
Or, 161
Pause, 60
Preferences, 194
Print, 184, 189
Process, 296
Properties, 122, 160, 184, 194-195, 201-203, 292
Queue, Calendar and History Options, 86-87
Release, 162
Remove License, 110
Reports, 181
Reset, 48
Reset All, 198
Review, 306
Save as Defaults, 185
Save Settings, 188
Schedule, 57, 149
Screen Fields, 128
Search All, 159, 162

Select, 147
Set All, 198
Show Topic in KnowledgeBase, 261
Sort, 184
Start Timer, 46
Stop, 60
System, 16
Today, 28
Undock Users, 110
Zoom, 224

C

Calendar
    deleting activities, 147
    displaying, 142
    rescheduling activities, 147
    scheduling activities, 146-147
calendar (Opportunity Manager), viewing, 213-214
Calendar command (View menu), 52, 142
Calendar Data panel, 187
calendar records, 187
Calendar Report Options dialog box, 184
Calendar tab, 50, 280
Call Back dialog box, 250
calls, private, 149
Calls tab, 138
Cancel button, 198
Cancel command (Field tab local menu), 203
categories (reports), choosing, 180-181
Cc button, 86
CGI (Common Gateway Interface), 100
changing field labels, 125
check boxes
    Alarm, 88, 148
    Allow File to Synchronize, 214, 254
    Allow Hot Link, 78
    Always Auto Refresh Field List, 65

333

Attach VCard, 87
Build Group, 170, 197
Confirm Each Recipient, 88
Create Duplicate Record, 37
Delete Merge DBF When Done, 65
Delete Old History Records, 250
Detailed View, 140
Discard Message After Importing Data, 101
Exchange the Values of Two Fields, 247
Expand Partial Contact Records, 245
Import Data on Background E-mail Retrieval, 101
Import Data When Retrieving E-mail Center Mail, 101
Issue SQL Queries, 197
Link, 24
Link to Doc, 69, 78
Log Updates in History, 245
Merge This E-mail to a Group of Contacts, 88
Merge/Purge Using a Predefined Profile, 239
Merge/Purge Using New Criteria, 239-240
Net-Update Connections, 197
Output to Menu, 197
Page <<ContactName>>, 92
Page by Dialing a Terminal Phone Number, 93
Page by Sending an Internet E-mail to Address, 93
Primary, 99
Private, 87, 136, 149
Prompt for Group Merge Destination (Print Only), 65
Prompt for Response, 306
Rebuild and Pack the Database Files, 236
Request a Return Receipt, 87
Rich Text, 87
RSVP, 24, 87
Save History, 78
Save in History, 92
Send a Copy of the Aattached File(s) to GM Recipients, 88
Send as MIME, 87
Show Bubble Help, 30
Show Button Text, 30
Show Send Screen, 65
Show Status Bar Help, 30
Sort the Database Files, 236
SQL Logon Name, 197
SQL Password, 197
Sync 3rd Column w/Sort, 153
Sync Contact Window, 153
Sync Using the Settings of a Sync Profile, 274
Toolbar Settings, 197
Update a Field Using Advanced Options, 247
Convert To options, 248
global replacement options, 247
Update Linked Fields (Based on lookup.ini), 245
Update Registration Information, 111
Use Fine Resolution, 65
Verify the Data and Synchronization Information, 236-237
Wrap lines, 87
checking
duplications of contact records, 105
license status, 114-115
choosing report category, 180-181
Clean Up DOS Notes command (Import/Export Wizard menu), 58
Clear button, 160
Clipboard command (Toolbars menu), 35
Clipboard toolbar, 35
Clipboard Viewer, 35
Clone button, 130, 203
Clone command
Contact Group menu, 169
Reports Menu dialog box local menu, 185
cloning, 130
records, 37-38
templates, 70
Close button, 184
Close toolbar button, 190
Closed Activity tab, 27
Closed tab, 138-140
Code field, 141
code listings (HTML), 103
cogwheel icon, 290
collecting contact data (Web), 102
colon (:), 281
comma (,), 118, 279
commands
Activate Groups local menu
Edit, 171
Find, 171
New, 171
Output To, 171
Sort Members, 171
Sync Contact, 171
View, 171
Analysis menu
Forecast Analysis, 210, 219
Graphical Analysis, 219
Leads Analysis, 219, 224
Quota Analysis, 219-220
Sales Analysis, 219, 227
Statistical Analysis, 219
Automated Processes menu
Execute Processes, 58, 296

Index

Set Up Automated Processes, 58, 290-292, 297
Competitors tab local menu
  New Linked Contact, 217
  New Unlinked Contact, 218
Complete menu
  Scheduled Call, 250
  To-do, 27
Configure menu
  Custom Fields, 126
  Custom Screens, 129, 203
  License Manager, 15, 110
  Resources, 123
  Users Groups, 193
  Users' Settings, 120, 123, 192, 195, 200
Contact Group menu
  Activate Group, 168
  Add Members, 168
  Clone, 169
  Delete, 169
  Edit, 169
  Find, 169
  New, 169
  Output To, 169
  Release Group, 168
  Select User, 169
Contact menu
  Assign a Process, 295
  Create E-mail, 54, 67, 85, 92
  Insert a Note, 39
  Lookup, 166
  Write, 66, 69, 75, 79
Create E-mail menu
  Customize Templates, 68
  E-mail Merge, 68
  Message to Contact, 67, 85
  Outlook Message to Contact, 67, 92

Pager Message to Contact, 68, 92
Date and Time menu (Date), 71
Details menu (Launch Web Site), 99
document context menu (Customize Templates), 54
Edit menu
  Copy, 35
  Copy Contact Details, 36
  Custom Templates, 48
  Cut, 35
  Delete Contact, 36, 249
  Edit Contact, 36
  Paste, 28, 35
  Preferences, 30, 49, 89, 120, 148, 200
  Record Details, 47
  Record Properties, 195
  Toolbars, 48, 60
  Undo, 35
Field menu (Date and Time), 71
Field tab local menu
  Cancel, 203
  New Field, 203
  Screen Design, 203
  [Screen name], 203
  Screen Setup, 203
File menu
  Computer, 319
  Configure, 15, 34, 110, 120-123, 192, 195, 200, 203
  Exit, 34
  Files or Folders, 79
  Log Away, 34, 148
  Log in Another User, 34, 121
  Maintain, 236
  Maintain Databases, 34, 205, 321
  New Database, 34, 125
  New Record, 34, 37, 60
  Open Database, 34, 125, 201

Print Reports, 34, 180, 183, 189
Save as HTML, 102
Setup Printer, 34, 189
Synchronize, 34, 236, 273-274, 278, 282-284, 312
GoldMine menu
  Insert GoldMine Field, 79
  Save as GoldMine Form, 69-72
  Save as GoldMine Linked Document, 73
  Setup GoldMine Link, 66
  Uninstall GoldMine Link, 66, 322
  Update GoldMine Form, 70, 73
Help menu
  About, 16, 109, 114
  GoldMine Newsgroups, 323
  GoldMine Web Site, 314, 322
  Update GoldMine, 233
Import/Export Wizard menu
  Clean Up DOS Notes, 58
  Import Contact Records, 58
  Import Zip Codes, 58
Influencer local menu
  Delete, 216
  Edit, 216
  Go to Contact Record, 216
  New Linked Contact, 215
  New Unlinked Contact, 215
  Relink to Another Contact, 215
InfoCenter topic local menu
  Delete, 264
  Edit, 264

335

Launch, 263
Link Contact, 263-264
New, 264
Options, 264
Print/Fax, 263
Search, 263
Insert menu (Fields), 71
Links tab local menu
  Delete, 254
  E-mail Document, 254
  Edit, 254
  Find, 254
  Launch, 254
  Move, 254
  New, 254
  Output To, 254
Lookup menu
  Company, 53
  Contact, 53, 143, 146, 216, 254
  Detail Records, 53, 155
  Filters, 53, 158-160, 167
  Goto, 54
  Indexed Fields, 53
  Internet Search, 54, 96
  Last, 53
  Phone1, 53
  SQL Queries, 53
  Text Search, 54
main menu
  Complete, 14
  Contact, 13
  Edit, 13
  File, 13
  Help, 14
  Lookup, 13
  Schedule, 13
  Tools, 14
  View, 13
Merge/Purge Records menu
  Merge Tagged Records, 59
  Merge Visible Records, 59
  Merge/Purge Wizard, 59
Options menu (View, Detailed View), 25

Org Chart local panel menu
  Create a New Organization, 256
  Link to Organization, 256
organizational tree local menu
  Activate Section, 257
  Delete, 258
  New Link, 257
  New Organization, 257
  New Section, 257
  Options, 258
  Properties, 258
  Release Section, 257
  Replicate Data, 257
Programs menu (Accessories), 35
Query menu (Contact), 36
Record Details menu (Resize), 47
Reports Menu dialog box local menu
  Clone, 185
  Delete, 185
  Find, 185
  Layout, 184
  New, 185
  Options, 184
  Output To, 185
  Print, 184
  Properties, 185
  Saved, 185
  Sorts, 185
Sales Tools menu
  Opportunities, 52, 210-212
  Scripts, 52, 304-306
Schedule menu
  Forecasted Sale, 209
  GoldMine E-mail, 84
  Literature Request, 264
  To-do, 24, 136, 140
Server Agents menu
  Agents Administrator, 58
  Start Server Agents, 58

Start menu
  Explore, 319
  Find, 79
  Programs, 12
  Run, 9, 114
Synchronize menu
  Copy/Move Records, 236, 312
  GoldSync Administration Center, 273
  Sync with Outlook, 278
  Sync with Pilot, 282-283
  Sync with Windows CE PDA, 284
  Synchronize Wizard, 274
Tasks local menu
  Complete, 212
  Delete, 213
  Edit, 213
  Find, 213
  Go to Task, 212
  New, 213
  Output To, 213
Team tab local menu
  Delete, 216
  Edit, 216
  Go to Contact Record, 216
  New, 216
  New Linked Contact, 216
Timer menu (Stop Timer), 46
Toolbars menu
  Clipboard, 35
  Insert Item, 48
Tools menu
  Automated Processes, 58, 290-292, 296-297
  BDE Administrator, 59, 321-322
  Delete Records Wizard, 59, 249-250
  Find, 319
  Global Replace, 244, 247
  Global Replace Wizard, 58, 251

Index

Import/Export Wizard, 58
Mail Merge, 74
Merge/Purge Records, 59, 239
Server Agents, 58
Strategic Solutions, 59
System Performance, 59, 234
Territory Realignment, 58
Year 2000 Compliance, 59
View Filters menu (public), 167
View menu
  Activity List, 25-26, 52, 136-137, 140, 219
  Analysis, 52, 210, 219, 224
  Calendar, 52, 142
  Contact Groups, 52, 157, 165-167, 170
  E-mail Center, 52, 90, 101
  E-mail Waiting Online, 52
  GoldMine Logs, 245-246
  InfoCenter, 17, 52, 259, 268
  Literature Fulfillment, 52, 264
  New Contact Window, 47, 51-52, 154
  Personal Rolodex, 22, 52
  Projects, 52
  Sales Tools, 52, 210-212, 304-306
  Source, 102
  Toolbars, 35
Window menu (Status Bar), 46
Write menu
  Customize Templates, 66, 69
  Letter to Contact, 66
  Mail Merge, 75, 79

Common Contact Set, 22
Common Gateway Interface (CGI), 100
Compact installation, 10
Company command (Lookup menu), 53
Company field, 215
competition, depicting, 259
competitors, documenting, 217-218
Competitors tab, 217
Competitors tab local menu commands
  New Linked Contact, 217
  New Unlinked Contact, 218
Complete command
  main menu, 14
  Task local menu, 212
Complete curtaining, 194-195
Complete menu commands
  Scheduled Call, 250
  To-do, 27
completed To-do tasks, marking, 27
completing activities, 57-58, 141
Computer command (Find menu), 319
Conduit tab, 283
Configure command (File menu), 34, 110, 120-123, 192, 195, 200, 203
Configure GoldMine command (File menu), 15
Configure menu commands
  Custom Fields, 126
  Custom Screens, 129, 203
  License Manager, 15, 110
  Resources, 123
  Users Groups, 193
  Users' Settings, 120, 123, 192, 195, 200
configuring
  licenses, 110-111
  resources, 123-124
  Time Clock, 122
  toolbars, 48-49

user groups, 123
workstations, 319-320
Confirm Each Recipient check box, 88
confirming HotSync settings, 284
connected synchronization sessions, 274
Contact button, 54
Contact command
  Lookup menu, 53, 143, 146, 166, 216, 254
  main menu, 13
  Query menu, 36
contact data, collecting (Web), 102
contact databases, 22
  access, controlling, 201-202
  default, 122
Contact field, 36, 87, 215
contact file logs, viewing, 245-246
Contact Groups command (View menu), 52, 157, 165-167, 170
Contact icon, 86
Contact Info button, 93
Contact Listing
  tagging contact records, 156-158
  untagging contact records, 158
Contact Listing dialog box, 146, 152
Contact Listing display, 152-153
contact lists, 23
contact managers, 6
Contact menu commands
  Assign a Process, 295
  Create E-mail, 54, 67, 85, 92
  Insert a Note, 39
  Lookup, 166
  Write, 66, 69, 75, 79
contact record groups. *See* groups

337

contact records, 22. *See also* contacts
　active, 36
　cloning, 37-38
　copying, 235-236
　databases, copying/moving, 235-236
　deleting, 249
　duplicate, merging, 239
　duplications, checking, 105
　filtered, 162-163
　　deleting, 250
　　deleting histories, 250
　filtering, 172
　finding, 36-37
　global changes, 243-245, 251
　　account numbers, 244
　　logging, 245
　history
　　deleting, 249-250
　　monitoring, 289
　maintaining, 239
　merging, 240, 242
　moving/copying, 312-313
　notes, adding, 39
　owning, 194-195
　Pilot, selecting, 284
　previewed, 174
　properties, editing, 42-43
　purging, 243
　searching, 152-153
　　details, 155-156
　　indexed files, 153-154
　　narrowing search, 154
　SQL Query, 174
　synchronizing, 289
　tagged, 157, 175
　tagging, 156-158
　tracks, attaching, 295
　untagging, 158
Contact Report Options dialog box, 184-185
Contact reports, 185
Contact Set Database dialog box, 201
Contact Set Profile dialog box, 201

contact windows, 51-52
　opening, 154
　spin buttons, 155
contacts. *See also* contact records
　active, 152
　editing Web site addresses, 99
　emailing, 67, 85-86, 92
　linking
　　activities to, 141-142
　　to documents, 73
　　folders to, 255
　　from Links tab, 254-255
　locating, 53-54
　making through Web sites, 100
　managing, 7
　scanning, 296
　sending literature to, 264
　sorting, 166
　tagged, 146
　tagging, 166-167
　writing letters to, 66-68
　writing to templates, 72
Contacts tab, 242, 280
controlling
　access
　　contact databases, 201-202
　　menus, 199
　sublicenses, 110
　user access, 194
　Web import, 101
CONTSUPP files, 277
[ContSupp] header, 104-106
CONTTLOG file, 245
Convert To options, 248
Copy All button, 16
Copy command (Edit menu), 35
Copy Contact Details (Edit menu), 36
Copy/Move Records command (Synchronize menu), 236, 312
copying
　database records, 235-236

records (Industry templates), 312-313
corrupt indexes, preventing, 235
costing (source of leads), 225-226
Create a New Mail Message icon, 91
Create a New Organization command (Org Chart local panel menu), 256
Create a Table of Contents toolbar icon, 261
Create Duplicate Record check box, 37
Create E-mail command (Contact menu), 54, 67, 85, 92
Create E-mail menu commands
　Customize Templates, 68
　E-mail Merge, 68
　Message to Contact, 67, 85
　Outlook Message to Contact, 67, 92
　Pager Message to Contact, 68, 92
Create Folder icon, 91
creating
　Automated Processes, 297-298
　books, 260-261
　databases, 125
　details, 214
　events, 297
　fields, 126-128
　Group Profiles, 168-170
　groups, 166-167, 173
　　filters, 167
　　Group Building Wizard. *See* Group Building Wizard
　HTML forms, 102-103
　licenses, undocked, 110
　literature, 266
　macros, 60
　screens, 129-130
　scripts, 306
　shortcuts, 114

signature bitmaps, 79
sublicenses, 110
template forms, 68
templates, 69-70
To-do lists, 24
user groups, 192
curtaining
    Complete, 194-195
    Partial, 194
Custom Fields command (Configure menu), 126
Custom installation, 10
Custom Screen Profile dialog box, 130, 203
Custom Screens command (Configure menu), 129, 203
Custom Screens Setup dialog box, 130, 202-204
Custom Templates command (Edit menu), 48
Customize dialog box, 12
Customize Templates command
    Create E-mail menu, 68
    document context menu, 54
    Write menu, 66, 69
customizing, 30
    database fields, 118-119
    screens, 125
    templates, 54-56
Cut command (Edit menu), 35
Cutoff Date/Time dialog box, 277

D

D GoldMine dBASE license (D-*xxxx* users), 14
.D* file extension, 235
D- licenses, 112
data
    backing up, 234-235, 244
    purging (Pilot), 283
    reports, sorting, 188-189
    standardized, entering, 40
    synchronizing, 271-272
        GoldMine, 273
        GoldSync, 273
        Microsoft Outlook, 278-279
        Palm Pilot, 281-282
        Sneaker Net, 275
        Windows CE devices, 284
    verifying, 237
data collecting forms (Web sites), 100-101
data entry (scripts), directing, 307
[Data] header, 104-105
Data sections, interpreting, 105-106
database files, 236-237
database languages
    dBASE, 175
    SQL, 174-175
Database Type field, 201
databases, 33
    assigning optional passwords, 122
    contact, 22
        controlling access, 201-202
        default, 122
    creating, 125
    fields, customizing, 118-119
    indexing, 238
    records, copying/moving, 235-236
date
    inserting (Word fields), 71
    setting (tasks), 28-29
Date and Time command (Field menu), 71
Date and Time menu commands (Date), 71
Date command (Date and Time menu), 71
Date field, 186-187
date format, setting, 28
dating activities, 143-145
dBASE, 175
dBASE condition trigger, 300
dBASE expressions, 248
DDE Command field, 69
DDE Launch Options, 69
deactivating toggle options, 38-39
default contact database, 122
Default Contact Database field, 122
Defaults tab, 283
defining
    retrieve options (transfer sets), 278
    tracks, 293-294
    transfer cutoffs, 277
    transfer set send options, 277-278
Delete button, 249
Delete command
    Activate Groups local menu, 171
    Contact Group menu, 169
    Influencer local menu, 216
    InfoCenter topic local menu, 264
    Links tab local menu, 254
    organizational tree local menu, 258
    Reports Menu dialog box local menu, 185
    Task local menu, 213
    Team tab local menu, 216
Delete Contact command (Edit menu), 36, 249
Delete Folder icon, 91
Delete icon, 128
Delete Leads Analysis Profile dialog box, 229
Delete Merge DBF When Done check box, 65
Delete Old History Records check box, 250
Delete option (Leads Analysis [Last Run] dialog box), 226
Delete Records Wizard command (Tools menu), 59, 249-250
Delete Selected Message icon, 91
Delete toolbar icon, 261
Delete Wizard dialog box, 250

339

deleting
  activities (Calendar), 147
  histories, 250
  history records, 249-250
  leads analysis, 229
  macros, 61
  records, 249-250
depicting competition, 259
Description field, 201, 265, 320
descriptions, attaching, 41
detail record trigger, 299
Detail Records command (Lookup menu), 53, 155
Detail tab, 57
Detailed View check box, 140
details
  activities, viewing, 26
  creating, 214
  searching for contacts, 155-156
Details menu commands (Launch Web Site), 99
Details Properties dialog box, 214
Details tab, 146, 214
dialog boxes. *See also* windows
  About to Delete Records, 251
  Add a Group Member, 298
  Add a New Record, 37, 250
  Automated Process Setup, 297
  Automated Processes Execution, 296
  Automated Processes Setup, 290-292, 297
  Automatic Maintenance, 237
  Branching Script Profile, 304-306
  Branching Script Question, 304-306
  Calendar Report Options, 184
  Call Back, 250
  Contact Listing, 146, 152

Contact Report Options, 184-185
Contact Set Database, 201
Contact Set Profile, 201
Custom Screen Profile, 130, 203
Custom Screen Setup, 130, 203-204
Custom Screens, 202
Customize, 12
Cutoff Date/Time, 277
Delete Leads Analysis Profile, 229
Delete Wizard, 250
Detail Properties, 214
Edit Macro Button, 61
Entry, 41
Event Properties, 297-298, 301
Expression Builder, 297
Field Properties, 124, 127
Fields of Screen:[screen name], 203
Filter:[filter name], 160
Filters and Groups, 52, 157-158, 161, 165, 172
form Template Properties, 69
Global Replace, 245
GoldMine Link Preferences, 66
GoldMine Pilot Synchronization Wizard, 282
GoldMine User Recipient, 86
GoldMine: Find IDAPI32.DLL, 322
Group Membership Setup, 193
Group Profile, 157, 169
HotSync, 282
Influencer, 215
Insert GoldMine Field, 71
Insert Toolbar Item, 48
Internet Preferences, 101
Issue, 218
Leads Analysis [Last Run], 225-226

Linked Document, 73, 254
Literature, 265
Literature Request, 264
Look Up a Contact Based on a Detail, 156
Look Up Detail, 156
Macro, 61
Mail Merge Properties, 76-77
Maintain Files, 237
Merge/Purge Criteria Setting, 241
New Field, 128
New Filter, 160-161
New Opportunity, 217
New Record Ownership, 194
Open Leads Analysis File, 225
Opportunity Properties, 210
Optional Settings, 173
Outlook Synchronization Options, 278
Place Field, 127, 205
Preferences, 30
Processes Listing, 290
Properties, 192, 196, 292-293
Queue, Calendar and History Options, 88
Quota Listing, 220
Quota Profile, 220
Ready to Synchronize, 279-281
Recipients, 79
Record Selections, 278
Reference Note, 305
Registration, 114
Report Profile, 181-185
Report Sorting, 184-185, 188
Reports Menu, 180, 183
Sales Team Member, 216
Save Script, 305
Schedule a Call, 250
Schedule a Forecasted Sale, 209

Index

Schedule a To-do, 216
Schedule an Appointment, 56
Scheduling, 146
Search, 262-263
Select a User, 169
Select Activities to View, 145
Select Components, 10
Select Report File to View, 185
Select User, 227
Send a Pager Message, 68, 92-93
Setup Type, 318
Task, 213
Telemarketing Scripts, 52
Template Properties, 69
Toolbars, 48
Transfer Set Retrieve Options, 278
Transfer Set Send Options, 277
User Groups, 193, 195
User Groups Setup, 123
Users' Master File, 120, 123, 192-195
Web Sites, 99
Zip Code Profile, 42
directing data entry (scripts), 307
directories
  GoldMine, 104
  home, 121-122
  sharing, 319
disabled trigger, 300
disabling Time Clock, 201
Discard Message After Importing Data check box, 101
disconnected synchronization sessions, 274
displaying
  Calendar, 142
  fields, 129
  help text, 29-30
  status bar, 46

displays, Contact Listing, 152-153
DMC (Document Management Center), 48, 66-67, 76
document context menu commands (Customize Templates), 54
Document Management tab, 78
document templates, 66. *See also* forms
documenting
  competitors, 217-218
  issues, 218
documents
  attaching, 86
  linked, editing, 255
  linking to contacts, 73
  managing, 78
  printed, reviewing, 267
  queued, 267
double slash marks (//), 41
downloading free support, 18
drafts of Web sites, viewing, 107
Drill Down button, 159
Drive drop-down list, 319
duplicate records, merging, 239
duplications (contact records), checking, 105
dynamic IP (Internet Protocol), 273

E

E- licenses, 112
E-mail Center, 90, 100-101
E-mail Center command (View menu), 52, 90, 101
E-mail Center toolbar, 91
E-mail Document command (Links tab local menu), 254
E-mail Merge command (Create E-mail menu), 68

E-mail tab, 138
E-mail Waiting Online command (View menu), 52
Edit button, 69, 123, 220, 304-306
Edit command
  Activate Groups local menu, 171
  Contact Group menu, 169
  Influencer local menu, 216
  InfoCenter topic local menu, 264
  Links tab local menu, 254
  main menu, 13
  Task local menu, 213
  Team tab local menu, 216
Edit Contact command (Edit menu), 36
Edit E-mail Rules icon, 91
Edit E-mail Templates icon, 91
Edit field, 266
Edit icon, 128
Edit Macro Button dialog box, 61
Edit menu commands
  Copy, 35
  Copy Contact Details, 36
  Custom Templates, 48
  Cut, 35
  Delete Contact, 36, 249
  Edit Contact, 36
  Paste, 28, 35
  Preferences, 30, 49, 89, 120, 148, 200
  Record Details, 47
  Record Properties, 195
  Toolbars, 48, 60
  Undo, 35
Edit Source Cost option (Leads Analysis [Last Run] dialog box), 226
Edit toolbar icon, 260
editing
  fields (Report Profile window), 181
  filters, 159-160
  linked documents, 255

341

macros, 61
permissions, 120-121
preferences, 120
properties (records), 42-43
questions and answers (scripts), 306
scripts, 304-305
templates, 66
toolbars, 30
user preferences, 49-50
Web site addresses, 99
elapsed days trigger, 299
ellipsis (...), 13, 29
email
    attaching documents, 86
    GoldMine, 84
    Internet, 84
    options, setting, 86-87
    queuing, 88
    writing messages, 54
email merges, 75-78
email=value entry, 106
emailing
    contacts, 67, 85-86, 92
    GoldMine users, 84
    mail merge, 88-89
emulators, 8
End User screen, 126, 129
entering standardized data, 40
entries
    email=value, 106
    multiple (fields), 41
    Password=value, 106
Entry dialog box, 41
entry fields, Pager ID (PIN), 93
envelope icon, 85, 296
Event Properties dialog box, 297-298, 301
events, 293-294
    actions, 294, 301-302
    creating, 297
    P (preemptive), 294
    sequencing, 294-295
    triggers, 294, 299-301
Events tab, 138
Exchange the Values of Two Fields check box, 247

.EXE file extension, 235
Execute Processes command (Automated Processes menu), 58, 296
Execute Script [contact name] window, 306
Exit command (File menu), 34
Exit icon, 128, 203
Expand button, 199
Expand Partial Contact Records check box, 245
expanding menus, 199
explanations, attaching, 41
Explore command (Start menu), 319
Export Contact Records command (Import/Export Wizard menu), 58
Expression Builder dialog box, 297
expressions
    dBASE, 248
    filter, building, 158-159
extracting information (InfoCenter), 263

F

faxing topics (InfoCenter), 263-264
Field Code field, 201
Field command (Insert menu), 71
field comparison methods
    selecting, 241-242
    Soundex Value, 241
Field Mapping tab, 280
Field menu commands (Date and Time), 71
Field Properties dialog box, 124, 127
field view, 202-205
fields
    Actv, 187
    adding to Fields tab, 129
    Allow File to Synchronize, 265

App Identifier, 69
Associated Document File Name, 214
automating, 70
Code, 141
Company, 215
Contact, 36, 87, 215
creating, 126-128
Database Type, 201
databases, customizing, 118-119
Date, 186-187
DDE Command, 69
Default Contact Database, 122
Description, 201, 265, 320
displaying, 129
Edit, 266
editing (Report Profile window), 181
entries, multiple, 41
Field Code, 201
Filename, 265
Find Contact, 36
GoldMine, placing, 71
Grant Access from This GoldMine License Only, 201
Grant Access to This File For, 201
Item, 214
labels
    changing, 125
    global, 124, 128
    local, 124
Logon Name, 202
moving, 125
names, 68, 124
navigating, 10
Notes, 24, 215
Oppty, 87
Page GoldMine User(s), 92
Password, 202
Path (Alias), 201, 320
Perform Action, 301-302
Primary Sort, 188
Reference, 214

Index

Replace, 247-248
Replace Field, 244
Result, 141, 187
Role, 215
Secondary Sort, 188
Success, 141
Tertiary Sort, 188
Title, 215
To, 86, 186-187
To-do, 24
Trigger On, 298
Type, 265
Type Message to Send to the Pager, 93
User, 186-187, 218
values, substituting, 246-247
Web Site, 99
With Value, 244
Word
   inserting date, 71
   placing, 70-71
Fields button, 128, 203
Fields of Screen:[screen name] dialog box, 203
Fields tab, 125-126, 129, 202, 204
Fields tab local menu commands
   Cancel, 203
   New Field, 203
   Screen Design, 203
   [Screen name], 203
   Screen Setup, 203
File Browse button, 214
File command (main menu), 13
file extensions
   .D*, 235
   .EXE, 235
   .FP, 235
File in History tab, 76-78
File menu commands
   Configure, 15, 34, 110, 120-123, 192, 195, 200, 203
   Exit, 34
   Log Away, 34, 148
   Log in Another User, 34, 121

Maintain, 236
Maintain Databases, 34, 205, 321
New Database, 34, 125
New Record, 34, 37, 60, 250
Open Database, 34, 125, 201
Print Reports, 34, 180, 183, 189
Save as HTML, 102
Setup Printer, 34, 189
Synchronize, 34, 236, 273-274, 278, 282-284, 312
Filed tab, 140
Filename field, 265
files
   contact, viewing logs, 245-246
   CONTSUPP, 277
   CONTTLOG, 245
   GM5SETUP, 9
   GMTLOG, 246
   GoldMine, viewing logs, 246
   GoldMine.exe, 113
   identifying, 235
   index, 235
   ISearch.ini, 98
   license.dbf, 113
   Web import, 104-107
Files or Folders command (Find menu), 79
Filled tab, 138
Filter button, 298
filter expressions, building, 158-159
Filter:[filter name] dialog box, 160
filtered contact records, 162-163
filtered records, 250
filtering
   Activity Lists, 138-139
   records, 172
filtering for transfer sets, 276
filters, 156, 161, 167
   building, 158-160
   creating groups, 167

editing, 159-160
releasing, 162
Filters and Groups dialog box, 52, 157-158, 161, 165, 172
Filters command (Lookup menu), 53, 158, 160, 167
Filters icon, 160
Filters tab, 250
Find command
   Activate Groups local menu, 171
   Contact Group menu, 169
   Links tab local menu, 254
   Reports Menu dialog box local menu, 185
   Start menu, 79
   Task local menu, 213
   Tools menu, 319
Find Contact field, 36
Find menu commands
   Computer, 319
   Files or Folders, 79
Find Messages icon, 91
Find option (Leads Analysis [Last Run] dialog box), 226
Find Value window, 53
finding contact records, 36-37
First toolbar button, 190
first-level problems, troubleshooting, 320
folders
   alphabetizing, 261
   linking to contacts, 255
Forecast Analysis command (Analysis menu), 210, 219
Forecasted Sale command (Schedule menu), 209
forecasted sales
   inspecting, 210-211
   scheduling, 209-210
Forecasts tab, 138, 210, 218-219
Form Designer toolbar, 182
Form Templates Properties dialog box, 69
formats
   date, setting, 28
   .TXT (Text), 266

343

formatting Web import files, 104
forms
　data collecting (Web sites), 100-101
　HTML, 102-104
Forward icon, 91
.FP file extension, 235
free support, 16-17
　downloading from GoldMine Web site, 18
　online knowledge base, 17
full backups, 235

G

G GoldSync license (G-*xxxx* sites), 14
G- licenses, 112
General Access permissions, assigning, 197
General tab, 279-281, 284
global changes
　options, 247
　records, 243-245, 251
　replacing with dBASE expressions, 248
global labels (fields), 124, 128
Global Replace command (Tools menu), 244, 247
Global Replace dialog box, 245
Global Replace Wizard, 243-244, 247
Global Replace Wizard command (Tools menu), 58, 251
GM5SETUP file, 9
GMLink, 309
GMTLOG files, 246
Go button, 312
Go to Contact Record command
　Influencer local menu, 216
　Team tab local menu, 216
Go to Tasks command (Task local menu), 212

GoldAlarm, 50
GoldMine, 5-7
　add-ons, 15. *See also* GoldSync
　administering, 119
　advantages, 23
　backing up, 8
　fields, placing, 71
　file logs, viewing, 246
　free support, 16-17
　　downloading from GoldMine Web site, 18
　　online knowledge base, 17
　installing, 7-9
　　in local path, 114
　　to networks, 317-318
　　registering license, 10-11
　　selecting installation type, 9-10
　　system requirements, 8
　launching, 320
　license status, checking, 114-115
　licenses, registering, 111-112
　linking to Word 97/2000, 64-65
　logging in, 11-12
　maintaining, 233-234
　Personal Rolodex, 22-23, 135
　premium support, 18
　Remote Synchronization, 15
　searching Web, 96-98
　shortcuts, creating, 114
　starting, 12
　synchronizing data, 273
　technical support
　　GoldMine Web site, 322
　　newsgroups, 323
　template forms, creating, 68
　updating, 8, 112-115, 233
GoldMine button, 16
GoldMine directory, 104

GoldMine E-mail command (Schedule menu), 84
GoldMine email, 84
GoldMine link, 65-66
GoldMine Link Preferences dialog box, 66
GoldMine Logs command (View menu), 245-246
GoldMine Master License, 14
GoldMine menu commands
　Insert GoldMine Field, 79
　Save as GoldMine Form, 69-72
　Save as GoldMine Linked Document, 73
　Setup GoldMine Link, 66
　Uninstall GoldMine Link, 66, 322
　Update GoldMine Form, 70, 73
GoldMine Newsgroups command (Help menu), 323
GoldMine Pilot Synchronization Wizard, 282
GoldMine Pilot Synchronization Wizard dialog box, 282
GoldMine Search Engine, 98-99
GoldMine Service and Support messages, 84
GoldMine Sublicense (S-*xxxx* users), 14
GoldMine Tools CD Catalog, 314-315
GoldMine Undocked (U-0001 user) license, 14
GoldMine update server, 112
GoldMine User Recipient dialog box, 86
GoldMine users
　emailing, 84
　locating, 148
GoldMine Web site, 17, 64, 95, 322
　downloading free support, 18
　Industry Solutions list, 314

Index

GoldMine Web Site command (Help menu), 314, 322
GoldMine: Find IDAPI32.DLL dialog box, 322
GoldMine.exe files, 113
GoldSync, 11, 15
   licenses, 111
   synchronizing data, 273
   updating, 112
GoldSync Administration Center, 273
GoldSync Administration Center command (Synchronize menu), 273
GoldSync Sublicense (Y-*xxxx* sites), 14
Goto command (Lookup menu), 54
Grant Access from This GoldMine License Only field, 201
Grant Access to This File For field, 201
Graphical Analysis command (Analysis menu), 219
group building methods, 172-173
   active set of records, 174-175
   optional settings, 173
Group Building Wizard, 167, 172-175
Group Membership Setup dialog box, 193
Group Profile dialog box, 157, 169
Group Profiles, 165
   accepting, 170
   creating, 168-170
Group Schedule tab, 57
groups, 165
   activating, 167-168
   creating, 166-167, 172-175
   Group Profiles, 165
   members, adding, 168, 172
   synchronizing, 170
   working with, 170

Groups (upper panel) local menu commands
   Activate Group, 168
   Add Members, 168
   Clone, 169
   Delete, 169
   Edit, 169
   Find, 169
   New, 169
   Output to, 169
   Release Group, 168
   Select User, 169
Groups tab, 165-167

H

headers, 104
   [ContSupp], 104-106
   [Data], 104-105
   [Instructions], 104-105
Help, 59
Help command (main menu), 14
Help menu commands
   About, 16, 109, 114
   GoldMine Newsgroups, 323
   GoldMine Web Site, 314, 322
   Update GoldMine, 233
help text, displaying, 29-30
histories
   activities, viewing, 140
   filtered records, deleting, 250
history activity trigger, 300
History Data panel, 186-187
history records, 186
   deleting, 249-250
   monitoring, 289
History tab, 27, 218, 306
history triggers, 299
hits, 96
home directories, 121-122
HotSync settings, confirming, 284
HotSync dialog box, 282

HTML (Hypertext Markup Language), 98
HTML forms
   creating, 102-103
   interpreting, 104

I

icons
   academic mortarboard, 259
   assigning to macros, 61
   binoculars, 261
   cogwheel, 290
   Contact, 86
   Create a New Mail Message, 91
   Create Folder, 91
   Delete, 128
   Delete Folder, 91
   Delete Selected Message, 91
   Edit, 128
   Edit E-mail Rules, 91
   Edit E-mail Templates, 91
   envelope, 296
   Exit, 128, 203
   Filters, 160
   Find Messages, 91
   Forward, 91
   Index, 321
   InfoCenter, 17
   Internet E-mail Preferences, 91
   ISearch.ini Properties, 97-98
   Layout, 182
   Mail Merge, 88
   Mark Message as Unread, 91
   moving, 12
   New, 39, 128
   New Literature, 265
   Open Selected Message, 91
   Org Chart, 256
   Preview, 182
   Print, 79
   Print Selected Message, 91
   Proc, 297
   Rebuild, 128

345

Record, 154
Redirect, 91
Reload, 97
Reply, 91
Reply to All, 91
Reports, 180, 183
Rocket, 234
Schedule, 209
Scripts, 304-306
Search Now, 96
Synchronize, 274
Toggle Data View, 96
user, personalizing, 320
identifying files, 235
immediate trigger, 299
Import Contact Records command (Import/Export Wizard menu), 58
Import Data on Background E-mail Retrieval check box, 101
Import Data When Retrieving E-mail Center Mail check box, 101
Import Zip Codes command (Import/Export Wizard menu), 58
Import/Export Wizard command (Tools menu), 58
Import/Export Wizard menu commands
　Clean Up DOS Notes, 58
　Export Contact Records, 58
　Import Contact Records, 58
　Import Zip Codes, 58
improving browse lists, 41
In dBASE option button, 159
index files, 235
Index icon, 321
Indexed Fields command (Lookup menu), 53, 153
indexed files, searching for contacts, 153-154
indexes (corrupt), preventing, 235
indexing databases, 238
Industry Solutions list, 313-314

Industry templates, 125, 310-311
　installing, 311-312
　moving/copying records between, 312-313
Influencer dialog box, 215
Influencer local menu commands
　Delete, 216
　Edit, 216
　Go to Contact Record, 216
　New Linked Contact, 215
　New Unlinked Contact, 215
　Relink to Another Contact, 215
Influencer tab, 215-216
influencers, 215
Info tab, 302
InfoCenter, 253, 259-260, 267-269
　extracting information, 263
　KnowledgeBase, 17
　opening, 259
　searching, 261-262
　topics, printing/faxing, 263-264
InfoCenter button, 304
InfoCenter command (View menu), 17, 52, 259, 268
InfoCenter icon, 17
InfoCenter topic local menu commands
　Delete, 264
　Edit, 264
　Launch, 263
　Link Contact, 263-264
　New, 264
　Options, 264
　Print/Fax, 263
　Search, 263
initializing GoldMine Search Engine, 98
Insert a Note command (Contact menu), 39
Insert Condition button, 161
Insert GoldMine Field command (GoldMine menu), 79

Insert GoldMine Field dialog box, 71
Insert Item command (Toolbars menu), 48
Insert menu commands (Field), 71
Insert Toolbar Item dialog box, 48
inserting date in Word fields, 71
inspecting
　forecasted sales, 210-211
　Master Licenses, 15
　permissions, 120-121
Install Locally tab, 114
installation, 9
　Compact, 10
　Custom, 10
　selecting type, 9-10
　Typical, 9
installation disc, starting, 9
installation images, 8
installing
　GoldMine, 7-9
　　in local path, 114
　　to networks, 317-318
　　registering license, 10-11
　　selecting installation type, 9-10
　　system requirements, 8
　Industry templates, 311-312
　links, 64-65
　Pilot conduit, 283
[Instructions] header, 104-105
Instructions section, interpreting, 105
insufficient memory, troubleshooting, 321
intermediate backups, 235
Internet E-mail Preferences icon, 91
Internet email, 84
Internet email accounts, setting up, 89-90
Internet email via Microsoft Outlook, 84

Index

Internet Preferences Advanced tab, 101
Internet Preferences dialog box, 101
Internet Protocol (IP), 273
Internet Search command (Lookup menu), 54, 96
Internet Search window, 96
Internet service providers (ISPs), 8, 89, 98
Internet tab, 50, 89, 101, 120
interpreting
   HTML forms, 104
   leads analysis, 224-225
   process listings, 291-292
   sections
      Data, 105-106
      Instructions, 105
IP (Internet Protocol), 273
ISearch.ini file, 98
ISearch.ini Properties icon, 97-98
ISPs (Internet service providers), 8, 89, 98
Issue dialog box, 218
Issue ID, 18
issue records, 218
Issue SQL Queries check box, 197
issues, documenting, 218
Issues tab, 218
Item field, 214

J-K

Jump toolbar button, 183, 190

keys
   Application, 40, 168
   Local Menu, 40
KnowledgeBase, 17
KnowledgeBase tab, 260

L

labels (fields)
   changing, 125
   global, 124, 128
   local, 124
Last command (Lookup menu), 53
Last toolbar button, 190
Launch Attached File toolbar icon, 261
Launch command
   InfoCenter topic local menu, 263
   Links tab local menu, 254
Launch Web Site command (Details menu), 99
launching
   applications, 106
   GoldMine, 320
   scans, 296
Layout button, 182-184
Layout command (Reports Menu dialog box local menu), 184
Layout icon, 182
layout of reports, viewing, 182
Layout toolbar button, 190
leads
   analyzing, 223-224
   costing source, 225-226
leads analysis
   deleting, 229
   interpreting, 224-225
   maintaining, 229
Leads Analysis command (Analysis menu), 219, 224
Leads Analysis Zoom report, 224
Leads Analysis [Last Run] dialog box, 225-226
Letter to Contact command (Write menu), 66
letters, writing to contacts, 66-68
License Manager command (Configure menu), 15, 110
License Manager window, 110, 114

license status, checking, 114-115
license.dbf file, 113
licenses
   adding, 110
   automatic registration, 112
   configuring, 110-111
   D-, 112
   E-, 112
   G-, 112
   GoldMine, registering, 111-112
   GoldSync, 111
   Master, 14-16, 109
      D GoldMine dBASE license (D-*xxxx* users), 14
      G GoldSync license (G-*xxxx* sites), 14
      inspecting, 15
      sublicenses, 14-15
   registering, 10-11
   removing, 110
   U-0001, 112
   undocked, creating, 110
   viewing, 16, 109
   Y-*xxxx*, 112
Link check box, 24
Link Contact command (InfoCenter topic local menu), 263-264
Link to Doc check box, 69, 78
Link to Organization command (Org Chart local panel menu), 256
Linked Document dialog box, 73, 254
linked documents, editing, 255
linking
   activities to contacts, 141-142
   contacts from Links tab, 254-255
   documents to contacts, 73
   folders to contacts, 255
   GoldMine to Word 97/2000, 64-65

347

links
  GoldMine, 65-66
  installing, 64-65
  to Word, troubleshooting, 322
Links tab, 73, 254-255
Links tab local menu commands
  Delete, 254
  E-mail Document, 254
  Edit, 254
  Find, 254
  Launch, 254
  Move, 254
  New, 254
  Output to, 254
lists
  Activity, 25
    filtering, 138-139
    tabs, 137-138
    viewing, 26, 137-140
  browse, improving, 41
  contact, 23
  Industry Solutions, 313-314
  To-do, 25-27
    adding items, 136
    creating, 24
    removing items, 136
    viewing notes, 25
literature
  creating, 266
  sending to contacts, 264
Literature dialog box, 265
Literature Fulfillment Center, 52, 264, 267-269
Literature Fulfillment command (View menu), 52, 264
literature fulfillment requests, reviewing, 266
Literature Request command (Schedule menu), 264
Literature Request dialog box, 264
local labels (fields), 124
Local Menu key, 40
local menus, 40

local paths, 114
locally updating GoldMine, 114
locating
  contacts, 53-54
  GoldMine users, 148
Log Away command (File menu), 34, 148
Log in Another User command (File menu), 34, 121
Log Updates in History check box, 245
logging global changes (records), 245
logging in to GoldMine, 11-12
Login tab, 50, 122, 201
Logon Name field, 202
logs
  Real-Time Complete Activities, 141
  viewing
    contact files, 245-246
    GoldMine files, 246
Look Up a Contact Based on a Detail dialog box, 156
Look up button, 156
Look Up Detail dialog box, 156
Lookup command (main menu), 13
Lookup menu commands
  Company, 53
  Contact, 53, 143, 146, 216, 254
  Detail Records, 53, 155
  Filters, 53, 158-160, 167
  Goto, 54
  Indexed Fields, 53, 153
  Internet Search, 54, 96
  Last, 53
  Phone1, 53
  SQL Queries, 53
  Text Search, 54
Lookup tab, 50

M

Macro dialog box, 61
macros, 56, 289. *See also* Automated Processes
  assigning icon, 61
  creating, 60
  deleting, 61
  editing, 61
  recording, 288
mail merge, emailing, 88-89
Mail Merge command
  Tools menu, 74
  Write menu, 75, 79
Mail Merge Helper toolbar, 74
Mail Merge icon, 88
Mail Merge Properties dialog box, 76-77
Mail Merge tab button, 88
Mailto messages, 100
main menu, 12-13
main menu commands
  Complete, 14
  Contact, 13
  Edit, 13
  File, 13
  Help, 14
  Lookup, 13
  Schedule, 13
  Tools, 14
  View, 13
Maintain button, 229, 290, 297
Maintain Databases command (File menu), 34, 205, 236, 321
Maintain Files dialog box, 237
Maintain Scripts button, 304-306
Maintain Source Cost option (Leads Analysis [Last Run] dialog box), 226
maintaining
  GoldMine, 233-234
  leads analysis, 229
  records, 239

Index

maintenance, automating, 237-239
Maintenance Wizard, 234-236
managing
  contacts, 7
  documents, 78
  sales, 207-209
Mark Message as Unread icon, 91
marking To-do tasks
  as complete, 27
  as private, 24
Master Licenses, 14-16, 109
  D GoldMine dBASE license (D-*xxxx* users), 14
  G GoldSync license (G-*xxxx* sites), 14
  inspecting, 15
  sublicenses, 14-15
Master number, 109
Master rights, 11, 120, 192
MASTER user, 11
Max Content spin button, 296
Max Events spin button, 296
Maximize button, 146
measuring system speed, 234
members of groups, adding, 168, 172
Members Setup button, 193
Membership tab, 123, 195-196
memberships
  assigning users (user groups), 193
  viewing, 195
memory, troubleshooting, 321
Menu tab, 196, 199
menu templates, saving, 199
menus
  controlling access, 199
  expanding, 199
  pop-up, 26
Merge and Edit button, 76
Merge Methods, 242

Merge Tagged Records command (Merge/Purge Records menu), 59
Merge This E-mail to a Group of Contacts check box, 88
Merge Visible Records command (Merge/Purge Records menu), 59
Merge/Purge Criteria Setting dialog box, 241
Merge/Purge Profile, 241
Merge/Purge Records command (Tools menu), 59, 239
Merge/Purge Records menu commands
  Merge Tagged Records, 59
  Merge Visible Records, 59
  Merge/Purge Wizard, 59
Merge/Purge Using a Predefined Profile check box, 239
Merge/Purge Using New Criteria check box, 239-240
Merge/Purge Wizard, 239-240
  Merge Methods, 242
  Purge Methods, 243
Merge/Purge Wizard command (Merge/Purge Records menu), 59
merges, 74
  email, 75-78
  paper, 75
merging
  duplicate records, 239
  records, 240-242
Message to Contact command (Create E-mail menu), 67, 85
messages
  GoldMine Service and Support, 84
  Mailto, 100
  pager, 84, 92
  sending, 85
  telephone, 84
Microsoft Outlook. *See* Outlook
Microsoft Word. *See* Word
minimal backups, 235

Misc tab, 50
Modem tab, 50
monitoring
  history records, 289
  users, 122
More Options button, 90
Move command (Links tab local menu), 254
moving
  database records, 235-236
  fields, 125
  icons, 12
  records (Industry templates), 312-313
multiple entries (fields), 41

N

names (fields), 68, 124
naming fields views, 204
narrowing searching for contacts, 154
navigating fields, 10
Net-Update connections check box, 197
Net-Update Now, 113-114
Net-Update Now button, 111
Net-Update tab, 111
networks
  installing GoldMine to, 317-318
  updating GoldMine, 113-114
New Book toolbar icon, 260
New button, 22, 48, 203, 306
New command
  Activate Groups local menu, 171
  Contact Group menu, 169
  InfoCenter topic local menu, 264
  Links tab local menu, 254
  Reports Menu dialog box local menu, 185
  Task local menu, 213
  Team tab local menu, 216

349

New Contact Window command (View menu), 47, 51-52, 154
New Database command (File menu), 34, 125
New Field button, 127
New Field command (Field tab local menu), 203
New Field dialog box, 128
New Filter dialog box, 160-161
New Folder toolbar icon, 260
New icon, 39, 128
New License button, 110
New Link command (organizational tree local menu), 257
New Linked Contact command
   Competitors tab local menu, 217
   Influencer local menu, 215
   Team tab local menu, 216
New Literature icon, 265
New Opportunity dialog box, 217
New Organization command (organizational tree local menu), 257
New Record command (File menu), 34, 37, 60, 250
New Record Ownership dialog box, 194
New Section command (organizational tree local menu), 257
New Site button, 110
New Topic Page toolbar icon, 260
New Unlinked Contact command
   Competitors tab local menu, 218
   Influencer local menu, 215
newsgroups, technical support, 323
Next toolbar button, 190

notes
   adding to contact records, 39
   To-do list, viewing, 25
Notes field, 24, 215

O

OK button, 198
one direction synchronization, 273
online knowledge base, 17
Open Database command (File menu), 34, 125, 201
Open Leads Analysis File dialog box, 225
Open Selected Message icon, 91
Open tab, 25, 138
Open toolbar button, 190
opening
   contact windows, 154
   DMC, 76
   InfoCenter, 259
opportunities, 288
   comparing to projects, 214-215
   details, creating, 214
   switching between projects and, 209
   tasks, updating, 212-213
Opportunities command (Sales Tools menu), 52, 210-212
Opportunity Listing window, 212
Opportunity Manager, 52, 209, 212-214
Opportunity Properties dialog box, 210
Oppty field, 87
Optimize tab, 161
optimizing record selection, 161-162
option buttons
   Additional Contact, 153
   In dBASE, 159
   Primary Contacts, 153

optional passwords, assigning to databases, 122
optional settings, group building methods, 173
Optional Settings dialog box, 173
options (email), setting, 86-87
Options button, 86, 184, 297
Options command
   InfoCenter topic local menu, 264
   organizational tree local menu, 258
   Reports Menu dialog box local menu, 184
Options menu commands (View, Detailed View), 25
Or button, 161
Org Chart icon, 256
Org Chart panel, 256
Org Chart panel local menu commands
   Create a New Organization, 256
   Link to Organization, 256
organizational tree local menu commands
   Activate Section, 257
   Delete, 258
   New Link, 257
   New Organization, 257
   New Section, 257
   Options, 258
   Properties, 258
   Release Section, 257
   Replicate Data, 257
organizational trees, 255-259, 267-269
   building, 256-257
   rearranging, 259
Others tab, 138
Out-Box tab, 138
Outlook
   advanced options, setting, 279-281
   emailing contact, 92
   synchronizing data, 278-279
   viruses, 92

Index

Outlook Message to Contact command (Create E-mail menu), 67, 92
Outlook Synchronization Options dialog box, 278
Output To command
    Activate Groups local menu, 171
    Contact Group menu, 169
    Links tab local menu, 254
    Reports Menu dialog box local menu, 185
    Task local menu, 213
Output to Menu check box, 197
Output To option (Leads Analysis [Last Run] dialog box), 226
Ownership tab, 42, 194-195
owning records, 194-195

P

P (preemptive) events, 294
packing database files, 236-237
Page <<ContactName>> check box, 92
Page by Dialing a Terminal Phone Number check box, 93
Page by Sending an Internet E-mail to Address check box, 93
Page GoldMine User(s) field, 92
Page Message tab, 92
Pager ID (PIN) entry field, 93
Pager Info tab, 93
Pager Message to Contact command (Create E-mail menu), 68, 92
pager messages, 84, 92
Pager tab, 50
pages, 95, 261

Palm Pilot, synchronizing data with, 281-282
panels, 129
    Access to Others, 198
    Action, 301
    Attached Documents, 86
    Calendar Data, 187
    History Data, 186-187
    Org Chart, 256
    Recipients, 86
    To, 86
    Trigger, 297-298
paper merges, 75
Partial curtaining, 194
Password field, 202
Password=value entry, 106
passwords
    databases, assigning, 122
    Web import files, 106-107
Paste command (Edit menu), 28, 35
Path (Alias) field, 201, 320
Pause button, 60
Peg Board tab, 148
Pending tab, 36, 57, 129, 210, 218, 288
percent sign (%), 41
Perform Action field, 301-302
permissions
    access to others, 198-199
    assigning
        access to user group users, 196-197
        General Access, 197
    editing, 120-121
    inspecting, 120-121
    users, viewing, 196
    widening, 121
Personal Base tab, 260
Personal Rolodex, 22-23, 135
Personal Rolodex command (View menu), 22, 52
Personal tab, 17, 49
personalizing user icons, 320
Phone Formatting tab, 42
Phone1 command (Lookup menu), 53

Pilot
    contact records, selecting, 284
    purging data, 283-284
Pilot conduits, installing, 283
Place Field dialog box, 127, 205
placing
    GoldMine fields, 71
    Word fields, 70-71
pop-up menus, 26
ports, TCP, 275
preferences
    editing, 120
    GoldMine links, setting, 65-66
    user, editing, 49-50
    viewing, 200
Preferences button, 194
Preferences command (Edit menu), 30, 49, 89, 120, 148, 200
Preferences dialog box, 30
Preferences tab, 49
premium support, 18
preventing corrupt indexes, 235
Preview icon, 182
Preview tab, 158, 174, 250
Preview toolbar button, 190
previewed records, 174
previewing
    filtered contact records, 162-163
    reports, 189-190
Previous toolbar button, 190
Primary check box, 99
Primary Contacts option button, 153
Primary Sort field, 188
Print button, 184, 189
Print command (Reports Menu dialog box local menu), 184
Print icon, 79
Print Preview toolbar, 189-190

351

Print Reports command (File menu), 34, 180, 183, 189
Print Selected Message icon, 91
Print toolbar button, 190
Print/Fax command (InfoCenter topic local menu), 263
printed documents, reviewing, 267
Printer toolbar button, 190
printing
    reports, 189
    topics (InfoCenter), 263-264
priority (tasks), setting, 24-25
private, marking To-do tasks as, 24
private activities, 136, 149
private calls, 149
Private check box, 87, 136, 149
probabilities of sales, assigning, 208
Proc icon, 297
Process button, 296
process listings, 291-292
Processes Listing dialog box, 290
Profile tab, 196
profiles, 240
    Merge/Purge, 241
    Sync, 274
program files, identifying, 235
Programs command (Start menu), 12
Programs menu commands (Accessories), 35
Project Manager window, 52
projects, 288
    comparing to opportunities, 214-215
    details, creating, 214
    switching between opportunities and, 209
Projects command (View menu), 52

Prompt for Group Merge Destination (Print Only) check box, 65
Prompt for Response check box, 306
properties, 42
    records, editing, 42-43
    tracks, 292-293
Properties button, 122, 160, 181, 184, 194-195, 201-203, 292
Properties command
    organizational tree local menu, 258
    Reports Menu dialog box local menu, 185
Properties dialog box, 123, 192, 196, 292-293
(public) command (View Filters menu), 167
Purge Methods, 243
Purge tab, 283
purging
    data (Pilot), 283-284
    records, 243

Q

Query menu commands (Contact), 36
questions and answers (scripts)
    editing, 306
    saving, 305-306
Queue, Calendar and History Options button, 86-87
Queue, Calendar and History Options dialog box, 88
queued documents, reviewing, 267
queuing email, 88
Quota Analysis command (Analysis menu), 219-220
Quota Listing dialog box, 220
Quota Profile dialog box, 220
quotas, analyzing/assigning, 220

R

Ready to Synchronize dialog box, 281
Real-Time Complete Activities Log, 141
Real-Time tab, 138-140
rearranging organizational trees, 259
Rebuild and Pack the Database Files check box, 236
Rebuild icon, 128
rebuilding database files, 236-237
Recipient tab, 76
recipients (email), selecting type, 85
Recipients dialog box, 79
Recipients panel, 86
Record Details command (Edit menu), 47
Record Details menu, 43
Record Details menu commands (Resize), 47
Record icon, 154
Record Properties command (Edit menu), 195
record selection, optimizing, 161-162
Record Selections dialog box, 278-279
Record tab, 49
record window, resizing, 47
record with input focus, 36
recording
    macros, 288
    time (tasks), 27-28
records. *See* contact records
Recurring tab, 57
Redirect icon, 91
Reference field, 214
Reference Note dialog box, 305
Referentia Tutorial, 9
Referral tab, 258

Index

registering
   GoldMine licenses,
     111-112
   license, 10-11
Registration dialog box, 114
Registration tab, 111
Release button, 162
Release Group command
   (Contact Group menu), 168
Release Section command
   (organizational tree local
   menu), 257
releasing filters, 162
Relink to Another Contact
   command (Influencer local
   menu), 215
Reload icon, 97
reminders, 25
remote synchronization,
   15-16
remote users, 14
Remove License button, 110
removing
   items from To-do list, 136
   licenses, 110
Replace field, 247-248
Replace Field field, 244
Replicate Data command
   (organizational tree local
   menu), 257
Reply icon, 91
Reply to All icon, 91
replying to activities, 141
Report Generator, 179-180
report options, saving, 188
Report Preview toolbar, 183
Report Profile dialog box,
   181-185
Report Sorting dialog box,
   184-185, 188
reports
   Analysis, 185
   categories, choosing,
     180-181
   Contact, 185
   data, sorting, 188-189
   identifying, 235
   layout, viewing, 182

Leads Analysis Zoom, 224
previewing, 189-190
printing, 189
templates, 181-182
Reports Categories window,
   180
Reports icon, 180, 183
Reports Menu, 184
Reports Menu dialog box,
   180, 183
Reports Menu dialog box
   local menu commands
   Clone, 185
   Delete, 185
   Find, 185
   Layout, 184
   New, 185
   Options, 184
   Output To, 185
   Print, 184
   Properties, 185
   Saved, 185
   Sorts, 185
Request a Return Receipt
   check box, 87
rescheduling activities
   (Calendar), 147
Reset All button, 198
Reset button, 48
Resize command (Record
   Details menu), 47
resizing record windows, 47
resources, configuring,
   123-124
Resources command
   (Configure menu), 123
Resources tab, 57
Result field, 141, 187
retrieve options (transfer sets),
   defining, 278
Review button, 306
Review Script window, 305
reviewing
   literature fulfillment
     requests, 266
   printed documents, 267
   queued documents, 267
Rich Text check box, 87

Rich Text Format (.RTF), 266
rights, Master, 11
rocket icon, 234
Role field, 215
RSVP check box, 24, 87
.RTF (Rich Text Format)
   format, 266
Run command (Start menu),
   9, 114

S

sales
   forecasted
     inspecting, 210-211
     scheduling, 209-210
   managing, 207-209
   probabilities, assigning,
     208
Sales Analysis command
   (Analysis menu), 219, 227
Sales Analysis window, 227
sales funnel, 223
sales performance, analyzing,
   227-228
sales pipelines, 219-220, 223
Sales Team Member dialog
   box, 216
Sales Tools command (View
   menu), 52, 210-212,
   304-306
Sales Tools menu commands
   Opportunities, 52, 210-212
   Scripts, 52, 304-306
Save as Defaults button, 185
Save as GoldMine Form command (GoldMine menu),
   69-72
Save as GoldMine Linked
   Document command
   (GoldMine menu), 73
Save as HTML command (File
   menu), 102
Save History check box, 78
Save in History check box, 92
Save Script dialog box, 305
Save Settings button, 188

353

Save toolbar button, 190
saving
    menu templates, 199
    questions and answers
        (scripts), 305-306
    report options, 188
    tagged contact records as
        group, 157
    templates, 72
SCANDISK.EXE, 235
scanning contacts, 296
scans, launching, 296
Schedule a Call dialog box,
    250
Schedule a Forecasted Sale
    dialog box, 209
Schedule a To-do dialog box,
    216
Schedule an Appointment
    dialog box, 56
Schedule button, 57, 149
Schedule command (main
    menu), 13
Schedule icon, 209
Schedule menu commands
    Forecasted Sale, 209
    GoldMine E-mail, 84
    Literature Request, 264
    To-do, 24, 136, 140
Schedule tab, 50
scheduled activity triggers,
    300
Scheduled Call command
    (Complete menu), 250
scheduling
    activities, 56-57, 137,
        146-147
    forecasted sales, 209-210
scheduling conflicts, 147
Scheduling dialog box, 146
Screen Design command
    (Field tab local menu), 203
Screen Designer toolbar, 128,
    205
Screen Fields button, 128
[Screen name] command
    (Field tab local menu), 203

Screen Setup command (Field
    tab local menu), 203
screens, 126-129
    creating, 129-130
    customizing, 125
    End User, 126, 129
    Tech Support, 126, 129
    user-defined, 202
scripts
    creating, 306
    data entry, directing, 307
    editing, 304-305
    questions and answers
        editing, 306
        saving, 305-306
    selecting, 303-304
Scripts command (Sales Tools
    menu), 52, 304-306
Scripts icon, 304-306
Search All button, 159, 162
Search command (InfoCenter
    topic local menu), 263
Search dialog box, 262-263
search engines, GoldMine
    Search Engine, 98-99
Search now icon, 96
Search Results tab, 262
Search toolbar icon, 261
searching
    contact records, 152-153
        details, 155-156
        indexed files, 153-154
        narrowing search, 154
    InfoCenter, 261-262
    Web, 96
        GoldMine, 96-98
        hits, 96
Secondary Sort field, 188
sections, 104
    Data, 105-106
    Instructions, 105
    [WebImpPassword], 106
Select a User dialog box, 169
Select Activities to View dia-
    log box, 145
Select button, 147
Select Components dialog
    box, 10

Select Report File to View
    dialog box, 185
Select User command
    (Contact Group menu), 169
Select User dialog box, 227
selecting
    actions for events, 301-302
    contact records (Pilot), 284
    field comparison methods,
        241-242
    home directories, 121-122
    installation type, 9-10
    scripts, 303-304
    trigger (automated
        processes), 298-299
    type of email recipient, 85
semicolon (;), 41, 118
Send a Copy of the Attached
    File(s) to GM Recipients
    check box, 88
Send a Pager Message dialog
    box, 68, 92-93
Send as MIME check box, 87
Send envelope icon, 85
send options (transfer sets),
    defining, 277-278
sending
    email merges, 78
    literature to contacts, 264
    messages, 85
    pager messages, 92
sequencing events, 294-295
Server Agents command
    (Tools menu), 58
Server Agents menu com-
    mands
    Agents Administrator, 58
    Start Server Agents, 58
sessions, synchronization,
    274
Set All button, 198
Set Up Automated Processes
    command (Automated
    Processes menu), 58,
    290-292, 297
setting
    advanced options in
        Outlook, 279-281

354

Index

alarms, 148-149
date (tasks), 28-29
date format, 28
email options, 86-87
preferences (GoldMine links), 65-66
priority (tasks), 24-25
time
    activities, 145-146
    tasks, 27-28
timer, 46
setting up
    Internet email accounts, 89-90
    synchronizing sessions, 272, 274
settings
    HotSync, confirming, 284
    optional (group building methods), 173
setup files, identifying, 235
Setup GoldMine Link command (GoldMine menu), 66
Setup Printer command (File menu), 34, 189
Setup toolbar, 297
Setup Type dialog box, 318
sharing directories, 319
Sharing tab, 319
shortcuts, creating, 114
Show Bubble Help check box, 30
Show Button Text check box, 30
Show Send Screen check box, 65
Show Status Bar Help check box, 30
Show Topic in KnowledgeBase button, 261
signature bitmaps, 79
slash (/), 281
slash marks, double (//), 41
Sneaker Net, 275
software, add-on, 309-310
Sort button, 184
Sort Members command (Activate Groups local menu), 171

Sort option (Leads Analysis [Last Run] dialog box), 226
sort order (Contact Listing display), 153
Sort the Database Files check box, 236
sorting
    contacts, 166
    database files, 236-237
    report data, 188-189
Sorts button, 184
Sorts command (Reports Menu dialog box local menu), 185
Soundex Value, 241
source (leads), costing, 225-226
Source command (View menu), 102
spin buttons, 37, 155
    Max Contact, 296
    Max Events, 296
    Terminal's Maximum Character Width, 93
SQL (Structured Query Language), 174-175
SQL Logon Name check box, 197
SQL Password check box, 197
SQL Queries command (Lookup menu), 53
SQL Query records, 174
SQL tab, 175
standardized data, entering, 40
Start menu commands
    Explore, 319
    Find, 79
    Programs, 12
    Run, 9, 114
Start Server Agents command (Server Agents menu), 58
Start Timer button, 46
starting
    GoldMine, 12
    installation disc, 9
static IP (Internet Protocol), 273

Statistical Analysis command (Analysis menu), 219
status bar, displaying, 46
Status Bar command (Window menu), 46
Stop button, 60
Stop Timer command (Timer menu), 46
storing signature bitmaps, 79
Strategic Solutions command (Tools menu), 59
strings, 96
Structured Query Language (SQL), 174-175
subdirectories, identifying, 235
sublicenses
    controlling, 110
    creating, 110
    GoldMine Sublicense (S-*xxxx* users), 14
    GoldMine Undocked (U-0001 user), 14
    GoldSync Sublicense (Y-*xxxx* sites), 14
substituting values (fields), 246-247
Success field, 141
Summary tab, 38, 151, 242
support. *See* technical support
switching between opportunities and projects, 209
Sync 3rd Column w/Sort check box, 153
Sync Contact command (Activate Groups local menu), 171
Sync Contact Window check box, 153
Sync Profile, 274
Sync tab, 50
Sync Using the Settings of a Sync Profile check box, 274
Sync with Outlook command (Synchronize menu), 278
Sync with Pilot command (Synchronize menu), 282-283

355

Sync with Windows CE PDA command (Synchronize menu), 284
synchronization
　bi-directional, 273
　one direction, 273
　remote, 15-16
synchronization information, verifying, 237
Synchronization Wizard, 272-274
Synchronization Wizard command (Synchronize menu), 274
synchronizations sessions, 274
Synchronize command (File menu), 34, 236, 273-274, 278, 282-284, 312
Synchronize icon, 274
Synchronize menu commands
　Copy/Move, 236
　Copy/Move Records, 312
　GoldSync Administration Center, 273
　Sync with Outlook, 278
　Sync with Pilot, 282-283
　Sync with Windows CE PDA, 284
　Synchronize Wizard, 274
synchronizing
　data, 271-272
　　GoldMine, 273
　　GoldSync, 273
　　Microsoft Outlook, 278-279
　　Palm Pilot, 281-282
　　Sneaker Net, 275
　　Windows CE devices, 284
　groups, 170
　records, 289
synchronizing sessions, setting up, 272-274
System button, 16
system information, viewing, 16

System Logs window, 245-246
System Performance command (Tools menu), 59, 234
system requirements, installing GoldMine, 8
system speed, measuring, 234

T

tab buttons, Mail Merge, 88
Tab Name Data Entry window, 204
tabs, 42
　Access, 192, 196-198
　Actions, 138
　Activity Lists, 137-138
　(Additional) Contacts, 242
　Alarm, 50
　Alarmed, 138
　Alerts, 43
　Appts, 138
　Attached File, 268
　Available Time, 57
　Build, 160, 250
　Calendar, 50, 280
　Calls, 138
　Closed, 138-140
　Closed Activity, 27
　Competitors, 217
　Conduit, 283
　Contact, 242
　Contacts, 280
　Defaults, 283
　Detail, 57
　Details, 146, 214
　Document Management, 78
　E-mail, 138
　Events, 138
　Field Mapping, 280
　Fields, 125-126, 129, 202, 204
　File in History, 76-78
　Filed, 140
　Filled, 138
　Filters, 250
　Forecasts, 138, 210, 218-219

　General, 279-281, 284
　Group Schedule, 57
　Groups, 165-167
　History, 27, 218, 306
　Influencer, 215-216
　Info, 302
　Install Locally, 114
　Internet, 50, 89, 101, 120
　Internet Preferences Advanced, 101
　Issues, 218
　KnowledgeBase, 260
　Links, 73, 254-255
　Login, 50, 122, 201
　Lookup, 50
　Membership, 123, 195-196
　Menu, 196, 199
　Misc, 50
　Modem, 50
　Net-Update, 111
　Open, 25, 138
　Optimize, 161
　Others, 138
　Out-Box, 138
　Ownership, 42, 194-195
　Page Message, 92
　Pager, 50
　Pager Info, 93
　Peg Board, 148
　Pending, 36, 57, 129, 210, 218, 288
　Personal, 17, 49
　Personal Base, 260
　Phone Formatting, 42
　Preferences, 49
　Preview, 158, 174, 250
　Profile, 196
　Purge, 283
　Real-Time, 138-140
　Recipient, 76
　Record, 49
　Recurring, 57
　Referral, 258
　Registration, 111
　Resources, 57
　Schedule, 50
　Search Results, 262
　Sharing, 319

Index

SQL, 175
Summary, 38, 151, 242
Sync, 50
Tasks, 211, 280
Team, 216
Time Clock, 122, 196, 199
To-do, 138
To-do List, 25
Toolbar, 30, 50
Tracks, 295-296
Users, 57, 147
What's New?, 260-261
tagged contact records, 157
tagged contacts, 146
tagged records, 175
tagging
    contact records, 156-158
    contacts, 166-167
tags, 166
task codes (Automated Processes), 291
Task dialog box, 213
Task tab, 280
tasks. *See also* activities
    opportunities, updating, 212-213
    priority, setting, 24-25
    recording time, 27-28
    setting time, 27-28
    To-do, 24, 27
Tasks local menu commands
    Complete, 212
    Delete, 213
    Edit, 213
    Find, 213
    Go to Task, 212
    New, 213
    Output To, 213
Tasks tab, 211
TCP ports, 275
Team tab, 216
Team tab local menu commands
    Delete, 216
    Edit, 216
    Go to Contact Record, 216
    New, 216
    New Linked Contact, 216

teams, assembling, 216-217
Tech Support screen, 126, 129
technical support
    free, 16-17
    downloading from GoldMine Web site, 18
    online knowledge base, 17
    GoldMine Web site, 322
    newsgroups, 323
    premium, 18
Telemarketing Scripts dialog box, 52
telephone messages, 84
template forms, creating, 68
Template Properties dialog box, 69
templates, 287-288, 309-310
    cloning, 70
    creating, 69-70
    customizing, 54-56
    DDE Launch Options, 69
    document, 66. *See also* forms
    editing, 66
    industry, 125, 310-311
        installing, 311-312
        moving/copying records between, 312-313
    macros, 56
    menu, saving, 199
    reports, 181-182
    saving, 72
    writing to contact with, 72
Terminal's Maximum Character Width spin button, 93
Territory Realignment command (Tools menu), 58
Tertiary Sort field, 188
Text (.TXT) format, 266
Text Search command (Lookup menu), 54
time
    activities, setting, 145-146
    tasks, recording/setting, 27-28

Time Clock
    configuring, 122
    disabling, 201
Time Clock tab, 122, 196, 199
timer, setting, 46
Timer menu commands (Stop Timer), 46
Title field, 215
To field, 86, 186-187
To panel, 86
To-do command
    Complete menu, 27
    Schedule menu, 24, 136, 140
To-do field, 24
To-do list, 25-27, 135
    adding items, 136
    creating, 24
    removing items, 136
To-do List tab, 25
To-do tab, 138
To-do tasks, 24-27
Today button, 28
Toggle Data View icon, 96
toggle options, activating/deactivating, 38-39
toolbar buttons, 190
toolbar icons
    Attach a File, 260
    Create a Table of Contents, 261
    Delete, 261
    Edit, 260
    Launch Attached File, 261
    New Book, 260
    New Folder, 260
    New Topic Page, 260
    Search, 261
    Write, 72
Toolbar Settings check box, 197
Toolbar tab, 30, 50
toolbar text, 29
toolbars
    Basic, 29, 39
    Clipboard, 35
    configuring, 48-49

357

E-mail Center, 91
editing, 30
Form Designer, 182
Mail Merge Helper, 74
Print Preview, 189-190
Report Preview, 183
Screen Designer, 128, 205
Setup, 297
Tools, 234
undocking, 30
Toolbars command
Edit menu, 48, 60
View menu, 35
Toolbars dialog box, 48
Toolbars menu commands
Clipboard, 35
Insert Item, 48
Tools command (main menu), 14
Tools menu commands
Automated Processes, 58, 290-292, 296-297
BDE Administrator, 59, 321-322
Delete Records Wizard, 59, 249-250
Find, 319
Global Replace, 244, 247
Global Replace Wizard, 58, 251
Import/Export Wizard, 58
Mail Merge, 74
Merge/Purge Records, 59, 239
Server Agents, 58
Strategic Solutions, 59
System Performance, 59, 234
Territory Realignment, 58
Year 2000 Compliance, 59
Tools toolbar, 234
topics (InfoCenter), printing/faxing, 263-264
tracks. *See also* Automated Processes
attaching, 293-295
defining, 293-294
properties, 292-293

Tracks tab, 295-296
transfer cutoffs, defining, 277
Transfer Set Retrieve Options dialog box, 278
Transfer Set Send Options dialog box, 277
transfer sets
browsing, 276
filtering for, 276
retrieve options, 278
send options, 277-278
Trigger On field, 298
Trigger pane, 297
Trigger panel, 298
triggering actions, 294
triggers, 294
Automated Processes, selecting, 298-299
dBASE condition, 300
detail record, 299
disabled, 300
elapsed days, 299
events, 299-301
history, 299
history activity, 300
immediate, 299
scheduled activity, 300
troubleshooting
BDE errors, 321-322
first-level problems, 320
insufficient memory, 321
link to Word, 322
.TXT (Text) format, 266
Type field, 265
Type Message to Send to the Pager field, 93
Typical installation, 9

U

U-0001 licenses, 112
uncompleted activities, viewing, 25
Undo command (Edit menu), 35
Undock Users button, 110
undocked licenses, creating, 110

undocking toolbars, 30
Uniform Resource Locator (URL), 96
Uninstall GoldMine Link command (GoldMine menu), 66, 322
untagging contact records, 158
Update a Field Using Advanced Options check box, 247-248
Update GoldMine command (Help menu), 233
Update GoldMine Form command (GoldMine menu), 70, 73
Update Link Fields (Based on lookup.ini) check box, 245
Update Registration Information check box, 111
updating
GoldMine, 8, 112-115, 233
GoldSync, 112
tasks, 212-213
URL (Uniform Resource Locator), 96
Use Fine Resolution check box, 65
user access, controlling, 194
User field, 186-187, 218
user groups, 123
configuring, 123
creating, 192
General Access permissions, assigning, 197
memberships, viewing, 195
users
access permissions, assigning, 196-197
assigning, 192-193
membership, assigning, 193
user permissions, assigning, 196
User Groups dialog box, 195
User Groups Setup dialog box, 123, 193

Index

user icons, personalizing, 320
User Logs, 199-201
user preferences, editing, 49-50
user-defined screens, 202
users
   assigning
      access permissions, 196-197
      user groups, 192-193
   MASTER, 11
   monitoring, 122
   permissions, viewing, 196
   remote, 14
   user groups, assigning memberships, 193
Users Groups command (Configure menu), 193
Users tab, 57, 147
Users' Master File dialog box, 120, 123, 192-195
Users' Settings command (Configure menu), 120, 123, 192, 195, 200

V

values (fields), substituting, 246-247
Verify the Data and Synchronization Information check box, 236-237
verifying data/synchronization information, 237
View command
   Activate Groups local menu, 171
   main menu, 13
View Filters menu commands (public), 167
View menu commands
   Activity List, 25-26, 52, 136-137, 140, 219
   Analysis, 52, 210, 219, 224
   Calendar, 52, 142
   Contact Groups, 52, 157, 165-167, 170

E-mail Center, 52, 90, 101
E-mail Waiting Online, 52
GoldMine Logs, 245-246
InfoCenter, 17, 52, 259, 268
Literature Fulfillment, 52, 264
New Contact Window, 47, 51-52, 154
Personal Rolodex, 22, 52
Projects, 52
Sales Tools, 52, 210-212, 304-306
Source, 102
Toolbars, 35
View option (Leads Analysis [Last Run] dialog box), 226
View Saved command (Reports Menu dialog box local menu), 185
View, Detailed View command (Options menu), 25
viewing
   Activity List, 26, 137-140
   calendar (Opportunity Manager), 213-214
   contact file logs, 245-246
   details (activities), 26
   drafts of Web sites, 107
   GoldMine file logs, 246
   history (activities), 140
   licenses, 16, 109
   memberships, 195
   notes (To-do list), 25
   Opportunity Manager, 212
   preferences, 200
   report layout, 182
   system information, 16
   uncompleted activities, 25
   user permissions, 196
views, 51-52
viruses (Outlook), 92

W

Web, 95
   contact data, collecting, 102
   searching, 96
   GoldMine, 96-98
   hits, 96
Web import, controlling, 101
Web Import Data, 100
Web import files, 104
   formatting, 104
   passwords, 106-107
Web Import Gateway, 100-102
Web site addresses, editing, 99
Web Site field, 99
Web sites
   data collecting forms, 100-101
   drafts, viewing, 107
   GoldMine, 17, 64, 95, 322
   downloading free support, 18
   Industry Solutions list, 314
   making contacts through, 100
Web Sites dialog box, 99
[WebImpPassword] section, 106
What's New? tab, 260-261
widening permissions, 121
Window menu commands (Status Bar), 46
windows. *See also* dialog boxes
   activity, 26
   Activity List, 137
   Advanced Options, 279-281
   arranging, 46-47
   Automated Process Monitor, 296
   Browse List, 41
   contact, 51-52, 154-155
   Execute Script [contact name], 306
   Find Value, 53
   Internet Search, 96
   License Manager, 110, 114
   Opportunity Listing, 212

359

Project Manager, 52
Properties, 123
record, resizing, 47
Reports Categories, 180
Review Script, 305
Sales Analysis, 227
System Logs, 245-246
Tab Name Data Entry, 204
Windows CE devices, synchronizing data with, 284
With Value field, 244
wizards
   Global Replace, 243-244, 247
   GoldMine Pilot Synchronization, 282
   Group Building, 167, 172-175
   Maintenance, 234-236
   Merge/Purge, 242-243, 239-240

Synchronization, 272-274
Word, 70-71, 322
Word 97, 64-65
Word 2000, 64-65
working with groups, 170
workstations, configuring, 319-320
World Wide Web. *See* Web
Wrap Lines check box, 87
Write command (Contact menu), 66, 69, 75, 79
Write menu commands
   Customize Templates, 66, 69
   Letter to Contact, 66
   Mail Merge, 75, 79
Write toolbar icon, 72
writing
   contacts, 72
   email messages, 54
   letters to contacts, 66-68

X-Z

Y-*xxxx* licenses, 112
Year 2000 Compliance command (Tools menu), 59

Zip Code Profile dialog box, 42
zip codes, 42
Zoom button, 224
Zoom option (Leads Analysis [Last Run] dialog box), 226

ASAP International Group Plc

The **ASAP International Group Plc** is an IT services group providing consultancy, training, and recruitment support for businesses implementing technology-driven change programs. The Group comprises eight companies:

- **ASAP GoldMine Consultancy, ASAP World Consultancy**
  GoldMine/SAP change management and systems implementation
- **ASAP Institute**
  Education, Training, Membership Services, Research
- **ASAP Worldwide**
  Recruitment and Resourcing Services

These are supported by a very high standard through the following companies:

- **ASAP Authors, Documentation Consultants (UK)**
  Authoring and Publishing
- **ASAP Standards and Assessment Board**
  Standards and Assessments Services
- **ASAP Concept**
  Change Management

Having broken records at its flotation, the Group is geared to dominate CRM (Customer Relationship Management) best practice through its commitment to its staff and its customers as the core business asset. Historically aligned to the interests of the enduser rather than the IT vendors, **ASAP International Group** combines excellence in operational implementation and educational fields. **ASAP** is a partner of **GoldMine Software Corp.**, the biggest provider of CRM user licences worldwide. It delivers cultural change, infrastructure, and technical solutions to companies that:

- Are committed to achieving service excellence
- Motivate staff through vision, values, and efficient processes
- Embrace the challenges of IT and enable mastery through a learning environment
- Recognize CRM as the key to long-term success

The **ASAP International Group** prides itself on its unique training for its consultants; a high standard of service delivery with innovative solutions as its hallmark. It has designed a CRM methodology called **ASAP GoldStrike™** in its commitment to share best practice with end users everywhere. Every company in the group is ISO accredited.

CONTACT CENTERS

Tel: ++ 44 (0) 1491 414 411
Fax: ++ 44 (0) 1491 414 412
Email: asapcenter@asap-group.com
Web: www.asap-group.com

Tel or fax ASAP 24 hour virtual offices in: • New York, USA 212 253 4180 • Sydney, Australia 61 (0)2 9475 0551 • Brussels, Belgium 32 (0)2 706 50 04

ASAP GoldMine Consultancy

ASAP GoldMine Consultancy team has been formed by a strong commitment to recruiting and cross-training its consultants from different areas of business expertise into the field of CRM (Customer Relationship Management).

ASAP GoldMine consultants undergo its own month-long training program based on the **ASAP GoldStrike™** methodology. This enables them to understand its client's needs in a wider business context. Instead of an inflexible technology implementation, it outlines phased implementations according to its client's budgets and business requirements based on the capabilities of the GoldMine FrontOffice 2000 (GMFO) suite and GoldMine 5. The company's achievement lies in maximizing GoldMine's functionality to deliver a powerful integration of the four key customer-facing areas:

- Telephony
- Sales and marketing
- Services and support
- Accountancy

The Consultancy term has completed GoldMine implementations in a variety of industry sectors and can deliver:

- **Increased profitability through customer retention and low marketing spend**
- **A reduction in operational deficiencies**
- **Increased sales performance**
- **Improved service response times**
- **Customer segmentation and profiling**
- **Remote system configuration, report writing, consultancy, and support**

With a grounding in service orientation, its GoldMine consultants will help you face the challenges of your own CRM culture change, achieve a quick implementation within an affordable price range, and deliver customized training with GoldMine's user-friendly interface. The integration of sales force automation and helpdesk technology will leave your business with the competitive edge necessary to shape future business policies and plans.

CONTACT CENTERS

Tel: ++ 44 (0) 1491 414 411
Fax: ++ 44 (0) 1491 414 412

Email: asapcenter@asap-group.com
Web: www.asap-group.com

Tel or fax ASAP 24 hour virtual offices in: • New York, USA 212 253 4180 • Sydney, Australia 61 (0)2 9475 0551 • Brussels, Belgium 32 (0)2 706 50 04

The ASAP GoldStrike™ Implementation Methodology

GoldStrike

This product offering from the **ASAP GoldMine Consultancy** team is a sharing of best practice in the CRM (Customer Relationship Management) field. **ASAP GoldStrike™** is drawn from its collective business experience in project management, sales, marketing, customer services, training, accountancy, ERP (enterprise resource planning), and GoldMine product and implementation knowledge. It distils in a highly practical and easy-to-understand manner the principles, practices, procedures, and protocols which will deliver success in CRM technology implementations using the GoldMine FrontOffice 2000 Suite and GoldMine 5.

With **ASAP GoldStrike™** it does not repeat old formulas indiscriminately. Instead, it shows you how to:

- Understand and integrate telephony, sales, marketing, services, and accountancy functions
- Adopt a structured approach to GoldMine implementation that maximizes business benefits
- Enable individuals to undertake their own GoldMine configurations
- Enable companies to resolve infrastructure and operational process issues pre- and post-implementation
- Understand and transform internal resistances to CRM culture change
- Minimize time spent by consultants in companies by simplifying technical issues with powerful and efficient solutions
- Establish the structure and reap the rewards of quick knowledge and skills transfer in training
- Achieve business excellence through service orientation

From practical hardware audits and system documentation procedures to strategic issues in change management, from individuals to companies, **ASAP GoldStrike™** keeps you in the loop of the latest practice and thinking in CRM.

CONTACT CENTERS

Tel: ++ 44 (0) 1491 414 411
Fax: ++ 44 (0) 1491 414 412

Email: asapcenter@asap-group.com
Web: www.asap-group.com

Tel or fax ASAP 24 hour virtual offices in: • New York, USA 212 253 4180 • Sydney, Australia 61 (0)2 9475 0551 • Brussels, Belgium 32 (0)2 706 50 04

Why join the ASAP GoldMine Consultancy team?

ASAP ™
GoldMine Consultancy

The **ASAP GoldMine Consultancy** team is a dynamic and international company taking the lead in changing the consulting world. We are capitalizing on the hottest application growth market – Customer Relationship Management (CRM). We recruit candidates with specialist skills or expertise from a wide variety of business and professional backgrounds to cross-train into **GoldMine FrontOffice 2000** and **GoldMine 5**. We aim to become unrivalled practitioners in customer centered business strategies.

As a subsidiary of **ASAP International Group plc**, **ASAP GoldMine Consultancy** has a training center in South Africa and others opening in Europe, the Caribbean, USA, the Middle East, and Australia. We are looking for like-minded individuals to join us in the adventure of dominating the CRM market with best practice procedures, innovative and creative thinking, and anticipating future market trends through knowledge management. Our Mission Statement is:

To be a third millennium, world class leader in technology-driven change.

ASAP employee values:
- honesty and openness in communication
- always acting in the customer's best interests
- maximizing the system's value to customers
- continuous service cycle improvement
- continual personal development
- interpersonal and group skills development
- respect for others in every encounter
- encouraging happiness and fun
- integrity • self motivation

Customers experience **ASAP** as:
- **Customer centered** – engaging in quality listening
- **Dialogue dependent** – developing successful partnerships
- **Committed to service excellence** – not just passing quality awards
- **Delivering innovation in solutions** – not just repeating an old formula
- **Committed to delivering value**

The **ASAP** culture:
- Global and multi-cultural approach
- Innovative, dynamic, and exciting teams
- Freedom and individual choice to develop specialist skills
- Flexibility with high professional standards
- Vision and values as the driving force
- Flat management structures to allow thriving entrepreneurialism

If you are highly skilled and experienced in: CRM systems implementation, sales, marketing, customer services, project management, business process engineering, call center management, IT support and helpdesk, programming and developing, human resources and personnel, accounting, Enterprise Resource Planning (ERP)

OR

wish to cross-train from Pivotal, Siebel, Vantive, Clarify, SAP, BAAN, Peoplesoft, Oracle, SSA, and other CRM or ERP applications—

Call us now!

CONTACT CENTERS

Tel: ++ 44 (0) 1491 414 411
Fax: ++ 44 (0) 1491 414 412

Email: asapcenter@asap-group.com
Web: www.asap-group.com

Tel or fax ASAP 24 hour virtual offices in: • New York, USA 212 253 4180 • Sydney, Australia 61 (0)2 9475 0551 • Brussels, Belgium 32 (0)2 706 50 04